P9-CDN-959

MEDIÆVAL CULTURE

AN INTRODUCTION TO DANTE AND HIS TIMES

BY
KARL VOSSLER

TRANSLATED BY
WILLIAM CRANSTON LAWTON

VOLUME TWO

NEW YORK
HARCOURT, BRACE AND COMPANY

Published in Germany as "Die Göttliche Komödie"

PRINTED IN THE U. S. A.

CONTENTS

VOLUME II: THE LITERARY BACKGROUND AND THE POETRY OF THE "DIVINE COMEDY"

IV: THE LITERARY BACKGROUND OF THE "DIVINE COMEDY"

1. The Position of the "Divine Comedy" in the History of Literature

Adolf Gaspary closes the chapter on Dante in his *History of Italian Literature* with the words: "Italian literature, which, in so many respects, took a course different from that of other modern literatures, has also this peculiarity, that it produced, near its beginning, a work of such supreme importance, uplifted itself to such a height, as it was never destined to attain again, so that all which followed is subordinated, in a certain degree, to that earlier masterpiece. All Italian literature is full of Dante."

If it is natural that such greatness towers high above its after-time, yet it does seem strange to see at the very beginning of a national literature and of an immature literary language almost without preparation such a Colossus as the *Divine Comedy*. A mountain peak of granite rises from a sandy plain.

The religious, philosophical, and ethico-political antecedents of the poem were seen to be long, rich, and complicated. Its literary forebears appear, by comparison, brief and scanty.

A comparative survey of the popular literatures of the Middle Ages immediately reveals the peculiar and remarkable position of Italy. The striking feature is the relatively late and dull beginning and then the sudden and unrivalled blossoming of Italian literature. A long-hidden and quietly accumulated force suddenly released itself in the poetry of Dante—not a growth, but an outbreak. Mighty forces, therefore, must have been pressing against strong obstacles.

The analysis of this historical situation resolves itself therefore into a twofold task. First: How did it come to pass that Italian literature begins so late—not until the opening of the thirteenth century—and so weakly and with so little independence? To that end we must study the forces which impeded the æsthetic life of the people. But as we endeavour to discover the mysterious growth of literary treasures and acquisitions, and the force behind them, we obtain the reply to the second question: How is it to be explained that Italian literature grows so rapidly that at the beginning of the fourteenth century it can produce such a masterpiece as the *Divine Comedy?*

2. The Late Beginning of Italian Poetry

England, Germany, Northern and Southern France, had all reached the culmination of their first phase of literary activity when Italy, the land of classic literature, had produced hardly so much as one song in its vernacular. That people especially which stands nearest to the Italian in speech and intellectual disposition, perhaps also in race, the Provençal, had far outstripped their cousins beyond the Alps.

As early as the tenth century we have an example in Southern France of a cleric who derives the material for a Provençal didactic poem from a biographical and philosophical book in Latin (*Vita Boëthii* and *Consolatio Philosophiae*). There are sufficient traces of other such adaptations of moral and theological works to popular forms of expression. We find them, indeed, in all mediæval literatures, and they are always among the oldest linguistic monuments. Whether they presuppose a still older, purely popular poetry in Latin lands is a problem not to be determined here. But at that moment it was certainly the clerics, familiar with Latin, who developed the new popular dialects into literary form. Ecclesiastical and popular didactic poems such as the Old High German *Otfrid*, the Old French *Passion Christi*, the *Leodegar*, the Boëthius just mentioned, and others, can hardly be found in Italy, and in particular in Upper Italy, before the middle of the thirteenth century, and so from two to three hundred years later than in the neighbour land of France!

If one does not hesitate to force the most original of masterpieces into a traditional class of works, the *Divine Comedy* may be characterized as the most perfect example of this popular mediæval religiously didactic poetry.

Not only in didactic poetry, but in courtly lyric as well, in epic composition, in the short story, in novel, and in drama, in short in all creations of poetic imagination, we find the Italians equally belated. Italian patriots have vainly tried all means, even forgery, and serious scholars have exerted themselves in vain, to trace the beginnings of their native literature back to an earlier date. We cannot speak of Italian literature at all before the beginning of the thirteenth century. Even if the date of this or that artistic work should be successfully assigned to an earlier age, little would be gained, for one lone swallow is by no means the harbinger of spring, nor does one minor poet constitute a national literature. Dante himself, apparently, does not trace Italian poetry back of the time of the Hohenstaufen emperor, Frederick II (1215–1250).[1]

But how are we to explain this long, enigmatical silence of the Italian muse? Was there, indeed, no Italian language until the thirteenth century? Was Latin still generally spoken, as Tiraboschi (1731–1794) surmises? By no means. The Italian language must have taken shape by the seventh century and even have attained, in the main, its present form.

If, nevertheless, it did not until long after assume written and, even later, literary shape, it may be assumed that Latin still met completely the needs of the time. The knowledge of Latin may, in fact, have been more extended, and the understanding of it easier, even for the uneducated, in Italy than in other Romance lands, just as the classic tradition in general is better preserved on Italian soil than anywhere else.

Yet the fact remains that the North Italian and in part also the Southern dialects had become perhaps as remote from written Latin, even in the earliest Middle Ages, as Provençal, French, or Spanish. Furthermore, the mastery and comprehension of another language, however closely akin, is attained only by the educated man, while the untrained mind is confused by the slightest variation in sound or sense. For instance, a speech delivered in Latin in the year 1189 by the Patriarch of Aquileia had to be interpreted to the people in their own dialect by the Bishop of Padua. Religious instruction and pastoral work were not possible, even in Italy, without the aid of the vulgar speech. This may well have been realized even by those who wrote, as a title of honour, upon the grave of Pope Gregory V (*ob.* 999):

> Using the vulgar speech, the French and also the Latin,
> He, with a threefold tongue, various peoples has taught.

One may have the most favourable impression as to the knowledge of Latin among the Italians, may assume the continuance

[1] *De vulgari Eloquentia*, I, 12, and *Vita Nuova*, § 25.

of Roman manners and habits in the widest sense; but even this will at best only explain the continued use of Latin in legal documents, in the Catholic ritual and the like—the late appearance of literature in the vulgar speech still remains a riddle.

The assumption that Italian was crushed by the overwhelming rivalry of Latin is a common error. It is founded upon the mistaken notion that the poet can choose between two forms of speech to express what is in his heart; that he decides according to caprice, expediency, or habit in favour of Italian or Latin.

In that case, the loss suffered by Italian should have been all gain for Latin literature. It should have flourished the more richly and gloriously in Italy the longer and the more completely the Italian speech remained debarred from poetry. But the opposite was true! Not only in literature but in the plastic arts there was a similar lack of creative originality, and, as compared with the people of the North, an equally late appearance was to be noted. Almost as surprising and unannounced as the *Divine Comedy* in the one field is the appearance of Giotto's masterpieces in the other.

Just as architecture does not arise merely out of the presence of stone, so poetry is not created simply by the existence of languages. Our problem is not merely linguistic, but pertains in the largest sense to the history of culture. It is necessary to put it more accurately and fittingly: *How does it happen that the Italians of the Middle Ages shared so rarely and hesitatingly in those thoughts and feelings which elsewhere, especially in France and Germany, developed an original literature in the vulgar language?*

3. The Isolation of Italy in the Middle Ages

CHARACTER OF POLITICAL LITERATURE

Besides the oppressive weight of Latin, the unhappy political doom of the peninsula, the invasions and raids of the Goths, of the Lombards, of the Saracens and the Huns—in short, the wars and anarchy which devastated the land from the fifth century to the eleventh—have been made responsible for the lack of poetry in the popular speech. This too is an error. It may be that science and the arts of design require for their growth rich economic soil. But poetry is a flower that prospers cheerily amid rocks and ice, in frost and tempest.

So the vicissitudes of political and military history can detain us only in so far as they act upon the feelings and imagination of the peoples.

The ancient imperialistic idea still ruled all men's hearts. It outlasted the unity and the visible existence of the empire. The division between Eastern and Western Rome was never recognized in the Middle Ages, nor even by Dante, as an essential separation.[1]

Two forces in particular tore to pieces the aging structure of world-rule: Christianity, whose anti-imperial spirit was revealed in St. Augustine's *Civitas Dei,* and the Germanic barbarians, whose childish political ignorance was satisfied for centuries with the primitive military organization improvised for the purpose of waging war.

But precisely these two inflexible forces, as soon as they had laid the mighty frame of world-empire prostrate, came under the control of its mightier spirit. The idea of the Roman monarchy captivated German warriors and Christian priests alike. The first German who attained unlimited power on Italian soil, the Frank, Arbogast, did not himself venture to ascend the imperial throne, but instead set a Roman upon it. The same drama was repeated with different outcomes in the following centuries. Alaric tried to elevate the Greek Attalos to the throne, and his successor, Ataulf, is said to have made the remarkable confession that "he had at first intended to make himself lord of the empire, to make the Roman state Gothic, and Ataulf a Roman Augustus. But experience had soon taught him that it was impossible; that Rome had ruled the world not merely by armed force, but through laws and order; that the Goths, in their unbridled barbarism, were not capable of submitting to justice and law. But since without justice and laws a state was no state, he had determined to use the force of the Goths to uplift the Roman name once more to its ancient glory." [2]

Theodoric the Great endeavoured with politic shrewdness to spare the national pride of the Romans and did not disdain to flatter them. His historian, Cassiodorus, as he himself says, set himself the task "to draw the old Gothic kings out of the night

[1] Dante represented it under the figure of the eagle that rends the young twigs, the blossoms, and the bark upon the tree of world-rule, as something that should not be. *Purgatorio,* XXXII, 113–114.

[2] Orosius, *Historia adversum Paganos,* VII, Chapter 43.

of forgetfulness into the light, to restore the Amals to the eminence of their origin . . . and make the early history of the Goths a part of the Roman annals." [1]

Such fraternizing efforts from above never became popular on either side, but they testify to the winning power of the ancient Roman tradition.

If ever a barbarous people broke this power, it was the Lombards. But, with all their contempt for the Roman name, they were unable, for their part, to put any political idea in the place of the ancient one. Their sway had only power enough to shatter the weakened unity of Italy and to let loose the maddest individualisms. Under them the peninsula fell to pieces, yielding to its own centrifugal forces. It is the fault of the Lombards that the South, including Benevento and Naples, diverged for a long time, in political and ecclesiastical developments, from the main portion of the peninsula, and became subject to Greek and Saracenic influences. While intermarriage between Goths and Romans was never legally recognized, the Lombards, after their conversion to Catholicism (about 670–700), slowly united with the natives, forming a new race, so that the ethnographical features of the land also became more and more variegated. Old German ideas of law were revived, and in every direction the unity of Roman character was broken down.

With the dissolution of the Byzantine exarchate (780), the last material tie between Italy and the ancient imperial idea is sundered. Germanic feudalism comes in with the rule of the Franks.

Graeco-Roman gave place to Germanic-Roman imperialism. This new institution, lacking in historical or legal foundation, stood in need of divine consecration from the hands of the pope. Although this was not the intention of Charlemagne, it quickly became the ruling one. In order to wear the imperial crown, it is no longer necessary to be a Roman or a Greek, for the priestly oil sanctifies German heads as well.

For this second empire, with its centre of gravity north of the Alps, the Italian people, naturally enough, could never be roused to enthusiasm. How public feeling regarded the German emperor is difficult to trace in detail; the prevailing sentiment must have been indifference, very often hostility. Certainly hardly

[1] L. M. Hartmann, *Das italienische Königreich*, Leipzig, 1897, I, 185.

one of the earlier German emperors received a literary eulogy in the grand style.[1]

The actual glorification of the emperor in legend and song comes from Germany and France, not from Italy. It is true that in Northern Italy the figure of the great Frankish ruler seems to have appealed to the popular imagination, but by no means in a kindly light.[2] When the French Charlemagne-epics found their way into Italy, they promptly received a very significant revision. The figure of the alien ruler became an ignoble and ridiculous caricature, his enemies, even his own paladins, towering high above him. The treatment of Theodoric, long before, seems to have been not much kinder. Attila, for whose heroic greatness even the conquered Germans could become enthusiastic, remained always for the Italians merely *flagellum Dei* (scourge of God). The feeling for martial glory vanished with the coming of foreign rulers. Joy over the new empire, whose splendour glorified alien peoples, was constantly diminished by the jealous nationalism of the Italians. "Why are we oppressed under the sway of the Franks?" asked the people of Benevento just after the Emperor Louis II had freed them from the Saracens.

While the Italian heroic legend drags on with scant additions, the independent feeling of the city dwellers already makes itself heard in the ninth and tenth centuries. About 850 a Venetian priest expresses himself vigorously in a Latin poem against the rival city of Aquileia.[3] About 892, a writer of Modena composed on a popular model a Latin watchman's song, intended to encourage the warriors, recalling to their minds classical examples of watchfulness, e.g. the Trojan Hector and the geese of the Capitol. The singer also entrusts his city to the protection of Christ, Mary, and St. John.[4]

Hardly has the burgher come to realize his own strength when his political feeling is fired by memories of Troy and Rome. It is, however, no longer imperial but republican Rome that attracts him, and which is no longer set below, but by the side

[1] The monk of Bobbio, author of an elegy on Charlemagne's death, was probably a German.

[2] Many curious legends, which present Charlemagne in quite an unheroic light, are preserved in the *Chronicon Novalicense*, credited to a monk of Novalesa, on the southern slope of Mont Cenis.

[3] *Monum. Germ. hist. Poet. lat. med. aev.*, II, 150 sqq. "The race of Venetians ever illustrious and noble," etc.

[4] *Ibid.*, III, 703 sqq.

of sacred and biblical history. The first glimmer of the Renaissance!

For in politics Renaissance means the elevation of the ideas of republican Rome above the imperial conception. Strictly speaking, therefore, Italy never passed through a political Middle Age. Not until Dante's day did the love of this people draw somewhat closer to the Roman empire of the German nation.

Why are practically all the eulogies of the emperors, as far as we can see, of a learned, courtly, scholastic, or purely personal character? So, for instance, the *Gesta Berengarii Imperatoris*, a piece of rhetorical bravura, and, for that age, a notable example of erudition; so, above all, the writings of the most important chronicler of that day, Bishop Liutprand of Cremona. Liutprand does not see things with the eyes of his fellow countrymen; he expresses no popular feeling. He sees in all things their relation to himself. Thanks to his keen vision and lofty outlook, as the emperor's friend and official, he is able to analyze critically the political attitude of the Italians. At the beginning of his *Antapodosis* he sets, with significant intention, the following example: the town of Frassineto could be captured (in the year 888) by a horde of Saracens only because the inhabitants quarrelled and one party was not ashamed to call in the heathen to their aid. So God's justice willed that both factions should live in servitude. "The Italians always wish to have two masters, so that they may control the one through his fear of the other." [1]

Liutprand is, at the same time, in his personality a vivid and premature example of that aristocratic individualism which, in the days of the Renaissance, dissolved social and political bonds and bade the smaller units flourish at the cost of the greater, the individual at the cost of the community.

It might be supposed that the conflict between emperor and pope, and the enthusiasm of the Crusades, would bring nearer to the Italians the question of theocratic world-rule. But even then, as late as the eleventh and twelfth centuries, the old drama is repeated. Precisely those dreams and feelings which in France and Germany are most popular, are in Italy cherished only by the learned, clerics and schoolmen.

[1] *Antapodosis*, I, 2 sqq. and 37.

The Crusades hardly found an echo in poetry.[1] Instead of being dragged into venturesome crusading expeditions by the fanaticism of the Northern nations, the Italian seaports, especially Genoa and Pisa, were intent upon giving a more profitable turn to the martial valour of their warriors. In a series of warlike undertakings (1015, 1034, 1113, and 1187) they swept the Mediterranean clean of Saracens, and made their own commerce safe.

These exploits, on the other hand, met with poetical praise. A poem by a Pisan on the capture of Mehdia (1088) may be considered one of the most significant examples of popular poetry in the Latin language. As in the poem on the watchman of Modena, so here the local civic patriotism is mingled with memories of republican Rome:

> I who would write the tale of famous Pisans
> Renew the memory of ancient Romans.
> For Pisa now extends the glorious fame
> That Rome of old by conquering Carthage won.

It may be assumed that poetry in the vulgar tongue is about to appear, that it will claim for its own such local and municipal events, and will become the rival of the poetry of daily life and strife in rhythmical Latin—which, in fact, continued to flourish far into the thirteenth century.[2]

On the other hand, learned poetry, which appears with some philological pretensions, begins to win for itself an ever larger field. The next great victory of the Pisans over the Saracens (1113) is not celebrated in the trochaic rhythms of popular poetry, but in highly ornate classic hexameters in eight books. The author, Laurentius, otherwise Henricus, deacon to the Archbishop of Pisa, has brought together with rhetorical pedantry a quantity of classic frills in order to give epic dignity to his tale, which is not uninteresting, but inspired rather by religious than by civic zeal.

The great struggle between emperor and pope did indeed call into life a rich literature of canon law and theology and sharpen

[1] A monk of the monastery Nonantola composed a dirge on the capture of Jerusalem by Saladin. Two or three other similar attempts are mentioned by chroniclers, but have vanished.

[2] The oldest trace of a poem in Italian is a satire on the Cremonese who drowned in the river Oglio, sung by Milanese boys, in the year 1109. Fifty years later we hear of a second popular song which the women of the rebellious city of Crema sang in the public squares against the Emperor Frederick Barbarossa.

to biting satire the pens especially of the learned monks of Monte Cassino and Farfa, as well as of the pugnacious bishops in Central and Northern Italy. The people, however, took no share in this world-wide controversy. The fundamental side of the matter did not interest them. Their whole attention was directed to the special advantages which resulted, according to the turn of events, for their own town, party, or family. The major aims and the great contestants in the duel between monarchy and church hardly ever come before the narrow vision of the popular poets of the day. Just as in the Trojan war the gods contend high above the people, while the battle of mortals in the valley of the Scamander splits up into countless single encounters, so it seems, in the Italian Middle Ages, the contest for sceptres and tiaras went on high above the people's heads, while the Italian was conscious only of the momentary outcome of some petty war, and only in rare instances and as if startled by war-cries becomes aware of an emperor's or a pope's mailed fist. The Ghibelline imperial legend in the time of the Hohenstaufens seems to point rather in the direction of the Greek and even Tartar East than in that of the Germanic North.

The subdivisions and complications of political interests reached their height about the time of the Emperor Frederick Barbarossa. The cities resisted the suzerainty of their bishops, or feudal lords. The bishops opposed the pope; the feudal lords and the pope fought against the emperor; the lower clergy held out against the bishops; the cities, in turn, were at war with one another, and even within the walls of a town civil strife was kept up. The threads crossed and recrossed in every direction, The political capacity of the Italian was developed to the utmost cleverness by the practice of this complicated game. But this keenness of insight and cunning were ever accompanied by that selfishness and short-sighted eagerness which still today characterizes the Italian in his business dealings.

Under these circumstances it was to take a long time before a serious effort toward national unity could be made. Some decades after Dante's death, about the middle of the fourteenth century, it did at least come to utterance as a sentiment, and found poetic expression in the verses of Fazio degli Uberti and, with a bolder sweep, in Petrarch's poems.

But the narrower the range of view, the clearer and nearer the political goals, so much the greater is the passion which they arouse. Ever louder, ever more bitterly and harshly, resounds in popular and scholarly poetry, occasional and polemic, an irreconcilable hatred for foreigners, especially for the German rulers; ever more self-conscious grows the remembrance of the Roman ancestors, ever more jealous the pride in the home city, until this firmly rooted and prevailingly Guelfic satire found complete development, sometimes in Latin rhythms, sometimes in Italian speech, in the course of the thirteenth century.

The great question of Church politics, however, is at most only touched upon in poems of this character, never treated fundamentally.[1] The Italians left this abstract material partly to French and German troubadours, partly to the learned dignitaries of their own land. Had there been in Latin a plentiful stock of such popular poetry, then the popular muse would certainly have seized more quickly and with greater ease upon questions of ecclesiastical and world-politics. As it was, down to the time of Dante it remained limited to petty factional politics.

Only the learned rise to a wider horizon. It might appear as though political consciousness, and hence the style of political poetry, had been divided into two separate levels. On the lower we find the authors of city chronicles and local poems, who are usually Guelf, republican, and particularistic in their tendencies. Their historical knowledge and even their religious feeling are directly and wholly devoted to their party or their narrower fatherland.[2] Hence their diction is usually halting, harsh, and directly to the point—simple, passionate, rude.

It is quite otherwise with the poets and publicists of the second and higher level. Here we find, for example, Bishop Benzo of Alba, with his panegyric on Henry IV.[3] In passion and fury he is not a whit behind the roughest of the popular poets. But his antipapal zeal is doctrinaire, his style ornamented with boundless pretentiousness. Prose, rhymed prose, leonine hexameters, distichs, rhymed strophes, and series of iambs, trochees, and dactyls whirled noisily together; a many-coloured patchwork,

[1] The single notable exception is the famous Ghibelline rhythm, "All too deeply stirred by grief" (*Vehementi nimium commotus dolore*), which must be attributed, if not to Pier della Vigna himself, at least to some eminent partisan of Frederick II.

[2] Occasionally, in conflict with a foreign enemy, this Guelfic muse assumes a somewhat higher national tone, foreshadowing Dante's famous outburst, *Ahi serva Italia* (*Purgatorio*, VI, 76 sqq.).

[3] *Monum. Germ.*, Pertz, II, 598 sqq.

only in part to be explained by the scattered and diffuse sources of the work, and quite as much by the contradictory, overstrained, egotistical individuality of the author. The more imperialistic the feelings of these poets and rhetoricians, the remoter they are from their people, the more ornate and forced their style becomes. The author of the *Gesta Berengarii*, Liutprand, Benzo, the anonymous master of Bergamo with his *Gesta per Imperatorem Fridericum Barbam Rubeam*, and Peter of Eboli, all of them bear out the soundness of this remark. The epic-lyric poem by the last-named on the sanguinary conquest of Lower Italy by Henry IV is a masterpiece of devotion, imperial loyalty, flattery, and learned embellishment. The emperor appears as thundering Jupiter, his spouse as Juno. One might imagine that the poet was writing in the days of Caligula or Nero.

Quite apart from this group of imperial humanists stands Geoffrey of Viterbo. By education, nature, and sympathy, he is so thoroughly German that one is disposed to doubt his Italian descent. Furthermore, he appears with his *Pantheon* as the sole author of his time engaged in writing world- and imperial chronicles. It is significant that this type of historical writing had been replaced by a rich literature and local annals and biographies, generally of eulogistic type.[1] Compared with the philosophic and comprehensive character of German historical writing—for example, Otto von Freising—the Italian compositions appear very narrow, often more like memoirs or fictions.

Such political divisions as we have noted in Italy throughout the later Middle Ages are, to be sure, bridged over temporarily in the *Divine Comedy*, but traces of them can be discovered even there. It is easy to perceive that the Florentine party-spirit of the poet dwells, so to speak, in a lower story than, and speaks a different language from, his theocratic universalism. The former is more at home in Hell, the latter in Paradise; the one appears embodied in sturdy and tangible forms, Ciacco, Farinata, Brunetto Latini, and Ugolino; the other, divested of its rhetorical trappings, and revealing only in the person of Virgil any of the ordinary literary, imperial, and humanistic traits, finds its chief expression in allegories and religious symbols.

[1] The first attempt to compile a world-chronicle was made in Italy by Bishop Sicard of Cremona (later than 1212).

CHARACTER OF RELIGIOUS LITERATURE

Neither was religious feeling in Italy forceful and original enough to give rise to a typical and important literature. From the founding of the Benedictine order down to the time of the Franciscan movement, no powerful religious current had its source in Italy.

"It is a fact fully assured by historical investigation that the spiritual and religious life of Italy, during the ninth and tenth centuries, was at heart pagan. Christianity was indeed the recognized religion, but it was only externally a traditional inheritance, without profound influence; all spiritual life was still under the domination of heathen antiquity. The very fact that a form was preserved almost wholly destitute of substance, that two such sharply contrasted human creations were forced to stand, in some fashion, side by side, is highly characteristic of the age." [1]

Even after the great reform movements of Cluny and Assisi, a mighty and indestructible inheritance of naïve heathenism, of superstition and of religious indifference, was left in the heart of the Italians. So it came to pass that later historians, such as Jakob Burckhardt and Carducci—to mention only the greatest—saw in this very lack of Christian and religious feeling an innate quality and even a natural advantage of the Italian race. The Italians appeared to these writers to be the classic people of heathenism, of antiquity, and of the Renaissance. This exaggerated notion is matched by the fanciful claims of the Romantic School that would make the greatest artists of Italy, Dante and Michelangelo, products of Germanism.

It is true that religious indifference, together with an inclination to superstition, was long prevalent in Italy, from about the fifth to the twelfth century, and later, again, in the fifteenth and sixteenth. If this general division be accepted, then the age of the philosophic and religious revival at the end of the Middle Ages, that is, at the time of Francis, of Thomas, of Bonaventura, and of Dante, will appear a brief interlude.

The great historic age of Christianity came to an end in Italy with Gregory I—at the time, that is, when the peoples of the North had become acquainted with the new teaching. Heathen

[1] A. Dresdner, *Kultur- und Sittengeschichte der italienischen Geistlichkeit im zehnten und elften Jahrhundert.*

ideas and customs, however, still persisted in large measure and were intermingled with Christianity. Something like this did indeed occur in the North; but the German religions were less sensuous in their nature, less artistic, anthropomorphic, and idolatrous than Graeco-Roman polytheism. Hence, in those regions the supersensuous Jewish and Christian spirit of the new religion was by no means so crudely distorted and falsified as it was in the South.

That which most promptly and clearly characterizes the artistic utterances of religious feeling in mediæval Italy is the varying relation between the Christian and the ancient forms and motives. Sometimes it is a relation of hostility, sometimes of indifference, sometimes of friendship.

The hostility soon ended—as soon as the actual, external victory of Christianity was assured. It was, to be sure, customary, following the fashion of the early Church Fathers, to inveigh long and loudly against pagan and worldly ornamentation of art and oratory. But not long after the death of Gregory intellectual life ran wild and became altogether worldly. The educated devoted themselves not to the Scriptures, but to Terence. Ratherius, the Belgian Bishop of Verona, is horrified at the godlessness of the Italian clergy and the superstition of the people. He characterizes his folk as "despisers of the canon law and vilifiers of the clergy." The cult of the saints is nowhere so lax as among the Italians. These sly Southerners, instead of praying to the bones of martyrs, barter them away. The learned world is accused by other lands of lacking interest in theology and metaphysics. The most important monasteries are erected and administered by foreigners. In Southern Italy the Christians and Mohammedans live in peace, side by side. Even Innocent III did not succeed in stirring up the faithful of Sicily against the Saracens.

The great Church reform which begins in the eleventh century in France as an essentially active and in the Greek world as an essentially meditative mysticism, exerts its influence on the Italians, so that at last their literature also gives the first notable evidences of a revived piety.

The most prominent religious poet and author is, without doubt, Peter Damian. His inspiration came, apparently, from Ravenna and France. The strongest note in his song is piety. Brief, changing, swift images rise out of the depths of his thoughts and feelings regarding a future life. The thronging impressions overwhelm the listener. It is rather movement than colour, more action and rhythm than painting and clarity. In Damian's descriptions of the next world we admire the glowing temperament rather than the warmth of feeling, and it all passes in a rush that leaves no time for learned embellishment.

> Evermore by seven tortures
> Are their agonies renewed:
> Thirst and hunger, smoke and stench,
> Heat and cold and flaming fire,
> Nevermore the worms are sated,
> At their vitals gnawing still.
>
> There is agony and torture,
> Weeping, gnashing of the teeth.
> There is heard the roar of lions,
> There the hissing too of serpents,
> While with them confused and mingled
> Is the cry of those who weep. . . .
>
> They would fain be done with living,
> Yet they may not cease to be.
> Dead they live who wish to die,
> Yet it nevermore shall be.

In the same rhythm, full and strong, the peace of Paradise is revealed:

> Harmonies, forever changing,
> With melodious voice are uttered,
> While in jubilee eternal
> Organ notes delight the ear.[1]

The poetry of the Franciscans may be more tender and delicate, more moving and effective, but no other before Dante showed such vigour and impulsiveness.[2]

The monks of Monte Cassino, in particular Gaiferius (*ob.* 1089) and Alphanus (*ob.* 1086), are praised by the historians of literature. However, their religious poetry is fired not by personal piety, but by the oratorical fire of classical scholarship. Their piety endeavours to forget ecclesiastical language and to pray in the idiom of Horace, Ovid, Virgil, Juvenal, and Cicero.

This fluctuation between Christianity and antiquity did not

[1] Migne, *Patrologia latina*, CXLV, pp. 980–82.
[2] That Dante was acquainted with Damian's verses is possible, but not certain.

remain limited to Monte Cassino. The crudest example is perhaps the Pisan deacon, Laurentius or Henricus. At the close of the sixth book of his *De Bello balearico* he portrays a scene in Hell. The fallen Saracens stream in great masses to the underworld. Cerberus howls so fiercely that the King of Tartarus asks him why. Aeacus and Rhadamanthus devise the tortures: fire, venom, cold, and tantalizing thirst. It is a grotesque medley of heathenish and Christian fancies. The classical element is decidedly larger, but the reckless lack of form betrays the mediæval barbarian who is more concerned for his Christian argument than for linguistic embellishment. Only the excess of decoration, not his art, marks him for an Italian.

This inartistic syncretism grows ever madder with time. Meanwhile, religious poetry in Italy withers before it has blossomed. Fallen to the lowest stage of degeneracy, it is seen at the beginning of the thirteenth century in a certain Bongiovanni, a Minorite monk of the monastery Santa Maria della Incoronata at Mantua. His work is a dismal didactic poem in rhythmic Latin verses of varying structure. It bears the proud title *Anticerberus*, for the prologue announces that the poet's shafts are aimed at the hound of Hell. The first three books deal with the dogmas, the sacraments, the Commandments, prayer, moral perils, deadly sins, and asceticism. The favourite satirical moral and religious rhymes and notable verses of Latin literature in the Middle Ages are capriciously tagged together. But in the fourth and last book, in the descriptions of the Hereafter, there appears also, prominently and unannounced, side by side with the apocalyptic visions of the Bible, the whole classical scenery of the Virgilian underworld. "At the creaking door of Hell, Bongiovanni sets, instead of the noisy and savage devils of the Mysteries, the harpies, the chimeras, centaurs, and, beside them, all the pallid band of Virgil's personifications: Sleep, Death, Revenge, and—by an incredible error—*turpis Egestas:* poverty! A Franciscan monk who chooses dear Poverty, the 'bride' of Assisi's saint, to be a horrible guardian of Tartarus! And there in Hell the mythical sinners, Tantalus, Sisyphus, Ixion, and the Danaïdes, are punished." [1] In Paradise the monastic brethren of the uninspired poet actually wear laurel wreaths upon their heads.

[1] F. Novati, *Un poema francescano del dugento*, in *Atlra verso il medio evo*, Bari, 1905, pp. 9–102.

In Germany and France, also, ancient forms and motifs are taken over into religious art, but in a quite different spirit. Even in the religious dramas of the nun Hroswitha of Gandersheim, in which the classical element of form has the widest scope and appears at least as prominently as with the Italians—even there it is merely the technique, by no means the inspiration, that can fairly be called classical or heathen. The antique and the Christian element appear here as means and end. Even what is most alien is subordinated to a mighty, an irresistible, faith. No matter how rude and helpless this poetry is felt to be, it is not inorganic; it is not unpoetical. Its whole life springs out of a superabundance of divine miracle. Contrasted with this the Italians usually seem wavering in their feelings. Their imagination flutters uncertainly between a Christian Heaven and a Roman earth.

As the contrasts are not duly emphasized, since no decision ever results either in favour of the Bible or of the Aeneid, there is no powerful impulse in either direction. For the soul of Anselm of Bisate (*circa* 1050) the blessed in Paradise and the literary muses contend. He would fain surrender to both. But since human nature does not permit prolonged association with a sensuous world, he chooses the muses.

This is no longer mediævalism and not yet the Renaissance.

Meantime, it was not merely the divided and uncertain mentality of learned men, only half conscious of historical exigencies, that brought about such a mixture of Roman and Christian ideas. The reawakening of practical and political thinking, especially in the bourgeois class of the Italian people, was working in the same direction.

In our day it is no mystery how closely the anti-Catholic and heretical movements from the eleventh to the fourteenth century were connected with the struggles for economic, social, and political freedom of the burghers, of the artisans and labourers.

At first, that is, in the Gregorian age of reform, the Roman Curia utilized the power of the lower classes and managed to direct their revolutionary violence against the feudal strength of the empire and against the aristocracy of the bishops. In the course of the twelfth century, however, the alliance between ecclesiastical absolutism and the lower classes came to an end. The upheaval of the popular masses took, more and more decidedly, an heretical and anti-ecclesiastical turn. Northern Italy, in particular, was full of Patarini, Catharists, Waldenses, Poor Men of Lyons, Poor Men of Lombardy, and Arnoldists. In almost all the cities religious struggles were combined with economic and social disorders. Gradually even Central Italy, Umbria, and especially Orvieto and Florence showed traces of heretical infection. In the years 1240 and 1246 there was bloody religious strife between Florentine factions.

The growth of the commune is accompanied by heterodox movements and religious civil war. In Southern Italy, however, where the free development of the cities failed, heresy has taken no such strong root.

Religious convictions were involved in the contests of classes in the cities. The democratic and republican memories of ancient Rome were associated with the gospel of the mystics. Such a figure as Arnold of Brescia (*circa* 1150), who was at once tribune of the people and ascetic, or such a combination of republican Romanism with mystical Christianity, is imaginable only on Italian soil.

To what extent, in Italy, the heretical movements from mysticism to the Enlightenment, from Petrus Waldus and Arnold to Averroism, fostered the introduction of antiquity among the lower social classes and hastened the coming of humanism, is a question the investigation of which promises abundant results. They also stimulated poetry in the vernacular.

In many Italian cities, where, in the course of the thirteenth century the masses, without rights, restless and always inclined to heresy, were apt to unite with the magnates in a contest against the prosperous and orthodox bourgeoisie, nobleman and heretic, consul and misbeliever, Ghibelline and Averroist, proletarian and religious visionary, became, only too often, equivalent terms. Mystical popular tribunes and apostolic party-leaders appear. How gladly must these people have united the biblical doctrine of penance with the eloquence of ancient Rome, and the spirit of Christ with that of the Gracchi! For, in the essential idea of freedom, the evangelical spirit was in touch with the republican or municipal movement.

In opposition to this, the dogmatic spirit of conservative minds, whether devoted to emperor or to pope, unites itself no less closely with Roman imperialism.

The poet of the *Gesta per Imperatorem Fridericum Barbam Rubeam* makes his divine Frederick pray as though he were a Caesar Augustus, to whom religion and the welfare of the state are one and the same:

> God, king eternal, ruler of the world . . .
> Thou gavest me, unworthy though I am,
> The scepter and the diadem to wear
> Of Roman empire: therefore, I beseech,
> Support me in the task by thee imposed.
> Permit that I subdue the savage tribes,
> That I rule the humble in settled peace,
> Taming the haughty spirits with the sword.
> If this thou grant not, and my fault prevents,
> Give, Sire, a sign revealing what shall be.

A mighty voice replies from above:

> Thy prayer to quell the nations is fulfilled
> And many a year thy empire shall endure.[1]

In fact, the Italians, from the pope to the humblest craftsman or peasant, from the eleventh to the middle of the thirteenth century down to the Franciscan movement, are too much influenced in their religious beliefs by political, social, and economic passions to be able to rise to that inward freedom and elevation which is essential to a great and pure religious art. Instead of inspiring poetry, we find biting satire. "As soon as religious problems reach Italian soil, they are transformed into social and political questions." [2]

At best, their poetry strays into moralizing. In the last decade of the twelfth century (*circa* 1193), a Tuscan scholar, evidently a layman, Henricus Pauper of Settimello, wrote a most remarkable and significant didactic poem, *Elegia de Diversitate Fortunae et Philosophiae Consolatione.* Henricus, absolutely a heathen philosopher, an Epicurean and Stoic soul, quarrelled with fortune over the misery of human existence, and hid himself at last, haughty and defiant, in the consciousness of his moral independence. Nervous impatience, a truly modern irritability and weariness of life, urge and struggle toward the classical equanimity of a purely rational morality. What is to be thought of the Chris-

[1] Monaci's edition in *Fonti per la storia d'Italia*, Rome, 1887. Verse 1905 sqq.
[2] U. Ronca, *Cultura medioevale e poesia latina d'Italia nei secoli XI e XII*, Rome, 1892.

tianity of a man who, with noisy pathos and in academic despair, cries out:

> What have I done against thee, great Jupiter?
> Whence comes thy thirst for harm?
> I've wrested from the sky no thunderbolts, nor sought nor craved
> The couch of Juno. Nor have I supplied
> Ferocious weapons to the Giants' race.
> Why dost thou harm me, cruel one? Why? Why?
> Tell me; I know not; and if thou dost not know
> Why harm then, Jupiter, the innocent?
> . . . How petty a victory,
> To have the power to rack a wretched man!

And what a difference between the pious Philosophia of Boëthius and the cool, sententious wisdom of Henricus's cultured imitation of her! This later Philosophia will hear not a word of Church or pope: "If Peter's rock should turn to ice, what then? More useful to thee were a pagan than the sharp-clawed man who bears the keys." [1]

She hates credulity as most fatal; she commends virtue and discerning modesty to her pupil.

No less precocious than the poet is his style: sententious, sober, abstract, pointed, and querulous. How remote from the amiable simplicity of the Franciscans!

In the thirteenth century, Henricus's *Elegia* was one of the most popular textbooks in the schools. Who knows but that Dante learned his Latin from it? Who knows but that in the description of his Fortuna,[2] along with his recollections of Boëthius there is hidden a reminiscence of the disdained and justified Fortuna of Henricus, of the *generalis oeconoma rerum?* [3] And may not the example of so learned a fellow countryman, who discussed, poetically and publicly, his own unhappiness, and indeed the whole state of the world, have excited the ambition and self-consciousness of the youthful Dante?

To be sure, only ambition and egotism, indeed, only literary inspiration, but no religious art, could have developed from such models.

So then the Christian ideal in Italy was not sufficiently pure, deep, and popular to bend to its needs the vernacular of the land—

[1] *Studi medievali*, IV (1912–1913), Book IV, verse 51 sqq.
[2] *Inferno*, VII.
[3] *Op. cit.*, Book II, verse 181.

and the less so when the Church persistently favoured Latin. It may well be that here and there a preacher made use of Italian. But the more boldly pious heretics and visionaries seized upon the speech of the people, the more strictly did orthodoxy limit itself to Latin and accept no other speech. Even Dante in his *De vulgari Eloquentia* could not bring himself to intrust divine and theological subjects to a poet of the vulgar tongue.

POETRY OF LOVE AND SOCIETY

It might be supposed that at least love, the passion of man for woman, and the social impulse, which is so strong in the Italians, should have expressed themselves in artistic form. But just here, the history of literature records an all but complete silence.

A dull, artificial love-idyll was laboriously composed, at the close of the eleventh century, by a scholar, presumably a priest, from Northern Italy. Whether other literary trifles of a similar character should be credited to Italy or not is of little importance. For a clerk, following in the footsteps of Petronius, Catullus, or Ovid, to express himself in lascivious fancies and extravagant metres, might happen anywhere in the mediæval Occident. Wherever there are celibates and scholars, we need not fear a lack of obscene trivialities and furtive and erudite toying with erotic literature.

The Italians, it appears, participated only indifferently, tardily, and under the inspiration of the French goliards, in the social love-songs and drinking-songs of the strolling scholars and unfrocked priests.[1] As there probably was no native goliard poetry in Italy before the thirteenth century, it was taken for granted that there could hardly have been before that time native and colloquial popular poetry.

Yet it is hard for us to believe in a complete barrenness in this field; to explain it is impossible. Certainly Italian lyrics were sung before the thirteenth century, but no pen was found to record them. Among the first to record popular poetry were perhaps the bored notaries of Bologna, who filled up the blank paper of their deeds and the idle intervals in their official schedule with such amusements. Their precious *memoriali*, however, do not antedate the year 1265. The popular poetry received more thorough or

[1] The presence of strolling scholars in Italy is attested by a bull of the Antipope Victor IV in the year 1160.

loving notice only long after Dante's death, and then at the hands of the accomplished humanists, Guistiniani, Politian, and Lorenzo the Magnificent.

How could Dante, the opponent of all dialect, the apostle of the noble and courtly form of common speech, have other than a chance, incidental, and more or less unconscious acquaintance with the popular poetry of his home?

The first social requisite for artistic, romantic, and popular love-poetry was lacking—knighthood. And even when the land became completely feudalized, the Northland customs and ideals of the nobility still continued to be regarded as foreign. Especially the position of woman in Italy was a different one. On this subject the popular tales, though they belong to a later age, give us perhaps the most truthful picture. The social intercourse between the sexes was unhampered. The step from love to gratification was swifter, easier, and more lightly taken than, for example, in Provence, where the nobleman kept his wife secluded as in a harem. The Italians seem to hold, as a rule, a happy and natural middle course between dreamy longing, love-service, and extravagant deification of woman, to which the knight is accustomed, and brutal contempt and maltreatment as practised by the peasant of the North.

Even at the end of the thirteenth century (*circa* 1276) this purely bourgeois feeling may be perceived in the manner in which the judge, Guido delle Colonne, recast in Latin prose the Trojan romance of Benoît de Sainte More. A scientific, critical spirit has supplanted the fantastic and romantic one; instead of erotics and gallantry, there are ethics and morality.

Boccaccio was the first who gave the Italians a light literature of their own. Just as at the present day, so in Dante's time it was the privilege of the French to feed and poison the idle fancy of young people with erotic pictures and to carry on in all civilized lands the business of the literary pander. "Galeotto was the book and he that wrote it!" [1]

The Italians, it would seem, were satisfied to relate orally brief, witty, pathetic, and fascinating tales to each other in a merry circle. For a long time, from the thirteenth century till far into the age of the Renaissance, their collections of short stories retained the fresh traces of conversation and social life.

[1] *Inferno*, V, 137.

So there doubtless must have been a strong disinclination to record love-poetry and light literature in Italian. The thoughts of those men who were in a position to handle the pen had been directed to quite different matters.

EDUCATION

Not only were the great, fresh, and elemental feelings and passions lacking, but even the actual intellectual tendencies, the chief educational forces among the people, were unfavourable, almost hostile, to all lively poetry.

In the North, in France and Germany, all education was under the control of the clergy. They live a scholarly life, and Latin suffices them. But the layman, excluded from study, requires diversion, amusement, stimulation, instruction in his own fashion, in his own language, and according to his own taste. For his sake, on his account, and in his service, literatures in the vulgar languages arise. Were it not for this striking cultural divergence, the need and demand for a popular written literature would doubtless never have arisen.

In Italy, however, these sharp distinctions were much slighter and less pronounced. There scientific education and activity were probably at no time the exclusive privilege of the clerics.

An inheritance from the imperial age of Rome had survived, however enfeebled and impoverished, into the Middle Ages, and still held its vitality—the schools of the grammarians and rhetoricians. These remained as lay schools, independent of the Church. They cultivated an essentially worldly, academic, formalistic, and, in a certain sense, humanistic spirit. The great ecclesiastical and Christian aspirations, dry, heavy, and disciplinary though they were, yet lent a profound sense of seriousness and conscientiousness to the clerical schools which was absent from these lay institutions. A self-satisfied, sensuous, pretentious, leisurely, haughty, and luxurious education, a mediæval æstheticism, asserted itself largely. The instruction was usually costly, while the dull monastic schools stood freely open to those without means. Indeed, in Italy, even the Church schools—for example, the famous Scola Cantorum at Rome—was influenced by humanistic and rhetorical preoccupations in the darkest mediæval days. How a scholar trained in the spirit of the Italian schools could be irritated by the homespun education of the sturdy monks of St.

Gall may be seen from the *Epistola Gunzonis ad Augienses Fratres* (965).

In his much-cited and much-debated *Panegyricus*, the chaplain Wipo demands of King Henry III that he see to it that in Germany also noblemen send their sons to school and have them instructed in writing and law. So, he declares, the old Romans did, and so the Italians do today.

> All of the boys are sent to school to sweat.
> Only to Germans seems it vain or base
> That any should be taught except the clerks.

About the same time Otto von Freising testifies to a greater height and breadth in the German schools and lay education than any other people's could boast.[1]

How large a share, on the other hand, was taken by the clergy in profane science, can be seen from the fact that in the decrees of the Councils of the years 1131, 1139, 1163, 1179, and 1180—all held, to be sure, outside of Italy—all monks and canonists were forbidden to study Roman law or medicine. The unseemly preference of the Italian clergy for the *trivium* of grammar, dialectic, and rhetoric, as well as their neglect of theology, is repeatedly assailed. The great theologians, Lanfranc, Anselm of Canterbury, Gerard of Cremona, and Peter Lombard, belong to the Italian nation more by birth than because of their studies, inclinations, and activities.

Certainly the Italians, especially in the eleventh century, were surpassed by the French and Germans, not only in ecclesiastical but even in classical learning and knowledge. But in the North there were only a few, in Italy there were many: clergy, knights, noblemen, burghers, notaries, judges, merchants, yes, even handicraftsmen, who shared in intellectual wealth and enjoyment.

Almost every city traced its origin back to Rome, Troy, or some other ancient greatness. Historic, no less than the soil, was the consciousness of its inhabitants. What connected the Italians with antiquity was not so much acquired knowledge as innate feeling. Virgil was the guardian spirit of Naples; Mars, of Florence; Fabius, of Bergamo. The great universal memory of Rome, still vital everywhere, created, as it were, an ideal soil in which the profound differences in the culture of the people were bridged

[1] *Gesta Friederici*, Book II, Chapter 13.

over. Even the ignorant man, in so far as he knew himself to be a descendant and heir of a great and advanced nation, uplifted himself from the depths of that barbarism without traditions in which the laity of the North lay.

But memories did not satisfy them. They desired, in the present also, to possess learned men and their own educational institutions.

As early as the eleventh century, the university—the *studium generale*—developed out of the lay school. All these higher institutions in Italy, except Salerno and Naples, owe their origin and prosperity to the communes, not to the Church, not to the emperor. Rhetoric and, what was then most closely associated with it, jurisprudence, and usually also medicine, made up the chief subjects of instruction. In Bologna, for example, it was not until the year 1360 that theology was included in the curriculum.

Rhetoric, law, and medicine—that is, the formalistic, practical, empirical, and natural sciences—interested the Italians. Medicine flourished in Salerno, mathematics and astronomy at Monte Cassino, in Pavia and Bologna the civil law, in Rome canon law, and throughout the whole peninsula, rhetoric. In these fields Italy leads the other nations as a pioneer. In the speculative and historical sciences she is behindhand.

Now it is precisely in these subjects, in theology, philosophy, and history, that the feelings and intuition play by far the chief part and fill the largest space. So an age which cultivates formalism and naturalism, but on the other hand neglects speculation, may fairly be described as sober, sagacious, liberal, shrewd, and essentially unpoetical. This state of mind was predominant during the tenth, eleventh, and twelfth centuries.

France and Germany also entered upon such a stage of enlightenment—lay education, naturalism, and formalism—but much later: in the fourteenth and fifteenth centuries. There, too, a corresponding decline of poetry accompanied it.

Regarded from this side, the absence of native poetry in the vulgar tongue in Italy no longer appears as tardiness, but rather as leadership, in the race for culture; and from this standpoint we may well approve the judgment of an eminent Italian scholar when he says, "One of the characteristics which reveal, even in the Middle Ages, the historical and cultural superiority of the

Italian people over all the rest of Europe consists in the fact that imaginative production is scantier in Italy than elsewhere." [1]

Various and complicated circumstances, then, condition the unique position of Italy in the Middle Ages, and check, until the beginning of the thirteenth century, the development of native poetry; these may be summed up as follows: the divided nature of political views, the disintegration of religious feeling, the aversion to a feudal order, the democratic spirit among the triumphant bourgeoisie of the cities, the effacement of the distinctions in education between layman and clergy, the weight of classical traditions and memories, the sober and enlightening progress of science, the barren æstheticism of the rhetoricians: we might say, in a single epigrammatic phrase, the universal lack of naïveté.

4. Dante and the Literary Inheritance of Italian Mediævalism

Not merely in the history of the rise of Italian poetry, but even in the *Divine Comedy*, these adverse conditions can be traced. What did the intellectual life of Italy from the eighth to the beginning of the thirteenth century provide for the construction of the great poem? Essentially nothing but raw material, rigid, shapeless blocks without living form, obstacles that must be surmounted, dissensions that must be reconciled. More unfavourable preliminary conditions for the creation of a literary masterpiece could hardly be imagined. The copious and easy poetical harvest which Ludovico Ariosto was able, two hundred years later, to reap with a light hand and to bind up in pleasing sheaves, was denied to Dante. It was crude ore that he had to forge, so that if, despite the fiercest fire and the mightiest of hammers, the form did not issue from his workshop in rounded perfection, who shall marvel?

We have already seen how the discordance of political poetry left its traces in the *Commedia*, how personal and party spirit and universal theocracy, the one embodied in all too local, the other in all too abstract, shapes and colours, oppose each other.

We again discern the disintegration of religious poetry. It betrays itself in the allegorical parallels and in the biblical and classical, ecclesiastical and heathen images and illustrations, all set, without question, side by side. Especially through the *Pur-*

[1] Domenico Comparetti, *Virgilio nel medio evo*, 2d ed., II, 16.

gatorio the alien threads run often closely intertwined. Frequently the reconciliation of such various and discordant forms is accomplished not by art but by philosophy, not formally but materially.

Now and again the prosaic, dogmatic, mathematical, and overclever spirit of the preceding centuries passes into the *Commedia.* The numerous detailed astronomical reckonings, the strong infusion of natural science, all the precision of the chronological structure, often appear rugged and scholastic. They do indeed lend to the poetical illusion its peculiar consistency, but they remind us at the same time of the good Italian schools.

Finally—and for any other poet this would have been the most difficult burden—the school satchel of the mediæval Italian was crammed with endless, wearisome scraps of Latin dialectic and rhetoric. Dante was not the man to cast aside, with a gesture of contempt, this hard-won and painfully retained ballast. For this he lacked the levity with which noisy and boastful young talents or so-called artistic geniuses relieve themselves of the burden of inherited goods. It is precisely the strongest spirits that drag along, patiently and persistently, their inheritance from many generations, until it becomes their own living treasure. So Dante struggled with rhetoric, dialectic, and the theory of poetry. In the *Vita Nuova* and in the *Convivio* he takes delight in the barren readiness with which he picks his own poetry to pieces in true scholastic fashion. His Latin letters are full of pompous embellishment. In the *De vulgari Eloquentia* he has attempted to systematize the rules of the formalists and to make them available for Italian poetry. Not until the composition of the *Commedia* does art, for him, become nature. But even here we are still disturbed at times by a bit of artificial decoration amid the living foliage. In order to see, figuratively, how Dante, out of the rigid idols of the Italians, out of the old beldame Rhetorica, has made a smiling, fresh, and yet somewhat prim child of Heaven, one should read the charming little song:

> A little child, lovely and young am I,
> And hither am I come that men may see
> The beauties of the place whence I am come.[1]

The summing up would be, thus far, mainly negative. Everything that is tasteless, hard, formalistic, and pedantic in the

[1] *I' mi son pargoletta bella e nova.* That Dante's ballad was meant to refer to Rhetoric is not certain but probable.

Commedia, everything that is poetically burdensome, is to be charged to Italian mediævalism.

But matters in this world—thanks be to God!—are so ordained that every loss is also a gain, all opposition is power. For so happy a toiler, so cheery a fighter, and so impetuous a giant as Dante, the chilliest opposition was the most precious of boons. For in the thin and frosty air wherein little talents perish, genius breathes and strives all the more mightily. Rigid strength grows pliant in action.

> Even as one well versed in song and music
> Binds fast with ease each harpstring to its peg,
> And makes the cord secure at either end,
> So did Odysseus string the mighty bow,
> With utmost ease, and then, with his right hand
> Plucking the cord, made trial of its sound.
> Clear as the swallow's voice the note he heard.

5. The Literary Influence of Foreign Lands

THE FRENCH

So long as science belongs to the few, there is danger of inbreeding. But when intellectual life becomes general and is multiplied, as it were, throughout the entire people, then interchange of ideas with other lands is vigorously carried on.

Toward the end of the twelfth century, education in Italy was more general and accessible than anywhere else. Much was to be learned, so that students gathered there from all parts of Europe. The foreign teacher who brought with him something new or valuable might count on a hospitable and intelligent reception, so that presently the brisk intellectual market of the Italians attracted French theology, Arabic philosophy and natural science, and, first of all, Northern art; they were eagerly received.

Even the French minstrel, who spoke not a word of Italian, found willing and appreciative ears among the burghers and handicraftsmen of the cities in Northern Italy. When the French boast of having brought to Italy their popular and knightly poetry, it seems to me that the merit of the Piedmontese, the Lombards, the Venetians, and the Romagnoles should also be remembered. It is no slight evidence of the adaptability, the interest, and the patience of the Northern Italian that he mastered the foreign, though closely related, language of the French street-singers. Listening is also an art.

By the end of the eleventh century the greater part of French Carolingian epic poetry must have been known in Northern Italy.

Later, more slowly and less profoundly, the knightly Arthurian romances found their way into the various classes of society. About the same time the romances of Troy, of Thebes, of Caesar, of Alexander the Great, and of Aeneas, as well as the Oriental tales of the seven wise men, the animal epics, and innumerable French farces or *fabliaux*, found numerous zealous readers and listeners in Italy.

A veritable flood of light French literature spreads over the peninsula, rises higher and higher during the thirteenth century, and rolls far on to Florence and Siena. It is taken for granted that an educated Italian, in the Northern half of the land, knows French. The greatest extension of this language occurs precisely in the time of our poet, and continues from about 1230 to 1350.

DANTE AND THE FRENCH

Of course Dante also understood French and read French books. That he made a journey to Paris is not so easy to believe after the impressive refutation by Arturo Farinelli. With the help of quotations, allusions, and reminiscences in Dante's works, the attempt has been made to define the extent of his acquaintance with light literature in French. It may fairly be inferred that the most important parts of the Charlemagne epics, the Guillaume epics, perhaps also the epics of the Crusades and of the Arthurian romances, certainly those of Tristan, Lancelot of the Lake, and the death of Arthur, were known to him, either in writing or orally, either in French or Italian.

All this did not, however, exert a decisive influence upon him. Somewhat as, at the present day, an imaginative boy is affected by tales of Indians or of Robinson Crusoe and a dreamy youth by love-stories, so, perhaps, the French national epics and somewhat later the romances of knighthood and adventure may have influenced Dante's childhood. Slumbering imagination is awakened, stirred, and heated. It is indeed strongly moved, but not turned in any decisive direction.

What could a popular epic like the *Song of Roland* offer to the most personal and meditative of poets, outside of isolated pictures and momentary stimulation?

Even an artistic poet like Chrestien de Troyes, or his supplementers and imitators, for example, the author of the *Lancelot of the Lake*, could hardly be Dante's guide or master. One who hides, as Chréstien does, like a magician behind a curtain, and with a thousand novelties and bewilderments takes his audience captive as if it were a troop of eager-eyed children, is no guide and leader for a serious philosopher. Dante called the Arthur romances of the French *ambages pulcherrimae*—a wondrously beautiful labyrinth, or lovely elaborated fantasies.[1] He took with him, on his way toward truth, only a few blossoms from the French pleasure-gardens, as they chanced to cling to his prophet's robe.

Superficial study of the sources has suggested that the well-known inclination of the French to a cyclic and genealogical chain of epics or romances had been the model for the construction of the Dantesque trilogy. But what is there in common between the commercial art of a collector, of an editor, or of a publisher, and the organically philosophical poetry of this most profound masterpiece?

It is of comparatively minor importance to set forth in detail the forms and shapes of narrative French literature that may have influenced Dante. The essential thing was to establish the fact of that influence. For the effect was chiefly indirect; that is, not so much on the finished work as on the implements. These French romances were the strongest, richest, and almost the only nourishment available in mediæval Italy for a youthful lay imagination. Without some such food, even the most gifted artist may pine; but his physiognomy is not, as a rule, determined by his nourishment.

FRENCH PROSE AND DIDACTIC POETRY

Along with narrative and imaginative literature, France early sent to Italy instructive and enlightening works in prose and verse. Its scientific prose was regarded, and is so expressly characterized by Dante, as a particular asset of the French language.[2]

A number of Italians in the thirteenth century, among them four Tuscans, wrote in French prose: the physician Aldobrandino,

[1] *De vulgari Eloquentia*, I, 10. [2] *Ibid.*

Rusticiano da Pisa, Frate Guglielmo of Florence, and the friend and master of Dante, Brunetto Latini.

It may well be, then, that the first scientific food of our poet was matured in French form. Dante was quite aware that the excellence of a language, that is, its literary perfection, appears more clearly unveiled in prose than in metrical use.[1] So it is more than probable that he composed the commentary of the *Convivio* in conscious rivalry not only with Latin, but also with French prose, and particularly with the great encyclopædic *Trésor* of Brunetto Latini. Not only from the respectful and grateful mention of the *Trésor* in the *Commedia*,[2] but also from certain undoubted echoes and citations, we decide that he had studied this favourite and imposing compilation and popularization of mediæval knowledge.

In the most famous French poem of the thirteenth century, the *Romaunt of the Rose*, the narrative and didactic motives are merged in a great and many-sided allegory. Considering the immense circulation and popularity of this work (before the close of the thirteenth century, we have two Tuscan adaptations of it, *Detto d'amore* and *Fiore*), it would be remarkable if Dante had not become acquainted with it. He may well have read, in particular, the first part, composed in 1237 by Guillaume de Lorris. An absolute proof, indeed, cannot be offered. At any rate, the poem is indirectly connected with the *Commedia*. For it made poets and lay audience familiar with the devices of allegorical constructions and personifications, theretofore little used in Italy. How often since then have such aids and expedients been repeated in popular prose and verse! Whether the influence was direct or indirect, it was limited to the technique. For the true source of inspiration is, in the first part of the *Romaunt of the Rose*, knightly gallantry, and in the second part a civic liberalism; while, in the *Commedia*, it is Christian piety and world-embracing speculation.

The entire wholesale literary importation from France would seem to have brought to our poet not much more than certain imaginative suggestions and some minor technical improvements.

THE PROVENÇALS

The strongest, the most decisive impulsion to artistic poetry, came from Provence. If the lyric of Northern France played a

[1] *Convivio*, I, 10.

[2] *Inferno*, XV, 119 sqq.

notable rôle in Italy, it is due entirely to its close connection with the troubadours of Southern France.

From court to court, from city to city, from one knightly castle to another, these song-loving minstrels wandered with lyre and sword. To Spain, to Hungary, to the farthest Orient, love of adventure led them on. Remembering the close commercial relations between Marseilles and Genoa in the stirring age of the Crusades and during the Albigensian wars which devastated their homeland, how could they fail to seek their fortune among the cultivated aristocracy of Upper Italy? Soon native Italians also, especially Genoese, were composing love-songs in the Provençal language. Indeed, this courtly occupation extended into Central Italy.

For whatever one may say, the art of the troubadours was aristocratic, and for that very reason suited to international extension. In a land like Italy, where even the lower classes were attracted to foreign poetry, much was to be expected from the nobility. In fact, from the last decades of the twelfth century until late in the thirteenth, troubadours who sang in Provençal found a hospitable welcome with the lords of Este, with the counts of Malaspina—and who knows where besides? Many a song of Peire Vidal, of Raimbaut de Vaqueiras, of Guilhem de la Tor, Aimeric de Pegulhan, of Uc de Saint-Circ and of Gaucelm Faidit teaches us how well they fared, how little they felt themselves strangers, how easily, I might almost say how warmly, they played their part in both the political and the gallant affairs of their hosts.

With their clever assurance, with their poise, with their noble independence, these troubadours educated the Italian noblemen to appreciate artistic talent and intellectual personality; taught them how to play the rôle of Maecenas—an advantage which presently was to come to the aid of the homeless poet of the *Commedia.* That same house of Malaspina which, at the beginning of the thirteenth century, was honoured in Provençal song by its troubadour guests, received Dante's royal gratitude, a hundred years later, in Italian verses.[1]

And, like the troubadours, Dante too seems to have addressed some songs purely out of courtesy and without amorous intent to the lady of a noble house. The wandering minstrel had to

[1] *Purgatorio,* VIII, 121 sqq.

make poetic love to the noble ladies of a hospitable court and pay homage of affection to them; it was a question, curiously enough, of good manners.

When Dante dedicates his *Paradiso* with a Latin inscription to Can Grande della Scala, is it not a final remnant of Provençal manners and at the same time a first breath of Renaissance courtesy?

THE OLDEST TROUBADOURS

(PEIRE D'AUVERGNE)

The troubadours introduced widely in Italy not only their social usages, but also their literary conventions; for the latter were most closely associated with the former. If a large portion of the troubadours' poetry remains, down to the present day, psychologically unintelligible or ambiguous to us, it is chiefly because their elaborate social customs are inadequately known to us.

Quite apart indeed from all fashionable life, the troubadour was a man of whims and fancies. As in Italy the puffed-up grammarians and rhetoricians, so in Provence the poet-knights may well have been the first who voluntarily put their trust in their own thoughts and feelings, and made their individuality interesting. On the one hand, they set themselves in opposition to everything commonplace and traditional, and preached the gospel of Nature. On the other hand, in their effort after distinction and originality, they narrowed nature once more to a caricature. With all its refinement, this was in reality a crude, premature, and arbitrary emancipation of the individual, in which nature became caprice, and this, in turn, unnatural convention. No wonder that, in this wilful and unjustified assertion of individuality over all general norms, mental balance was often lost, and that such an astonishing number of troubadours were regarded as daft or insane, or pretended to be, or really were so.

Even the few poems of Guillaume, the ninth count of Poitiers (the eldest of the troubadours known to us), justify this view. Dante regards Peire d'Auvergne as one of the oldest.[1] Even he had, however, a long tradition behind him, especially the artificial school of Marcabru, Cercamon, and Raimbaut d'Aurenga. His datable songs fall approximately into the years 1158–1180.

[1] *De vulgari Eloquentia,* I, 10.

Before he became a troubadour, Peire belonged to the priestly class. His elaborated forms of expression betray his training in Latin and the gradual development of a verbal art on the foundation of which even Dante stands.

Peire d'Auvergne is much further removed from popular songs than Guillaume de Poitiers. Even his most popular bit of verse, the much-admired bird message (*Rossinhol, el seu repaire*) spins out quite too long its fragrant motif. It is not in these light verses nor in his religious songs that his peculiar quality and strength lie. If he attempts to bid us be merry (*L'airs clars e.l chans dels auzelhs*), he writes a didactic treatise; if he would glorify the power of love (*Lo fuehls e.l flors e.l frugz madurs*), he grows most emphatic, heaps up his words, repeats himself, arrays his homonyms before us, and tries to conceal the conventionalism of his material by overloading it. But the moment he begins to analyze the complicated conditions of his soul in the service of love (as in *Ab fina joia comenza*), as soon as he brings into the old love-motifs the new art of reflection and analysis, in short, the intelligent self-consciousness that wholly controls him, his verse acquires a remarkable firmness and strength. His sentimental dialectics create a style hitherto unknown in the popular speech of the day, in which the logic hides rather behind the forms than in them. The intertwined relations of his thoughts are rather hinted at than clearly revealed. There is a progress, but we presently realize that it leads into darkness. If Peire and many of his predecessors and imitators pride themselves on this obscurity, it is not always vanity that is in question, but usually also the consciousness that they are wandering in untrodden ways and steering toward the new artistic ideal of a poetry heavily laden with thought. Because they have not yet the means to be clear—consider the syntactic ambiguity and vagueness of many Provençal constructions!—they pride themselves on obscurity and make a virtue of their linguistic poverty. They are conscious of the multiplicity of their feelings, but they mistake the confused for the complex, pedantry for profundity, and the artificial for the artistic. These obscure poets (*chantar ab motz serratz e clus*) have striven in every way to make progress. Their laborious quest and effort in all directions and with all devices prepare, in a way, the ground for Dante's stylistic accomplishments.

Even the most painfully warped songs of these troubadours

conceal poetic pearls. How powerful in its harshness is Peire's song:

> Be m 'es plazen
> e cossezen
> qui s'aizina de chantar
> ab motz alquus
> serratz e clus
> que om tem ja de vergonhar.

Defiant and tender, he withdraws into himself, sets himself upon a pedestal, teaches mastery through limitation.

> I truly think
> And do believe
> And everything make clear to you,
> Who much begins
> Is little worth
> And his affairs are backward still.
> A garden well
> And safely watched,
> Wherein may no man steal from me,
> Is better than
> An open field
> Whereon I gaze, but own it not.

In a final strophe, notably condensed and difficult to understand, the poet's will is expressed: to collect himself within himself, escaping from the distractions of an empty life:

> Whatever comes,
> Of my free will
> Through life I choose to be a fool.
> When I am dead,
> Berate me not
> For that which I would fain forget.[1]

They are verses hard to translate, of surprising profundity and significance of expression. Long trains of thought are hidden behind a single phrase. The translator is in continual doubt which

[1] The meaning seems to me to be: The inward concentration on which I am now determined may seem to you foolishness. Such a fool I wish to be, because of my wisdom, for the rest of my life. But after my death, cease to make my earlier life, which I desire to forget, a reproach to me.

> Si mal m'en pren,
> per eis mon sen
> Cug a ma vida folleiar.
> Apres ma mort
> no'm fass' om tort
> d'aquo qu'ieu ai ad oblidar.

of the numerous impressions packed together in curt utterances he should bring out.

This epigrammatic, sententious, and oracular style is a creation of the Provençal poets. Here the idea is not revealed in white light and full detail; it lives and works in the fervour of sentiment, and pierces through the mystery of struggling affections. We meet phrases and entire poems which, like riddles, appeal both to our understanding and to our imagination.

Dante learned much in this Provençal school. Many of his lyric poems resemble these early notes of Peire d'Auvergne. Is not the entire *Commedia*, to some extent, a great, subjective, didactic and love-poem in the most compressed or conundrum-like style?

DANTE, PEIRE D'AUVERGNE, AND THE PROVENÇAL "CLASSICISTS"

A notable work of art by Peire d'Auvergne, which had a lasting influence on the development of lyrical forms and was also studied by Dante, is the winter love-song, *De josta .ls breus giorns e.ls loncs sers.*

The contrast between dead Nature in the cold season and the defiant vitality of love in the fervid heart of the singer was a favourite motif. Dante treated it twice.[1] It fitted his temperament as well as it did that of his master. Both loved the rough happiness of feeling themselves at strife with all things, Nature included. Such contests, or discords, between the ego and the non-ego, the troubadour was fond of expressing in shrill, strange, complicated rhymes. Thus Peire in his winter love-song ventured to use the endings *-ers*, *-is*, *-ics*, *-eis* as rhymes. Dante vies with him in harshness of sounds such as *-orca*, *-arco*, *-etra*, *-egue*, *-olti*, *-alto*, *-armo*, and the like. This naïve but often very effective manner, which is determined at any price to have a close connection between sound and mood,[2] may often be recognized in the *Commedia*, especially in the *rime aspre e chiocce* of certain cantos of the *Inferno*. Indeed, it was even carried so far that a distracted state of the soul, particularly an unrequited love, was indicated by a mixture of several languages or dialects in one and the same poem (*descort*). Even in this tasteless device, Dante

[1] In the sestina *Al poco giorno*, and in the canzone *Io son venuto al punto della ruota*.
[2] Cf. *De vulgari Eloquentia*, II, 7.

imitated the Provençal poets if the canzone *Ai faux ris!* is really his.[1]

If we disregard such torturing of language, the admiration above expressed for Peire's poem must still seem justified today. Here too there is a thoughtfulness, enlivened by self-consciousness, which evidently urges the poet to an extraordinarily condensed and epigrammatic treatment of his thoughts. It is not the strength of passionate love, nor the peculiarity of the mood, but rather the zeal and force with which the thoughts are moulded and forged, that gives the song its inner life. The lover vanishes behind the technical exertions of the artist. We are affected not by what he says, but by his manner of saying it, of preaching it, and by his insistent assurance of it. Here, perhaps for the first time in vernacular poetry, the interest becomes exclusively artistic, chiefly formal, in both the good and evil senses of the word. We admire successful stylistic power and cleverness in verse, which reminds us directly of Dante and Petrarch. For instance:

I eu vei e crei e sai qu'es vers
qu'amors engraiss 'e magrezis. . . .

Quar no m'enquier de dir? M'en ven destrics:
Tan tem que.l mielhs lais e prenda.l sordeis;
On plus n'ai cor, mi pens: Car no ten gics?

I see, believe, and know it to be true,
That love doth make us lean, or fat. . . .

Why does she ask me naught? That grieveth me.
Yet fear lest I not better fare, but worse.
The more the pain, I say: "So let it be!"

How assured, firm, and bold is the syntax in the passage:

Qu'anc tant no fui mais coartz ni mendics,
ab qu'ieu la vis alques, aqui mezeis
no.m saubes far de gran paubretat ries!

And ne'er was I so base and beggarly
But that, if I could simply look on her,
In utmost misery I could be strong!

Dante has appreciated these purely formal touches. It is most notable that he entirely ignores the lovelorn, sentimental, direct,

[1] His model may have been the famous *descort* of Raimbaut de Vaqueiras.

graceful, amiable, or humorous troubadours, who affect us more by their mood than by their art, and, above all else, by the natural freshness and simplicity of their utterance: men like Guillaume de Poitiers, Jaufré Rudel, Bernard de Ventadour, Peirol, and Peire Vidal.

What he most admires and quotes as models in his *De vulgari Eloquentia* [1] is songs of pomp and splendour that gloriously overcome some great difficulty, such as the artful piece of Aimeric de Pegulhan, *Si cum l'albres que per sobrecargar*, or the ingenious love-casuistry of Folquet de Marseille, *Tan m'abellis l'amoros pensamens*, or two French songs which Dante believed he must ascribe to the most spiritual of Northern troubadours, King Thibaut IV of Navarre. "This type of construction we call most perfect!" Dante cries enthusiastically. This is, he declares, essentially the same noble, artistic, and regular style that we admire in the ancients, in Virgil, Ovid, Statius, and Lucan, and in prose writers like Livy, Pliny, Frontinus, and Paulus Orosius.

One might feel tempted, by this allusion to the ancients, to distinguish between a classical and a romantic school in Provençal literature, as is customary in the case of modern poetry. Of course such a distinction can be applied, in this case, only to the temperament and style of the singer, not to the material. It should therefore have only a psychological and æsthetic, not a cultural and historical significance.

The psychological and the æsthetic significance need not coincide. Regarded psychologically, all the troubadours might, doubtless, be classed, with few exceptions, as romanticists; that is, as isolated, divided, sentimental, in one way or another jostled out of the natural balance of their feelings. Courtly love and the life of chivalry are in their very essence the opposite of naïve, and therefore highly unclassical. Yet even the most whimsical feelings admit, according to the character of each artist, a more subjective, direct, unreflected, spontaneous, offhand, nonchalant, unforced, in fact, romantic treatment; or, again, a more artistic, artificial elaboration controlled by the norms of the mind, of wit, of understanding, or in other words the objective, classical manner of handling. In this æsthetic sense we may reckon a poet like Peire d'Auvergne, or passages like those cited as models by Dante, as unquestionably classical.

[1] II, 6.

The king of these classicists, whom Dante has set high above all the rest, is Arnaut Daniel. Others were of the opinion that the crown belonged to Giraut (Gerardus) de Bornelh. Dante decides for Arnaut, in the most solemn manner, by the mouth of his father in poetry, Guido Guinizelli:

"O brother," said he, "he whom I point out,"
And here he pointed at a spirit in front,
"Was of the mother tongue a better smith.
Verses of love and proses of romance,
He mastered all; and let the idiots talk,
Who think the Lemosin surpasses him.
To clamour more than truth they turn their faces,
And in this way establish their opinion,
Ere art or reason has by them been heard." [1]

In order to understand an æsthetic judgment by Dante which so sharply contradicts the general opinion, we must endeavour to comprehend the æsthetic nature of Giraut as well as of Arnaut. Both of them influenced Dante's poetry decisively and profoundly, but in quite different directions.

GIRAUT DE BORNELH

Giraut's poems were composed approximately between 1165 and 1195. At first, evidently under the influence of Peire d'Auvergne, he was content to follow the obscure style. His biography tells us that he was a learned poet, and that "his manner of life was to spend the whole winter in study, and in summer to pass from court to court." It is accordingly to be expected that the conventional element would be prominent in him, as in most of the troubadours. Against this grey background of customary love-service and the professional artistic performance, it is not easy to trace the outlines of a truly original poetry.

But even in his imitation of the obscure manner Giraut's temperament seems to reveal itself. It is not, as in the case of Marcabru, bitterness; it is not, as with Peire, the intensity of his nature; nor, again, is it the struggle with his thought, nor inner depth, nor even a defiant self-consciousness that inclines him to obscurity of utterance. It is only superficially that he imitates the most striking quality of his models. Hence his obscurity often becomes vagueness and caprice. Ambiguous, half-finished images and unintelligible allusions keep pressing forward.

[1] *Purgatorio*, XXVI, 115–123.

Giraut must soon have noticed that such efforts were unsuited to his nature. Even the sentiments of hopeful love and fear, which were usually expressed in obscure verses, he determines to utter in an easy song "which every one may understand."

I could make it difficult,
But a song has fullest worth
When it is for all mankind.
Blame who will, I like it well
When from happy mouths I hear,
Plain and rudely sung, my song,
As they to the fountain go.[1]

This state of mind accords ill with a Dante who, as the story-tellers relate, was beside himself when, instead of a musician like Casella, a donkey-driver or a smith, rough-throated, sang his good verses.

But that Giraut at a definite point in his development (before 1173) renounced positively, once for all, affectation and obscurity, I cannot believe, in the light of his discussion of this subject with the troubadour Linhaure (Raimbaut d'Aurenga). He did liberate himself from his inbred reverence for the learned style, but his capricious humour and a certain impulsive nonchalance may well have beguiled him, now and again, into obscurity of expression. Only, it was not the solemn and epigrammatic obscurity of the classical stylists, but rather a jesting game of hide and seek, or the "genial" negligence of a nature inclined to romanticism. He obeys his own mood and caprice:

Que no m'azaut de trop sen
N'en trop foldat no m'enten.
Pero sens, pretz e folia
  Chascus a sas vetz
Qui be.ls assembla ni.ls tria,
  Segon mo veiaire.[2]

In spite of his studies, in spite of his culture, despite his high regard for knightly usage and custom, Giraut is a child of nature. He has an inborn, good-humoured amiability. The exasperated self-consciousness of a Marcabru, of a Peire, Arnaut, or Dante, is alien to him. Although he, low-born, loves a lady of the higher nobility, there is nothing heroic in his love-service. Modesty,

[1] *Sämtliche Lieder des Trobadors Giraut de Bornhel*, ed. A. Kolsen, Halle, 1910, I, 14 sqq.
[2] *Ibid.*, p. 310.

discretion, and reticence are the virtues which he most eagerly approves and practises without effort:

Car pos c'om no pot dir
So cor ni descobrir
Lai on es sos entens
Pauzatz, drechs es niens
    Totz als bobans,
C'om pot far en fols mazans.[1]

And if we may not dare
Reveal our heart to her
Who in our thought abides,
Then surely nothing worth
    Is vain display
Of fervid utterance.

It almost sounds a bit bourgeois. Compared with the brilliant wit of ingenious virtuosos of love-service, this honest man finds himself at a disadvantage.

Que per us prims entendedors
    Me tol paors
    E frevoltatz,
Car no cut esser be amatz,
Mans gaps, mans dichs, mans fachs ginhos,
Per qu'eu fora bautz e joios.[2]

Where love's more lofty liegemen are
    Fear summons me
    And humble mind,
Since less I deem myself beloved
For many a merry quip and jest
Wherewith I too might give delight.

But he accepts humorously the limitations of his temperament. With childish gaiety and sometimes with elaborate loquacity, he knows how to carry on a dialogue with his abashed heart, and again he sings in the gentlest tones of humorous melancholy, and smiles cheerily at himself.

When he praises his lady's features for their calm simplicity and modesty, verses come to him which remind us of the tenderest sonnets in the *Vita Nuova*.

C'umilitatz
Don es chargatz
Sos cors prezatz,

[1] *Op. cit.*, p. 28.

[2] *Ibid.*, I, 26.

La ten en patz
E.lh ditz: Parlatz!
E: No gaire! [1]

Humility
Still keepeth veiled
Her noble form,
And gives her peace,
And bids her: Speak!
Yet: Not too much!

Though still pent in rigid rhymes, it is Beatrice's portrait.

The more freely such a man allows himself to be borne on by the clear current of folk-song, so much the safer fares the poet's little bark. Perhaps the completest thing that Giraut created is the watchman's morning song: *Reis glorios, verais lums e clartatz.*[2] On much thinking and much study, so delicate a muse cannot thrive. She cannot, indeed, cease from inborn dreams and fancies, but often she does not permit herself to utter them save in clever and elaborate phrasing.

DANTE AND GIRAUT

Here the young Dante of the *Vita Nuova* could learn both dreaming and interpretation.

"On a night in spring," so Giraut tells the tale, "I dreamed a dream that entranced me, of a wild falcon that perched upon my fist, and seemed, indeed, tame, but never saw I one at first so wild that later grew so familiar and confiding, so clever on the wing. I told the dream to my lord, as one should do to his friend. He interpreted it to me as a vision of love, and said it could not fail that I should peacefully win a beloved in lofty station. . . . Now I feel shame and fear, I weep and watch and sigh and account the dream great folly and have no faith in its fulfillment. Yet from a foolish soul a vain, proud, and audacious dream cannot part, for to myself I say: 'After our journey, the dream will come true, even as it was interpreted to me.'" There is much here to remind us of the first dream in the *Vita Nuova*, except that in Dante even the obscurest images and the strangest comparisons are still more sharply outlined, and more firmly set in their proper connection.

Giraut's fancy, however, has in it something undisciplined; it eludes control, gladly runs at large, and lights on trivial things.

[1] *Op. cit.*, p. 36.

[2] *Ibid.*, p. 342 sqq.

The moment it seeks new paths it grows bewildered, uncertain, and, amid images, forgets its own goal. How swollen, for instance, and inwardly how empty, is the figure of the beleaguered castle in the canzone *Can lo glatz e.l frechs e la neus.*[1] How haphazard in its construction is the moralized romance of the three maidens (*Lo dolz chans d'un auzel*),[2] compared with the mighty structure of Dante's canzone of the three symbolic ladies, *Tre donne intorno al cor mi son venute.* If there is a relation between the two, it is the palest possible: a union, in each, of the idea of three feminine beings with a complaint concerning the moral degeneracy of the times and injustice suffered—no more than that.

Giraut was much too good-natured to attack the evils of his time with lashing satire. He strikes, like all men who do not wish to harm, not at anything definite, but always at general ills. Therefore his satire becomes unctuous, sermon-like, prosaic, argumentative, and Philistine. We understand at once that in his age, and in general amid the harsh realities of life, he could not be at ease. But presently we perceive, also, that he has not the strength to take revenge upon them, or to protect himself against them. He cannot even suppress the suspicion that his complaints over the decay of knightliness remain unprofitable, to himself and to other men. And then, with lightened heart, he overleaps it all:

E tenh m'a joc
Lor falhimen![3]

Compared with the war-songs of a Bertran de Born, how good and worthy, but how lukewarm, are the two crusaders' songs of our Giraut!

But Dante, curiously enough, valued Giraut most highly as the poetic eulogist of virtue. To be sure, virtue was the one subject upon which the lovesick, dreamy troubadour could become sober, thoughtful, and serious enough to file his verses according to all the rules of the art, to polish his words, and to arrange his sentences in due order. On the other hand, as an honest soul, which he surely must have been, he feels the desirableness of virtue enough to be able to put some fluency into the dryness and some colour into the pallor of moral and didactic verse. So Dante may be quite right when, from the purely formalistic point of view of the

[1] *Op. cit.*, p. 62. [2] *Ibid.*, I, 348. [3] *Ibid.*, p. 84.

De vulgari Eloquentia, he cites Giraut's moral poems as the most regular examples and models.

We, however, are to be forgiven if, from a less scholastic point of view, we count among the weaker performances of our poet precisely the poems praised by Dante, particularly the songs

> Per solatz revelhar . . .
> Er auziretz encabalhitz chantars. . . .

and

> Si per mon Sobretotz no fos.

The theme *O tempora, O mores!* is disposed of in faultlessly rhymed, lifeless prose. Neither with indignation nor with bitterness, but, as a rule, merely with edifying peevishness, the querulous critic of morals contrasts the gloomy and world-weary materialism of his own time with the chivalry, the dignity, and the cheerfulness of days gone by. His sharp antitheses, his generalizing exaggerations, are the unpoetical creation of a discontented nature, if not mere rhetorical exercises.

What Dante could learn from him was chiefly superficial verbal devices, such as critics have attempted to point out in his moral canzones (*Le dolci rime d'amor*, *Poscia ch'Amor*, and *Tre donne intorno al cor*): figures of speech, like the sudden transition from contemplation, from complaining, from the elegiac tone, to the apostrophe, the transition from the love-song to the sermon, the mingling of long eleven-syllable verses with short ones of five or seven syllables; a certain mobility in syntax and metre, as well as in particular images and ideas—all in all, rather mannerisms than style.

Giraut's style is more romantic than classical; hence he may well have exerted a profound influence upon the youthful poetry of the *Vita Nuova* and of the *stil nuovo*, not upon the philosophic poetry contemporaneous to the *Convivio* and the *De vulgari Eloquentia*.

The visionary mood, the popular and dreamy tone that Giraut often reveals in the opening stanzas of his songs, we recognize again in the love-poems of the youthful Dante. And it is perhaps no accident that with him also, the employment of pathetic tones is most successful in the introductory verses. With the Provençal poets this nowise rare phenomenon is accounted for by the metrical structure of the canzone. In the first strophe the poet was still free, in the following stanzas he was under obligation to repeat exactly not only the metrical scheme, but the rhymes of the introductory strophe.[1] The Italians, on account of the greater scarcity of rhymes in their speech, held only, from the earliest times, to the metrical sequence, not to the identity of rhyming sounds, from one stanza to another. But if Giraut, like Dante, was apt to be happier at the beginning of the song than during its continuance, this may be explained by a special circumstance. They were both poets born and, for that very reason, able to strike in the first note the lyrical tone of each particular mood. But they were both apt to permit the independent development of poetic motifs to suffer through their desire to be instructive. However, Dante's art was less fragmentary and appears worked out in unified form, with power to keep the goal in sight.

The romantic appeal to the imagination and the gentle, lovable, delicate, humorous heart-tones which here and there, almost unnoted, emanate from Giraut's songs, just because they are part of a profounder movement have been less clearly recognized either by the historians of literature or by Dante than have certain rhetorical and metrical features of his art. These can be learned one by one and accordingly observed and pointed out.

But in the devices of their art, Arnaut Daniel was immeasurably superior to Giraut de Bornelh.

ARNAUT DANIEL

With Giraut these devices are something alien and disturbing; with Arnaut they spring out of the natural impulse of the poetry itself, and crown it like gloriously unfolded blossoms. With Arnaut everything is artificial—even Nature. He was so fortunate as to live among a people and to compose his poetry in a time (*circa* 1180–1200) when artistic technique had attained a high, but not the final, degree of refinement, and to be able therefore to bring it to its highest culmination.

"Born a nobleman, bred a Latinist, he lived a musician and poet." So Canello, the worthy editor of Arnaut's poems, sums up his life.[2]

Arnaut, like Giraut, does homage to a lady in lofty station, and following his example, commends austerest reticence. Indeed,

[1] Only here and there a troubadour—for example, Arnaut Daniel—occasionally ventured to break this rule.

[2] *La Vita e le opere del trovatore Arnaldo Daniello*, ed. U. A. Canello, Halle, 1883.

in the few (altogether eighteen) songs of his which we possess, he cannot do enough to proclaim his absolute subjection to the laws of love-service, and to assert his most unconditional devotion to the will, ay, to every whim, of his mistress. He is at ease only under the tyranny of fashion and convention. He is not satisfied to leave his love unuttered; he must, as a pretext, and to deceive the inquisitive, acclaim another lady. The revelation of his feelings must be made under false pretence, so that his love may abide purer and truer in his heart's inmost cell. Without the quiver of an eyelash he will endure the grimmest tortures of unsated longing. Desire pierces him to his heart's core; yet is he mute.

Car, si m'art dinz la meola,
La fuocs non vuoill que s'escanta.

E qui de parlar trassauta
Dreitz es qu'en la lenga.is morda.

Fire may through my marrow rage,
Nor would I desire it quelled.

Who in speech is over-hasty
Shall be doomed to bite his tongue.[1]

In such love there can be no question of rights, or of requital. In favour or disfavour, you are subject to your lady—even if it be her pleasure to revile you and to cast the blame on you that the Franks are not Gascons, or that a ship is wrecked before it reaches the harbour of Bari. Like an heroic penitent, Arnaut delights in the servitude of such love. He boasts:

Non sai un tan sia e Dieu frems,
Ermita ni monge ni clerc,
Cum ieu sui e leis de cui can.

There is no hermit, no, nor priest,
That is so loyal to his God
As I to her that hath my love! [2]

Don Quixote, the knightly fool, castigated himself and pined in the wilderness of the Sierra Morena, because his Dulcinea seemed ungracious. But centuries earlier Arnaut declared:

So long as she was wroth with me
I would do penance in the wilds
Where never bird hath made its nest.[3]

[1] Canzone VIII. [2] Canzone XIV. [3] Canzone XI.

In truth this heroism in love has something of Don Quixote in it; it is the conventional lie, the hyperbolic contrast between semblance and reality. Don Quixote, however, constantly forgets this contradiction, and whenever his esquire reminds him of it, ignores it; Arnaut, on the other hand, remains fully aware of it, and from that very contradiction draws the stress and vigour of his verse. In Arnaut, Don Quixote and Sancho Panza are merged, so to speak, in a single soul. On the one hand he boasts and exalts himself as the perfect artistic servant of love, as the *parfait amant;* on the other hand he calls attention, in mingled vanity and self-derision, to the senseless, unnatural, and foolish nature of his behaviour, as in the winged verses:

> Ieu sui Arnautz qu'amas l'aura,
> E chatz la lebre ab lo bou
> E nadi contra suberna.
>
> Arnaut am I who clench the air,
> Who would with oxen chase the hare
> And swim against the stream.[1]

Stimulated passion, overstrained sensuousness, forced eagerness on the one side, sturdy realism on the other; and, between them, a constant interchange of clever, ironic, reflective wit: these are, if I am not mistaken, the vital forces of Arnaut's lyrics. Everything, sublime as well as commonplace, appears in his verse exaggerated, often distorted. More than with his lady he seems to us to be in love with this inborn morbid state. One could hardly imagine a more romantic nature. That this man was regarded as a sexual pervert and was placed by Dante among the sinners against Nature[2] need not surprise us.

And nevertheless, although Arnaut's romanticism extends even into his sexual relations, his poetic ideal is classical. To be sure, he rarely, perhaps never, attained it; it is true there is much that is disjointed, obscure, whimsical in his songs. Often he cares more for emphasis than for harmony. Often the contrasted elements of his style—learned Latinisms and popular proverbs, the dialect of Don Quixote and that of Sancho—stand unreconciled side by side. But before Dante another can hardly be found who

[1] Canzone X.
[2] *Purgatorio,* XXVI, perhaps on account of an obscene poem of Arnaut's, *Puois en Raimons e'n Turc Malecs* . . . which was, as a matter of fact, uttered merely in jest.

strove more earnestly and intelligently for their artistic reconciliation. What he brought together, out of his home-field and out of his school textbooks, he kneads together with unwearying patience and effort. "Only seldom do we find in Arnaut, despite the great difficulty of his rhymes and metres, those superfluous words and meaningless makeshifts of which the troubadour lyric poetry is so full." [1] Yes, Dante is right, and we now understand the full meaning of his judgment: "He was the greatest welder of his mother-tongue."

Because Arnaut has the power to reconcile them, he seeks out contradictions. No less than four of his eighteen songs treat of the contrast between glowing love and perishing Nature in autumn and winter. He delights in the social obstacles which his passion meets. If other men do not oppose him, if spies and chatterers do not stand in his way, then he seeks his pleasure in self-devised pain.

Light tones, simple and kindred rhymes, easy rhythms, are distasteful to him. He seeks out novel, rich, more difficult harmonies. How artfully and yet how clearly is he able to indicate in his rhythm the longer or more hurried flood or ebb of the feelings:

Bona es vida
Pos joia la mante,
Que tals n'escrida
Cui ges no vai tan be;
No sai de re
Coreillar m'escarida,
Que per ma fe
Del mieills ai ma partida.

Sweet is this life
When it happiness brings.
Let others lament
If it be not so blest.
No fault may I find
With my own happy fate.
Verily mine
Is the luckiest lot.

Arnaut selects the remote instead of the obvious rhymes; their echoes do not appear until later strophes. Instead he offers assonances nearer at hand.

With the utmost profusion of rhymes he combines the most

[1] Canello, *op. cit.*, p. 16.

assonances

painful accuracy of sound. He beguiles the ear wonted to harmony, bewilders it, only, after prolonged suspense, to give it the richer satisfaction, and to lull it to rest as if in a mysterious, all-sided symphony.

He is accounted the inventor of the sestina, which must not be hastily decried, at least in Arnaut's art, as a senseless elaboration. Its significance in his hands has been capitally set forth by Canello: "In the first stanza the rhymes are lacking but are replaced by light vocalic or consonantal equivalents: *arma—cambra*, *oncle—ongla*, *intra—verga.* In the following stanzas they are still floating in the troubadour's mind; he is haunted with certain fixed ideas which are carried on by the final words of the verses: in a changing order, he strives to harmonize them. In this fashion he gradually accustoms himself and his readers to a sympathy with the hidden harmony, which lurks also within the strophes, in the assonances. In the three verses of the finale, he at last succeeds in bringing together all the six haunting ideas, and in so attuning them to each other that the effect is perceptible to every ear. Now the tortured soul is satisfied with harmony and finds repose." [1]

DANTE AND ARNAUT DANIEL

The sestina was imitated by several troubadours, among them a native Italian, Bertolome Zorzi. But in Italian speech Dante was the first who attempted to reproduce it. He expressly declares himself to be, in this matter, an imitator of Arnaut.[2] And, not content with composing, in his poem *Al poco giorno ed al gran cerchio d'ombra*, a regular sestina in Arnaud's form, he complicates the scheme, already so elaborate, in a double sestina (*sestina rinterzata*), the song *Amor tu vedi ben che questa donna.* He would outdo the master and cannot therefore resist the temptation at the end of this performance to refer, with scholastic pride, to the unheard-of feat; to "the novelty that never has been attained in any age." [3]

The troubadour virtuoso had set a dangerous example, and Dante permitted himself to be misled by him, at least temporarily, into the most painful distortions of form.

He who thus follows his leader through thick and thin must

[1] *Fiorita di liriche provenzali tradotte*, Bologna, 1881, p. 35.
[2] *De vulgari Eloquentia*, II, 10 and 13.
[3] Repeated in similar words, *De vulgari Eloquentia*, II, 13.

have a high regard for him. In fact, one can hardly realize the full extent of Dante's enthusiasm for Arnaut.

An external circumstance may have intensified it. Arnaut was not regarded, either at home or abroad, as a troubadour of the highest rank; his fame grew dim with time, so that Dante could flatter himself that he had discovered him anew and brought him into fashion again.

He must have made his acquaintance early in life. At first it was doubtless the content rather than the form of Arnaut's songs that made an impression on him. The austere reticence of the troubadour, his devotion, his feverish longing, his diffidence in the presence of the beloved, his unwillingness to address her directly in verse, the religious colouring of his homage, his strife with eavesdroppers and slanderers, his trick of pretending allegiance to another lady—in short, all the morbidness and exaggeration of love-service—found an echo in the *Vita Nuova.* To be sure, Dante could have found these and similar traits in the songs and in the biographies of many other troubadours, in Aimeric de Belenoi, for example, in Bernard de Ventadour, and most especially in Folquet de Marseille, whose life and poetry Dante studied very attentively.

Among Arnaut's forms of expression he accepts, as a rule, only what is most striking, for example, the personification of Amor, and the fashion in which the latter gives advice and commands to the servant of Love,[1] a poetic fiction which was as yet so unusual in the lyric poetry of Provence and Italy that Dante considered it necessary to justify it in detail.[2]

When Dante came to write the *Convivio* and the *De vulgari Eloquentia,* and began to devote himself to philosophic investigation, to conscious refinement, to linguistic training, to the accumulation and the mastery of difficulties, and therefore decisively turned from the popular and romantic to the classic norm, and even to academic virtuosity, then the full power and brilliancy of Arnaut's forms appeared to him and compelled him to revere this "master in self-limitation."

It is no superficial mimicry if he, like Arnaut, seeks out difficult, rich, ambiguous, elaborate rhymes. Rather is it a close artistic kinship that impels him to this technique. Hence, it is not only the form of the strophes, but the whole tone of certain songs, and

[1] Arnaut's Canzone XVI.

[2] *Vita Nuova,* § 25.

especially of the "stone canzoni," that reminds us constantly of Arnaut. An unsatisfied, rude, sensuous passion groans and strives to assert itself within narrow, rigid verse-forms, and finally in the sestina and double sestina—and just here the strongest Provençal influence has been noted. But the superficial investigator falls into grave error if he insists upon finding in these "stone canzoni" nothing more than a stylistic exercise. The imagination of him who wrote these poems was possessed and tortured by love-madness; whether the object of his longing was a woman, or, what is quite credible in the case of Dante, an idea, his poetic struggle with sensuous images and shapes was decidedly stronger and more passionate than his literary ambition to rival Arnaut the troubadour. It was only because Dante had fallen into the same spiritual condition as Arnaut that the thought came to him to imitate him by forcing the most violent sensuousness into the most elaborate forms of art.

There was one difference: the morbid exaggeration which in Arnaut was chronic and, so to speak, constitutional, appears in Dante as a temporary indisposition. Hence his expressions are more forceful, more direct, not so over-refined, less elaborated and complacent, and not so ironic.

In the *Commedia*, Dante is emancipated from the tortuous art of the troubadours. So it is hardly credible that the system of rhymes in the great poem, the Dantesque terzina, is but a simplified modification of Arnaut's sestina, as some would have it.

But Dante remembers lovingly the priceless inspiration that came to him from the art of this Provençal poet. He shows him the greatest honour that could fall to the "welder of his mother-tongue." In the midst of his own thoroughly Italian poem he lets Arnaut speak in Provençal! And what a simple, clear, lovely Provençal! The painful ban is lifted. An Arnaut quite restored to moral and artistic health comes to meet us.

> "Ieu sui Arnaut, que plor e vau cantan;
> Consiros vei la pasada folor,
> E vei jausen lo joi qu'esper, denan.
> Ara vos prec, per aquella valor,
> Que vos guida al som de l'escalina,
> Sovenha vos a temps de ma dolor!" [1]

[1] *Purgatorio*, XXVI, 142–147.

"I am Arnaut, who weep and singing go;
Contrite I see the folly of the past,
And joyous see the hoped-for day before me.
Therefore I do implore you by that power
Which guides you to the summit of the stairs
Be mindful to assuage my suffering!"

DANTE AND THE TECHNIQUE OF THE TROUBADOURS

No troubadour influenced Dante's art more profoundly than Arnaut. But our poet knew and studied many others. We may even assume that he had before him richer and completer collections of their songs than we. This fact alone would prevent us from defining with accuracy the extent of his knowledge. Furthermore, the most important poetical motifs common to him and the troubadours were so generally used that it would be rash to trace any of them back to a special original. Much also which seems to be of Provençal origin may have come to him through Italian imitators, especially poets of the Sicilian, Bolognese, and Tuscan schools, all of which he knew. So, it will only be possible to trace particular, prominent traits in Dante's art, with proximate probability, back to Provençal sources.

For example, the remarkable mingling of narrative and lyric in the *Vita Nuova* has been explained as a Provençal usage. To especially difficult poems the troubadours attached prose explanations (*razos*) in which they set forth the historical occasion, the allusions, and the general meaning of their own poems, or those of others. The authors of the troubadour biographies, on the other hand, tried to connect the songs of their poets by means of half-historical, half-romantic information. So it came to pass that an especially beautiful or impressive song stood forth as the highest point, or as a turning-point, in the life of its author. The *razos* of the troubadours would, at best, furnish only an additional, fortuitous, and uncertain suggestion for the artistic form of the *Vita Nuova*.[1]

Even the philosophic canzone of the *Convivio* rests upon presuppositions characteristic of the troubadours. For it also appears as occasional poetry and seeks, especially in its opening and in its close, to establish a personal relation between the author and the individual to whom it is addressed, or a circle

[1] Such a theory is unnecessary, as mediæval Latin literature offers abundant examples of prose and verse commingled.

of listeners. The manner of introducing oneself and one's poem into society, and of assuring to the work of art the proper, that is, the desired, circulation, was invented by the troubadours.

The authors of the old French national epics were a part of their public. As they shared its interests, they did not need to seek it by artifice. The material was in the memory of the whole people, and the form was, so to speak, already given in the matter. There was no need of preface, introduction, or epilogue, and, in general, no arrangement was required other than that of the events and the feelings aroused by them. Each new incident suggested fresh utterance. Since it was not the poet but his hearers who determined the occasion on which he was to appear, he himself had no arrangements to make. Under such circumstances, he was the best artist who best knew how to suit his public and to devote himself to it, not he who drew it to himself most imperiously. The most impersonal, least pretentious, and most self-evident poem won the prize.

But the more readily the singer divested himself of all personality, and the more humbly he sued for the favour of his hearers, the lower his importance and social position became.

The minstrel was listened to but despised. He had made himself too common. The rift between poet and public became ever wider.

In Southern France this gulf was bridged by the technique of the troubadours. According to his social rank the troubadour assumed his relation toward a public which he sought only in knightly circles. The acceptance of his rank was the only concession that he must make to his listeners. So far as his birth did not make him a knight, he must win his position by his knightly spirit.

In earlier days everything, and especially sentiment, was common to all. Now the poet shares with his listeners only the consciousness of rank. The material and obvious presuppositions of poetry rest on the customs and manners of chivalry, not on the common grounds of religion or nationality.

Such conditions, however, demanded a suitable and helpful opportunity to call forth the utterance, and, as it were, an interlocutor. Only in modern times has the poet gradually reached the point where he can give voice to his inmost sentiments without preamble, without special explanation, without any particular audience in view.

To be sure, the folk-song also flows straight from the emotions of the soul. It is, however, essentially musical and lacks reflectiveness. It breaks forth out of the happy abandon of the dance, out of the rhythms of toil, of march and procession.

Undoubtedly the troubadours appropriated the musical form of the folk-song. But they could not, like the peasant, spontaneously send their song heavenward. They must, in the presence of a cold and alien public, introduce themselves, excuse themselves, make themselves agreeable and interesting. Through stubborn social barriers the musical and lyrical content of the poet's soul must seek its way, by artistic meanderings, into publicity.

As a cultivated social individual, however, a man can give his heart free utterance only through conversation: and, as a poet born, only in song. The troubadour was at once courtier and poet. His art has a double character. It is half conversation, discussion, wit, spirit, and understanding; half music, lyric poetry, feeling, and mood. Out of the mingling of these different sources an exceedingly rich and complicated technique issued. The innumerable external and internal social and personal circumstances had each one of them peculiar verse-forms. And thus, athwart custom and courtly life, was spun a network of available ties between the soul of the troubadour and the ears of knighthood. These poems fraught with sentiment and thought do not, however, like modern lyrics, flow out of the very heart of experience, but rather spread over it on every side.

So the troubadour, for example, who had a due sense of his own importance, maintained his own minstrels and envoys. He did not himself take his poetry to market; he bade others sing it where he pleased. With Dante, who can hardly have had a single minstrel at his disposal, the actual sending of the canzone, usually intimated in the closing strophe, became a mere poetic fancy. But the question whether it is befitting or not, in certain circumstances, to approach the beloved lady with direct utterance, or to send her greeting through a third person, even Amor himself, was doubtless not merely of literary but of practical importance to him.[1]

Together with this ceremonial, Dante took over from the Provençal poets, with Italian modifications, to be sure, a great part of their artistic forms: above all, the solemn canzone, the half canzone, and the *cobla esparsa* (single canzone-strophes), which

[1] *Vita Nuova*, § 12.

appears earlier in Italy as the sonnet. The sonnet served the Italians, also, for the discussion of a debated question or for an exchange of ideas, while the Provençal poets had shaped for this purpose the *joc partit*. In the dancing song (*ballata*), also, Dante holds more closely to the Italian than to the Provençal form.

In the sixth section of the *Vita Nuova*, Dante relates that in a certain missive, in the form of a sirventes, he recorded a list of sixty of the loveliest Florentine ladies, with Beatrice's name in the ninth place. It has been surmised that this youthful work, which is, unfortunately, lost to us, was composed in imitation of similar social poems by Raimbaut de Vaqueiras and Guilhem de la Tor. By sirventes was meant a poem written for a political, religious, or instructive purpose, which in form and melody recalled some famous canzone, but was usually divided into relatively simple and regular stanzas. There were moral, political, satirical, personal, and various other sirventeses; only the lover's greeting was excluded. The Italians, however, of the thirteenth and fourteenth centuries, used this name especially for a narrative poem on passing events, and gave their sirventeses a still simpler construction in strophes: for example, *aa*, *bb*, or *a bb a*, *a cc d*, *d ee f*, or *a aa b*, *b bb c*, and the like. Accordingly the terzina strophe of the *Divine Comedy*, with its scheme *aba*, *bcb*, *cdc*, . . . *yxy*, would appear to be nothing more than a special form of the Provençal-Italian *sirventes*, and more especially of the *sirventes incatenato*. So, from the standpoint of mediæval metrics, the *Commedia* might be characterized as a great complex of narrative, personal, religious, moral, satirical, and didactic sirventeses in the form of chain-strophes.—Why Dante decided in favour of the triple rhyme (*terza rima*), which has not been discovered in this special form in any earlier poem, is easily explained by his predilection for the symbolism of numbers and especially for the sacred Trinity.

DANTE AND THE TROUBADOURS' ARTISTIC CREED

After the art of the troubadours had attained so high a degree of refinement, the theory of technique as a necessary aid to artistic poetry, including grammar, rhyming-dictionary, *ars poetica*, etc., came to the fore. Artistic consciousness awoke. The question arose: What are the aims, the problems, the methods, the value, of poetry? Such expositions of a half-dogmatic, half-critical theory of art, whether in verse or in prose, become more and more frequent from the thirteenth century onward. About 1240, the first Provençal grammar appeared (*Donat proensal*). It was written in Italy and for Italians. The *Razos de trobar* of Raimon Vidal strove to further a pure, poetical written language. These were presumably composed in Catalonia, but soon became known in Italy.

Whether Dante studied these and other theoretical compositions by Provençals, we do not know. But it seems to me impossible to doubt that it was by the spirit of Provence, above all, that his artistic consciousness was awakened and his attention called to questions of the language, style, origin, and purpose of poetry.

Dante, to be sure, gave his attention almost exclusively to the troubadours of the most brilliant period. Such poetry in the Provençal language as appeared in later decades, for instance after the Albigensian wars, is practically ignored by him—with the exception of Sordello. But even in the oldest singers, even in Raimbaut d'Aurenga, Peire d'Auvergne, and the rest, he could have discovered an awakened consciousness of their art, and a discussion, as yet somewhat superficial, indeed, and capricious, of its æsthetic quality.

In the *Vita Nuova*, he certainly shows that he is still strongly influenced by the views of the poetic art current among troubadours. The first who composed artistic poetry in the popular language, he declares, did so in order to make himself intelligible to his lady, who knew no Latin. Homage to women seems to him to be the real purpose and object of poetry in the vulgar tongue.[1] The entire mediæval literature of entertainment and instruction is left unnoticed; Dante values only the courtly love-poetry of the troubadours. But while he discusses the æsthetic question of the rhetorical privileges which are granted to a troubadour, the ancient classical poet is set by him beside and above the mediæval minnesinger (*dicitore d'amore*) as his model.

So here, perhaps for the first time, the artistic consciousness and poetic doctrine of the troubadour come in contact with the ideas of the Renaissance.

Finally, in the *De vulgari Eloquentia*, Dante united the theory of the troubadours with those of Horace and Cicero in a philosophically elaborated system. This scientific statement of prin-

[1] *Vita Nuova*, § 25.

ciples rises heaven-high above the mass of rules, the "laws of love" (*Leys d'Amors*), in which the Toulouse school of Provençal masters laid down, some fifty years later, their grammatical, metrical, and stylistic requirements.

But both treatises have their oldest roots in the artistic consciousness of the troubadours. They were the first, within the circle of the lay vernacular, in whom artistic individuality, interest in art, and criticism were aroused. Without their leadership not even Dante could have attained to his classic ideal of art or become the Virgil of Italy.

FOLQUET, BERTRAN, SORDELLO, AND OTHERS, IN REAL LIFE AND IN THE "COMMEDIA"

How could one or the other of the artistic individualities of Provence fail to be included in so rich a collection of character portraits as Dante's *Commedia?* For not only in song but in life the troubadours had strongly and audaciously revealed their unique character. What was lacking to round out their existence into a complete work of art was often supplied by the troubadour biographies. After such patterns, but with a master's freedom, Dante sketches the features of Folquet de Marseille, Bertran de Born, and Sordello.

FOLQUET DE MARSEILLE

Folquet, who is honoured, not without reason, in the *De vulgari Eloquentia* as an artist of classical form, is illustrious as a finished servant of love, as *letizia* and *preclara cosa*, in the third Heaven of the *Paradiso*.[1] He is honoured, likewise, as a man of noble appearance in the troubadour biographies. As he had paid homage to three different ladies, one after another, so he narrates his earthly love-service by means of a three-fold comparison: Dido, Phyllis, and Iole. In detailed biographical statements he indicates the environment wherein his stirring life was spent. Born a merchant's son, he rose to the rank of bishop, retired from worldly life to a monastery in 1195, and died a very famous man. All this Dante sums up in the verses:

> See if man ought to make him excellent,
> So that another life the first may leave!

[1] *Paradiso*, IX, 37–42 and 67 sqq.

Probably soon after his entrance into the monastery, Folquet composed a penitential poem in which he says: "Always I have loved bitterness and had my joy in acquiring wealth; greedily have I accumulated, and not always in righteous ways, greedily have I grasped for myself the goods of others, and did not consider to whom they belonged." [1] And behold, the Folquet of the *Paradiso*, too, inveighs against greed. Dante probably also knew of the important part Folquet had played as collaborator of St. Dominic in the founding of the Dominican order, and therefore makes him preach against the worldly interests of the priesthood.

As a bishop, Folquet preached the crusade against the Albigensians, and as a blessed spirit, he demanded an expedition to Palestine. Just as his life was a transition from the love-service to crusading against heretics, so in Dante's *Paradiso* he stands between Cunizza, the friend of the troubadour Sordello, and Rahab, who shared in a holy war. This figure becomes fully intelligible to us from a study of the sources. It is viewed and delineated by Dante rather historically than poetically.

BERTRAN DE BORN

So much the more vividly appears in one of the circles of Hell the fomenter of discord, Bertran de Born.[2] He is of all the troubadours the most natural, the most powerful, the harshest, a strong contrast to Giraut's tenderness and Arnaut's artfulness. Therefore in the *De vulgari Eloquentia* he is contrasted with the former, who is a poet of virtue, and with the latter, who is a minstrel of love, as the foremost representative of martial poetry. He closes and completes, in Dante's evaluation, the trio of greatest and most representative troubadours.

Even at the present day he must be accorded an unique position; for among all the Provençals, there is hardly another who banished so completely the conventional, reflective elements from his poetry. Love-longing and elaborate fancies are not for him. Hence, he lacks the most important characteristics of the troubadour. And he disdains also something closely connected with these, the highly developed technique of the canzone. "He was

[1] Diez, *Leben und Werke der Trobadors*, pp. 250–51.
[2] *Inferno*, XXVIII, 113 sqq.

a master of the sirventes and composed in his whole life only two canzoni," so his biography tells us.

The honeyed love-song grew ever remoter from reality; it stiffened into a scholastic social diversion, or took refuge in religious mysticism. But Bertran's poetry has its roots in mother earth. It exhales a pungent odour of iron and blood. It is too personal and too occasional to be called classic, but quite too naïve and elemental to be classed as romantic. If the annotations to his sirventeses were not extant, we should be quite at a loss.[1] If his disposition had been as rudely bestial as he boastfully assures us, he would be detestable. But he had not fought all the battles that he glorifies, nor committed all the atrocious deeds he proudly claims. Indeed, some years before his death (*circa* 1215) he took refuge, a pious man, in a monastery. And though he was an audacious and quarrelsome fellow, he more often rattled his sword than drew it. It is not so much war itself as its dramatic pomp that delights him:

> How glad am I when scouts draw nigh
> While frightened folk and cattle flee,
> And when the clashing armèd hosts
> Are on their way it gladdens me.
>   Delightful is it to mine eyes
> When they a fair-built castle storm,
> When crashing fall each tower and wall,
>   Or when upon the plain I see
> A goodly army girt about
> With deep-sunk moat and strong redoubt. . . .
>
> Neither in food nor drink have I
> Nor yet in sleep such full delight
> As when from either side the cry
> I hear, of "Onward to the fight!"
>   When riderless the horses neigh
> Along each shadowy woodland way,
> When here and there the desperate shout
>   "Help! We are perishing!" rings out,
> And when the green turf of the grave
> Covers the coward and the brave.[2]

[1] These notes are indeed often remote from reality, as Bertran early became a legendary character.

[2] We are reluctant to question the authenticity of this truly Bertranesque poem, but its authorship is not certain. The reader may accept in its stead another which is certainly his:

> To peace is all the world inclined,
> An ell for feud suffices me:

As the Italian *condottiere* made the battlefield, in some sense, a work of art, even so Bertran's enthusiasm for feud and bloodshed is chiefly an æsthetic impulse. He has been fitly called the *condottiere* of poesy.[1] Not that he developed an objectively perfected art in depicting battlefields; it is his imagination, rather, that plunges him into the thick of the fight. He does not portray war; he fans it, urges both sides on, shouts, dashes about, and finally uprises like a joyous flame out of the fury of the crashing onslaught. It is not like a painter but like an incendiary that his muse revels in destruction. His poetry is all movement, action, passion. Hence the utterance also savagely, insolently, and directly matches the event. Thing and name, image and presentation, are, so to speak, one and the same. This art is certainly not symbolic. One might be tempted to call it absolutely realistic or impressionistic, if these designations did not so insistently call to our mind a pictorial style of art. The naturalism of Bertran is on the other hand stirring and oratorical, but while most agitators are forced into rhetoric, this troubadour remains comparatively—that is to say, for an orator and agitator—natural and frank. His exaggerations are not hyperboles, his images are not metaphors, his comparisons are not similes. His inward if not his outward life coincides with his words. The actual content of his poems may be questioned; their æsthetic content is as genuine as gold, as truly lived and felt as it is formally expressed.

No wonder that even his contemporaries, the troubadour biographies, the short stories, and finally Dante, took him literally. He has been regarded as actually the dangerous and savage man he described himself to be, but doubtless was not. His cynical invectives and naught else was held responsible for the uprising of

---

May he go blind who seizes it
Although the fault shall be mine own!
Peace irketh me,
I am for strife.
No dogma else
Has worth for me. . . .

Another man may till the heath,
Early and late am I intent
How I may gather swords and horse,
Missiles and all the gear of war:
Because my sole estate
Is tourney and assault.

Both poems are in Diez, *op. cit.*, pp. 188 and 210.

[1] The expression is applied to him by A. Thomas, though from a different viewpoint.

young Henry against his father, Henry II of England (1182–1183). His sirventes were accepted as the cause of countless feuds and wars. For that very reason it is in a poet's Hell that this poet suffers the penalty for the poetic sins of an imagination athirst for deeds.

> And so that thou may carry news of me,
> Know that Bertram de Born am I, the same
> Who gave to the Young King the evil comfort.
> I made the father and the son rebellious;
> Achitophel not more with Absalom
> And David did with his accursed goadings.
> Because I parted persons so united,
> Parted do I now bear my brain, alas!
> From its beginning, which is in this trunk.
> Thus is observed in me the counterpoise.[1]

A poet who casts forth his ideas and images with such elemental force, almost as unworked raw material, will hardly have any technique worth mentioning. If, nevertheless, Bertran's verses are sufficiently correct, that only proves how highly, in his time and among his audiences, the technical requirements were appraised for artistic mastery. But Bertran never was an inventive technician. He has, accordingly, been unable to exert any notable influence upon Dante's technique, unless, indeed, primitive rudeness be regarded as an acquisition. So it is perhaps more than mere chance that precisely the twenty-eighth canto of the *Inferno*, precisely the description of Bertran's circle in Hell, begins with an expression which was a favourite with Bertran.

Bertran loved to produce his effects by accumulation of kindred images, or by the representation of a kind of poetic massiveness. It is a crude and childish substitute for loftiness and greatness. Carried to the extreme of mannerism, it appears in the love-song, *Domna, pois de mi nous chal:*

> But, as I find no other like you, none so beautiful, none who is so high-hearted, whose noble figure is so gracious, whose bearing is so attractive or so cheerful, whose fame is so well grounded, therefore of every other lady I will beseech some fair feature, and shape for myself a composite figure wherein I may find your semblance.[2]

[1] *Inferno*, XXVIII, 133–142.
[2] Diez, *Leben und Werke der Troubadours*, p. 185.

The famous lament over the death of Prince Henry of England begins:

> If all the tortures, all the tears and pain,
> The sorrow, the bereavement and the grief
> That men throughout the course of time have known
> Were heaped together, they would seem but light
> Beside the death of England's youthful lord.[1]

Similarly Dante, in order to give an idea of the punishment of the fomenters of discord, would fain gather up all the horrors of countless historic battlefields.[2]

But we are less concerned with such simple and obvious devices of art than with the peculiar psychology of Bertran's poetry. It must have influenced Dante as a rude violent natural phenomenon, not as an æsthetic creation. What attracted him was rather the man than the artist. And therefore, fittingly, in the awful realm of horrible discord, Dante evokes this remarkable man. He himself has something of this violence in his own flesh and blood. While he is completely absorbed in Bertran's dæmonic figure, his own great-uncle threatens him from afar. It is the terrible Geri del Bello.[3] But he also was aware of Bertran's noble, lofty, and generous side.[4]

Whether and to what extent Bertran's sirventeses influenced Dante's political invectives can hardly be determined. In personal bitterness, in cynicism and sarcasm, he does not lag behind the troubadour. Perhaps this very example encouraged him in his vehemence. But the egoistic, unphilosophic arbitrariness of Bertran's political utterances, his lack of idealism, must surely have repelled him.

In this respect other troubadours, those devoted to the emperor and to his cause, such as Aimeric de Pegulhan, Guilhem de Figueira, Folquet de Romans, Peire Cardinal, and Bertolome Zorzi, appealed to him more strongly. For these men, above all others, gave to the Holy Roman Empire that poetic and romantic splendour which is reflected in the *Commedia*.

I would call attention especially to the sirventes *Caritatz es en tan belh estamen*, by Peire Cardinal. In this poem there occurs

[1] Diez, *ibid.*, p. 204. Some question has been raised as to the authorship of this poem, but it seems to me clearly Bertran's.
[2] *Inferno*, XXVIII, 7 sqq.
[3] *Ibid.*, XXIX, 18 sqq.
[4] *Convivio*, IV, 11.

before an allegorical court, before Love, Piety, Truth, Justice, Mercy, Peace, Power, Wisdom, and Goodness, a polemic discussion between Right and Wrong (*Dreitz* and *Tortz*), and the poem closes with a dedication to noble lovers:

> A belh amador
> que a belh' Amor
> a donat son cor e se
> ai donat m'amor e me.

This seems to call to mind Dante's solemn canzone in which, again in the presence of Amor, Justice makes complaint: *Tre donne intorno al cor mi son venute.* Amor, whose usual attendants, *Cortezia*, *Largeza*, *Jois*, and *Solatz*, were to be brought into the Christian company of *Caritas*, *Misericordia*, *Justitia*, and *Pax*, could only be accepted by a troubadour versed in theology, like Cardinal. He is perhaps the first to do this, at the beginning of the thirteenth century. Since the famous first sermon of St. Bernard, *In Festo Annuntiationis Beatae Mariae Virginis*, the subject of the trial before the assembled Christian virtues was a favourite. Cardinal's direct source I cannot point out, just as I have no further proof of any acquaintance of Dante's with Cardinal. We suspect here a connection the individual threads of which are concealed from us.

SORDELLO

The true political troubadour in Dante's eyes, however, is Virgil's fellow townsman, Sordello of Mantua (*circa* 1200–1270). Strangely enough, troubadour biography knows and honours him only as an adventurous lover and an adroit courtier. In fact, among the more than forty poems of his that are preserved, not more than three or four are of a political character. If on the other hand we examine Sordello's poetry from the viewpoint of its literary character and importance, the monument which Dante erects to him seems even less justified. Sordello's love-poetry, with all its lightness, fluency, and tenderness, has a certain weakness. Various reminiscences of Peire Vidal, Bernard de Ventadour, Giraut de Bornelh, and others who belong especially to the popular and romantic school, have been noted in his verse. His ideas seem to us, by comparison, more novel than his form, especially in so far as he is one of the first to uphold the chaste and supersensuous love of woman, and, in a certain sense, anticipates the attitude of the *dolce stil nuovo.* But this very affectation is in sharp contrast with the defiant figure of Sordello in the *Purgatorio.*[1] Such contradictions have led scholars to surmise that Dante's Sordello is a wholly different person from the historical troubadour.

However, the testimony of the *De vulgari Eloquentia* leaves no room for doubt. There a *Sordellus de Mantua . . . tantus eloquentiae vir* is mentioned, who, it is said, not only in poetry, but even in conversation, disdained the ignoble dialect of his own birthplace. Surely this can only mean the troubadour who, as we positively know, spent the greater part of his life in foreign lands and returned to Italy only in his old age.

On closer examination, we find that all the originality, all the eloquence of this Sordello lies in his personal, political, and moral satire. In fact, one of his many songs, but the most notable and most famous of them all, became, as it would seem, an example for Dante—the dirge for the Provençal knight Blacatz.

> Knightly Blacatz in lofty song I mourn!
> Sad is my heart and rent, as needs must be,
> For I in him my lord and friend have lost.
> And with him is all knighthood dead as well.
> A fatal loss, that brings to me despair
> That ever filled his place should be, unless
> The dead man's heart be offered for their food
> Unto our coward knights to make them brave.[2]

The most important princes of Europe: the emperor, the kings of France, of England, of Castile, of Aragon, of Navarre, the counts of Toulouse and Provence, are scornfully urged to take unto themselves a goodly portion of the knightly Blacatz's valiant heart.

Out of this single song Dante has created his ideal Sordello, his "lofty and disdainful Lombard soul." The troubadour who bids all the crowned heads of Europe stride through his song as faint-hearted cowards becomes in Dante's *Purgatorio* the judicious guide through the valley of neglectful monarchs forgetful of their duties.

The dirge for Blacatz, however, has not served Dante as an artistic model, but merely as a suggestion. Two almost accidental

[1] *Purgatorio,* VI, 58 sqq.
[2] Cesare De Lollis. *Vita e poesie di Sordello di Goito,* Halle, 1896, p. 153 sqq.

historic facts, namely, that Sordello was born near Mantua, the home of Virgil, and that he had written a satirical "mirror for princes," gave to the poet of the *Commedia* the opportunity for developing with a free hand, and in conformity with the poetic laws of his *poema sacro*, one of his most important and lifelike figures. Just as the romantic Sordello bows down in reverent humility before the classical Virgil, so also did the poetry of Provence with all its splendour wholly conform and subordinate itself to the nobler art of the *Divine Comedy*.

RETROSPECT

Dante familiarized himself with a century or so (1160 to 1260) of Provençal art-poetry, at first as a learner and imitator, then as a discriminating critic, and finally as a master, controlling and transforming it with complete freedom. The romantic troubadours, Giraut de Bornelh, perhaps also Bernard de Ventadour, Peire Vidal and others, offer him motifs and moods; the classic poets, for example, Peire d'Auvergne, Arnaut Daniel, perhaps also Folquet de Marseille and others, provide him with forms, technique, and criticism; men of personal and historic importance, like Bertran de Born and Sordello, offer him merely the raw material of their lives, and must, like all mortals whomsoever, serve as models for the creative artist of the *Commedia*.

Just as the gifted pupil of painting, after he leaves his school, as a proof of his gratitude and of the mastery he has acquired presents former teachers with their own portraits executed with an unerring hand, so did Dante treat the troubadours.

6. The Beginnings of Italian Literature

THE SICILIAN SCHOOL OF POETS

The artistic poetry of Provence had, by the end of the twelfth century, become so petrified in courtly manners and rhetorical forms that it retained its artistic character under altered conditions of life and under the alien skies of Northern France, Catalonia, Castile, and Upper Italy. The Genoese, Venetian, and Lombard knights and burghers who played the part of the troubadour in Provençal speech were hardly distinguishable from their predecessors in Southern France. The songs of Manfred Lancia, Alberto Malaspina, Rambertni Buvalelli, Lanfranco Cigala, Perceval

Doria, Bertolome Zorzi, Sordello, and the rest, have the flavour of their literary source, not of their native land. To some extent original with them is, at most, the political song of attack and censure (sirventes).

In order to become really Italian, the Provençal love-song was compelled to penetrate into the peninsula by a circuitous path through the South, a land quite remote in language and culture.

There, especially in Sicily under the rule of the Arabs, later of the Normans, and finally of the Hohenstaufens, a rich civilization had developed. A many-sided, brilliantly coloured, luxurious life, without deep social roots, somewhat international in character, must have exercised with its superficial splendour a powerful attraction on the wandering troubadours and minstrels of France and Provence.

To detail the sources of this mixed courtly brilliancy would be out of place here, the more since it never attained to positive and direct expression in the songs of the so-called Sicilian school of poets. Only indirectly and in a limited fashion does it make itself felt. In the kingdom of Frederick II, where a half-Oriental, new, alien absolute monarchy was based not on a national or religious community but on bureaucracy and officialdom, only that singer could be welcomed at court who avoided all historical, political, and ecclesiastical subjects. All that was left to him was to glorify by his song the single universal human passion which was, nevertheless, capable of certain social and intellectual refinements: sexual desire, love-service. So it comes to pass that the Sicilian imitators of the Provençal troubadours limit themselves, even more exclusively than their predecessors, to the service of woman. Whether, and to what extent, Arabian poets, side by side, perhaps, with the lyrists of Northern and Southern France, also exerted a stimulating influence on the Sicilian love-song, can hardly be determined, on account of the cultural poverty and lack of colour of its content.

The especial originality of the Sicilian poets lies in the form, particularly in their language. They are, in a certain sense, the creators of literary Italian; that is, the first who uplifted themselves out of the limitations of isolated dialects to artistic composition. Latin, Provençal, and French models stimulated them. All else was discovered and developed of itself, so to speak. The "Sicilian" minnesingers who were active at the court of Frederick

II were by no means all Sicilians. Pier della Vigna, for example, was born in Capua, several others in Apulia. The earliest among them were officials of the emperor, secretaries, notaries, councillors, judges, falconers, and officers, far-travelled and educated folk. So even in daily conversation the speech of the Sicilian country became fused with the kindred dialects of the southern mainland. Furthermore, this nominally Sicilian court led an unsettled, wandering life, and moved about with all its hangers-on throughout the entire peninsula. It has been reckoned that out of the forty-two years of his reign, Frederick spent about seven in all on Sicilian soil. Thus arose, by a gradual formation, a courtly speech whose forms, starting from the South, came more and more to resemble the dialects of Central Italy, and particularly the Tuscan type. Through artistic imitation and written records, Provençal idioms, Gallicisms, and Latin archaisms streamed in abundantly.

Accordingly, Dante might even today be justified in regarding literary Italian as a *vulgare aulicum*, as the vernacular of the imperial court, as a language of cultivated folk, which, strictly speaking, is not to be identified with any one of the extant dialects. We cannot, however, approve what is unhistoric and *a priori* in his conception of a literary language. He rejects as a *patois* the Sicilian dialect, along with all the rest. For he is not interested in the linguistic and local origin, but only in the cultural elevation, of the Italian language.

He does not give the credit for this elevation to the Sicilian people, but, quite justly, to the court, and above all, to the Emperor Frederick and his son Manfred,[1] since they, he says, encouraged the Italian love-song, and probably contributed to it themselves. Indeed, all the troubadour and literary poetry that precedes the *dolce stil nuovo* in every part of Italy is characterized by Dante as Sicilian.

Of course this enlarged conception cannot be fully maintained. Even in the oldest poets, the dividing-line between artistic and popular poetry is uncertain. Among the poems that are ascribed to the Emperor Frederick, to Jacopo da Lentino, to Rinaldo d'Aquino, or to Odo delle Colonne, and above all, in those of Giacomino Pugliese, side by side with stiff repetition of Provençal ideas there are genuine folk-songs full of fresh Southern sensuousness. It may be that Provençal and French models, which, with

[1] *De vulgari Eloquentia*, I, 12.

all their polish, often retain a minstrel-like genial humour, strengthened in their Sicilian imitators a taste for folk-lore; but the mere transfer of an outworn motif to a new language might suffice. Again, a mere change of climate is capable of producing fresh fruit from an old plant. The melodious Italian seems of itself to give to the familiar tones a clearer, more open sound of sensuous delight. In these first Italian singers we discover less self-consciousness, less individuality, less extravagance, and less technical finish, but a stronger appeal to popular feeling than exists in most Provençal poets. They do strive to be refined, ingenious, and elaborate, but the vigorous popular speech often breaks forth through their courtly polish, and sings and versifies for itself. In the midst of the fanciful artistry of their canzoni a cheery tone, a minstrel's jest, a warm familiar merriment and joy, will often take us by surprise.

A good example is the responsive song, *Rosa fresca.* Dante also knew this delightful poem. And yet, since it is the tongue of Apulia, and not the language of the court, that speaks, he is disdainful.[1]

Dante regards the notary Jacopo da Lentino as the first representative of the Sicilian school. In fact, he does seem to be one of the most fertile, clever, correct, but also the most wearisome, of the minnesingers. His merit is essentially technical. How deficient he is in warmth and freshness of feeling was neither overlooked nor passed over in silence by the poet of the *Commedia.*[2]

LITERARY SYNCRETISM IN CENTRAL ITALY

The love-song of the troubadours, transferred to Italian speech, might have amused a courtly society for many a year, if the singers and audience had not been swallowed up by war. In the battle of Benevento (1265), the knightly splendour of Ghibellinism went down to destruction. Guelfism and the bourgeoisie rose in their place.

At the court of Anjou, to be sure, there was still room for love-songs and the service of woman. It was, however, no longer Italian, but Provençal and French song that found a hearing there. Indeed, it may be assumed that the Angevin court, on account of its relations with the Guelfic cities, was the medium

[1] *De vulgari Eloquentia,* I, 12.

[2] *Purgatorio,* XXIV, 56.

for a renewed and increased importation of Provençal art-poetry, especially into Tuscany.

At least, the Tuscan heirs of the Sicilian school reveal even more artificial and over-elaborated Provençalisms than the poets of the age of the Hohenstaufens; it matters not whether they obtained their foreign models through Genoa, Venice, and Bologna, or Naples. Probably it was through all of them.

Instead of the emperor's officials and Ghibelline knights, it was city magistrates, jurists, notaries, and the whole upper class of citizens who continued the traditions of the Sicilian poets. Arezzo, Siena, Lucca, Pisa, Pistoia, and, foremost, Florence, become the important centres of artistic poetry. The person who contributed especially to the extension of courtly poetry and who was not only the political but also the literary mediator between feudalism and the bourgeoisie was he who held the office of *Podestà*.

The more the poetry of the troubadours became, in this manner, urban and Italian, the more was it inevitably modified by that intelligent, dry, formalistic spirit of the Italians, educated in law, natural science, grammar, and rhetoric, which I have already characterized. Even from its native home in Southern France, this poetry had already derived a strong tendency to introspection and didacticism.

A pleasing and highly characteristic combination of the Provençal-Sicilian culture with the urban and Italian learning is to be seen in the poetry of Guittone d'Arezzo.

Guittone d'Arezzo

Guittone was born of bourgeois parents between 1225 and 1230. By his many-sided literary activity, which lasted down to the end of the century (he died in 1294), he acquired a reputation and influence superior to that of all others.

He was an upright man, but an inferior poet: unamiable, dry, prosaic, pedantic, and tasteless. In his youth he devotes himself to love-songs which betray a ponderous scholastic imitation of the Provençals, though inspired by a spirit quite unlike that of chivalry. The vigorously lyrical canzone is driven out by the compact sonnet. All the sensuous freshness which still remained in the Sicilian versifiers becomes heavily overlaid with Provençalisms and Latinisms. A native simplicity and a practical sense for common things show themselves in coarse epithets and in a keen insight into human weakness. An unpleasing and perhaps merely theoretical acquaintance with the *Ars amatoria* of Ovid is betrayed in his theory of love. The unknightly youth had evidently learned the courtly and refined principles of love-service more from books and poems than from association with noble ladies. His homage comes from an empty heart. The suspicion that it is not addressed to any particular noblewoman and that this was merely a literary love forces itself on us, and is only strengthened by Dante's judgment.[1]

Since there was no actual person in his thoughts of love, the outlines of the imaginary lady were blurred in haze. The women of the troubadours themselves had not been very vividly individualized. But with Guittone the last vestiges of physical charms vanish. He retains only those parts of the body that are closely associated with the theory of love: the heart and the eyes, which as the abode and as the windows of the love-god could hardly be dispensed with. So that, at least negatively, by this disembodiment he prepared the way for the symbolic and mystical conception of the *dolce stil nuovo* and for the apotheosis of Beatrice. The last sensuous colours of the old love-song perish in Guittone's bourgeois simplicity.

Yet he did achieve something positively new. Because it was not granted him to unbosom himself freely and spontaneously, he endeavoured, partly through lack of skill, partly through ambition and self-consciousness, to profit by over-elaboration, artificiality, and oddity of form. What he handles worst is just what lies nearest at hand, the Italian language itself; he cannot make himself master of the courtly refinement which it had received from the hands of the Sicilians. Dante saw this: *nunquam se ad curiale vulgare direxit.*[2] He does not seem, either, to have been especially gifted musically, and was eager therefore to substitute the sonnet for the canzone of homage, which required a melody of its own. As the lady is bereft of her charms, so too the texts of the love-song begin to lose their melodies. Poet, composer, and singer had, even in the days of the troubadours, to some extent parted company; but in Italy the division of labour went still further. Doubtless many of Guittone's pieces existed on paper only, and were intended to be read. Indeed, his poetry is actually intermingled with prose. His letters are a notable attempt to bring over into Italian

[1] *Purgatorio,* XXIV, 52 sqq.

[2] *De vulgari Eloquentia,* I, 13.

the rhyme and the rhythmic close of the period which are characteristic of artistic mediæval Latin prose. So he decks out his native and traditional material in every fashion, now with foreign words from the Provençal, repetitions and leonine rhyme, now with figures of speech from mediæval Latin, now with names of ancient authors and with maxims from Aristotle, the Bible, or the Church Fathers. He knows and boasts that he is wandering on untrodden paths:

> Scuro saccio che parlo
> meo detto; ma che parlo
> a chi s'entend'a me;
> chè lo 'ngegno mio dà me
> ch'e 'me pur prove nd'onne
> mainera e talent'onne.[1]

> I speak, I know, obscurely,
> My sayings, but I speak them
> For those that understand me.
> Because my nature bids me
> In utterance to make trial
> Of every style and fashion.

Certainly one must give him credit for novel and manifold experiments.

After his youth had passed, he strove yet more zealously to enrich himself with knowledge. He forsook love-service in disdain. In middle life, like the poet of the *Commedia*, he too departed from

> That ugly, evil, and unseemly place
> Where I was quite pent in,

and entered the monastic order of the Knights of Mary.

His poetry becomes didactic, querulous, ascetic, but at the same time acquires a sincere and genuine ring. He really possesses the spirit of the teacher and preacher and in happy moments rises to pathos. He has a gift for admonition and argument, and with it the ability, not indeed lyrical, but highly effective, to put a twist on words and ideas, to play with them laboriously, to analyze his subject logically, to compress it into brief and vigorous expressions, and to give a spice of sophistry even to the stalest commonplaces. Thanks to this nowise trivial dialectic equipment, he is the chief forerunner of philosophic poetry. This honest Philistine, who practises the arts of utterance like a dancing bear, is certainly not beautiful; but historically he is important and instructive.

[1] *Le Rime di Fra Guittone*, ed. F. Pelligrini, Bologna, 1901, I, canzone XI.

With all his efforts he never acquired the sense of proportion. Dante is right when, with an emphatic gesture, he excludes this inartistic man from the company of the classic poets of Provence and of antiquity.[1] But the very severity of this judgment proves how greatly Guittone was admired even in Dante's time.

Apart from the foolish display of pedantry which might dazzle the eyes of many an ignorant man, Guittone really was the first Italian poet who possessed a personality of his own: "no talent indeed, but a character." Character always asserts itself, especially in Italy, the land of individualists.

As a personality, Guittone had firm political and religious convictions. He was a Guelf and loathed the Ghibellines, who brought destruction upon their fellow countrymen, their children and their parents by the alien and mercenary sword of a German prince. His satiric poem on the Ghibelline victory at Montaperti is sustained by a political, ethical, and almost national pathos, which has no kinship with the occasional poems of Provence, and recalls rather Dante than Bertran de Born.

The attempt has been made to discover even in the *Divine Comedy* reminiscences of Guittone's religious poetry, which, though destitute of intensity and pious enthusiasm, yet strives with sound instinct to strike the chord of the popular dance-song.

However that may be, Guittone represents, in the history of literature, a transitional stage of fundamental importance for Italian poetry, and therefore also for the *Divine Comedy*. No one worked more zealously to bring to the cities of Tuscany the courtly poetry of Provence and Sicily and to establish it there. No one embodied more vigorously than he the intelligence of the layman and burgher, the independent feeling of the Guelf, and the true character of the mediæval Italian.

Therefore Dante is indebted to him indirectly, perhaps also directly, for considerably more than he is willing to express.

The School of Guittone

There was soon an abundance of imitators of Guittone. In Pisa and Lucca, in Pistoia and Florence, they were in constant evidence. To exaggerate the most prominent traits of the master was alluring and easy. Along with the jurists, magnates, and merchants, the less educated handicraftsmen could master the

[1] *De vulgari Eloquentia*, II, 6.

cruder side of this art. One can hardly realize the wooden dryness and intricacy of the poems of a Meo Abbracciavacca, of a Dotto Reali, of a Monte Andrea, and particularly of Guittone's Pisan imitators. A goodly portion of the odium which has rested on Guittone, from Dante's condemnation of him down to the present day, is to be charged not to him, but to his disciples.

And yet, they too have their significance. They came into literary relationship with each other, exchanged sonnets on problems in mechanics, physiology, philosophy, ethics, theology, politics, poetics, etc. They handled with their rough and awkward fingers all possible objects of curiosity. Sometimes they even appended to their sonnet a letter in Italian prose. The place of the troubadour canzone was taken by the dedicatory epistle, of which Dante too made repeated use. Poetry, which was at first confined to oral utterance and social gatherings, lost this character, and freed itself from local limitations. There gradually arose a widely extended literary public, above all at Bologna, the most important intellectual centre of Northern Italy, which now came into closer contact with the poets of the Tuscan cities. Even in Faenza, about 1280, we find two poets striving for the mastery of the literary language.[1]

The Poets of the Transition

The simpler half-courtly and half-popular style of the Sicilians continued in vogue in Central Italy, side by side with the mannerism of Guittone. The stilted style of the latter aroused not only admiration, but also opposition and ridicule. There was no lack of fresh, delightful dance-songs or of notable efforts to enliven Guittone's didacticism, in a purer, simpler, and nobler speech, by the lyric lilt of the Provençals. The most gifted and happiest in this regard may well have been the Florentine Chiaro Davanzati. The notary of Lucca, Bonagiunta Orbicciani, must also be reckoned among the poets of the transition. He is quite lacking in originality and even his contemporaries charged him with servile dependence on the Sicilians. His language betrays, even to us, the colouring of that dialect for which Dante criticized him.[2] Although he lived long and composed poetry for forty years (1250–1290), we can trace in him no artistic development, indeed, but the progressive changes in the prevailing fashion al-

[1] *De vulgari Eloquentia*, I, 14.

[2] *Ibid.*, 13.

most down to the period of the Dantesque lyric poetry. If, however, in the *Divine Comedy* he is relegated to the old school on much the same footing as Jacopo da Lentino, it is because Dante sharply distinguishes between individuality and imitation.[1]

Thus, just about the time of Dante's youth, in the seventh and eighth decades of the thirteenth century, the few lyrical forms current in Italy, the canzone, the ballad, and the sonnet, show an extraordinary poetical diversity, which widens in every direction and breaks away from the technique of the troubadours. New wine is continually being poured into the old bottles. Philosophical and theological subjects are treated in the musical forms of the canzone and even of the ballad. The favourite form, however, with these bourgeois poets, is the sonnet. Like a well-cut democratic uniform, the sonnet fitted every body. It did not commit the composer to any definite style or content; it was not burdened with any artistic tradition. It had no fixed character, and adapted itself to every key. Alone, it voiced maxims or epigrams; in series, it became a didactic poem; in dialogue form, it served the purposes of poetic discussion; it finally constituted in itself a lyric unit. It was the fitting vessel for literary *potpourri*.

Comprehensive Didactic Poetry

But it was not the Guittonians alone who effaced the distinction between art and science, poetry and prose. Dante's teacher, Brunetto Latini, the Florentine notary, was himself a terrible example of slipshod style.

He compresses the scientific contents of his French encyclopædia into monotonous Italian verses. Whatever does not fit into the rhymes he leaves in prose. One can hardly imagine a ruder conglomeration of art and science than Latini's *Tesoretto*. The outward allegorical form is a mere pretext, a ready-made wooden scaffolding from the top of which the author pours all his knowledge down on us as if from a potato sack. He wishes to get rid of his scientific knowledge, no matter how. Guittone and his school do at least reveal in their struggle with language and in their quest for new means of expression an honest good will for art. Brunetto, on the contrary, borrows his poetical garment heedlessly out of the great allegorical wardrobe of mediævalism. Sometimes he draws the decorations for his personifications from

[1] *Purgatorio*, XXIV.

Boëthius's *Consolatio*, sometimes from the *Planctus Naturae ad Deum*, sometimes from the *Anticlaudianus* of Alain de Lille, or again from the *Romaunt of the Rose* of Guillaume de Lorris, and into the midst of these he thrusts, without introduction or imaginable reason, his own experiences, and preferably his political convictions. He had given his best in his great French *Trésor*. Now he spins out the most important scraps of his information, like an absent-minded schoolmaster, in a rhymed, yet cruder form, to a less cultivated Tuscan audience. It seems, even to him, so little to the purpose that he never brings it to an end.

Nevertheless, this wretched patchwork, even if it exercised no direct artistic influence, may yet have given a considerable literary impulse to the *Divine Comedy*. At any rate, there is a remarkable similarity between the historical and psychological settings of the two poems. Brunetto, like Dante, composed his poem in exile and not long after his party and his political hopes had suffered a heavy blow at the battle of Montaperti (1260). Like Dante again, in distress and despair, he strays from the right path, wanders into an inhospitable wood, and meets an allegorical creature—in his case, Nature. After prolonged many-sided instruction, she directs him to the realm of the worldly virtues, where he listens to a series of sermons and is accompanied by a well-bred knight. He arrives at the court of Amor, from subjection to whom he is released by Ovid, with his familiar counsels. There follows a confession of sin and a moral admonition. Thence the pilgrim passes to Olympus, where Ptolemy is to instruct the traveller in the observation of the starry Heaven. Here, however, the story breaks off.

It is evident that just as the *Divine Comedy* may be regarded as a profounder repetition of the *Tesoretto*, so the latter, if it had been a later creation, might be held a silly imitation of Dante's masterpiece. What makes it worthy of our attention is its date and its Florentine origin. Of secondary importance is the probability that Dante was acquainted with it—all this having, however, no æsthetic significance, but merely a cultural and psychological interest. The more highly we value the symptomatic importance of the *Tesoretto*, the slighter and more doubtful must its direct influence on the *Commedia* appear. For us as historians of the *Commedia*, the *Tesoretto* is of the utmost importance. For Dante as creator of the *Commedia*, it hardly has a value worth reckoning. There remains nothing more than a remote family likeness, which might be sufficiently explained merely by the proximity in time and place and by kindred mental attitudes, without the supposition of direct contacts.

In fact, about the same time as the *Commedia*, there appeared in the Florentine tongue still other allegorical and didactic poems: the *Intelligenza* of Dino Campagni (??), the *Documenti d'amore* and the *Reggimento e costumi di donna* of Francesco da Barberino. A certain family resemblance with the *Commedia* is here also unmistakable, and yet there is hardly a possibility of imitation.

Perhaps the most interesting creation of this type, from the purely symptomatic point of view, is an allegorical prose romance which is ascribed, under the title *Introduzione alle virtù*, to the Florentine Bono Giamboni, and accordingly would be of about the same date as the *Tesoretto*.

Like Latini, like Henricus Pauper, like Boëthius, Giamboni too feels unhappy and desperate. Still, his wretchedness of soul is more imitative than sincerely felt. And sure enough, his consoler too is my lady Philosophia. But it is no longer the independent Prudence of Henricus; it is the guide to pious belief. So she at once conducts her charge to the palace of Christian Faith. Here at a social supper, the man in need of comfort is put through a test on the sacraments, the Commandments, and the creed. "And a notary who is present writes down every word." The journey is continued. Upon a great plain, just as in the *Psychomachia* of Prudentius, the personified virtues and vices are seen contending with each other. Then the moral battle broadens to a world-wide religious war. Christian faith fights in regular succession against Judaism, against heresy, and finally against Islam.

The reader is to imagine all this as narrated without personal enthusiasm or moral sympathy, in the clear, fluent, objective prose of a chronicler; it is to be remembered that the allegorical dress and the form of personal narrative remain external and adventitious in the most famous mediæval models, and that here too we find the usual lack of style, the same uncertain mixture of subjectivity and objectivity, of poetry and truth, idealism and realism, poetry and prose. Only toward the close of the romance, and when historical exigencies make themselves more prominent, does the orderly prose of the author (or editor?) come to its own proper rights. It is not unthinkable that this ecclesiastical and historical vision may have made some impression upon Dante. He may have taken a scholastic pleasure in the threefold examination. But how Dante, as Kraus surmises, could have constructed his Virgil and his Beatrice upon the model of Giamboni's Philosophia and Christian Faith, I cannot imagine. In Giamboni's work Philosophy and Faith are freely confused. Each of these figures reiterates that it is utterly powerless without the other (Chapter 15). In Dante they are distinct independent personalities, quite aware of their proper spheres of influence. In the *Introduzione* chaos rules: in the *Commedia*, order. Out of chaos one can only create, there being nothing to imitate there. And when once a form is shaped, who can recognize chaos in it?

All these works of Brunetto, of Bono, of Dino, of Francesco, are chaotic. Whether Dante had precisely these, or others of the same type, in his hands, matters little.

Education and Poetry

All these works bear testimony to us how greatly the bourgeoisie of Florence took delight in this medley of art and science, of poetry and philosophy; and how they were always attracted to the allegorical combinations of poetry and prose.

They desired to pour the educational ideas of the Arabian natural scientists and philosophers, the achievements of the scholastics and historians, all Aristotle, the ancient rhetoric, and all sorts of theoretical and practical knowledge, into the handy vessels of Italian prose and poetry; and on the other hand, to elevate the lyrical and musical song of the Sicilians and of the people to the plane of metaphysical and psychological speculation. Science must become popular and concrete, poetry intellectual and abstract. The remote was made accessible, and the familiar difficult. The former tendency finds expression in the *Tesoretto*, as also in numerous translations and recastings of Latin and French works, the second in the elaborate hide-and-seek and linguistic contortions of the Guittonians. Even Dante permitted himself to be carried away by one or the other of these currents. His investigation of the popular speech is recorded in Latin; his didactic treatises on scholastic and ancient philosophy are in Italian, and take on, though only partially, the form of the love-song.

Such an interchange presupposes that between the educated and uneducated a sufficient series of transitional stages, a ladder of the quarter, the half, the three-quarters educated, acts as intermediary, and passes the ideas up and down. If one surveys the writings of that age, the literary market of Tuscany reveals a truly modern, picturesque diversity. At the bottom, translations and extracts from French light literature, minstrel epics, crudely recast; somewhat higher up, the Breton material—*Tristan, Tavola rotonda;* romantic tales—*Libro dei setti savi;* classical romances—*Fatti di Cesare, Istorietta troiana;* tales of conversion and miracles—*Dodici conti morali;* anecdotes—*Conti d'antichi cavalieri;* the *novellino* and animal fables. One story higher, French didactic literature in Tuscan dress—the *Tesoro*, the *Disciplina clericale;* vulgarizations and compendiums of Latin texts—the *Trattati morali* of Albertano of Brescia, the *Istorie* of Paulus Orosius, the *Arte della guerra* of Flavius Vegetius, the *De Regimine* of Aegidius Romanus, the *Miseria dell' uomo* or *De Contemptu Mundi* of Pope Innocent III, the *Giardino di consolazione* (*Viridarium Consolationis*), Aesop, the *Retorica nuova;* compilations—*Fiore e vita di filosofi, Composizione del mondo*, and so forth.

Along with these, French and Provençal literature in the original, which was not only read, but even in part preferred by the Tuscans. A Lanfranchi of Pistoia, a Dante da Maiano, and probably various others, even composed poetry in Provençal. The French language, as we have seen, was in even freer and commoner use. So, not less that four idioms—native dialect, cultivated Italian, French, and Provençal—were united in Tuscan production.

And above them all, a fifth element; the great Latin literature together with the recent gigantic philosophic and theological works of Albertus and Thomas. In the Dominican school of Santa Maria Novella, at Florence, the mighty volumes stood in long rows, and were accessible even to laymen. There was no lack of books of maxims and dictionaries. Already at the beginning of the thirteenth century, Uguccione of Pisa had compiled such a work, under the title *Magnae Derivationes*, with the aid of the *Origines* of Isidor of Seville and of Papias's *Elementarium Doctrinae Rudimentum.* From this work Dante acquired the greater part of his etymological knowledge. It would be surprising if the Dominicans of Florence had not also secured the greatest of mediæval encyclopædias, the amazing work of a brother of their order, Vincent of Beauvais. The arts of letter-writing and of rhetoric were cultivated and taught by lay teachers.

But all this wealth of books, minor poets, authors, writers, teachers, readers, and intellectual workers, did not constitute a fine art. On the contrary, it only bewildered and spoiled the popular taste. It produced, at best, a Guittone or a Giamboni. Just as in the great cities of the present day, there was a host of literati, but no poets. Social and technical materials abounded; a fertile soil was strewn plentifully with seeds; but the muse had not yet given her benediction. Only by chance here and there on the edges of the field a poetic blossom appeared.

The most characteristic and promising artistic motifs, however, originate from crude beginnings: the chronicle, the short story, the didactic poem. But a truly gifted poet like the Florentine, Rustico di Filippo (*circa* 1235–1295), held himself aloof. With the serious and fashionable love-song he was but fairly successful. Only where he lets his sensuousness express itself with fresh wit is he genuine. But in his more important verses, in his picturesque, grotesque, malicious satires, he cripples himself by adhering too closely to personal and local topics.

Similarly of the poems of Guittone or of Chiaro Davanzati, those that are conditioned by time and place, the political satires, have a lasting artistic value. Their interest is exclusively partisan and local. The freshest and clearest springs of poetry were, therefore, at the same time the most limited ones. Even the popular song is stifled under the weight of general culture, unless it be promptly given free air.

7. Dawn of the "New Style"

Florence, despite her many priests, monks, notaries, grammarians, and rhymers, was essentially a city of large proprietors, merchants, and craftsmen. Intelligence was alert, desire for education general; wit was keen, curiosity insatiable. The loquacious populace looked for spiritual food as well as for sensuous satisfactions. Nevertheless, genuine enthusiasm, passion, deep love and reverence for the inner life of the spirit, were still lacking, as they are wont to be, at first, in all peoples devoted to industry and trade. Religion and science lived here in an atmosphere which was some degrees too cool to produce the flower of poetry.

In Umbria, the pious land of St. Francis and Jacopone, came the first blossoming of religious art; and philosophic poetry flourished earliest in the university city of Bologna. Bologna and Assisi are the spiritual homes of Virgil and Beatrice.

THE POETRY OF THE FRANCISCANS

Francis as a Poet

Art and poetry did not come to the pious soul of St. Francis from without; it was rather his piety that sprang from his lyrical and rapturous embrace of the universe. He became a saint, but he was a poet born. His prayer is no deliberate begging, but pure feeling: no function or task, but contemplation and poetry; it is not a sacrificial offering, it is a song of joy.

O Thou, most high, almighty kindly God,
To Thee belong all blessings, glory, praise and honour.
Praiséd be my Lord God, His creatures all,
And most of all the sun, who is our brother,
Who brings the day to us and brings the light;
Fair is he and with glorious splendour shines,
And is to us, O Lord, a sign of Thee!
And for the moon, our sister, praise the Lord,
And for the stars which He as well has set
Brightly and beautifully in the sky,
For the wind, too, our brother, praise to God!
For air, calms, clouds, all weather, be Thou praised,
Whereby Thou in all creatures life upholdest.
For fire, our brother, praise to God no less,
Whereby to us in darkness light is given,
Delightful, bright, mighty, and strong is he.
For earth, who is our mother, praise the Lord,
Who doth sustain our life and keepeth us,
Producing grass and flowers and varied fruits.
Praise be to God my Lord for those who grant
Forgiveness in love's name to one another,
In weakness and in hardship patient still.
Blessed are they that peacefully endure,
For they receive a crown, Most High, from Thee.
Blessed be Thou, O God, for death our brother,
Wherefrom no human body may escape.
Woe unto him that dies in deadly sin!
Blest they who die in Thy most holy will,
On whom the second death may work no harm,
Praise ye and bless the Lord and give Him thanks,
And do Him service in humility.

In a hundred figures a single feeling. We may change the order, or omit any strophe, and the artistic unity of the song of praise hardly suffers at all. Indeed it would be easy to imagine it continued indefinitely. Its construction and outlines are vague, indicated somewhat in the order, and also after the manner, of Psalm CXLVIII. The whole effect is in the colour of the feeling and in the urgent directness with which the manifold diversity of life is attuned to a single harmony. This art is not constructive, not reflective, neither scholastic nor classical; it is without rules, direct, musical, and picturesque, and impressionistic rather than thoughtful.

Much the same may be said for most of the Franciscan poets. Whether, for example—to mention only the most famous pieces—we recall the *Dies Irae* of Thomas of Celano, with all its nineteen strophes, or select merely a few striking verses, for instance, those used by Goethe for the cathedral scene of Gretchen, the mighty imaginative picture of the Last Judgment is hardly affected at all, for here also the spiritual situation is felt rather than developed. In fact, the majority of these poems, even the *Ave coeleste Lilium* and the *Stabat Mater*, would be improved by abridgment.

However, the Latin sequences and hymns of the Franciscans are quite artistic in comparison with their vernacular poetry. Ever ruder, but mightier, uprose the voice of song when Franciscan piety, nourished by hunger, war, pestilence, and madness, flew like a great conflagration through the Umbrian cities and villages. A holy frenzy seized upon mankind (*circa* 1260). Naked or clad in a sack, as the penitents of Jesus they marched through the land, scourged themselves to the quick, and shed floods of tears. The cross was borne before the throng, amid earnest chants of penitence and praise. Dancing- or marching-songs, dramatic responsive strains, rose from the gatherings of these penitent brothers—simple and childish paraphrases of the gospels, anonymous and impersonal.

Jacopone da Todi

The most individual and important singer of sacred *laudes* is Jacopone da Todi (ob. 1306). As a prosperous jurist, he enjoyed life with his pretty, young wife. One day he attended a wedding celebration. In the midst of the dance, the floor fell with a crash. His wife lay before him a corpse. When her festal dress was removed, a penitent's haircloth shirt was found upon her tender body. Jacopone, profoundly shaken, sold his possessions, fled from the world, tortured and mortified himself for ten years in measureless penitence. Then he entered the Franciscan order, attached himself at once to the austerer sect, and became, as a "spiritual," one of the sternest opponents of Pope Boniface VIII.

All ideas and thoughts appear as religion in Jacopone's songs. He is a religious monomaniac. Not a trace of that Central Italian literary *potpourri!* Holy passion, the only one in his nature, gives to his poetry its unity, its material, its style. And yet he too falls only too often into gross violation of all style. But his artistic shortcomings do not spring, as with Guittone or Giamboni, from distracted feelings, from wavering uncertainty between art and science, antiquity and Christianity. Jacopone does not have the inartistic complexities of the literati, no; his is a simple, rude, barbaric lack of art, despite all his learning. He sings by compulsion from within, out of his need for religious activity. Whether the song is pleasant or ugly, he cares not, if only it lightens his heart, and stirs, edifies, and betters his fellow men. The troubadours laid claim to artistic originality, but the Franciscan poets called themselves minstrels (*giullari*), not troubadours (*trovatori*), of God.

It has been shown that Jacopone's lauds are sharply distinguished from those of the Umbrian penitential brotherhoods, and that they are at times anything but popular. Rich and varied in their rhythms, strongly influenced by the Latin hymns of the Church, and often excessive, even unintelligible, in their mysticism, they soar high above the calm, monotonous, solemn tone of the anonymous collections of lauds and make their appeal less to the average piety of the mass than to the virtuosos in piety and ecstasies. Jacopone, however, is no learned, abstruse poet, but only the leader of a divinely inspired choral dancing-band, and his figure is often lost in the throng. Whatever one may say, his song is essentially popular and collective. It has the irresistible enthusiasm, the force, the glowing heat, the insistent repetition, the sensuous picturesqueness, the simple naturalness, the rudeness and the wide range, of popular art. They both resemble a natural phenomenon. Like a torrent it rushes on and carries everything with it. The love of a mother for her child, all the tenderness and intimacy of domestic life, is glorified in the Holy Family. God himself is no philosophically purified being, but a gigantic man with all the human passions. The virtues and other personifications appear as normal women with such thoroughly feminine adornment and manners that we often can but smile at them. There is nothing so delicate and noble, nothing so vulgar and foul, that it may not be seized upon by Jacopone's resistless religious anthropomorphism.

For us, one side in this humanizing of the metaphysical is especially important: the figurative use of sexual love for the relation of the Christian to the Godhead.

We have seen how the later troubadours, yes, even Arnaut Daniel, loved to ennoble and elevate their homage to woman by a religious colouring. The result was an abstract, vague, and artificial style. Jacopone goes in somewhat the opposite direction. He sensualizes and materializes his mystical fervour with the colours of sexual passion and of chivalrous love. Here the result is a popular, natural, and forceful style. So Jacopone summons us to the divine dance of love:

> Ye lovers who love your Lord,
> Come ye with song to the dance of love . . .

and, like the servant of love, he addresses his ballad to the Holy Virgin:

> Go, my ballad, in my name,
> And greet in all humility
> The fragrant queen of roses all,
> The Virgin Mother Mary.[1]

Both these tendencies and styles, the glorified love-service of the knight and the sensualized devotion of the Franciscan, meet in the *stil nuovo*. Beatrice, the Florentine lady, becomes a religious symbol; a philosophic conception becomes a Florentine lady, and the glorified Beatrix becomes now a jealous, now a devoted motherly woman. The tendency to symbolism of the later troubadours and to anthropomorphism on the part of the Franciscan popular poet unite, in the *Commedia*, to form a harmonious whole.

In political poetry also Jacopone, as compared with the troubadours, offers something altogether new. He does not revile his opponent, as did the troubadour, from mere political, ethical, or even personal points of view. In the religiously heated imagination of this zealot, Boniface VIII becomes a myth, an embodied Satan, a new Lucifer. In this respect Jacopone does not stand

[1] Cf. A. D'Ancona, *Jacopone da Todi*, in *Studii sulla letteratura italiana dei primi secoli*, Ancona, 1884, pp. 41 and 47 sqq.

alone, but is in accord with the spirit of the Franciscans. Like the pope in Jacopone's invectives, so the emperors and kings become, in the anonymous Franciscan prophecies, according to their behaviour either representatives of the Lord or incarnations of Antichrist. It is the theocratic style of the prophet and seer that speaks through Jacopone's mouth, for the first time, in an Italian idiom. And once again, it is the *Commedia* that fuses in one the personal sirventeses of the knight and the theocratic prophecy of the monk.

The Indirect Significance of the Franciscan Movement for Dante's Art

We do not know, to be sure, whether Dante was acquainted with the Umbrian lauds and, in particular, with Jacopone's songs. Direct imitation of them cannot be pointed out, either in Dante or in the other representatives of the *stil nuovo.* An indirect influence, however, is beyond question. For brethren of the Franciscan order were to be found in Florence after 1218, and three years later St. Francis founded there the first group of Tertiaries, or lay brethren, the penitent friars, as they called themselves. It is probable that Dante became a member of this "third order," either in his early youth or later in Ravenna. From the year 1244 there existed also in Florence a sort of choral union, the *Compagnia dei Laudesi di Santa Maria Novella,* which was followed, in the time of Dante's youth, by a series of similar brotherhoods, devoted to songs of praise to God and to the saints. It even seems that the Laudesi were earlier in Florence than the Disciplinati in Umbria. How deeply and permanently Dante was affected by the Franciscan spirit is revealed by the history of his religious and moral convictions and character. The ethos of a man must inevitably display itself, in some fashion, in his poetry.

And yet the Franciscan poetry was too formless, that is, on the one hand too direct, fresh, and transparent, on the other hand too crude and wooden, to be of much help to an artist. It is impossible to imitate or acquire either spiritual enthusiasm or awkwardness in technique, for the one is a divine gift, the other a natural failing. So one cannot speak of a Franciscan school of poetry which Dante or any one else might have attended. It was a school of the heart, of character, of the disposition, of the spirit; not of art. If Dante reveals the same force, the same power and tenderness as Jacopone, and more, he does not, however, derive it from Jacopone, but partly from a common background, partly from Franciscan piety, and, in the last analysis, from himself. Jacopone as artist and stylist must, if we know him aright, have been loathsome or ridiculous to him.

Even that graphic humanizing of the metaphysical which we have characterized as the Franciscan poets' most important trait was never acquired by Dante. Indeed, in his description of the other world, and especially in the *Paradiso*, he avoids as far as possible all anthropomorphisms. His God is philosophic, even impersonal; the heavenly spirits ethereal, intangible. Compare with them, for example, Brother Jacopone's *Ballata del Paradiso*, where the blessed dance in rhythm, the angels "wear garlands" and "look like youths of thirty years," and the saints stand like "kings and counts" about their "emperor." Or recall even the description of Heaven and Hell as represented by a Franciscan monk, Giacomino da Verona, in a rude didactic poem in the Veronese dialect, written toward the end of the thirteenth century. His Paradise is a city, with walls of precious stones, battlements of crystal, streets and open squares of gold and silver, and marvellous fragrant trees and songs of birds in gardens where "saintly knights" roam at ease. Angels and apostles stand before God's throne, maidens before Christ and knights before Mary; the Mother of God presents her adorers with a white banner and a battle steed. But the city of Hell is an eternal fire of pitch and sulphur; a vault of steel, iron, and brass spans it. Trifon, Mocometo, Barachin, and Satan guard the gate. When the sinner arrives, he is most cordially received, but presently bound hand and foot, beaten, cast into a noisome stream full of serpents, dragons, and basilisks. Out of the cold water he is suddenly plunged into fire. Baçabu, the cook, roasts him on the spit like a choice pig, seasons him with salt, soot, wine, vinegar, and venom. Then he sends the roast to the table of the king of Hell. But the latter becomes furious and complains that the meat is too rare and the blood too fresh. The sinner must be plunged again headlong into the eternal fire. Devils shear the flock, making a horrible uproar.

> So dread is there the agony of fire
> That even had I fifteen hundred mouths
> Repeating it forever day and night,
> I nevermore could rightly tell the tale.

What a contrast between this monkish crudeness and the *Divine Comedy*, between the anthropomorphism of this idea of Hell and the lofty imaginings of the eternal spirit!

They have in common only the material and the determination to use it in moral warning and for the betterment of the world about them. But utterly diverse is the treatment, the art. Strictly speaking, Franciscan poetry of the future life has no place in the history of the artistic development of the *Commedia*. Upon the structure and the æsthetic value of the poem they have hardly exerted any demonstrable influence. They have nowhere been utilized or imitated by Dante.

In some fashion, however, there is always a connection between the material and the art. We cannot wholly separate the history of the former from that of the latter. To what extent, therefore, the material is to be brought into the discussion can only be determined by a study of the historical development of the form: not through any historical study of the motif—which has no existence!

In other words, we must find in the æsthetic character of the poem itself the measure and the limitations within which we require the material. Thus it becomes clear that, for the construction of the *Divine Comedy*, the dialect poetry of the Italian Franciscans has furnished hardly one artistic idea, hardly a poetic principle, hardly a complete figure, hardly one assured traditional vision of the next world, hardly one hewn stone. So much the greater and more significant is the mass of habits of thought, traditional tendencies of feeling, more or less fixed channels of ideas and beliefs. It is what might be called lyrical anthropomorphism and symbolism; not perfect art, but the conditions for it.

Perhaps our conclusion will be clearer if we express it hypothetically or negatively. Imagine all the poetry of the Franciscans in the Umbrian dialect, or with it this or that Latin hymn, or one or another of their literary productions, effaced from the history of literature: it would hardly cause any serious gap in the æsthetic history of the *Divine Comedy*. But imagine all the activities of Francis and his disciples, or what is much the same thing, the whole Franciscan movement, effaced from the history of Italian culture and literature: what would then remain save romantic love, political satire, secular and classical formalism of rhetoricians, and the allegorical gallicized didacticism of rationalistic notaries and burghers? Pre-existing poetry of chivalry explains certain poems in Dante's *Canzoniere;* rhetoric accounts at the most for the consistency, the harmony and ornamentation, of the Dantesque period; the *Convivio* in general, and the crudest and most jarring part of the machinery in the *Commedia* itself, may be traced back to allegorizing tendencies.

But the passionate directness with which our poet breathes into the events of his life their eternal meaning, the deeper religious significance given to his love for the Florentine maiden, the transformation of his political opponents into diabolical beings—in short, everything which can only be explained by his personal faith in the sacredness of his own destiny, and that means, in terms of literature, the victory of the artist over rhetoric and allegory—that profoundest peculiarity of Dante's art, the entire supernatural sense of the *Commedia*, no matter how truly it is the personal creation of the poet—all this, but for the previous Franciscan movement, would have been an incomprehensible, unnatural innovation. Even the courage to force such a pre-eminent ecclesiastical and religious content into a secular, earthly vernacular would have appeared, without the Franciscan poets, an unexampled anachronism.

So Dante owes to the Franciscan poetry, directly and specifically, nothing: but indirectly, and in general, he owes to it practically everything. We find united here the utmost cultural and psychological indebtedness and the profoundest poetical originality. Nowhere is it clearer that the *Commedia*, in its inmost essence, is a work of art, poetry, an absolutely independent æsthetic monument; or in other words, that almost all cultural values, and especially those of Franciscan piety, are completely transmuted, in the *Divine Comedy*, into pure, transparent shapes of art.

The Transmission of Franciscan Influence

But there must have been some demonstrable channel, surely, by which that spiritual attitude toward art, characteristic of the Franciscans, which we have called lyrical symbolism and anthropomorphism, was conveyed to our poet. And indeed such channels were far more numerous than is commonly taken for granted.

In the first place, it is more than probable that songs of praise in the popular tongue, or lauds, came directly to Dante's ears, in city or country, in the churches or in the open air.

Furthermore, not only the popular but the Latin literature of the Franciscans contained abundant strains of religious poetry. In Bonaventura, in Ubertino da Casale and numerous imitators or predecessors, in Augustinian and Victorine mystics, Dante might and must have found them. There is no lack here of definite points of contact and direct borrowings.[1] But of this, more hereafter.

Thirdly, even the rationalistic didactic poetry of the French and Italians, made use, together with allegorical elements, of a mystical and symbolic language. Hardly a book appeared so prosaic as to be wholly uninfluenced by the spirit of Francis.

Fourthly and chiefly, the later troubadours in Provence, in France, and in Italy blended their mysticism with unmistakable anthropomorphism in their most worldly poems, and clothed religious motifs in the most alluring, charming, courtly, gallant, and fashionable forms of the love-service. In the second half of the thirteenth century, say from 1260 onward, some troubadours, and especially those of Italian stock, Peire Guilhem de Luzerna, Lanfranco Cigala and Bertolome Zorzi, and later also those of Southern France, Folquet de Lunel and Giraut Riquier, begin to give a religious turn to the whole figurative language and phraseology of the courtly love-song and to the whole technique of the service of woman, and to refer them to the Virgin Mary. The worldly bottle is filled with spiritual wine, and the profane form acquires religious meaning. This novel spiritualization of the decadent love-song is, to be sure, no poetic achievement; rather the reverse. But it gives the first impulse to the gradual formation of a new style, and creates a contact with French poetry. Jacopone also, as we saw, widened the sensuous language of homage to women by giving it a religious meaning. About the same time we find, even in Tuscany, villanelles and pastorals with mystical content in the simple forms of popular song.

This state of things, from an æsthetic point of view unnatural and untenable, and brought about especially by the Franciscan popularizing of piety, gave rise, toward the end of the thirteenth century, to a great artistic question, the problem of the *Commedia:* how to cast essentially religious thoughts in a vernacular familiar to the laity. To that end, secular, artistic poetry must be spirit-

[1] It is well known, for instance, that the biography of St. Francis in *Paradiso*, XI, is given partly in the very words of Thomas of Celano and Bonaventura.

ualized in the service of a new idea, the conventionalism of the love-song must be broken up, and fresher, more plastic, more direct forms must be adapted to a loftier type of love.

The significance of the Franciscans, in the history of literature, lies in the presentation of this problem, that of the *dolce stil nuovo* in the partial solution of the problem, that of the *Commedia* in its complete solution.

For the creation of the required new style which should be neither ecclesiastical nor knightly, neither learned nor vulgar, neither purely religious nor merely worldly, but must, so far as possible, include them all, there was need not only of artistic power, but, along with it, of philosophic culture. For only he who was conscious not solely of the inner contradiction between sensuous and religious love-service, but also of their inner kinship, could reconcile them. The mere sensation, without clear comprehension, had been attained by the Franciscan poets, but with all the warmth with which they embraced at once the sacred and the profane, they had not been able to master the inarticulate confusion. Neither their imagination nor their mastery of language had sufficed. A philosophic poet and a new poetic thought were requisite, by which monastic and worldly ideals could be stylistically articulated with force and unity, without the ambiguity that had prevailed.

Nowhere were the conditions more favourable for such philosophic poetry than at Bologna.

Guido Guinizelli

At the close of the twelfth century, Bologna was already a European centre of culture of the first rank. Here scientific knowledge was not extended as in Florence, but more profound: knowledge was not exchanged, dealt in, harmonized, and blended, but made, created, multiplied, and developed. For this was the home of the specialists. Jurisprudence, above all, was taught and learned. And next in its service arose philology, that is, Latin grammar and rhetoric. The Florentine Boncompagno, one of the most important grammarians, taught in Bologna in the first half of the thirteenth century. At the instance of the Emperor Frederick, Aristotle was read and expounded in the university. There was, however, no chair of theology. Hardly anywhere else in Western Europe were the sciences handed down from Greek and Roman antiquity presented in such relatively pure form, unmixed with ecclesiastical and mediæval ideas, as in Bologna. And for that reason also they could exert on men's minds an influence which was new and quite different from that of Paris.

Even the ordinary inhabitants, owing to their constant contact with the university and with students, seem to have had a less prosaic, less Philistine spirit. From Bologna come the first sturdy, genuine, joyous examples of popular poetry; from Bologna, the first traces of goliard poetry in Italy. A Bolognese was one of the first Italians to compose love-poetry in Provençal—Rambertino Buvalelli—no marvel, for the records of the university testify to the presence there of numerous students from Southern France. In the palaces the troubadours sang their canzoni, in the streets the minstrels chanted the Carolingian epics.

Various representatives of the Sicilian school of poets were students in Bologna. Guittone's lyrics also found there the widest circulation and the promptest imitation. Indeed Guittone stood in a close relation to the city, as a member of the Ordo Militiae Beatae Mariae. This order, known under the nickname "Joyous Brethren" (*frati gaudenti*), was of Bolognese foundation (1261). Knights and wealthy folk joined it for benevolent purposes; for charity, for the armed defence of widows and orphans, to settle family quarrels, etc. The brethren of the order might be married and were not bound to any fixed abode. They enjoyed special privileges, were, in particular, relieved from military service for secular purposes, and need not submit to monastic discipline. So the people soon came to look upon them as a band of wealthy, self-seeking hypocrites.[1] In short, renunciation of the world was not the popular ideal in Bologna. The air was fresher and merrier there than elsewhere.

An aristocratic citizen, though not a Knight of Mary, was the creator of the *stil nuovo*—Guido Guinizelli dei Principi. Unfortunately, few of his poems are preserved; but these suffice to show us how in his clear mind the scientific training of the university was united with the beautiful art of the minnesinger, and how in his young heart there abode a warm metaphysical sensitiveness. Illumined by philosophic thought and brightened by

[1] Dante so treated them, not without reason. *Inferno*, XXIII, 103 sqq.

poetic images, this spiritual love breaks forth in the famous canzone, *Al cor gentil ripara sempre amore.*[1]

Here, for the first time so far as we can see, the style of Guittone, which Guinizelli too had acquired, is overcome, the wearisome pedantry of erudition is laid aside, the ascetic monastic piety is purified by philosophy and uplifted to a noble enjoyment of life. The knight's lady has become a nobler being, half Christian angel, half Averroistic intelligence, a pure, lofty, smiling figure, whose love ennobles. It is no longer the suitor's love, greedy for full enjoyment, it is the youth's pure contemplation: a spiritual love, supersensuous and visionary, like the ecstasy of the penitent, passionate, joyous, as free from jealousy as the devotion of a philosopher to his Idea. Brilliant, novel, and noble pictures speak out a marvellous delight of utter self-surrender. It is as if the Christian's Hereafter smiled upon us with Hellenic joyousness. The poet no longer takes his similes from the Bible, nor from history, but from Nature and her mysterious wisdom:

Foco d'amore in gentil cor s'apprende
como vertute in pietra preziosa:
che da la stella valor non discende,
avanti'l sol la faccia gentil cosa;
poi che n'ha tratto fore,
per soa forza lo sol ciò che li è vile,
la stella i dà valore.
Così lo cor, ch'è fatto da natura
eletto pur gentile,
donna, a guisa di stella, lo inamura.

Amor per tal ragion sta in cor gentile
per qual lo foco in cima del doppiero
splende a lo so diletto, chiar, sottile:
non li staria altrimenti, tant'è fero;
però prava natura
rincontra amor como fa l'acqua il foco
caldo, per la freddura;
amor in gentil cor prende rivera
per so consimil loco,
com' adamas del ferro in la minera.[2]

The pictures and comparisons crowd in, are heaped up and intertwined with each other, in long series. The philosophic theme is poetically varied, the artist, in his delight, is never fully satisfied;

[1] See translation, Vol. I, p. 304.
[2] Strophes 2 and 3 of the canzone above cited.

in order to mirror the mystery of this new love, he goes again and again upon the quest for new figures. Guinizelli will not, like his predecessors, develop the supersensuous doctrine of love, he will not justify, defend, or prove; he possesses it, beholds it, displays it, ever the same, to his hearers, in beautiful coloured glasses. Through this visible delineation and attentive attitude, face to face with an ideal, science becomes art, abstract truth becomes living poetry. It is the overcoming of didacticism, the silencing of the preacher and the critic, the dramatic power, that give this canzone its significance. Guinizelli did in miniature what Dante achieved on a far mightier scale; he crystallized and made eternal the whole mediæval doctrine of God and wisdom in one clear and harmonious picture.

There is indeed to be felt, here and there in Guinizelli, a restless struggle, a complicated and unsuccessful search for expression. He seeks to depict the intangible and falls sometimes into Guittone's awkward, over-ingenious obscurity, or he plays with his subject like an æsthetic lover, who paints without feeling. Hence, along with the obscurity, a cold allegorical splendour. But where he feels what he sees, he attains—especially at the close of his song—a wholly novel, vivid, truly dramatic poetic power of mystic quality.

With this canzone, the cycle begins to which the *Vita Nuova* and the *Commedia* belong; the new style is born. All its possibilities of development, its merits and defects, lie here enclosed in a tiny bud. The simple syncretism of the Tuscan burgher is fused in lyric fire, the common anthropomorphism of the Umbrian monk is purified. Dante's art-form, the poetry of contemplative love, of the sincere and pious vision of the supersensuous, is born.

RETROSPECT AND PROSPECT

It is true that Guinizelli's brief love-song is a long way from the all-embracing poem of Alighieri. Granted that the style is spiritually and artistically akin, still its application is as diverse as could be imagined. It is as though we compared a miniature to a fresco.

The example of Guinizelli may enable us to comprehend some poems in Dante's *Canzoniere:* but for the interpretation of the *Commedia*, especially on its technical side, all the antecedents from the history of Italian literature combined are still inadequate. Language, expression, and style, indeed the whole artistic spirit of the poem, we must recognize as completely and definitely Italian, even Florentine. But so far as concerns the sources, the material, the motifs, the technique, in short, the whole structure and purport of the *Commedia*, they are drawn not from Italy alone, but from all the lands of the old world of culture, and their significance and appeal therefore extend beyond all racial confines. In their origin and purpose they are as comprehensive as Catholicism.

The more intimate artistic history of the *Commedia* begins, if we choose to go so far back and to pass beyond the borders of Italian speech, not earlier than with the Provençals. For the Provençal troubadours are the first who, with full artistic consciousness, bring their own personality to expression and create a new poetic art.

Their Italian imitators fill these personal and courtly forms at first with an impersonal and conventional, then more and more with a scientific and uncourtly, bourgeois spirit. The types of poetry become uniform, mingle, and approach prose. Meantime, the old Italian spirit reaches its lowest level; there is a pause in the history of art, which, as is wont to happen, is filled with futile artificialities (Guittonists and allegorists).

The young language did indeed take to itself, out of the wealth of Provençal, French, and Latin literature, an abundance of poetic implements, artistic devices and formulæ, but it lacked creative genius. Poetic impulse and energy were absent.

It was the popular religious movement of the Franciscans that first introduced the poetic problem, and it was the poets of the *stil nuovo* who first attempted to solve it. In a narrower sense, the poetic evolution of the *Commedia* begins, accordingly, with Guido Guinizelli, with Dante's contemporaries—or even with Dante himself.

The remoter artistic history, on the other hand, that is, the history of the material and sources of the *Commedia*, divides and subdivides, losing itself in remotest antiquity. For that very reason, the results of extensive investigation in this direction are less important and valuable for the artistic understanding of the poem. They only illuminate and confirm what the criticism and history of art have to ask and to answer. He who enjoys this diversion—and fortunately, very many Dante lovers do—can so overburden the artistic problems with cultural data of motifs and sources as to render them all but unrecognizable. For unless the investigation of motifs and sources is directed by the exigencies of the art critic, the results, copious and variegated though they be, lack all connection, sense, and value. He who believes in the independent value of the history of subject-matter is consistent if he seeks for the sources of the *Commedia* in India, in China, or among the Hottentots; for isolated portions, comparable with each other, are to be found wherever men abide.

We, however, are concerned not with isolated motifs and insignificant *rapprochements*, but with the *artistic idea* of the entire poem. This, in every successful work of art, is nothing other than the concrete development of the fundamental poetic thought. Poetic technique, in the truest and best sense, is poetic inspiration attaining to self-expression. Where form and content have so completely permeated each other as in the *Commedia*, there can no longer be a question of an independent study of the materials.

When, therefore, we characterize the style or form of the *Commedia* as national, but its technique or motif as international, that means, in truth, nothing more than that the *Commedia* has behind it not only a national but also an international artistic development. It is now time to consider the latter.

8. The Bible

STYLE OF THE PSALMISTS AND PROPHETS

We have characterized the central motif of the *Divine Comedy* as essentially religious. All the art-forms, accordingly, created by Christianity, may fairly be considered, in connection with the history of the sources of the *Commedia.*

We remember that Egyptian, Assyrio-Babylonian, Hebrew, Persian, Greek, and Roman religion and philosophy made their contributions to the formation of Christianity. In fact, certain symbols and allegories of the *Commedia* can be traced, separately and abstractly, to the very remotest of these sources.

The study, in general outlines, of the influence of older religions upon Christianity was attempted in the first part of this work.

There two types of influences were distinguished: the one chiefly ethical, the other mainly æsthetic. The Jewish religion, for example, with all its extraordinarily powerful ethos, created hardly a new figure, hardly one fixed series of legends or characters to present vividly God or His kingdom; but it did utilize and interpret, in its own spirit, the formal religious elements which it took over from the Egyptians, Babylonians, Assyrians, and Greeks. On the contrary, what the religions with naturalistic tendencies furnished toward the development of Christian art seems to have been primarily connected with materials—symbols, allegories, figures—but to a less extent with the fundamental ideas.

In and for itself, to be sure, every religion is capable of creating its own art. But each one is more or less limited in character. Sensuous, plastic, architectural, picturesque, objectively descriptive, or even scientifically planned representations of the next world are most successful, as experience teaches, within those religions that we usually characterize as naturalistic. For only these religions create and bring about that intuitiveness and calm without which a clear objectivity can hardly be attained.

So the Egyptians, along with their magnificent architecture and sculpture, had also their sharply outlined pictures of the realm of the dead. The Babylonian-Assyrian religion begins, thanks to its remarkable astronomical character, to arrange scientifically its mystical cosmology. Along with a highly imaginative, picturesque symbolism, in which animal and human forms are combined, there appears, at once, a mathematical symbolism. "Beneath the earth lies the gloomy abode of the departed, the realm of the dead, with seven or twice seven well-guarded gates, whose queen dwells in a palace. The spirits of the dead on their way thither pass through a stream, and must undergo, before their entrance into their permanent abode, 'full of earth dust,' a sort of judgment." [1]

In order to purify the next world from the "earth dust," to uplift it from the depths of earth into upper air, there was need of a powerful religion, rather ethical than sensuous, such as that of the Persians. Over against the realm of the abyss a heavenly kingdom has its place, and between them a mountain and a bridge. The good and the wicked, demons, angels, and devils, form successive grades.

Religious art grows ever more plastic. Rigid and monumental

[1] Carl Bezold, *Die babylonisch-assyrische Religion*, in Hinneberg's *Kultur der Gegenwart*, Berlin, 1906, I, 3, p. 48.

among the Egyptians, fantastic, picturesque, but still mathematically limited with the Assyrians, enlivened ethically and dramatically among the Persians, it finally appears, in the flowing poetry of the Hebrew prophets and psalmists, as pure and highly lyrical hymnology. The language of the stones has been transformed into a language of the heart and spirit. The Word is become alive, all rigidity has vanished. The Hebrews may have been bad architects and painters, and in the narrower sense of the word, deficient as artists; their entire eschatology, cosmology, and mythology may be borrowed; but they are the first truly intimate and lyrical poets of religion. Possessed by the spirit of their god, they destroy the forms of objective art, shatter the naturalistic cosmology and theology, and whirl the fragments like toy balls through the air. They need no sensuously entertained conception of the other world, for they bear it within them. Their temple is a portable ark, their artistic forms a swift rushing song. In brief linguistic units, not in periods, but in paratactic and parallel phrases, wave on wave, their enthusiasm ebbs and usually dies away in a brief finale. Since the unity depends wholly on the firmness of feeling, it needs no elaborate connection of thought or composition.

Somewhat distinct from this lyrical emotion of the psalmist is the admonitory sermon of the prophet. The prophet seeks, in order to convert and to convince, the most intimate relation with the religious conceptions of the whole people. An old formula, a brief passing allusion to mythical figures, legendary memories, or eschatological imaginings, must awaken, in his hearers, intimate and widely-shared feelings. The oratorical effect of the prophet moves upon an objective and popular foundation of old traditions and beliefs. Hence it did not affect his hearers as violently and mysteriously as a reader of the present day might suppose. On the contrary, it had a strong reflective, critical, and prosaic element, in that it was compelled to give a new content and spiritual significance to the old figures of mythical origin.

As the religious ethos of the prophet rises above the ordinary thinking habits of the masses, the expression clears itself of all the formal and legendary elements of the tradition; oratorical subjectivity lends itself to freer and even more direct utterances of the heart. Allegory vanishes, thought and image are completely fused in a parable that carries its significance within itself, and needs no special explanation. The prophet's style reaches its perfection in the preaching of the last prophet, Jesus. The most unconditioned religious individualism and the most universal piety reach out heartily and instinctively for the commonest, everyday, universally human figures of speech. "All is yours" is the fundamental idea of this style. "In order to diffuse a clear light over what is lofty and divine, over the conditions and laws of God's kingdom, in order to make Heaven accessible to his earth-bound hearers, Jesus led them gently from what was familiar to all, upward to the unknown, lifted their souls, by the cords of resemblance, from the commonplace to the eternal. The whole world, and also what was worldly in them, he took into his service with royal magnanimity; in order to overcome the world, he smote it with its own weapons. He left no means untried, no word unuttered, to bring God's word into the heart of his hearers. Only allegory, which veils and does not proclaim; which does not disclose, but seals up; which instead of uniting, sunders; which does not convince, but repels—this form of speech the clearest, the mightiest, the simplest of all orators could not employ." [1]

DANTE AND BIBLICAL HISTORY

For Dante the Bible is divine truth, but also divine poetry. No other text carries out for him more freely and completely the fourfold method of interpretation of mediæval æstheticism. Hence, in the first place, his extreme reverence for the word and letter; secondly, his zealous effort to extract from the pictures of biblical story and poetry more or less general philosophic concepts; thirdly, to deduce dogmatically from it moral commandments; and fourthly, to force it into a mystical significance—in short, either stubborn insistence upon syllables, or a violent distortion, or at best a scientific dissection, of the meaning. One cannot imagine a less artistic procedure.

Accordingly, æsthetic theory certainly did not favour any serious influence of the style of the Bible upon Dante. Nevertheless, such an influence might well be conceived; for art is not the same in life as in theory.

In fact, how could the open mind of an artist so religiously inclined have escaped the tremendous influence of the language

[1] A. Jülicher, *Die Gleichnisreden Jesu*, 2nd ed., Freiburg, 1899, I, 118.

of the Bible? Especially in Dante's youthful poetry we recognize the deep impressions which it left upon his spirit. His memory is full of biblical reminiscences and pictures; the Bible is by far the most quoted book in his writings. He had it in his head and heart better than many professional clerics. And yet his muse asserts her independence!

Men not artistically gifted, nor independent, are wont to imitate even in their phraseology the authority which they revere in science, in morals, or in religion. A preacher devoid of taste thunders in biblical fashion, an unimaginative worshipper of Kant or Hegel makes his own the trailing sentence-structure of his masters. But a poet like Dante maintains the originality of his own words even in the presence of the majesty of "God's word." He might have been able to mould his language after the pattern of the Bible if he had regarded it, as did the youthful Goethe, not as metaphysical, but merely as poetical matter. Here, one may say that a faulty poetic theory has been helpful to a true poet, and has aided him to comprehend the spirit of the Bible, without submitting to the yoke of its form.

Whoever runs through the biblical references, reminiscences, and allusions in Dante's writings, will be amazed to see how great are the poet's debts in number, and how small in artistic importance. Single expressions, whole sentences, figures, comparisons, or the like, drawn from the Bible, are taken over unchanged, or they are so literally transferred from the Latin of the Vulgate into Italian words that it has been possible to utilize them in many details for the establishment of a critical Dante-text. Quotations, reminiscences, borrowed expressions, however, do not make up style, they do not form it, they only serve it. Employed with moderation and taste, they may spice it, but strewn too lavishly, they are harmful to it. Instead of heaping up inartistic masses of biblical quotations, as people were wont to do in the Middle Ages, Dante, at least in the *Commedia*, uses them in modern fashion, with artistic effect.

In his early writings, to be sure, and even in the *Convivio* and in his political letters, he also gives us too much of a good thing. Most especially in the *Vita Nuova* the biblical allusions make an unpleasant impression. They affect us, if not as a profanation, at least as out of place or superficially ornamental. They seem alien to his style. What an un-Dantesque lover is he who, on the death of his beloved, writes a Latin letter to the "Lords of the land" in the manner of the prophet Jeremiah, and begins: "How doth the city full of people sit desolate! The queen of nations is become as a widow." [1] What a patchwork stylist is he who compares the companion of his beloved to John the Baptist,[2] who characterizes his mistress as gloriously blessed, or lady of salvation, who lets Amor the love-god and the spirits of life of his own body grow eloquent in solemnly biblical Latin: "Vide cor tuum.[3]—Ecce Deus fortior me, qui veniens dominabitur mihi.—Apparuit jam beatitudo vestra," and the like. At the close of the sixteenth century, after religious consciousness had been notably sharpened by the Reformation and counter-Reformation, an editor of the *Vita Nuova* thought it fitting to remove these and similar biblical words from the text, or to alter them. This philologically obtuse but religiously and æsthetically keen censor might have found much more to expunge from our poet's Latin epistles.

In the *Divine Comedy* conditions are quite different. In the next world biblical words are in their proper place; there they have, even when applied to the relation of the poet to his beloved, a proper spiritual significance. For in Paradise the divine mission of Beatrice, which in the *Vita Nuova* was only a semblance, a gesture, or a claim, has become an evident and earnest reality. Latin as the Church language befits the Catholic Purgatory and Paradise. Especially the psalms, as the expression of our common worship of God, are in place here.[4] In fact, the poet could have employed here the words of the Bible without injury to artistic unity, even more freely than his purified and austere feeling for style actually permitted. But his piety had become personal and human rather than ecclesiastical and biblical.

To what extent the abandonment of the biblical style, or its subordination to that of the poet, is Dante's own act, we need not here decide. We wish for the present merely to know to what extent it was prepared and conditioned. Let us then recall how biblical thought underwent peculiar interpretations and radical transformations through the labours of the theologians,

[1] *Vita Nuova*, § 29.
[2] *Ibid.*, § 24.
[3] *Ibid.*, § 2.
[4] E.g. *Purgatorio*, V, 24; XX, 94 sqq.; XXIII, 11; XXIX, 3; XXX, 74 sqq.; XXXIII, 1; *Paradiso*, XXV, 98, etc.

ancient and mediæval. Let us call clearly to mind that habit of thought which we have recognized and characterized as theoretical intellectualism and moral illusionism. For this is the ground upon which Dante's poetry was to undertake and carry out successfully its struggle with the most powerful religious style in the world.

The biblical story begins with simple narrative: "In the beginning God created the heaven and the earth. And the earth was without form and void; and darkness was upon the face of the deep. And the spirit of God moved upon the face of the waters. And God said: Let there be light; and there was light." And it ends: "And God saw everything that he had made, and behold it was very good. And the evening and the morning were the sixth day." But in Dante's, that is, Beatrice's mouth, by the power of theoretical intellectualism, the chronicle becomes historical theology, and the straightforward description becomes a logical proof lyrically expressed: [1]

> "Not to acquire some good unto himself,
> Which is impossible, but that his splendour
> In its resplendency may say, '*Subsisto,*'
> In his eternity outside of time,
> Outside all other limits, as it pleased him,
> Into new Loves the Eternal Love unfolded.
> Nor as if torpid did he lie before;
> For neither after nor before proceeded
> The going forth of God upon these waters.
> Matter and Form unmingled and conjoined
> Came into being that had no defect."

Again that same theoretical intellectualism shapes the tale of Jacob's dream and the ladder to Heaven into a representation of contemplative monasticism.[2]

Moral illusionism on the other hand transforms the biblical chronicle at once into didactic articles of faith, so that the direct and picturesque language of the tale takes refuge in the colourless and sententious style of a jurist. One step farther and a long series of scriptural stories, regarded as moral models, shrink to meagre, brief exclamations, admonitions, warnings, and commands. Thus and so did this or that biblical hero or sinner behave!—conscience remembers, and punishes their souls with Purgatorial pains. Meantime, it may come to pass that the biblical

[1] *Paradiso,* XXIX, 13–23.
[2] Genesis 28:12 and *Paradiso,* XXI, 28 sqq.

fragments are quite stripped of their divine character, and with purely educational purpose are put upon one and the same level with the fables of pagan antiquity.

A comprehensive example of such Dantesque transformation of biblical forms is offered us by the mysterious tree of Paradise. Two shoots from this plant first appear on the sixth cornice of the Purgatorial mountain: first as actual means of punishment, secondly as magical mouthpieces of moral admonition and warning. Thirdly, we find on the summit of the mountain the tree of knowledge itself, as a comprehensive allegory, full of philosophic, ethical, and political instruction. All the transformations from sensuous materialization to moralizing, and even to intellectualizing, are here passed through, and according to its needs, the biblical tree receives the most varied and marvellous environment.[1]

No further examples are needed to reveal and characterize the complete independence of Dante's art, and the means by which it breaks up every expression of the Bible. In the Bible, a practical and collective spirit rules; in the *Commedia*, a contemplative and personal one. Hence, in the one, we find a chronicler's direct and eloquent style; in the other, a poetical, meditative, and philosophical form of expression—in the Bible an abundance of full, natural, and unforced phrases, in Dante elaborated, curt utterance packed into regular metrical units. There a god speaks in human, and here a man sings in divine, forms.

DANTE AND THE STYLE OF THE PROPHETS

Sometimes, however, Dante believes that he must put himself on a level with God. Then he does indeed have recourse to a biblical style—to that of the prophets, as befits his rôle of God's mouthpiece. Then he seeks to imitate that abrupt, obscure, mysterious, and direct subjectivity which we saw to be historically conditioned in the case of the old prophets. Now we admire not so much his poetic originality as the craftsmanlike cleverness with which he attains the antique colouring, the archaic patina, of his forerunners. In the Latin epistles, and in part also in the prophecies of Virgil, of Beatrice, and of the blessed in the *Paradiso*, this intentional imitation is unmistakable.

On the other hand, it must be conceded that Dante possessed

[1] Mediæval plastic art stands in quite the same relation to the Bible: now it clings to the letter and materializes the text, again it presents it with perfect freedom in symbolic and allegorical modifications.

not only the voice but the spirit of a prophet. Thanks to this inward genuineness, he attains a prophetic style of his own which is both classic and thoroughly Florentine, wherein the Hebraic elements acquire fresh and eloquent life, and are all but unrecognizable. The single sermon of wrath, *Ahi serva Italia, di dolore ostello*, suffices to convince us that the Old Testament prophets' language of moral indignation is the mightiest of all the artistic treasures which the Bible bestowed upon our poet.

9. Apocalyptics

ITS LITERARY CHARACTER

The style of the Hebraic prophets had a further development in two directions. Its practical and oratorical directness was perfected, as we have seen, in the preaching of Jesus. Its meditative, mythical, and imaginative elements, however, which had their origin largely in the natural religion of paganism, were reshaped in the later age of Judaism (*circa* 150 B.C. onward) after a new literary pattern, halfway between the sermon and revelation.

This remarkable, long-lived, composite development is known as apocalyptic literature. This literature extends from the closing days of antiquity to the end of the mediæval period.

We may distinguish, with sufficient accuracy, between a Jewish, a Jewish-Christian, and a pagan-Christian apocalyptic literature. This last group, again, breaks up into a Greek and a Roman type.[1]

Despite the utmost variety and diversity, the numerous apocalypses throughout this period of nearly fifteen hundred years have certain formal characteristics in common.

In the first place, they are nearly all artistically deficient, more or less confused and fragmentary. It is to some extent in the nature of an apocalypse to be neither art nor science, rhetoric nor lyric, satire nor didactic poem, fable nor history, but if possible, all these at once. It is approximately true that what mysticism is to philosophy, apocalyptics is to art, namely, an incomplete, vague, undifferentiated form. If we then reckon apocalyptic literature among the sources of the *Commedia*, we cannot expect

[1] There is also a fairly rich and strong Mussulman apocalyptic literature, which borrowed largely from Jewish and Christian sources, and which may in turn have influenced mediæval Christendom. A useful account of this literature will be found in M. Asín Palacios, *Islam and the Divine Comedy*, London, 1926; but I agree with Torraca (in *La Critica*, Naples, 1920, XVIII, 50) and other cautious Dante-scholars that a direct influence on Dante has not yet been established.

from it anything more than scattered fragments. As a collection of isolated fragments, however, it promises, precisely because of its bewildering diversity, the richest results.

From the æsthetic point of view, the apocalyptic concept appears as a concept of value or of non-value. Of course not all bad or imperfect poetry should be summarily classed as apocalyptic literature. The incompleteness must be in some particular and definable field; and the required definition is offered to us by no other poem than the *Divine Comedy*. A *Divine Comedy* without poetic unity and without artistic consciousness would properly be called apocalyptic. If Dante's mighty and firmly knit poem of the future life were a heterogeneous patchwork, then it would fall irrevocably and all but completely under the literary and historical rubric of apocalyptics. And if on the other hand the *Divine Comedy* had never been, I should like to see the historian of literature who would set much store by the whole mass of apocalypses.

Apocalyptic literature could in that case claim nothing but further psychological investigation by the historian of culture; for only he would be in a position to see anything of importance in its formal shortcomings.

A reason for the artistic incompleteness of apocalyptic literature may well be its pseudonymity. The authors have no longer the courage or the confidence to come forward in their own persons and to defend the validity of their prophecies and feelings about the Hereafter. They hide behind the majestic name of a great prophet, long and generally believed in by the public. They feel themselves inferior late-born heirs; they do not wish to be responsible for either the content or the form of their utterances; yet they claim, nevertheless, the highest religious prestige. They evade their own responsibility by giving their writings an archaic tone and the grey tint of venerable antiquity. Hence the oracular and sibylline obscurity and a more or less intentional vagueness. It is hard to decide where conscious deceit begins, and how far in each case the sincerely devoted and enthusiastically receptive ecstasy of these writers of revelations extends.

None of these latter, however, not even St. John himself, the most genuine of them all, was able to overcome wholly the inward contradiction between true piety and literary invention. Only Dante, the greatest combination of character and artistic genius that ever the sun has looked down upon, had that power. All the so-called forerunners of the *Divine Comedy*, however, tread between the precipices of dream and deception.

For there is to be noted not only an artistic, but a certain ethical, incompleteness or indolence that distinguishes the apocalyptist from the prophet. "For the apocalyptist the future does not depend on human action or inaction, as it does for the prophet; and therefore he never passes from his foreboding to a clear conception of present duties. What he announces is the action of God and of the superhuman powers. But since the apocalyptist does, after all, proclaim God's Judgment Day, moral motives of the strongest kind unite at this point with religious hopes. These motives, however, stand only in the loosest connection with the special content of the apocalyptic revelations. They do not, therefore, spring directly out of it, but appear quite independently beside it, loosely connected with it merely through the thought of God's Last Judgment. This explains the structure of most of the Jewish apocalypses. In them the ethical admonitions appear apart, side by side with the apocalyptic prophecies and revelations of transcendent mysteries." [1]

According as the apocalyptic spirit is predominantly visionary or hortatory, contemplative or doctrinaire, edifying or damnatory, it assumes a different outer garb. In fact, revelations present themselves sometimes in allegorical and symbolic form, as a vision, a dream, a parable; sometimes they claim actual, historical, personal verity, as an experience, an absence, a journey; sometimes they regard the condition of the dead as everlasting; sometimes they consider the end of this world as one to be expected soon or late; sometimes they assail the alien, sometimes the domestic, foes of their religion, sometimes a great host, sometimes a little group, etc. All this without counting the senseless compilers who throw together the most contradictory materials and methods.

Indeed, all apocalyptic literature works through compilations; that is, it brings together, in a more or less haphazard fashion, the religious ideas of the most diverse times and peoples. "If anywhere, it is in such apocalyptic, cosmological, and cosmogonic fancies and popular imaginings that national limitations play no part whatever." [2] Limitations of time, too, are hardly regarded. Ancient and modern, Oriental, Hebraic, Greek, Etruscan, Roman, Celtic, and finally, even German materials lie close together.

[1] W. Bousset, *Die Offenbarung Johannis*, p. 18. [2] Bousset, *ibid.*, p. 10.

Religious folk-lore digs and pokes about in apocalyptic literature as though it were an international deposit accumulated in the course of thousands of years.

Apocalyptics defies all limits in form, no less than in matter. There is talk, of late, of a special type of apocalyptic literature which is meant to include all non-heathen visions of future life, so far as they represent themselves as revealed, i.e. as inspired by the Divinity. That the greatest poem on future life, the *Divine Comedy*, however, on account of its artistic originality, which defies classification, absolutely cannot be included in this group, has been shown in an excellent essay by Francesco Torraca.

It is in fact only its creative, poetic power that frees the *Commedia* from the reproach of being apocalyptic. For in truth Dante, like all the apocalyptists, claims to have received a revelation, and to communicate a mystery unveiled by God to him, and to him alone. But he does not, like the apocalyptists, make this claim in advance. It is not in the name of a revelation or even of the Godhead, but in that of the muses and of Apollo, that we are to harken to him. Dante hides behind no authority, no pseudonym. Only by the clarity of his art would he convince. He makes no claim, he wishes to earn belief step by step, and is conscious that the effect of the *Commedia* depends not on what it says, but on how it speaks.

> O mind that didst record that which I saw,
> Here thy nobility shall be revealed.

After he has gazed into the eyes of his God, the artist awakens in him and prays:

> O Light Supreme, that dost so far uplift thee
> From the conceits of mortals, to my mind
> Of what thou didst appear re-lend a little,
> And make my tongue of so great puissance,
> That but a single sparkle of thy glory
> It may bequeath unto the future people.[1]

The artist's prayer was heard, and instead of a doubtful vision, we have the purest of poems.

The literary type of visions as such, accordingly, remains limited to fragmentary, immature, and hybrid imaginings of the Hereafter. It thereby gains in extent what it loses in artistic

[1] *Paradiso*, XXXIII, 67–72.

value. For what Christian sermon, what theological writing, what religious treatise fails to show some attempts or beginnings of eschatological poetry? Not written books only, but all the thousand tales and oral traditions of the next world, belong to the class of apocalyptic literature.

Like golden dust fallen here less, there more abundantly upon the earth and covering all the land, so the lore of Judaism and of older Christendom lies enfolded in visions. Out of this heavenly and earthly dust Dante has moulded the noble metal of his poem.

DANTE AND APOCALYPTIC LITERATURE

So, out of the inexhaustible storehouse of apocalyptic poetry, only so much is of interest to us as has demonstrably or probably been utilized by our poet. All else can be considered only in so far as it enables us to recognize and restore an apocalyptic tradition, now lost, which was known to Dante. In this process, the symbolic language of architecture, painting, and sculpture may be of service to us.

The Israelitic-Judaic Apocalyptic Literature

The oldest apocalyptic vision made use of by Dante is that of Ezekiel (Chapter I). The prophet's four apocalyptic beasts were connected by mediæval theology with those of Revelation (4:6), and interpreted as the four Gospels of the New Testament. It is in this modification that Dante accepted them, and included them, with a statement of his authority, in the triumphal procession of *Purgatorio*, XXIX: it is practically a quotation.[1]

More original and profound is the meaning which our poet has given to Nebuchadnezzar's dream (Daniel 2:31 sqq.), in the fourteenth canto of the *Inferno*. From Daniel's vision of the four kingdoms of the earth and the eternal kingdom of the Messiah (Chapters VII and VIII) he drew no concrete symbols, indeed, but doubtless some inspiration. Here he could see an apocalyptist representing a series of ethico-political powers under the figure of beasts. The choice of the three symbolic animals at the opening of the *Commedia* may have been suggested, to some extent, by the following passage from Jeremiah, Dante's favourite prophet: "For they have known the way of the Lord and the judgment of

[1]The picture of Paradise as "a tree that lives from its top, and always bears fruit" (*Paradiso*, XVIII, 29 sqq.) may well be a reminiscence of Ezekiel 47:12 and Revelation 22:2.

their God: but these have altogether broken the yoke, and burst the bonds. Wherefore a lion out of the forest shall slay them, and a wolf of the evenings shall spoil them, and a leopard shall watch over their cities" (Jeremiah 5:5–6).

Not directly used by Dante, but indirectly of great symptomatic importance is the Book of Enoch. It shows us what apocalyptic ideas were probably dominant in the Hellenized Judaism of the Dispersion. Since it was used by the Catholic Fathers as a genuine composition, it became fundamental for Christian apocalyptics. Here we find, for the first time, Hell depicted as an abyss full of fire, sulphur, and mud, inhabited by devils whose task it is to intensify the tortures of the damned. The blessed, however, have their abode in beautiful, richly adorned regions, and await the Last Judgment. How much of Greek and Oriental conceptions there may be in the Book of Enoch is not to be determined here.

More than from the Judaic prophets of the Old Testament, Dante drew from the Jewish-Christian apocalypse of John. It is undoubtedly the chief source for the triumphal procession of the Church, and for the vision of the Church's history, on the summit of the Purgatorial mountain. It excels all other apocalypses in artistic value. Though a compilation, it is by far the most unified; in eloquence it is the mightiest; in colour, movement, and picturesqueness the richest, in religious power and conviction the most genuine.

If no one of the later apocalyptists attains the height of John, and much less surpasses him, that is the best evidence that apocalyptics is no fixed form of literature, no cycle, with its own artistic motifs; that, in short, it does not develop, but crumbles away.

Hence Dante took from John details only, nothing entire. The largest fragment which can claim a certain independent completeness is the vision of the destiny of the Church's chariot (*Purgatorio*, XXXII, 103 sqq.). Here, and here only, the poet's inspiration approaches the apocalyptic frame of mind. After the pictures had become, in the previous scenes of the Earthly Paradise, rather magical than profound, they now begin to melt into each other and to take on a didactic and purposeful colour. The purely poetical connection is broken. Beatrice gives to her pupil, as God gave to John, an allegorical drama and, at the same time, the charge to make it known to mankind: "And what thou beholdest, write thou in a book." [1]

> "Therefore, for that world's good which liveth ill,
> Fix on the car thine eyes, and what thou seest,
> Having returned to earth, take heed thou write."

Dante did in part construct his vision independently; but the figure of the dragon, whose tail does such damage, the transformation of the chariot into a many-headed monster, and the figure of the harlot are taken directly from Revelation. Even the mysterious interpretation of the allegory, as it is given by Beatrice in the next canto, is imitated.

This unmistakable borrowing leaves no doubt as to the poet's intention. He wishes the reader to treat this and similar passages as the Revelation of John was treated in the Middle Ages. He ceases to be merely a poet, takes for a brief time the part of an imitator, and gives his reader a theological nut to crack.

The chief figures in the previous triumphal march of the Church (*Purgatorio*, XXIX) have the colouring of an apocalypse and are intelligible not in themselves, but only from the mediæval exegesis of the Bible: so, e.g. the seven lamps (Revelation 4:5), the four and twenty elders in white garments (*ibid.* 4:4), the four beasts, etc. Over the whole solemn procession there lies a warm glow of Oriental splendour.

Hellenistic Apocalyptic Literature

But with all its magnificence, Jewish apocalyptic literature—except where it is already under Hellenistic influence, like the Book of Enoch and John's Revelation—is lacking in constructive unity. The figures are somewhat misty, and blend into each other; they move dramatically in time, but they lend themselves to historic and prophetic vision, not to the representation of definite realms in the Hereafter, or of eternal conditions.

It was the Greek influence that first gave to the other world its foundation in space and a certain order. But this firmness was not, as might have been expected, brought into apocalyptic literature through the structural or plastic forms of classical art, but through philosophic conceptual elaborations and abstract thinking. Probably dramatic performances in the Eleusinian and Orphic mysteries

[1] Rev. 1:11.

aided not a little in the development of ideas as to the future life. But these performances influenced Dante quite indirectly, possibly through Cicero's treatment of them in the *Somnium Scipionis*, or through the sixth book of the *Aeneid*. By the side of the Jewish Hereafter as a super-historical event, rises the Platonic and Orphic Hereafter as a supernatural condition.

In Plato's philosophic mythology we already find numerous attempts to arrange definitely the condition of human souls in the Hereafter, according to their moral behaviour in this world, and to distinguish the realms of the pure and of the impure. Through ethical and theological speculation, the fantastic ideas of torture and punishment in the underworld are made symbolically more profound. Platonic, for example, is the thought that sins leave a scar upon the soul, or otherwise disfigure it. Perhaps we have here the first germs of a tradition made use of by Dante, and the first suggestion for the idea of the seven P's (*Peccata*) that are cut in the foreheads of the penitents.

Oriental, especially Gnostic, superstition of the influence of the stars unites in the Hellenistic period with the philosophic notions of the Stoics. In the popular tradition, more or less definite lists of crimes or sins take shape. It has been shown that the Gregorian scheme of the seven deadly sins is found even in Horace,[1] and this coincidence has been explained—perhaps correctly—by the assumption of a half-mystical, half-philosophical doctrine of the Hereafter, which might have made its way even earlier into Christendom through the Gnostic sects.

Accordingly, the Hellenistic contribution to Christian apocalyptics would appear to be chiefly speculative. It should be remembered that the idea of Purgatory is a creation of Neo-Platonic Christian theology and that already with the Orphics the process of future purification through pain appears in symbolic connection with present sins. In the so-called apocalypse of Peter we have, within the Hellenistic Christian apocalyptic literature, the first confused attempt to arrange the blessed and the sinners in space according to their deeds, misdeeds, and penalties.

Furthermore, the Christian Hereafter is not only enriched through Greek influences with conceptual and topographical elements, but endowed therefrom with a dramatic myth. I refer to the victorious descent of Jesus into Hell, as it presents itself to

[1] *Epistolae*, I, 33-38.

us in the so-called Gospel of Nicodemus. The rise, or rather the acceptance, of this legend may well have occurred early in the third century. A series of old Greek descents into Hell (Orpheus, Heracles, Pythagoras, etc.) furnish the probable prototypes. The notion of a neutral Elysian region in Hell (the Limbus), from which the patriarchs are ransomed by Christ, is also connected with this legend. For Dante the descent of Christ into Hell and the breaking down of Hell's gates is a fact well known and accepted by the Church. He is content to mention it merely in brief allusions.[1]

Finally, the first journey into the other world undertaken by a mortal, the so-called apocalypse of Paul, may date back to the centuries of Hellenistic Christianity. It was certainly suggested by the words of Paul in II Corinthians 12: 1 sqq.: "It is not expedient for me doubtless to glory. I will come to visions and revelations of the Lord.

"I knew a man in Christ above fourteen years ago (whether in the body, I cannot tell; or whether out of the body, I cannot tell: God knoweth); such an one caught up to the third heaven.

"And I knew such a man (whether in the body, or out of the body, I cannot tell: God knoweth).

"How that he was caught up into paradise, and heard unspeakable words, which it is not lawful for a man to utter."

The legend of Paul's journey to Hell and Heaven was certainly known to our poet, and was to him an historical fact.[2] Only an indirect influence from it, however, is demonstrable. Above all, the passage in the Bible just mentioned received, thanks to Paul's apocalypse, an historical and tangible significance for every mediæval reader that it no longer has for us. They who then read it thought of the journey, described at length and in detail in that apocalypse, which the apostle was said to have made, under the guidance of an angel, throughout the other world.

With this tale in mind, Dante may have read the Bible passage in question. Then it struck him that Paul himself did not wish to determine whether he had been in Paradise bodily or in spirit. This uncertainty—which, in the presence of a Greek congrega-

[1] *Inferno*, IV, 52 sqq.; VIII, 124 sqq.; XII, 37 sqq.; and perhaps also XXI, 112 sqq.

[2] Cf. *Inferno*, II, 28 sqq.

tion, inevitably incredulous as to a physical Hereafter, was very convenient—has been utilized and imitated by Dante. While Dante traverses Hell and Purgatory as a living man, he leaves it distinctly in doubt whether he flew through Paradise only in spirit or in the body as well.[1]

In true Platonic and Hellenistic fashion, he ascribes to his heavenly world a glorified, figurative, allegorical materiality.

The Paul-legend, furthermore, may be one of the first which also included the Earthly Paradise in the realm of the Hereafter, and placed it between Hell and the heavenly Paradise.

But the greatest, the artistically most vivid and most famous figures of the Hellenic Hereafter—Charon, Cerberus, Minos, the Erinnyes, the giants, the monsters, and the great criminals—are at first omitted from Christian apocalyptic literature. The classical rivers of the underworld and everything else associated with Greek mythology or otherwise recognized as heathen were, in the main, excluded. Not until near the end of the Middle Ages were these plastic shapes gradually taken over.

Here, however, we must distinguish the popular, or layman's, ideas of the Hereafter from the learned, ecclesiastical and more or less authorized apocalyptics of the Hellenistic theologians and Church Fathers. Only the latter is exclusive, endeavouring to make itself scientific and contemplative. Its most important systematizing achievement, besides the doctrine of Purgatory, may well have been the hierarchical ordering of the angelic choirs.

In angelology, as is well known, the *De coelesti Hierarchia* of the Greek mystic Dionysius the Areopagite was our poet's chief authority. This book is in the borderland between apocalyptics and theology.

From other and wholly unscientific sources came the demonology of the *Commedia*. Only the figure of Lucifer is elaborated theologically. All the other Dantesque devils are creations of popular superstition and of Virgilian art.

Roman Catholic Apocalyptic Literature

At this point we return to Italian soil. That which Hellenistic philosophy and Church theology strove to purify, or to re-

[1] *Paradiso*, I, 73–75:

> If I was merely what of me thou newly
> Createdst, Love who governest the heaven,
> Thou knowest, who didst lift me with thy light.

move altogether, lived on and persisted powerfully and stubbornly in the imagination of the humbler classes of Christendom.

After the Egyptians, hardly a nation of antiquity maintained such religious intercourse with their dead as did the ancestors of the Tuscans, the Tusci or Etrurians. Who knows how many monuments to the dead and how many demoniac pictures of the underworld the land wherein Dante was born still hides beneath it? And ought there not to be recognizable, here and there in the *Commedia*, a shadow of the colours in which the Etruscans painted their Hereafter?

In Etruscan art the figure of Charon, for example, assumes a decidedly demoniac or devilish character, such as it never had in Greek art, but which early becomes noticeable among the Romans, e.g. in Virgil. Under Etruscan treatment the pictures of the Hereafter derived from Greece are monstrously and horribly distorted. Terrible demons, armed with serpents or with a hammer, assailing the soul of the dead; evil spirits with bushy beards, crooked noses, savage claws, mighty wings, great pointed ears, and horn-like protuberances on their heads; struggles carried on between a good and an evil spirit for the possession of the soul—these and the like appear in Etruscan painting and sculpture.

But who can determine how much of this terrifying and grotesque gloom came down from Etruscan antiquity into Dante's art? How much is to be credited to Nordic, Celtic, or German representations, or to prehistoric Central Italian superstitions?

Certainly we know that ancient Italian fantasies of the Hereafter, heathenism, belief in demons and gods, lingered on through the last centuries of classical antiquity and the early Middle Ages, growing more and more vigorously as Christianity spread. The Roman Church, in its own flexible and shrewd fashion, tolerated, explained away, utilized, or even encouraged, what it could not root out.

So fauns, satyrs, centaurs, and Titans became devils; Diana, Venus, Mercury, and Vulcan, yes, even Apollo and Jupiter, hostile spirits. When Dante transfers the name "supreme Jove" to Christ, and uses the gods of Olympus not as demons but as rhetorical figures, he turns away from the popular ideas of the Middle Ages and places himself on the side of the humanists and the Renaissance.

Thanks to the superstitious and sly transformation of the

ancient divine world, a host of new motifs streamed into Christian apocalyptic writings. Picturesquely scattered and intertwined, we find them in Tertullian, Gregory I, Bede, and various others, whose writings became a mine for later visionary literature. The deterministic, contemplative, and objective character of Hellenic visions of the Hereafter faded out. "Instead of the frantic ecstasy of the pious appears the purposeful dream of the hierarchs."[1] Augustine (*De Civitate Dei*, XXII) insists with increased emphasis upon the physical reality of the resurrection, the physical pain of the penalties in Hell, and the beauty of the heavenly body which is to be restored to us at the Last Judgment. Apocalyptics becomes practical and realistic.

After paganism is vanquished and the Church has become all-powerful, the religious and renunciatory gain renewed strength. From the future of mankind the seer turns his eyes increasingly toward the future of individual men and the children of the Church; his dreams no longer threaten the foe without, but the foe within: lawless princes, insolent rulers, scoffers, and negligent servants of the Church. It is no longer Christianity as such, but this or that feudal lord, who endows a monastery or supports a bishop, that receives reward and praise in the eternal world. The drama of the Hereafter grows petty, moralizing, pedagogical, subservient, slanderous, personal, gossipy; in short, tendential. The consolatory features vanish, the range of vision narrows, the pictures grow ever more sensuous and punitive; ever more detailed and elaborate become the descriptions and scenes of future tortures.

As the Church rose to absolute power, the apocalyptist within it no longer needed to assure himself of authority and credibility by means of impressive pseudonyms. He no longer had novel religious truths or secrets to reveal, nor new symbols to create, but only old ones to multiply. He has ceased to be a prophet or a philosopher, and conducts himself above all as an educator. Every petty monk, every pious woman, every obedient lamb of the fold, can have his edifying visions. With the suggestions of these worthy people, the preacher makes Hell hot for the other sheep and goats. The old mythical, gigantic pictures fall part into countless legendary and anecdotic tales of horror. It was the great reform movements at the end of the Middle Ages

[1] A. d'Ancona, *I precursori di Dante*, Florence, 1874, pp. 69–70.

that checked this diffusion and secularization of apocalyptic literature.

In the works of Gregory I and of Bede we find, perhaps for the first time, the idea of a contest between devils and angels for the possession of a human soul. Dante has depicted it more than once, and never twice alike.

In the Roman Catholic apocalyptic literature the devils grow ever more insistent and bolder. They crowd upon the seer, who makes a purely contemplative journey through the regions of Hell, as they did about out poet, so that his guide, usually an angel, has to defend him.[1]

Purgatory, which was already fully established conceptually, now reveals itself picturesquely as a valley, as a spring, a river, a bridge, or again as a mountain.

The intention to educate or to convert makes it necessary for the ecstatic pilgrim to expose himself to the tortures of Hell, or of Purgatory; he must test them, force his way through them, doing and suffering; he ceases to be a mere observer, becomes himself a sinner among sinners, renews all his acquaintances and memories of this world in the other, and is finally regenerated by his numerous instructive experiences. Then he returns to earthly life as a messenger of divine instructions, provided with information, commands, threats, or greetings for princes, friends, and foes.

If in his *Inferno* Dante often feels himself imperilled or threatened by evil spirits, if in the *Purgatorio* he shows that he is physically affected by the purifying penalties, and even receives ethico-political and personal messages and instructions from the blessed in Paradise, and never wearies from beginning to end in performing the most manifold duties of messenger between his contemporaries and the eternal world—we recognize in all this the sturdy and practical spirit of Roman Catholic apocalyptic literature, as it held sway especially in the first half of the Middle Ages.

This period is closed by Gregory VII. In a sermon delivered at Arezzo, while he was still the monk Hildebrand and thundering against the simoniacs, he related how a German count, recently dead, despite all his merits and despite his great piety had been seen in Hell, standing at the top of a flaming ladder, and that every time a scion of his noble family died, his ancestor, in order

[1] So fares the Northumbrian, Dricthelmus, whose journey to the other world is described by Bede.

to make room for him, must move down a step deeper into the fire; for the progenitor of the dynasty, many years before, had encroached upon the lands of the Church at Metz.

Reference has often been made to the fact that Dante, whether consciously or unconsciously, literally reversed this punishment and transferred it from secular to spiritual simoniacs. In the nineteenth canto of the *Inferno*, the simoniac popes, Nicholas III, Boniface VIII, and Clement V, push one another ever deeper into a fiery grave. Whether Dante was or was not acquainted with Gregory's sermon just mentioned, we certainly see here, in typical form, how thoroughly the secularized apocalyptic writings of early mediæval times have been recast and reversed in the *Commedia*.

APPEARANCE OF APOCALYPTIC MATERIAL IN CHRISTIAN ART

From Music to Architecture

If this secularization had not occurred, if the priests had not systematically connected, by their ideas and their actions, the present with the future life, apocalyptic materials could hardly have become available for artistic purposes. How utterly inartistic the renunciatory and austerely ascetic apocalyptic literature is, may perhaps best be seen from the gloomy penitential treatise of Pope Innocent III, *De Contemptu Mundi*, a famous, much-read work, perhaps known to our poet. There the description of the Hereafter is given in clear, juridical, systematic fashion, neither poetically nor for edification, but chiefly to convert by terrorism.

And yet, as may well be imagined, despite the austere spirit of mediæval literature on the future life, there is no lack of tender, lyrical, and feminine voices. In North Germany, when Dante was a youth, there lived three women: Mechthild of Magdeburg, Mechthild of Hackeborn, and Gertrude of Eisleben, in whose writings quiet and charming pictures of hope and happiness in the Hereafter are to be found. If one considers the similarities and analogies to Dante's *Purgatorio* which these works reveal, especially in reference to his Earthly Paradise and its streams of oblivion and of consolation, its successive steps of purification, etc., it is hard to resist the surmise that Dante read the *Revelationes* of these Benedictine nuns, or heard of them, or even that the figure of his Matelda was created as a memorial to the two Mechthilds.

It is a question of suggestion, which is possible and probable, but defies proof and verification.

However that may be, so long as the future world remains an incomprehensible marvel, or a terrible threat, or a rosy dream, remote from earth and complete in itself, so long as it makes itself known only through inspiration or revelation to him who passively and devotedly lets it possess him, it will always remain limited to artistically crude and imperfect forms. The religious sign (symbol) cannot become a picture, nor the idol a work of art. This was uttered, in modest self-knowledge, by the apocalyptist Barontus, when he declared that he had only recorded, not elaborated, the vision which had been granted him, and that he could be accused of deficient skill in expression, but not of untruthfulness.

A religion so essentially transcendental and renunciatory as Christianity could, strictly speaking, create a "religious art" only through unsuitable compromises, only if it wedded the sensuous and sinful world, so to speak.

Therefore, original Christianity remained artistically barren. It either destroyed the fully developed forms of pagan painting, architecture, and poetry, or took them over externally, as a borrowed garment. It could at best recognize only a worldly, not a religious, art. Hence the Christian hymn in Horatian form; hence the intensest mysticism, even that of Augustine, in the graceful phrases of rhetoric; hence the Christian temple persisting for centuries in a structural type that was intended for civil law and business (the basilica); hence, in the catacombs, an art of painting and mural decoration borrowed from the airy rooms of the Roman dwelling-house, etc.

The one art, however, which on account of its especial materials is dependent most directly upon sincerity and feeling, and which therefore most easily frees itself from conceptual or material conditions, music, was, so far as I can see, the first which in, the course of its artistic development, became truly religious. Even in the fourth century it acquires, first in Ambrosian and later in Gregorian chants, its own thoroughly Christian character. "The liberation of melody from the fetters of metre broke the tie which until then had connected Christian with ancient music, and actually emancipated it from the poetical composition in which it had until then been merged almost as an essential portion without independent existence. Since tone was now set free from the syllable, it could go its own way, could shape itself upon the single syllable, which could now be variously and colourfully drawn out in rich passages, in coloratura phrases and figurations. The sculptural stateliness of classical tonality was opposed to this fantastic colouration, whereas the barbaric, i.e. non-Hellenic, Asiatic peoples undoubtedly took delight, even at that time, in such elaborations of melody. The Asiatic and African churches may have given the first impulse to those rich musical strains which were afterward taken over as Gregorian chant by the Western churches. 'The halleluja,' Durandus tells us, was sung from early days with the *pneuma;* that is, with coloraturas which made a serious demand upon the singer's breath (πνεῦμα). 'But the *pneuma*, as expressive of jubilation, sings, over and beyond the power of words, the delight of the spirit in things eternal, and the *neuma*, made only upon the final syllable of the antiphon, indicates that God's praise is ineffable and beyond our understanding. The *pneuma* betokens the joy of eternal life, which no words can express; hence it is an utterance without definite meaning.'"[1]

It was to be many centuries before this utterance could be wedded to beautiful and significant poetic words. For the word belongs to the common throng; it is worldly and characterless; it degrades the noblest content, turns it into chatter and commonplace. Therefore the Christian religion imprisons itself in an old and dying language which was presently to live only in books. Unnatural fetters were imposed upon poetry. The Latin peoples suffered most severely; for, on account of the close relationship between the classical language and their own dialects, the distinction of languages usually meant also a difference in style; while with Germans and Englishmen, each of the two languages could develop its own style independently. The Italians, finally, for reasons with which we have become acquainted, were the last to release themselves from the old bonds.

In short, the fundamental bilingualism delayed, where it did not prevent, the growth of a great, unified Christian poetry and pushed it on into an age in which the diverse styles, the vulgar and the learned, the worldly and the spiritual, after long interchanges had finally grown together.

[1] A. W. Ambros, *Geschichte der Musik*, 2nd ed., Leipzig, 1880, II, 61–62.

While the hierarchic isolation of religious thought was a hindrance to the poet, it was helpful to the builder, and made possible a magnificent ecclesiastical architecture.

For in architecture the problem took an essentially different form than in poetry. In the former the religious idea is the fast and fixed backbone and skeleton, but in the latter it must become flesh, warm blood and living word.

After the sixth-century Gregorian chant, it is the Romanesque and Gothic cathedrals of the twelfth and thirteenth centuries that give to the Christian idea a new, complete artistic expression. In forms of stone, the *corpus mysticum Christi* is here portrayed. It is dogmatic and hierarchic art, static as a canon of theology. The sobriety of decoration, the solidity of construction, such, for instance, as we admire in the cathedrals on the Middle Rhine dating from the Romanesque period, reveal to us that religious feeling has become wholly will, power, and embodiment. Nothing is left to the caprice of the individual. As every man has his social position and every class its sacred duty, so here every pillar, every arch, every tower, bears its appointed share of the general burden.

As early as 787, the second Council of Nicaea decided that the composition of sacred images should be determined in accordance with the fundamental traditions of the Catholic Church, not according to the taste of the artist; that only the execution of the picture belonged to the painter, its whole plan and arrangement to the ecclesiastical authorities. So, even in the Gothic cathedrals of France, where the sculptural decoration and coloured glass always took on richer forms, the priest, educated in theology, guided the artist's hand. Behind almost every figure, every drawing, there lies an official literary source. The result was a magnificent, unified, impersonal, solemn, serious, and yet childishly submissive, amiable, and credulous artistic language. What the Christian thinker taught was moulded, without initiative or vanity of his own, by a sensitive, devoted artist. Hence the indescribable combination of supernatural profundity and popular naïveté. Never again has a systematic religious view of life been portrayed with such rich and assured symbolism, with impersonal and harmonious artistic feeling, in stone and colours. A division of labour acceptable to God resulted in artistic perfection.

Apocalyptics in the Arts of Design

That which best attained expression in such rigid and monumental art was, of course, the persistent concept of faith. The ideas and pictures of so bewildering and changeful a world, however, as that of the apocalypse, could better come to their own in decoration.

There was no lack of attempts to express monumentally the vision of the ecstatic seer. In the mosaics of early Christian art, in the solemn, calm, representative mural pictures of the Byzantine-Italian churches of Rome and Ravenna, the cities of the Dantesque *Paradiso*, this problem is solved, so far as possible. But this was made possible only by the application of rigorous symbolism, intelligible to the initiated alone.

Even the walls of the catacombs show the mysterious emblems of the other world: the soul as a dove, a peacock, or a lamb, Paradise as a garden with few trees, or perhaps also represented with four rivers and a hill. The condition of the blessed is indicated by a banquet; resurrection and salvation by the Jonas motif, by Daniel in the lion's den, or by the men in the fiery furnace; or, again, by a phœnix, a cock, a harvest scene, and the like. In the mosaics, Christ sits on a lofty throne, in a typical position, among the twelve apostles, and surrounded by the four apocalyptic beasts. But it is precisely the art of mosaic that led the way to a calm, changeless, hieratic style. All dramatic liveliness or excitement, such as would be unavoidable in scenes of Hell or Purgatory, are as yet absent in early Christian art. This art, in general, does not attempt to depict, but to recall; not to excite or frighten, but to edify and soothe. The simplest things are so vivid in spirit that the slightest, remotest hint suffices, and anything more would be excess.

Hence, from the great church pictures intended for worship, the terrors of Hell or of Purgatory are excluded. These first come to their own in the illustrations of educational books. Representations of the Last Judgment are found in Byzantine and Occidental miniatures after the sixth or seventh century, and they do not seem to have made their way into church frescoes until the Carolingian age.

Demons, devils, dragons, and monsters are employed preferably for decorative purposes by Irish and Anglo-Norman, and then generally by Northern, art of the Romanesque period. A grotesque and elaborated art-language develops, especially under Celtic and German influence. The central Christian idea of salvation in the Hereafter is gradually overgrown and covered by fantastic decorations. From columns, friezes, crucifixes, and walls, masks and caricatures grin down at the congregation. That secularization of apocalyptics in literature which began about the age of Gregory becomes noticeable at this time, especially in the art of the Northern nations. The symbols of the next world become stylistic ornaments. But mediæval Italy, so long as it retained its contact with the austerely hieratic art of Byzantium, had little part in this romantic and grotesque development.

In France and Germany, however, this unchristian tendency in decorative art was, at least in part, suppressed by the Cistercian movement. "What do these ludicrous monstrosities mean in the monastery, before the eyes of the studious brethren? A strangely deformed beauty, and a beautiful deformity! Such a multiplicity of shapes induces them to study the sculptures rather than the Scriptures. Even if one is not ashamed of the folly, at least the burdensome expense should be deplored!" So thundered St. Bernard.

So, if we disregard decorative accessories and manuscript illustrations, no independent representation of Paradise, Hell, and Purgatory was produced, even in the late Romanesque and early Gothic period. A personal or even individual conception of the Hereafter could not be favoured by the Church as such. Its corporate and dogmatic character made it inevitable that it should set the realm of eternity before its believers' eyes only in close association with all Christendom and with world-history. Hence the pictures of the Earthly Paradise are closely associated with Adam's fall and the images of the Hereafter are connected with the Last Judgment or Christ's descent into Hell.

The first representations of the Last Judgment appear in the monumental art of the Occident soon after the year 1000, for example, in the Church of St. George at Oberzell on Reichenau, in French and in South Italian churches. The pictures are almost invariably divided into horizontal sections (from two to five). Christ, surrounded by angels, His figure usually recessed in an oval (*mandorla*), is enthroned at the top; somewhat lower the apostles; on the next grade below, the resurrection of the dead, with the damned starting for Hell on one side, and the elect on the opposite side moving toward Paradise. Each group, each grade, each section, is complete in itself, and has a merely formal and symmetrical dependence on the rest of the picture. Their simple construction, rigid and solemn, gives to the visions of Doomsday no opportunity for dramatic life.

Not until the thirteenth century is the law of symmetry violated. Then miniature painting took the lead with monumental art slowly and hesitatingly following. It arrives too late for our purposes. The greatest painters and sculptors of the apocalyptic realm, Orcagna, Signorelli, Grünewald, Dürer, Holbein, Michelangelo, are of course no forerunners of the *Commedia*, but its followers, in part its imitators.

Dante never saw a human, living, individualized picture of the Hereafter in ecclesiastical art except in miniature, unless possibly the famous reliefs by Nicolò and Giovanni Pisano, in the pulpits of Pisa and Pistoia.

The great Doomsday of Giotto in the Church of Santa Maria dell' Arena at Padua (1306), even if perchance Dante saw it, had no perceptible influence upon his art, nor could it serve as an illustration for the *Divine Comedy*.[1]

But what the monumental works of his time could teach the poet, and no doubt did teach him, is the magnificent, firm, and regular structure of his poem. If we did not know it already, the *Divine Comedy* would suffice to prove to us that at the end of the Middle Ages, the foremost art was still Church architecture.

Dante learned from it not only symmetry but symbolism. When he imagines his Lucifer with three ugly faces in contrast with the three beautiful aspects of God, when he plants the tree of knowledge in his Earthly Paradise as an antithesis to the cross of Christ in Jerusalem, when, finally, he distributes his entire theology analogically through spatial series, we may suppose that he was influenced far less by the literary fancies of the mystics than by the serious works of the architects. Without this massive realization of the symbolic habit of thought of the Middle Ages, the accuracy, the rigour and assurance of Dante's cosmic construction are hardly explicable. It has even been asserted that his particular feeling was fundamentally architectural, and that, of all great poets, he is the only one who unites a godlike structural firmness with human fluidity of words and colours.

[1] In the two works, however, the kinship in time and place is recognizable.

In comparison with this fundamental importance of Church architecture, the occasional symbols and pictures which our poet may have borrowed from painting and sculpture are of minor value.

It is known, for example, that his portrayal of angels and devils coincides with the usual representations of them, that the treatment of Hell as a city, the description of the Trinity and of fettered Lucifer, the symbol of the sirens, that of the Heavenly Rose, the picture of the Holy Virgin in a circle of angels, that of John, the author of Revelation, as an old man asleep, that of the martyr Stephen as a gentle youth, and probably those of many other figures, are repeated in mediæval miniatures, frescoes, and reliefs.

Apocalyptics in Poetry

After the arts of design, with their dogmatic, symbolic, and monumental tendencies, had shaped a limited portion of the apocalyptic thought, it was only natural that the ignored remainder should demand expression in other directions and by novel paths. That which lived so forcefully, though unexpressed, in the minds of mediæval men, the idea of a future world, could have no rest until it found artistic utterance. The mysteries of the other world were important not merely for Christendom as a corporate entity, not merely for the theologians and priests, not for the monumental artist alone. The mind of every believing mortal from the visionary hermit to the simple layman, whether in the monastic cell or in the nursery, was haunted and filled with the marvellous tales of a life to come.

About the same time and in the same lands where apocalyptic figures were shaped by artists for decorative purposes, monks, no less gifted with imagination, took delight, first of all in Ireland, in adventurous, fabulous, and awesome tales of the visionary future. It was Northern, barbaric, but genuine poetry. In the legend of Brandan, Northern sea-sagas are fused with apocalyptic visions.[1]

The so-called *Purgatorium* of St. Patrick is not so much a romance of travel as a history of a soul in legendary garb. As a brief account of this second Irish journey to the next world is

[1] Here, for the first time, so far as we know, a special abode and condition of neutral angels, neither evil nor blest, are mentioned: something like Dante's ante-Inferno. The Brandan-legend was brought to Italy, probably in the thirteenth or fourteenth century, but can hardly have been known to Dante.

included in the *Legenda aurea* of Jacopo da Voragine, the Northern legends may very well have been widely known in Italy in Dante's time. We find here a comparatively clear arrangement of the divisions of the next world (1, Purgatory and Hell; 2, the Earthly, and 3, the Heavenly, Paradise), we find here also penalties in Hell like Dante's. Sinners lie crucified upon the ground, others are devoured by serpents or driven by a chilling tempest, others are imprisoned in ice, others in hot streams with devils that smite and submerge with rakes those who attempt to rise.

The most important and most complete poem of future life, composed by Irish monks, is the *Visio Tnugdali* (*circa* 1150). It was well known in Italy, as in the rest of Europe, but probably not until after Dante's time. It has often been compared or associated with the *Divine Comedy*. And yet, what have its ingeniously horrible, uncanny, agonizing pictures and haphazard style in common with the austere art of the *Commedia?* No influence from it can be positively demonstrated: certainly not as a work of art, but only perhaps as a popular tradition, and indirectly, which may be true also of many another vision.

A long succession of such monastic poems from the eleventh, twelfth, and thirteenth centuries, in Germany, France, England, and finally in Italy, might be mentioned here. The vision of Fra Alberico of Monte Cassino was for a long time supposed to be the direct source of the *Commedia*. But here again, amid the utmost internal diversity, only a few more or less obvious coincidences are to be noted: e.g. in the local divisions of the other world, in the figure of Lucifer at the bottom of Hell, and the like.

Certainly all this monastic literature is to some extent poetic. Its interest is no longer edifying, as in the true apocalyptic writings, but chiefly entertaining and imaginative. The religious and mythical form of the apocalypse died out in the course of the tenth century, when its literary exploitation began. The transition is marked by the descriptive monastic visions. As art they are still crude and shapeless, as an unveiling or revelation quite inadequate, unoriginal, and pointless. They seek to create the impression of truth not by a tone of profound conviction, not by their weight of thought, but by the abundance and elaboration of their accounts. They aim rather at the semblance of truth than at truth itself. The unconscious and inspired lack of plan in the visions that true believers and frenzied votaries enjoyed gives place, with these half-believers, to a description of incidents that is systematically carried out and finished without a break. An ignorant man might regard all this as revelation; an intelligent person must consider it merely fabulous.

These literary apocalyptists, accordingly, seek their public among simple folk. In the course of the twelfth and thirteenth centuries, the visions find their way deeper and deeper into the humbler classes of the people, lose their ecclesiastical character, and take their place in the literature of the laity, in the vulgar tongue. For the less cultivated men are, the more gladly do they believe in prophecies, marvels, and legends; indeed, they feel no essential difference between religious edification and imaginative diversion.

If, in such advanced and enlightened times as the twelfth, thirteenth, and fourteenth centuries, the apocalyptic materials, instead of shrivelling, become ever richer, more comprehensive, and more popular, the reason doubtless is that the laity were coming to share in the intellectual life. Ideas and motifs which had been regarded as obsolete become more vital than ever as they pass into lower and larger classes, and unfold an abundance of unimagined possibilities.

The dramatic side of the future life, which was quite neglected in the arts of design, now comes to its own in shows and pageants. Partly within the churches, partly in the public squares, Hell's jaws and Heaven are displayed to the gaping multitude. Angels and devils show themselves upon the stage, heathen demons and profane jesters mingle in the spiritual drama.

When we read the coarse, vulgar, yet lively and dramatic comedy of devils in the *Inferno*, XXI–XXII, it is difficult to avoid the surmise that even the meditative Alighieri had sometimes attended the churchly and popular, comic and instructive, mystery plays or performances. He was not present, to be sure, when, in 1304, his uproarious fellow citizens enjoyed a "divine comedy" quite to their taste. "The people from the quarter San Friano, with whom it was a usage to be constantly planning new and various plays, let it be proclaimed throughout Florence: 'He who wishes to obtain news from the other world should come on May Day evening to the Carraja bridge or the near-by banks of the Arno.' They erected, upon skiffs and boats in the river, a stage on which they represented a fiery Hell, with all sorts of punishments and tortures, with men who were disguised as terrible devils; and others who appeared like naked souls, and seemed to be alive, were subjected to the most varied agonies. There was a mighty outcry, shrieking and uproar, so that it both looked and sounded terrifying and awesome." But, under the throng of spectators, the wooden bridge gave way. Many of the curious crowd met their death under the ruins or in the waves. But the wit of the survivors came to the conclusion that the people who had been so eager to get fresh news from the other world were having it now at first hand and quicker than they could have expected.[1]

After the eternal mysteries had once been caricatured and vulgarized by the rude hands of the mob, the comic element, whether as burlesque parody or grotesque satire, became part of the poetry of the Hereafter.

The tendency to the burlesque, to irony and parody, was developed especially in the farces of French actors or in the jesting verses of wandering minstrels. But with this light-hearted thoughtless folk, who had lost all respect for apocalyptics, Dante had nothing to do. To him belongs the ethically attuned, satirically spiced, grotesque, pathetic and coarse humour of the edifying mysteries, of the mendicant monks, "the Lord's actors," and of popular preachers. For, like them, he too retains his belief in and reverence for his subject. He can treat ironically, at most, and for once only, himself or a minor human sinner.

We recall how in Northern Italy the favour of the cities was won, in the course of the thirteenth century, by French players with adventurous legends, fabulous tales, and surely also with frivolous burlesque farces.[2] Faced with this immense importation of worldly and sinful means of diversion, the preaching monks, the shepherds of souls, found themselves obliged to invent a literary antidote. So they came before the people in conscious rivalry with the strolling minstrels, and sang to them in rude Italian verse of the Creation, of Adam's fall, of the sufferings of Jesus Christ, and of the Last Judgment. The best material, however, with which to rival successfully the fascinating minstrels' tales, was the apocalyptic. To depict and portray how

[1] Villani, *Cronica,* VIII, 70.

[2] The *novella,* or short story, in Italy is evidently based largely on French *fabliaux.*

things are in the other world must prove not only edifying and instructive, but also most interesting and absorbing. The brethren Pietro di Barsegapé, Bonvesin da Riva, and Giacomino da Verona were surely not the only ones who seized upon this congenial subject. Indeed, it even seems that the worldly minstrel, allured by the success of the spiritual one, devoted himself to a serious and systematic treatment of the future life. Uguccione da Lodi, with his five religious poems, was a layman, and in close relations with the heretical sect of the Patarini of Cremona.

Some thirty-five years ago a minstrel's song, a so-called *cantare*, more accurately an *atrovare*, was discovered, which was composed by a nameless rhymer of Reggio Emilia in the thirteenth century: an ill-preserved, tattered, wretched patchwork, in irregular eight-line stanzas. But for that very reason it is of importance in the history of culture, for it is unimaginable that the awkward, halting, anonymous writer invented the exact, systematic, relatively clear and regular arrangement of the realms of the other world. He makes known to us an elaborate, really systematic tradition. His *Purgatorio* is larger than four mountains piled one upon another; his *Inferno* is divided into eight sections, each of which has its distinct name and character. The first section, called *Ago*, is full of fire; the second, *Tartaro*, full of discord, the third, *Averno*, full of cruelty; the fourth, *Aciro*, full of evil memories; the fifth, *Gena*, full of sulphur; the sixth, *Grabasso*, a testing place, the seventh, *Baratro*, is very deep; the eighth, *Abisso*, contains fiery ovens and red-hot pitch. The entire extent amounts to more than a thousand miles. Ten gateways, a hundred miles apart, open downward. Each of these gates has also its special character and is intended for a definite class of sinners. There are volcanoes, seas, and lakes at the entrance. The first gate is called Gate of Tears, the others Gate of Grief, of Fear, of Chains, Sulphurous, of Serpents, of Thirst, etc.

It is evident that the feeling for monumental symmetry, which was developed first in theology and church architecture, finally affected popular poetry in the vulgar tongue. The learned tendencies of apocalyptic art were shared by the laity. A fairly intelligent popular poet, acquainted with Latin, Bonvesin da Riva, ventures to appear (*circa* 1274) before a Lombard public, which speaks a local dialect, with a comprehensive religious and didactic poem in extremely symbolic and symmetrical form. His recently discovered *Libro delle tre scritture* seems to have been planned for six hundred strophes. Their artistic arrangement has been compared to the ground plan of a cathedral. The nave, accordingly, would be represented by the "red writing," that is, the tale of the sufferings of Christ; the left aisle by the "black writing," that is, the description of the twelve punishments of Hell, in one hundred and eighty-five strophes; and the "golden writing," again in one hundred and eighty-five strophes, describing the twelve joys of Heaven, answers to the right aisle. At the end of the nave, an apse of twelve strophes is added, at the end of each side aisle, one of six strophes. Whether the plan is to be understood precisely so or somewhat differently is unessential for our purpose. Certainly the comparison between the twelve penalties and the twelve joys of the blessed stands before our eyes as clear and exact as any one could wish. The stench, for example, which must be endured by the sinner in Hell as his second penalty, corresponds to the "sweet fragrance" in Heaven; the outcry and shrieking of the sixth penalty offset the sixth blessing, which is harmonious song; the most terrible diseases (in the tenth place) answer to the most healthful beauty of the celestial body; the damned, who are tortured by devils, are contrasted in the same division (the seventh) with the elect, who are attended and served by Christ, etc. Even the chapters, devoted to the successive penalties and joys, seem to be arranged in fairly parallel order. First the poet gives a definite description of the penalties or blessings; then he indicates by exclamations or comparisons the impression that they make upon him, the chronicler; then he causes the sinner, or the just man, to speak, to lament, or rejoice, and to connect his present condition closely with his previous life. But the elaborate scheme is filled in with coarse monotonous phrases, with heavy materialistic pictures, with childish comparisons and exaggerations. There is a lack of vital connection between the various sections. The saved and the sinners are abstract beings under twelvefold conditions. We have only scenes in Hell, no Hell; only types of blessedness, no Heaven. With the help of his classification, the poet completes his task; not artistically, but systematically, after the manner, so to speak, of natural science. The rough and crude poet lets his hand be guided by an over-precise and fussy mechanician. The whole thing seems like a pale and feeble imitation of the *Divine Comedy.* Science is distorted into dry schematism, and poetry into coarse naturalism.

It can hardly be that Dante ever met this recent and least agreeable apocalyptic forerunner. In the literary evolution of the *Commedia,* Bonvesin's poem has no immediate, but much indirect significance. Symptomatically considered, it is perhaps the most instructive.

Above all, it gives us evidence of the fact that in Italy, the rudest dialect poetry, even at an early date, strove for regularity of form, that poetry in the popular speech, not only in the domain of love, but also in the religious and especially in the apocalyptic field, endeavoured to approach the didactic treatise as did allegorical and philosophic poetry. The monks, composing for the common people, made an effort to follow the same path as the notaries, the Guittonians and other more or less learned laymen. Spiritual and apocalyptic art, or the literature of the religious vision, is about to put itself in touch with the worldly and allegorical poetry of the grammarians and rhetoricians, or with the literature of the philosophic visionaries. The long line which, starting with Boëthius's *Consolatio,* with the *De Nuptiis Philologiae et Mercurii* of Martianus Capella, and with the *Psychomachia* of Prudentius, passes on to the *Anticlaudianus* of Alain de Lille, to the *Elegia* of Henricus Pauper, and to the *Romaunt of the Rose,* to Brunetto Latini's *Tesoretto,* to the treatises of Bono Giamboni, to the didactic poems of Francesco da Barberino, and to the *Intelligenza*—is at last beginning to merge on Italian soil with the equally long line of development of apocalyptic art.

10. From Allegory to Humanism

CHARACTER AND SIGNIFICANCE OF ALLEGORICAL POETRY

We should now tell, connectedly, the story of the allegorical or worldly literature of visions; but we are no better able to discover a clear and connected development here than in the case of the spiritual literature of visions.

No less than apocalyptics, allegory, on account of its artistic nature, is condemned to remain imperfect. What prevents apocalyptics from becoming a pure art-form is the passive attitude of the imagination, which receives pictures, but cannot shape them in accordance with its own laws. The apocalyptic artist is under religious pressure, undervalues his own poetic powers, uses them only hesitatingly and, in part, unconsciously. In allegory, on the other hand, poetry is too highly valued and forced into unfitting service. Scientific conceptions, abstract ideas, which, by their very nature, are thought out logically, and cannot be made visible poetically, are what the allegorist attempts to treat. Words philosophically fixed and defined, such as virtue, science, nature, destiny, chance, beauty, and the like, he believes he can incarnate by personifying them; that is, by putting the definite article before them, hanging a brilliant cloak about them, or putting some significant emblem in their hand.

Apocalyptics lies below and to one side of genuine art, allegory above and beyond it. The former remains in the sway of ecstasy and transport, the latter in that of abstinence. In the one the temper is too hot, in the other too cold, to win the muses' favour.

Accordingly, in so far as the history of art can be imagined as rationally progressive at all, apocalyptics should be regarded as a crude early stage in artistic development, and allegory as a useless epilogue. In fact, apocalyptics is a preparation for the blossoming of Christian art, allegory a soulless repetition or a dull imitation of antiquity. The allegorical poetry of Prudentius, Capella, Alain de Lille, and so on, is pagan form without heathen faith, classic drapery without bodies beneath it, a Graeco-Roman paper flower—in short, philological art.

For us, it has a significance of its own as a school, a tradition, a relic, and as a stylistic practice, not as poetry. The writers of allegory, consequently, take their place side by side with mediæval language teachers, grammarians, and rhetoricians, on whose dry soil humanism slowly grew.

From philology to humanism is, to be sure, a long step not easy to explain. The evolution of humanism also is as yet by no means adequately illuminated; for it is not merely a story of philological activities, nor is it a tale of pagan revolt against Christianity, but far more than the one or the other. The deepest roots of humanism lie in an essentially mystical, that is, more or less naïve, unconscious, and confident, bridging of the rift between antiquity and Christianity.

Reverence for a pre-eminently ethical personality was, for the pious Christian, always a necessity. That cheerful and optimistically ethical faith exemplified by Jesus or by the apostle Paul never lost its influence, even where the narrowed spirit of the Church held sway. Traces of it may be recognized in Augustine and his followers, in the Victorines, in the Franciscans, and also in many heterodox mediæval sects (Waldenses, Arnoldists, etc.). An inward tolerance, however much it had to conceal itself in the presence of orthodoxy, did exist in the Middle Ages. Many a quiet, noble nature was open and liberal enough to ascribe even to the heathen a certain holiness in so far as they were morally pure and high-minded. Noble men like Cato, Virgil, or Trajan, Plato, Aristotle, or Cicero, were revered and loved: more, perhaps, by the humble piety of the laity than by those made narrow by theological learning. The genuine, fresh, and as yet unphilological Renaissance begins, therefore, not with the æsthetic and literary leaders, but with the moral heroes, of antiquity. They who revived and awakened it were mystics and lovers. Only after the miracle was accomplished did the philologists and doctors come trooping in. Unfortunately we have as yet no comprehensive study which traces through the Middle Ages the growth of humanism in its contacts with the Augustinians, Franciscans, Arnoldists, and all the forerunners of the Reformation.

Such an investigation would perhaps enable us better to understand the meaning and the fate of the allegorical interpretations and art-forms. For if we observe how in Italy and in the more naïve Northern Europe the classical world was justified by pious, unwary monks, laymen, and heretics, how they made Virgil a prophet or a magician, Ovid a teacher of morals, Hades a Hell, Olympus a Paradise, Orpheus or Apollo a Redeemer, Horatian love-songs chants of the Church; how they prayed at Ovid's grave, as though at a sacred spot, and half-piously, half-inadvertently, regarded Cato, Seneca, Pliny, Statius, and Trajan as Christians, how they were edified by the humanity and greatness of these figures and their works without questioning their historical environment, how they took delight in what they had in common with them and ignored what was alien—when we weigh all this, we understand that there existed in the Middle Ages a spontaneous, blindly loving humanism, and beside it, a temperamental, uncritical type of allegory, and that this childish, fanciful attitude was the preparation for critical humanism and for the conscious, formal allegorical interpretations and compilations.

Everything that cannot be grasped and assimilated in this amiable, soulful, mystical, and lyrical fashion—and that is the entire crude and forbidding historical reality of the ancient world—is left to the philologists, the grammarians, and the rhetoricians. These were the mediæval guardians of classic form, and as the Church took sometimes an indifferent, sometimes a hostile, attitude toward such treasures, these scholars rescued, by consciously allegorical interpretation, at least the beauty of the outer shell, at the cost of sacrificing the pagan inner substance. The rift between classical antiquity and Christianity, which as critical thinkers they could not conceal from themselves, and which they often felt as a contrast, even a gulf, was bridged over by them systematically with the compromise of allegory.

Not always, but often enough, there were united in one and the same person the naïve and blind with the critical and learned love for antiquity. Then arose that inward discord, that divided conscience which reveals itself to us in allegorical poetry, sometimes as practical, sometimes as artistic, obscurity. Toward the end of the Middle Ages the number of such divided and sundered natures increased, and Dante, for a time, was one of them.

The most eminent and in a certain sense the last representative of this double attitude is Petrarch, in whose soul the inward wavering has become an open strife between Virgil and Augustine, between humanism and mysticism. This secret dualism of his reveals itself in the broad daylight of his art, and he becomes the foremost defender and singer of the divided heart and of the anxious dilemma of sensuous hedonism and spiritual eudæmonism.

DANTE AND ALLEGORICAL POETRY

Earlier than this, however, the minds of poets and scholars had wavered in painful indecision and compromises.

"Jupiter and the followers of Christ exchange ignoble kisses," is the complaint of a priest about the middle of the twelfth century.[1]

Even in ancient Greek and Roman art, wherever the Platonic negation of free and pure art was accepted, allegory occasionally appeared. So again and again with Virgil, Apuleius, Claudian, and many another.

[1] Bernard de Morlas, in his *De Contemptu Mundi*, a didactic poem on the penalties of Hell and the joys of Paradise.

The first and last comprehensive pagan allegory, however, was *The Marriage of Philology and Mercury*, by Martianus Capella (early in the fifth century after Christ). It is a didactic explanation and interpretation of ancient divinities, an illuminating analysis of the old art-form.

All the personifications of the sciences or of the seven liberal arts, as we find them in mediæval poetry, painting, and sculpture, are derived more or less directly from Martianus Capella. Only in the representation of Philosophia is Capella's personification superseded by that of Boëthius in his *Consolatio*. Capella can hardly have been known to Dante, who disdains his crude personifications. The allegorical representation of philosophy, of rhetoric, of law, etc., which Dante gives in a learned canzone, is less sensuous, less picturesque, more pallid in appearance, but much more spiritually alive. External description has been transformed, under the influence of the *dolce stil nuovo*, into a profounder inner characterization. The emblems and garments of the personified conceptions are superseded by the study of physiognomy, as it were, by the light of the eyes or the smile of the lips.

Within the sphere of classic art, allegory led to formlessness and prose. The example of Capella shows that. Within the Christian world of culture, on the other hand, allegory, no longer able to destroy what is already fallen in ruins, serves as a basin and depository for shapely fragments. Thus in the famous *Battle of Souls* (*Psychomachia*) of Prudentius (at the close of the fourth century), especial attention is devoted to description and to form. What the pagan allegorist Capella disdains, the Christian Prudentius carefully assembles.

Capella became the accepted model for the personification of the sciences, as Prudentius did for that of the virtues. He, too, was probably unknown to Dante, certainly not utilized by him. The only allegorical personifications of a moral nature in Dante's poem that are of any importance are Fortune and Poverty, the former modelled after Boëthius and Henricus Pauper, the latter after Franciscan types.

Even the most famous and brilliant allegorical poem of the Middle Ages, the *Anticlaudianus* of Alain de Lille (at the close of the twelfth century), remained unknown to our poet.

So utterly trifling are the stimuli and creations of allegorical art in comparison with those of apocalyptic art! It was not granted to allegory to create anything viable. Its problem and its importance in the history of art did not consist in the shaping of new forms, but in salvaging, preserving, and transmitting the old. The more faithfully it watched over them, the less it changed them, the more it abstained from free invention and limited itself to mere compilation, or at most to interpretation, the better did it fulfill its function.

DANTE AND ALLEGORICAL INTERPRETATION

In fact, it was as compilation and interpretation that allegory rendered its chief service to the construction of the *Commedia.* Wherever two or more contradictory authorities, whether philosophical, religious, moral, or artistic, are to be accepted without contrast and reconciled, allegory is of great help. Thus the Stoics put philosophy and popular belief, Philo, Greek science and Jewish religion, the Church Fathers, the Old and the New Testaments, under one allegorical cloak; that is, set them peacefully beside each other on parallel lines.

We are interested, at this point, only in that type of allegory which endeavoured to unite and reconcile the great art-forms, which served as mediæval models, the typical styles, divine and heroic figures, myths, legends, wonder tales and fables of the Greeks and Romans, with those of the Bible, of the prophets and the apocalyptists.

The first step in this direction is said to have been taken by the Emperor Constantine the Great with his allegorical interpretation of Virgil's fourth eclogue. The strongest impulse, however, toward the conquest of pagan art-forms was given by Fulgentius (late in the fifth century), with his abstract analysis of the Graeco-Roman myths and divinities in his *Mythologicon* and with his essay on the historical foundation of the *Aeneid*, known as *Virgiliana continentia.* Many other allegorical explanations and analyses, other attempts to moralize and spiritualize works of pagan art of antique or Oriental origin, appeared later. Along with Virgil, it is especially Ovid, the fabulist and story-teller, who was given a spiritual and Christian colouring.

The collections of golden maxims (*Florilegia*) and of instructive exploits (*Exempla* and *Gesta*), unite with moral purposes things profane and sacred. Only under the protection of allegory and only as suitable parallels could ecclesiastical and worldly art live side by side.

In mediæval world-histories, allegorical parallelism comes into use still earlier as one of the important methods of presentation. The inventor of this procedure was Paulus Orosius. In his *Historiae adversus Paganos* (A.D. 418), Orosius undertakes to point out a mystical connection and a symmetrical or parallel series of events in the history of Babylonian world-rule, of the Roman empire, and of Christianity, and thereby initiates a pagan-Christian form of parallelism. Dante made large use of Orosius, and borrowed from him the chief ideas of this mystical and numerically symbolical philosophy of history. In almost the exact words of Orosius he teaches that, in the very year when Caesar Augustus for the first time brought about universal peace on earth, the birth of Jesus Christ occurred. By means of this anything but chance coincidence the two lines of development, the worldly and the spiritual, are set side by side, both in retrospect and in prospect.

Nevertheless, with Orosius parallelism is only the fundamental principle of historical writing, but not yet realized as its form. We find this in the most famous biblical history of the Middle Ages, the *Historia scolastica* of Peter Comestor (middle of the twelfth century). Events of profane history are here introduced in the course of the biblical history, partly as a chronological guide, partly as spiritual explanation, and stand beside it, now as boundary stones, now as analogies. This work also, which became a model for many others, may have been known to our poet.

In the arts of design in the West, the juxtaposition of pagan and biblical figures is relatively late and did not become widely prevalent until after the date of the *Divine Comedy*. At most in the illustration of books, on the pavement of Italian churches, on capitals, and the like, our poet may have noted them. Whether such monuments really served as suggestions for his "setting face to face allegories and personifications of virtues and vices and parallel types illustrating them drawn from paganism and Judaism" cannot be determined with certainty.

After the principle of juxtaposition was once established and justified by the philosophy of history and had come into use in literature, partially also in the art of Oriental and Occidental Christendom, after it had proved useful, especially for encyclopædic works, it must naturally find place in a comprehensive didactic poem like the *Divine Comedy*.

If this parallelism is unintelligent, it deteriorates into syncretism. As such it was most prominent in Byzantine art and, as we have seen in frequent examples, in Italy also. For both in Byzantium and in Italy that discord between clerical and worldly culture which allegory was intended to allay was lacking. Allegorical poetry and allegorical thinking, long prevalent in France and Germany, had no great vogue in Italy until the thirteenth century. The poem of Alain de Lille and the *Romaunt of the Rose* were favourite models.

At about the same time, however, allegory accomplished its task in the history of art. The worldly art of the laity, of the wandering players and minstrels, of the knights, the grammarians, and finally the humanists, acquires sufficient strength to stand alone. The ancient beauty of form begins to doff its protective cloak of allegory. Allegory gradually becomes unnecessary. It ceases to be a practical and therefore requisite form of thought. The time of its misuse and decline begins.

In part it reverts to complete formlessness, *e.g.* with Brunetto Latini or Francesco da Barberino. Or it sinks to idle diversion and is lost in dainty elaboration, as with the French *rhétoriqueurs* of the fifteenth century. Or again, it becomes one with apocalyptic and symbolic art in a completely new and original form, as in the *Divine Comedy*.

To have mastered and united the two imperfect, visionary styles of mediævalism, namely, the religious and mystical symbolism of the apocalypses and the lay, moralizing, classical intellectualism of allegory—that is the distinction of the *Divine Comedy* in the universal history of art. It owes its effectiveness in international art to this twofold victory.

MYSTICAL AND ITALIAN HUMANISM

How does it come to pass that the international problem of art is solved poetically not in Latin but in the national language of Italy?

There was certainly no lack of apocalyptic and allegorical poetry outside of the peninsula. That patient, evangelical love for antiquity, that broad whitewashing of the pagan world, was surely practiced as much in Germany and France as in Italy, if not even more. And did not mystical humanism, in the second book of Dante's *De Monarchia*, employ the international language, Latin prose? Were not the antecedents for allegorical and apocalyptic compositions richer and more elaborate in the North of Europe than in Italy?

Surely! Yet a mighty and thoroughly popular movement took possession later, but all the more powerfully, of the Italian nature. It is the spring wind, which, to be sure, blows from the North, but grows warm only under Italy's classic sky. Here first, here alone, do the dry seeds of antiquity waken to life and blossom. In the Italy of the thirteenth century everything is eager for renewed life. Social order grows civic, piety becomes childlike, the Church turns mystic, dogma is made philosophical and science humanistic; even the old biblical style of prophecy and revelation cannot escape this first Renaissance. In the writings of Joachim's and of Francis's disciples apocalyptics undergoes a most remarkable, unheard-of transformation. The Jewish-Christian style of these new prophets and seers is associated with heathen, Celtic, and especially Roman ideas and with memories of Troy and Greece. Merlin and the sibyl become spiritual authorities; the legendary as well as the real history of antiquity is seen through a Christian veil; present and future are concealed in a half-biblical, half-classical language. There is formed a double manner of speech which is nevertheless highly suggestive for the mood of the Italy of that day. Let us hear how the tale of Troy, for example, sounds in the jargon of Joachimitic prophecy:

"Sudoris opus aggredimini, o Danay, sollicitudinis et cruoris, donec X pedes premensurati discurrant, Ylion depereat, Laumedontis proienies evanescat, preda redeat ad Atridem. Precedet siquidem sanguinis effusio inestimabilis Danaumque exanimatio, Frigiorum audacia, donec dolor impudicus Pellidem urgeat, duos leones Laumedontides fortissimos virtute prosternat; fietque Frigiis animorum debilitatio, donec virginalis concupiscencia Eacidem afficiat et enervet."

Of Emperor Frederick it is said in the same prophecy:

"Et veniet aquila habens caput unum et pedes LX, cuius color sicut pardi, pectus sicut vulpis et cauda sicut leonis, et dicet: 'pax,' ut pacifice capiat. Mamillis sponsae agni lactabitur, usque dum accrescat ei caput maius in Eneaden terciumque minus, eruntque sibilantia a Germanicis usque Tyrum," etc.

That such Joachimitic-Franciscan prophecies were read by Dante, and more or less closely imitated in the *Veltro* and *Dux* prophecies of the *Commedia*, can hardly any longer be doubted.

The style, also, in which the history of the Roman empire is given in the sixth canto of the *Paradiso* unites in similar fashion the pathos of the classic epic with the solemnity of prophecy. The language of Joachim's imitators is here elaborated oratorically and becomes, in the mouth of the Emperor Justinian, a pathetic-mystical, epic-prophetic, classic-biblical tirade.

> " In order that thou see with how great reason
>   Men move against the standard sacrosanct,
>   Both who appropriate and who oppose it.
> Behold how great a power has made it worthy
>   Of reverence, beginning from the hour
>   When Pallas died to give it sovereignty.
> Thou knowest it made in Alba its abode
>   Three hundred years and upward, till at last
>   The three to three fought for it yet again.
> Thou knowest what it achieved from Sabine wrong
>   Down to Lucretia's sorrow, in seven kings
>   O'ercoming round about the neighbouring nations;
> Thou knowest what it achieved, borne by the Romans,
>   Illustrious against Brennus, against Pyrrhus,
>   Against the other princes and confederates.
> Torquatus thence and Quinctius, who from locks
>   Unkempt was named, Decii and Fabii,
>   Received the fame I willingly embalm;
> It struck to earth the pride of the Arabians,
>   Who, following Hannibal, had passed across
>   The Alpine ridges, Po, from which thou glidest;
> Beneath it triumphed while they yet were young
>   Pompey and Scipio, and to the hill
>   Beneath which thou wast born it bitter seemed;
> Then, near unto the time when heaven had willed
>   To bring the whole world to its mood serene,
>   Did Caesar by the will of Rome assume it.
> What it achieved from Var unto the Rhine,
>   Isère beheld and Saône, beheld the Seine,
>   And every valley whence the Rhone is filled;
> What it achieved when it had left Ravenna,
>   And leaped the Rubicon, was such a flight
>   That neither tongue nor pen could follow it.
> Round towards Spain it wheeled its legions; then
>   Towards Durazzo, and Pharsalia smote
>   That to the calid Nile was felt the pain.

Antandros and the Simois, whence it started,
It saw again, and there where Hector lies,
And ill for Ptolemy then roused itself.
From thence it came like lightning upon Juba;
Then wheeled itself again into your West,
Where the Pompeian clarion it heard.
From what it wrought with the next standard-bearer
Brutus and Cassius howl in Hell together,
And Modena and Perugia dolent were;
Still doth the mournful Cleopatra weep
Because thereof, who, fleeing from before it,
Took from the adder sudden and black death.
With him it ran even to the Red Sea shore;
With him it placed the world in so great peace,
That unto Janus was his temple closed.
But what the standard that has made me speak
Achieved before, and after should achieve
Throughout the mortal realm that lies beneath it,
Becometh in appearance mean and dim,
If in the hand of the third Caesar seen
With eye unclouded and affection pure,
Because the living Justice that inspires me
Granted it, in the hand of him I speak of,
The glory of doing vengeance for its wrath.
Now here attend to what I answer thee;
Later it ran with Titus to do vengeance
Upon the vengeance of the ancient sin.
And when the tooth of Lombardy had bitten
The Holy Church, then underneath its wings
Did Charlemagne victorious succour her." [1]

Such a mystical and yet humanistic, romantic and yet classical, glorification of the Roman empire, at the beginning of the fourteenth century, is imaginable only in Italy. In Germany and France the vernacular poet, when essaying a classical subject, must have recourse to allegory, or he must, like Benoît de Sainte More, equip his classical heroes in knightly and romantic fashion; in short, he must treat antiquity didactically, drily, and prosaically, or entertainingly, gallantly, and in courtly manner.

To be sure, even in Italy, and with Dante, there are abundant traces of allegory, and also of a romantic and novelistic conception of antiquity.[2] The so-called *Tales of Ancient Cavaliers*, *Ex-*

[1] *Paradiso*, VI, 31–96.

[2] Allegorical passages are most frequent in the *Convivio* and especially in the eclogues.

ploits of Caesar, Trojan History, The Flower of Philosophers,[1] and the like, are throughout unhistorical diversions; but they are composed on French models, not from an Italian point of view.

Fragments of such romances and legends are found here and there even in the *Commedia*. Among the lustful in the *Inferno* we have the "ladies of ancient time and cavaliers." Achilles and Paris stand beside Tristan, Dido and Cleopatra beside Francesca da Rimini. The poets and sages of antiquity dwell in a mediæval castle, which is girt about by seven symbolic walls, doubtless betokening the seven free arts. In short, Gothic anachronism is abundantly illustrated.

That in Dante's philosophy of history and in his ethics the peculiar value of ancient culture is only partially and imperfectly realized, we have noted. But that which might then have seemed to us a lack, reveals itself, in the field of art and poetry, as a merit. The fine, unerring, naïve conscientiousness with which Dante absorbs himself in pagan antiquity, so that the enjoyment of study and of its fruits may not be embittered by the shadow of a scruple, this unswerving devotion to the world of his Virgil and Aristotle, relieves him of all need for allegory and enables him to comprehend and portray in his *Commedia* the very features of the antique world.

He who reads the description of Elysium is inevitably reminded of the most refined Renaissance paintings, Raphael's Parnassus and the "School of Athens."

> We came into a meadow of fresh verdure.
> People were there with solemn eyes and slow,
> Of great authority in their countenance;
> They spake but seldom, and with gentle voices.
> Thus we withdrew ourselves upon one side
> Into an opening luminous and lofty,
> So that they all of them were visible.
> There opposite, upon the green enamel,
> Were pointed out to me the mighty spirits,
> Whom to have seen I feel myself exalted. . . .
>
> The Master I beheld of those who know,
> Sit with his philosophic family.
> All gaze upon him, and all do him honour.
> There I beheld both Socrates and Plato,
> Who nearer him before the other stand.[2]

[1] *Conti di antichi cavalieri, Fatti di Cesare, Historia troiana, Fiore di filosofi.*
[2] *Inferno*, IV, 111–120 and 131–135.

The destiny of Ulysses is, to be sure, elaborated in mediæval legend; but listen to the fiery speech of this adventurer, who forgets his home and family, and hurries his crew forth on the "mad flight" over the untravelled ocean.

> "O brothers, who amid a hundred thousand
> Perils," I said, "have come unto the West,
> To this so inconsiderable vigil
> Which is remaining of your senses still
> Be ye unwilling to deny the knowledge,
> Following the sun, of the unpeopled world.
> Consider ye the seed from which ye sprang;
> Ye were not made to live like unto brutes,
> But for pursuit of virtue and of knowledge." [1]

Who does not at this point think of Christopher Columbus? How could such a clear, noble, free, and refreshing utterance have been heard in the "gloomy day" of the Middle Ages which enfolded the Northern lands of highly moral and Christian Germany? Turn wherever they will, to the Germans antiquity is something acquired, drilled into them. As they are good students, they attain to a considerable enthusiasm and a satisfying zest for this transmitted knowledge. The Italian is spared any such exertions and efforts. He has all antiquity in his native land and in his heart's blood; he has no need to conquer or rescue it allegorically, symbolically, or romantically; scientifically, morally, or artistically. He takes it into himself warm and sweet with his mother's milk.

So for him, even in his most pious, most Christian, most mediæval century, the thirteenth, everything, even prophecy and apocalyptics, became old Roman eloquence, and took on a classic splendour.

And that is why Christian and transcendental ideas could attain clear, intelligible, cosmopolitan and human forms only where such forms had been familiar for centuries. Therefore the international problem of the *Divine Comedy* could find a solution only in Italy.

11. Retrospect

We are at the end of our study. The international and the Italian developments of art have come together.

The worldly-ecclesiastical, Catholic culture elaborated, in po-

[1] *Inferno,* XXVI, 112–120.

etry, two visionary styles: the apocalyptic, mystical, symbolic, and the worldly, philological, allegorical. Through the great popular movement of the twelfth and thirteenth centuries, which may be characterized as pre-Renaissance, or pre-Reformation, or Franciscanism, or mystical humanism—according to each man's viewpoint—the demand for complete fusion of the two styles arises. This demand is met at first, in Italy, prematurely and imperfectly; namely, through a styleless hodge-podge of traditional forms. For creative genius, such confusion is welcome freedom and opportunity for a great unhampered venture. The stiff, formalistic, and prosy mass of rules of the Italian grammarians and rhetoricians of the ninth, tenth, and eleventh centuries grows limpid, opposition is overcome, the soil is opened up. The road is clear for Dante, but it is not yet defined.

Guido Guinizelli, the first Italian poet to emerge from this stylistic confusion, drew a short straight line, but only from one single point. The developed technique of the Provençal troubadours had made it possible for him to solve, at least in the narrow field of the love-song, the contrast of this world with a Hereafter that is the artistic problem of the *Commedia*, and to discover a new secular and yet religious devotion to woman and a "new style."

Out of such a love-song in the "new style" Dante's *Vita Nuova* grew, and out of that, the *Divine Comedy*. The Beatrice of the *stil nuovo* is the lyrical original source of the *Commedia*. What was accomplished in the *stil nuovo* for the love of woman, is accomplished in the *Divine Comedy* for the universal love of God; that is, the appropriate, perfect poetic expression, the earth-born form for a Heaven-scaling spirit.

12. Dante as Artist

THE MINNESINGER OF FLORENCE

What from thy fathers thou inheritest,
Earn ere thou shalt possess.

The innate Italian feeling for form needs education in order to become a work of art. Indeed, the richer and the more complex the capacity of an artistic nature, the longer and more laborious and tortuous is the path to harmonious form.

Just at the mid-point of the Italian stylistic medley, Dante was born and grew up. Florence was then, as Germany is today, the "home of all the paint-pots." Imitations and translations from all lands were welcomed and fused. In the general craving for culture and in the double effort to popularize science and to exalt poetry—prose, verse, and all literary genres were confused.

A rapidly developed economic prosperity beguiled the simplest bourgeois families into luxury. Sumptuous buildings, sacred and secular, were either recently completed, or in process of erection: Santa Annunziata, Santa Croce, San Marco, Santa Maria Novella, Santa Trinità, and the cathedral, Santa Maria del Fiore, the hospitals of the Innocenti, of Misericordia, and of Santa Maria Nuova, the Bargello or palace of the Podestà, and the palace of the Signoria. To the single bridge which Florence had possessed from the earliest times, the Ponte Vecchio, there were added, within the first half of the thirteenth century, no less than three new ones. How the city had grown some twenty years after the poet's death, we are told by the chronicler Giovanni Villani: [1] "The city was well planned, and contained many houses. Construction was going on constantly at that time, and the effort was to make everything richer and more comfortable and to display notable examples of a general improvement. Cathedrals, monastic churches, and splendid monasteries! Either among the common people or among the magnates, there was hardly a citizen who had not either built, or laid out, an extensive and rich estate in the suburbs, with a noble mansion and buildings, much better than those within the walls. Nobody resisted such temptation, and the outlay made it seem as if the folk were mad. But it all appeared so magnificent that strangers, who did not know Florence, when they approached it and beheld the rich buildings and beautiful palaces in a circuit of three miles round about it, believed that all this, just as in Rome, was part of the city itself: quite apart from the rich palaces, towers, courtyards, and walled gardens, which stood yet farther away, and in other regions might well be accounted castles. In short, it was reckoned that within six miles of the city there were so many rich and lordly dwellings that it amounted to more than double the number in the city itself."

But Dante, the dreamy youth, rapt in himself, had but a very casual eye for all this splendour. Only slowly and reluctantly is his imagination filled with the nearest shapes of his

[1] XI, 94.

surroundings. The first and, for the moment, the only thing in the present that absorbs him is the sight of lovely ladies; but even these he beholds through the coloured glass of fashionable love-poetry. His early poem, now lost, on the sixty most beautiful women of Florence, must have been exceedingly Provençal in tone.

He who set out upon the path of poetic devotion to woman soon won such luxuries as companions, envious competitors, rivals, and friends; for it was a social art. So Dante too, in the companionship of congenial bosom friends, sang his love and his homage. In fact, he made his entrance as one of the most up-to-date visionaries with a sonnet that related a dream of love. Amor, the love-god (then still a poetic novelty), holds the sleeping Beatrice upon his arm, awakens her, gives her the poet's burning heart to eat, and vanishes. . . . Sympathetic souls are asked to interpret the mystery!

So the youth of eighteen years (1283) tries to outdo the conceits of the troubadours. Provençal reminiscences and strange, wild impulses produce a whirl of cloudy shapes. Longings and visions swell into soul-experiences, and the more bizarre and fortuitous they are, the more important they are considered and the more hastily made public. Young artists who are in love with what is peculiar and unusual in their feelings, without yet recognizing it, find the dream-vision a convenient form of expression. It commits them to nothing, and permits everything. The poetical beginner who starts, not with oratorical and classical exercises, but with romantic compositions, is always aided by dreamy visions. So Dante's youthful poetry, especially the *Vita Nuova,* is full of dreams and all manner of visions.

To the sober imitators of the Provençal love-song and of the Guittonian bourgeois didactic verse, to whom love-poetry was merely a game of poetic rules, the fancies of the lovelorn youth must have seemed something queer and morbid.

> If thou art well and sane of wit,
> Then bathe thy groin befittingly
> So that the cloud may leave thy brain
> That to such fancies driveth thee.
> But if thou'rt truly ill, then know
> Thou art, methinks, delirious.

That was the scornful, not wholly undeserved retort with which Dante da Maiano, then an esteemed rhymster, paid his respects to his great namesake after the latter's first dream.[1]

Another Florentine minnesinger, however, younger and less sober than the one of Maiano, and gifted with a decided penchant for the unusual, Guido Cavalcanti, enshrined Dante in his heart because of this first vision.

Guido Cavalcanti

The friendship with Cavalcanti proved decisive for Dante's development. Guido may have been at this time (1283) twenty-five years old, so eight years Dante's senior. Knightly and proud of his nobility, sprung from one of the most aristocratic families, son-in-law of Farinata degli Uberti, contemptuous of the humble people, a feudal (white) Guelf, and fiercest enemy of the Donati, he had disdained to record his name in any of the bourgeois guilds. Wilful, headstrong, eager for broils, prompt with his fist as with his tongue, he was a dangerous disturber of public life, and had at last to be sent into banishment (June 24, 1300) by his own fellow partisan, nay, his personal friend, Dante, who at that time sat in the priorate. Not only as a politician, but also as a thinker and artist, he despised the lower orders, their dialect, their superstitions, their religion. Such a proud, clever, and violent man must have made a striking impression upon his fellow citizens. The chronicler Villani (VIII, 42) describes him as "a philosopher, and able in many ways, only that he was quite too sensitive and headstrong." Dino Campagni, the other chronicler, celebrates in a sonnet his many-sided physical and intellectual qualities, the keenness and learning of the man; and the writers of tales, Boccaccio and Sacchetti, relate characteristic anecdotes concerning him.[2]

He was reputed to be a heretic, and must have had more or less of a leaning to Averroism. When Dante characterizes him as a despiser of his Virgil,[3] we may, from the context of the much-debated passage and from what else we know of Cavalcanti, perhaps see an allusion to that philosophical self-esteem and

[1] The great Dante did not resent this jest of the lesser, as we see from a later exchange of sonnets between the two. Indeed he of Maiano finally published a dream-sonnet himself, which called forth a verily savage reply from other brethren in the craft, especially Guido Orlandi.

[2] *Decameron*, VI, 9, and *Le Novelle di Fr. Sacchetti*, 68.

[3] *Inferno*, X, 61 sqq.

self-glorification which was characteristic of the Averroists, and possibly also to a lack of classical culture.

However that may be, certainly the philosophic depth and chivalrous exaltation of homage to woman—the creation of Guinizelli—must have been well suited to a man like Cavalcanti, who was at once a knight and a thinker. Through him above all, it appears, the *dolce stil nuovo* was transplanted from Bologna to Florence and there developed.

He knew how to grasp both features of the new style, the mystical tenderness as well as the scientific profundity. For under his courtly and haughty demeanour he hid a soft, love-seeking heart. His mood is one of longing, unsated by scientific speculation; it is stronger than his will. His self-restraint put melancholy and longing for death into his desires, inward strife and agony into his sensuousness. But his sensuousness is not sober, his longing not gentle, his suffering not voluntary, his speculation not over-ingenious, his thoughts not playful, his pride not vanity. Hence the unevenness of his nature, which old Villani so well characterizes as tenderness with stubbornness, appears in his poems spontaneously and often artlessly direct and naked—and seems almost a hodge-podge. Reflection and feeling stand close to each other and do not intermingle.

> If I from death must draw my life,
> From melancholy my delight,
> How then amid such misery
> Can Amor lure my soul to love? . . .
>
> Amor, from mutual pleasure born,
> Makes in the heart his lair
> And from desire he fashions form,
> Yet quickly doth transmute his work
> Into perverseness, so he cannot love
> Who feels how ill he doth requite our service.
> Why should he then speak to me more of love? [1]

So disillusionment speaks, after it has become profound insight and has ceased to be feeling and lyric. The inmost contradictions are clearly comprehended and expressed; they have not yet become poetic. Petrarch, not Cavalcanti, was to be the first singer of the divided heart. The latter knows only the alternatives:

[1] *Quando di morte conven trar vita*, in G. Cavalcanti, *Le Rime*, ed. E. Rivalta, Bologna, 1902, p. 163 sqq.

either to pour forth his whole soul in loving homage, or to wrap himself in self-assertive aloofness; to melt in love, or to analyze the nature of love. This incapacity to heal with the poet's words the rift in his own breast makes him one of the incomplete and tragic poets of the *stil nuovo*.

In the foreboding of his early death (*ob.* 1300) he sends from banishment his last song, a beautiful, tender strain addressed to his beloved. He stands like a great and nobly conceived but broken column by the road which Dante followed to the end, to completion. Sometimes it seems as if he were only one stride from the goal.

> Who is the lady? All men gaze at her,
> And with her splendour trembles all the air.
> Love is her companion; and no man
> Can speak before her, though all sigh for her.
> And when she turns her eyes, oh, what a picture!
> Amor shall tell, for I have not the power.
> Mistress of all humility she thus seems
> That by her all the rest seem full of wrath.
>
> And of her graciousness one may not speak.
> All noble worthiness bows down to her,
> Beauty accepts her as her deity.
> So lofty hath our spirit never been,
> Nor in us have such virtues their abode,
> That we might rightly comprehend her worth.[1]

How much did Dante learn from this! With what slight changes did he shape the more intimate, more touching, more graceful figure of his Beatrice, without in any way dimming the light of his master's poem!

> My lady looks so gentle and so pure
> When yielding salutations by the way,
> That the tongue trembles and has nought to say,
> And the eyes, which fain would see, may not endure.
> And still amid the praise she hears secure,
> She walks with humbleness for her array;
> Seeming a creature sent from Heaven to stay
> On earth, and show a miracle made sure.
>
> She is so pleasant in the eyes of men
> That through the sight the inmost heart doth gain
> A sweetness which needs proof to know it by.

[1] Cavalcanti's sonnet, *Chi è questa che ven ch'ogni 'om la mira.*

And from between her lips there seems to move
A soothing essence that is full of love,
Saying forever to the spirit, "Sigh!" [1]

When we compare Cavalcanti with Dante, the love-poetry of the latter almost invariably appears less rigid, less abstract, less highflown; somewhat warmer, more flexible, more natural, more intimate. It is true that Dante could hardly have sung a pastoral so light and fresh as Cavalcanti's

Within a dell I found a shepherd's lass
That lovelier than a star did seem to me.

Such diversions are not for him. Cavalcanti pays for them at the heavy price of his own inward unity. He seizes with a facile hand the charms of the folk-song—and lets them fall again: for his full heart they are too poor and superficial. He feels the lofty poetry that underlies philosophic speculation, but he cannot give it utterance, for he lacks the sensuous impulse in the presence of the abstract; he lacks the pious and comprehending delicacy of Virgil—

Whom it may be your Guido did disdain.

So his style is sometimes vigorous, picturesque, and brilliant, sometimes halting, pale, and hard; again flattering and caressing, or didactic and sharp. We miss in Cavalcanti the long, calm, full melody, the rhythmic and melodious harmony; what Leopardi calls *pastoso*. It is usually lacking in Dante also. Petrarch, at the cost of renouncing the philosophic element, was the first to perfect the *stil nuovo* in this musical direction.

In the last analysis, however, Cavalcanti and Dante seek the same end, namely, poetry made up of love and scientific knowledge. A common purpose unites the two, and gives loftiness and ideality to their friendship.

Dante and Cavalcanti

Guido replied to Dante's first poetic vision with serious and encouraging words: "The loftiest, loveliest, noblest of all things," he writes, "that can befall a man, Love, thou hast discovered. Good fortune on thy way!" [2]

[1] Sonnet XV, in the *Vita Nuova* (Rossetti's translation). Both sonnets go back to similar glorifications by Guido Guinizelli, especially the sonnet:

"I fain would laud the semblance of my lady,
Likening her to the lily and the rose."

[2] Cavalcanti's sonnet, *Vedeste al mio parere*.

"With so understanding a guide, with thee, O Guido! far from the world, upon a magic ship to the blue sea to fare, with our friend Lapo, and with our ladies, there, in happy harmony, only of love to talk—that would be bliss for me." [1] With such imaginative words young Dante clasps Cavalcanti to his soul.

The latter, however, responds with sad doubts as to the devotion of his beloved, and his friend Lapo's sincerity. More and more confidentially, in sonnets full of secret allusions, they exchange their dreams and visions of love.

But the evil days come when Dante, presumably after the death of Beatrice, sinks from the higher to lower and vulgar love, seeks the companionship of revellers like Forese Donati and of coarser men, and wastes his powers. And Cavalcanti sends to him the saddest and tenderest of sonnets. It is the last and the finest memorial of his friendship.

I come to thee so oft, so oft by day,
And yet I find thee in unworthy thought.
Then am I saddened for thy noble soul
And gifts so manifold that thou hast lost.
Thou heldest many a man once in disdain
And shunned the company of wretched folk,
And then did speak such hearty words of me
So that I treasured every song of thine.

Now is thy life so base I do not dare
To show thee that thy verse is dear to me.
To thee I come so that thou seest me not.
If thou this little song full oft wilt read
Then shall the ignoble life that hunteth thee
Lose its fast hold on thy degenerate soul.[2]

After the loss of his Beatrice (1290) Dante consoled himself with philosophy. If it is true that Cavalcanti guided him to the *stil nuovo*, he may have stood beside him also as he began to philosophize. The one could not go on at all without the other. Certainly Cavalcanti's most famous canzone, the didactic poem on the nature of love, exerted a powerful influence upon Dante, as upon all their contemporaries. He quotes it twice in his *De vulgari Eloquentia*,[3] as an example of the solemn style, wholly in

[1] Dante's sonnet, *Guido vorrei.*

[2] Cavalcanti's sonnet, *I'vegno il giorno a te infinite volte.* I find the surmise of Appel alluring: that this sonnet was put into the mouth of Beatrice, after her death.

[3] II, 12.

hendecasyllables. Solemn it is, indeed, and with its inner rhymes and complicated fourteen-line stanzas so elaborate, and with its intricate deductions so obscure and difficult, that, although in the Middle Ages and Renaissance no less than eight commentators and in recent times a whole series of Italian scholars have explored its meaning, we still stand before it in bewildered admiration. A prose translation of the introduction will suffice:

"A lady begs me; therefore I will speak of somewhat that befalls which is so cruel and haughty that it is called love; so that whoso denies it may hear the truth concerning it. And for the question before us, I require one who knows, for I do not believe that a man of commonplace mind brings with him understanding for such an exposition. For, without the guidance of natural philosophy, I have no inclination to set forth (1) where love abides, (2) who begets it, (3) what its nature, and (4) what its power, (5) its essence, and then (6) all its action, and (7) the service that gives it the name of love, and (8) whether it can be made visible to the eyes." In each of the next four strophes two of these eight points are successively treated. At the close the poet is well pleased with this accomplishment, and sends forth, in an envoi, his heavily laden song: "Without shame, my song, thou mayst go forth whithersoever it pleaseth thee. For I have adorned thee so that thy utterance must be praised by those that have understanding. To linger with others thou hast no desire."

That this song lingered long and oft with Dante cannot be doubted. The contempt of the ignorant and inexperienced in love, the close connection of ideas, the poetic evaluation of the philosophic conceptual terminology, the scholastic, compact, solemn treatment of theoretical questions concerning the nature of psychological faculties—all this we find again in a series of Dante's canzoni. And we find it not in the tortured, patched, cramped style of Guittone's followers, but in the austere, close-knit utterance, firm despite all its abstractness, of Cavalcanti. It is a preliminary training and preparation for the masterly treatment of the most difficult scientific problems in the *Divine Comedy*.

But what distinguishes Dante's didactic canzoni, despite their scholastic nature, from Cavalcanti's, is an essential and happy trait. Dante, both in propounding a problem and in discussing it, adheres less to natural philosophy, which Cavalcanti prefers, than to moral philosophy. And herein he found the best means to infuse warmth and enthusiasm even into the most prosaic subjects, and to overcome Cavalcanti's rigid intellectualism.

So an important part of our poet's development was due to the friendship, the counsel, and the example of Cavalcanti. In the middle of this period, which extends from Dante's first sonnet (1283) to the philosophic canzoni of the *Convivio*, the composition of which doubtless continues beyond Cavalcanti's death and over more than a decade (*circa* 1293–1308), comes the chief work of Dante's youth, the *Vita Nuova*. It is dedicated to Cavalcanti, whom he often calls the first of his friends. "He desired," says Dante, "that I should always write to him in the vernacular speech, not in Latin." [1] We see from this that the high value set upon written Italian, and with it the leading ideas of the first book of the *Convivio* and of the *De vulgari Eloquentia*, were inspired by Cavalcanti.

Cavalcanti's book of songs, so far as it is preserved, consists of two canzoni, thirteen ballads, and thirty-eight sonnets. The poet, in contrast with his predecessors, disdains the complex and intricate forms, such as the double sonnet, the sonnet with coda, etc. He strives unmistakably after pure and simple art-forms. Dante, who at first delighted in double sonnets and in the period of his moral aberration also followed metrically in the footsteps of Arnaut Daniel, was called back to simpler forms by the example of Cavalcanti.

But in contrast with this helpful influence upon the outward form, there was a serious danger as to content, namely, the dualism of heart and head, of faith and knowledge, of overflowing tenderness and intellectual arrogance, excessive use of figures and scholastic concepts; in short, the lifelong discord in Cavalcanti's soul and art. It was only for a time that Dante was misled by this double nature. We find isolated traces of it in his *Vita Nuova* and in his *Canzoniere*. If Cavalcanti had become, like Petrarch, fully conscious of this discord, if he had found it beautiful, if, as a poet, he had played with it—his example would have been far more seductive and harmful to Dante. But Cavalcanti was neither sentimental nor elegiac; his strongest impulse was not toward art; Love and Death faced each other, not as tearful brothers, but as irreconcilable rivals. The poet despaired and became mute, while the moral man wore himself out within him.

[1] *Vita Nuova*, § 31.

Instead of being one who led astray, Cavalcanti broke the strings of his lyre and died. And so all honour and fame to the noblest, greatest, bravest, and most unhappy friend of Alighieri!

As a poet who surpassed the creator of the *stil nuovo*, Guido Guinizelli, but was not himself unsurpassable, he has his monument in the *Commedia*.[1]

Guido Orlandi, Dino Compagni, Gianni Alfani, Lapo Gianni, Dino Frescobaldi, Cino da Pistoia, and Others

Compared with Cavalcanti, the other Florentine minnesingers with whom Dante came in contact are of slight importance.

A puffed-up, half-trained courtier today, tomorrow a fawning versifier who prided himself not a little on his knowledge of the love-rules of Ovid and of André le Chapelain and made much of his own petty talents, Guido Orlandi kept his two friends busy. He was too bourgeois to follow the lofty flight of the *stil nuovo;* so he devoted himself to belittling the poems of Cavalcanti and Alighieri, and to interrogating the former on all sorts of subjects in ill-constructed sonnets.—Dino Campagni also, the sturdy chronicler and Dante's fellow partisan, attempted the love-song and the didactic canzone. But he lacked the requisite culture to make an impression upon Dante.—Gianni Alfani moved among the conventions of love-service with childlike simplicity and freshness, but without notable force. Whether he was in personal relations with Dante is uncertain.—But the most lovable and facile minstrel of the new style was that Lapo Gianni dei Ricevuti whom Dante desired to make the third in his company of friends. In fact, with his soft and melodious songs he offers a welcome relief to the profound and brilliant but somewhat rigid art of Cavalcanti. In his longer canzoni he is often heavy, hollow, and garrulous; but the ballad acquires in his hands a charming, coquettish, daintily stiff movement. The courtly ceremonial of the service of woman is refined by yearning, by admiration, by greeting and homage. How delightfully Lapo composes a dance-song which is to bear a message of love to his lady!

> If thou dost see a blush upon her face,
> Then speak no word! It may be she is wroth.
> But if thou dost behold her milder grown,
> Utter thy gentle message without fear.

[1] *Purgatorio*, XI, 97 sqq.

And if thou courteously hast addressed her,
Bending with grace and fitly greeting her
Before her cheerful and most gracious brows:
Note well the answer that, angelically
Framed in her noble soul, flows from her lips
As from within a veil of tender grace. . . .
So, go thou, my ballata, noiselessly,
And hasten forth upon thy path of love.
And when thou'rt come, speak thou with bended head:
From treacherous jealousy protect thou me.[1]

Purely spiritual emotions of a loving heart, the charms of the soul of the adored lady, are set forth with fragrant picturesqueness. Lapo Gianni possesses what Cavalcanti lacked: sensuous simplicity in the presence of the abstract. In him Dante could find such fine and pleasing turns as *benignamente di umiltà vestuta* and such transparent grace as he himself later developed in his charming ballads:

I am a little child, lovely and young,
And hither come to show myself to you.[2]

Or again:

Because of a little garland which I saw
Every flower will make me breathe a sigh.[3]

Lapo was not, indeed, a profound thinker, and Cavalcanti may well have been right when he doubted the genuineness of his Platonism. But upon Dante's artistic nature, Lapo's natural grace could have only helpful influence.

Another devotee of the *stil nuovo*, Dino, of a famous Florentine family, the Frescobaldi, was probably too young to have influenced Dante with his poetry. He must, on the contrary, be regarded as Dante's imitator.

The same is true of Cino da Pistoia. He was born rather after than before 1270, and so was at least five years younger than Dante. His poetical correspondence with the latter is difficult to date, but it can hardly have begun before the completion and publication of the *Vita Nuova*. Considerations drawn from art-criticisms also teach us that Cino learned something from Dante, but Dante nothing from Cino. The lyrics of the Pistoian have a

[1] *Ballata, poi che ti compose amore*, in *Liriche del dolce stil nuovo*, ed. E. Rivalta, Venice, 1906, p. 108 sqq.
[2] *Io mi son pargoletta bella e nuova.*
[3] *Per una ghirlandetta.*

remarkable iridescent character. As far as concerns purity of language and harmony of rhythms, his art, on the average, is higher than that of Dante. A full, resonant stream of utterance flows through his stanzas. But the effect is often weakened by ingenious trifling. The inwardness of the *stil nuovo* is gradually dissolving into a clearer, freer, cleverer, stronger, but more superficial form. That full-blown beauty is repeatedly praised by Dante in the *De vulgari Eloquentia.* And yet those very poems of Cino, which he cites as examples, are full of imitations of Dante, and are not among the Pistoian's best achievements: a proof that Dante was recognizing and praising, in his young friend's poems, rather his own art than the other's.

Together with the poets of the new tendency, Dante must also have known personally several of the elder ones, and with them a series of other artists and men of science. Brunetto Latini doubtless imparted to him grammar, rhetoric, and all sorts of practical knowledge, rather than a deeper appreciation of art. What his association with the painter Giotto and the musician Casella contributed to his poetic development is hard to determine. That Dante was a lover and no mean connoisseur of those arts is revealed in numerous passages of his work. We do not know whether he came into contact with the intellectual men of Bologna during his 'prentice years or later.[1] Indeed the external circumstances of his artistic education are veiled in deep obscurity.

The Florence of that day was even richer in oddities and singular characters than in poets and artists. Chronicles and tales are full of them. In the satires and the poetic correspondence of Florentines there is an abundance of personal allusions, gibes and offensive remarks, which we at the present day do not understand, but which prove to us how strongly the observation of one's fellows and the taste for caricature and for characterization were developed, how busily gossip and slander were carried on, and how fully informed people were as to their neighbours near or far. Florentine inquisitiveness, the closeness and narrowness of their city life, and not least the disciplinary penance of the Catholic Church, made it possible to keep oneself informed without effort on the way of living and habits of all individuals of any promi-

[1] An early visit in Bologna (1287?) is indicated by his sonnet, *Non mi poriano già mai fare ammenda.*

nence. Without these social conditions, it would be incomprehensible how Dante could, with such positive assurance, put one of his fellow citizens and contemporaries into Hell, another into Purgatory, a third into Heaven, and pass judgment upon them to a hair's breadth. We must suppose that, earlier in his life, his memory and imagination had begun to people themselves slowly and automatically with human and all too human shapes and destinies. Ciacco, Belacqua, Brunetto Latini, Forese Donati, and many others came very close to him. It was in his association with Forese, so far as we know, that our poet's pen was first sharpened for personal, biting, and scoffing verses. Then the greatest humourist and jester in the Italy of his day, Cecco Angiolieri of Siena, took him into his rough school.

Cecco Angiolieri

Cecco was perhaps ten years older than Dante, and died not long before 1313. His father, a miserly banker in Siena, belonged to the order of "Joyous Brethren." The son was a happy-go-lucky, dissolute blade. There is documentary evidence that he was punished with a fine for night vagrancy and for absence from the Sienese army, and that, at his death, he left nothing behind him but debts. His poems (138 sonnets) [1] complete the picture of this lawless life in the liveliest and most highly coloured strokes. Woman, tavern, and dice are his favourite subjects:

> Three things I love and none beside;
> But these I cannot well provide:
> A tavern, dice, a woman too:
> These make me gladsome through and through.

Against everything which hinders him in the indulgence of these three vices, he directs his hatred and his wits. As for his father, who locked his wine-cellar and closed his purse, he wishes him dead, and his mother no less. He has an exhaustless supply of comic expressions and witty comparisons to set forth the stinginess and tough constitution of the old man, his own poverty, and in general, everything that is hateful to him.

> Yet will I not indulge in melancholy,
> Nay, at my torments I will only laugh,
> Just as a savage does at evil weather.

[1] Cecco Angiolieri, *I sonnetti*, ed. A. F. Massèra, Bologna, 1906.

A fresh and vigorous joyousness and humour dwell in this spirit of denial:

> Were I the wind I'd tear the world to tatters,
> And if the fire, I'd crunch it into sparks.
> Were I the sea, full long ago 'twere sunken.
> If I were God, I should have hurled it in the abyss.
> Were I the pope, a jolly life I'd lead,
> I would annoy my Christian rascals!
> If I were king, I'd chase my people to the gallows!
>
> If I were Death, then straightway I would visit
> My precious father, once! If I were Life,
> Then nevermore I'd step across his threshold!
> If I were Cecco—ha! but so I am;
> I'd take the fairest maidens as mine own,
> To other men I'd leave the ugly ones.[1]

Such a man loved, not with angelic contemplation, but in absolutely sensual fashion: no Giovanna or Beatrice, but a Becchina, the ill-tempered, faithless, greedy, jealous, reckless, buxom, not quite chaste daughter of an "ass of a cobbler." His love for this lawless child of Eve is uttered now in the freshest language of the folk-song, now in a tone of knightly homage, which is exaggerated with capricious humour. The transitions from the one key to the other are made so naturally and so nimbly that we cannot note the exact point where earnest turns to jest. It is neither irony nor parody of the noble style; it is exuberant insolence, and it all seems to be done offhand. Whatever comes into his head, whether it be a homosexual declaration of love, or horrible accusations cast at his own mother, it has to be uttered. To sift, smoothe, and file his verses would be too wearisome for Cecco. He was perhaps even more frivolous in art than in his life, which we must beware of interpreting from his sonnets.

Dante became acquainted with Cecco probably at the time of his military service (1288–1289). His intercourse with this wastrel, which was evidently quite intimate, certainly did no lasting harm to his character, but widened considerably his knowledge of human nature, and in some sense even benefited him as a poet.

Of the correspondence in sonnets between the two, only three of Cecco's pieces have been preserved. In the first, he makes merry over a third person, who is known to Dante also. In the second, he points out, in the spirit of friendship, a contradiction

[1] Cecco's sonnet, *S'i' fosse foco, ardere' il mondo.*

which he claims to have discovered in the last sonnet of the *Vita Nuova.* We see from it that Dante submitted even his heavenly visions of love to Becchina's lover for criticism. That he paid careful attention to the external and superficial criticism of this friend, we see from the prose text which he later added, and from the manner in which he removed and excused a similar contradiction in the *Convivio* (III, 4).

Cecco's third and last sonnet was written in the time when Dante was living in banishment and Cecco was an insolvent spendthrift—both in misery. The general sense is: "Dante Alighieri, if I am a chatterer, you are not far behind me. If I breakfast at other men's tables, you dine at them; if I bite into the fat, you nibble at bacon; if I clip the cloth, you rub it with the thistle; if I am loose-mouthed, you wear a bridle but little; if I claim to be an aristocrat, you make pretense of learning; if I play the Roman, so do you the Lombard. And so, God be thanked! neither of us can well reprove the other. Such is our misfortune, and our folly. And if you will still make poetry of it all, Dante Alighieri, I'll tire you out in turn; for I am the ox-goad and you are the ox."

Dante was not, with his pride, so blind as to ignore in silence the scoffs of a poet whom he must have known to be of the cleverest. Does it not sound like an agonized reply to the coarse familiarity of Forese and Cecco when he, at the beginning of the *Convivio*, complains that his poverty and homelessness have been accounted a disgrace to him; that he has appeared ignoble in the eyes of many, and that he has all too rashly granted certain people his intimate acquaintance? "And, therefore, in the task that lies before me, I must show some dignity, so that it may win respect; and this may serve as sufficient excuse for the abstruseness of my commentary." [1]

The language of symbolic interpretation of love in the *Vita Nuova* had been misunderstood; Cecco had found contradictions where there were none: and this had led Dante to the profound doctrine of the inadequacy of all linguistic utterance in the domain of the supernatural. His misfortune had become a reproach to him; Cecco had made appear ignoble what was but unfortunate; and this had thrown Dante back upon his own resources, and finally carried him so far that he avoided all too tri-

[1] *Convivio,* I, 4.

fling friendships, uplifted himself above the rest of mankind, and no longer permitted any contemporary to exert a decisive influence upon his inward development. Association with the most natural and lowest of all minstrels had not dragged him down, but lifted him up, had not made his art laxer or more trifling, but profounder and more arduous, and had hastened his abandonment of social, courtly-bourgeois, and opportunistic poetry. The 'prentice years of the Florentine minnesinger are ended. They close with the *Vita Nuova.*

The "Vita Nuova"

Around a single figure, "Beatrice, the glorious lady of my mind," as though a sun now resplendent and now magically veiled, the youth's wistful dreams hover and sway. With her rising begins the "New Life," the life of the conscious spirit. Until then everything was vague, misty memory. In the radiance of her beauty the boy suns himself; to draw lovingly near her is the effort of the youth. Then she dies and vanishes into the heights of the Hereafter. To seek her there, with purified, supersensuous mind, to find her, to comprehend her, is possible only for the matured and fully developed man. So runs the dreamy curve of the *Vita Nuova;* uplifting itself from earth, rising in slow circles higher and higher, it loses itself in the future life and glides into the mightier and firmer curve of the *Divine Comedy*, which leads through Hell to the Godhead.

The *Vita Nuova*, taken as a whole, is the poetic embodiment of a spiritual development, actually and historically lived out, through who can say how many single experiences. He who composed the *Vita Nuova* must already have had the *Divine Comedy* more or less clearly in mind; as he gazed back upon his youth, he must have recognized or dimly felt in all its experiences an inner destiny, a divine guidance, that drew him on to something greater. To work out this appointed destiny from the motley material of a series of events and experiences which extend from the ninth to the twenty-second year of the poet's life, is if not the only, at least the chief, purpose of the *Vita Nuova.*

His spiritual destiny is not so clearly, so definitely, progressively, and connectedly revealed in this youthful work as to exclude the possibility of other critical interpretations. The great differences of opinion which have always existed and always will exist as to the meaning, that is, the artistic central idea, of the *Vita Nuova*, are an indication, even if not a proof, of a certain immaturity or obscurity in this work.

The thought of a development is clearly and distinctly expressed only in the introduction and at the end of the little book: at the beginning in the words which are attached to the first meeting with Beatrice, "The New Life begins," and at the close, in the announcement of the future master-work: "Soon after this (last) sonnet I had a wondrous vision, wherein I saw things which determined me to write nothing more concerning this blessed one until I should be prepared to treat of her in more worthy fashion. And she knows that I am exerting myself to this end, as much as I am able. Therefore I hope, if it shall please Him through Whom all things live, that my life shall last some years longer, to say of her something that was never said of any woman until now.

"And then may it please Him Who is the Lord of Grace, that my soul may go to behold the glory of its lady, namely of that blessed Beatrice who in glory beholds the face of Him Who is through all ages blessed."

Thus the beginning and the goal of the new life are stated. But no man can say wherein its content and peculiar value consist. A course of moral development it is not, nor yet a philosophic one; nor will any one venture to claim that it is, in the strict sense of the word, a religious one. We behold neither a story of improvement nor of enlightenment, nor of sanctification; indeed we see no story at all, but at first a mere loose succession of events: something halfway between a romance and a diary, something mediævally duplex, like a chronicle that would fain be development or upward progress step by step, but is not.

This uncertainty in plan is easy to explain and excuse historically. Dante's poetic idea was as yet too much confined within the one unifiedly developed form, the love-song. Homage to women was the only accepted convention and art-form, the only one which was mature, or, indeed, symbolically profound. And into this comparatively narrow, socially limited and conditioned language, he must compress the entire content of his early spiritual life, the entire result of his development. His heart held a universal romance of the soul, and the means of expression at his command permitted at most a love-romance. The result was that neither the one nor the other, but a combination of the two, came into being. How could it be otherwise when the man had grown beyond the poet, the spirit beyond the form, the thought beyond the convention? With the feeling of poetic inadequacy, the *Vita Nuova* closes:

> Beyond the sphere that widest orbit hath
> Passeth the sigh which issues from my heart . . .

and as it returns to tell his heart what it has beheld:

> It speaks so softly that I understand not,
> To the poor heart that forces it to speak.

The technical difficulty is aggravated by a remarkably fragmentary record of the origin of the work. It has now been established by detailed and accurate investigation that the prose text was, in the main, composed later than the poetic insertions. The first sonnet must be assigned to the year 1283, the last one to 1292, and the prose account to a date one or several years later. So this brief work is spread over at least nine years. In fact, of all the poems in the *Vita Nuova*, perhaps not one was composed primarily for the *Vita Nuova*, but each was written on a special occasion for its own sake. Out of quite a number of youthful poems, composed gradually and separately, which had perhaps not even been preserved by Dante himself, but by Cavalcanti, a selection was eventually made of those which could be tolerably well united by a prose account of events. If it is probable that the selection, arrangement, and connected treatment of the poems, in short, the prosaic element of the *Vita Nuova*, had for its purpose the justification of the author in the circle of Florentine love-poets, it is nevertheless certain that the poems themselves had no original connection with such a plan. Prose and poetry, in this case, go separate paths; and Dante, when he composed the *Vita Nuova*, was a compiler of his own productions.

Nevertheless, "you cannot dip twice in the same stream." So it came to pass that a historical and mental occasion for the separate poems was created as an afterthought, and many a poem acquired a new significance which coincided only partially, or not at all, with its original meaning. Such discordances have been repeatedly and convincingly pointed out. They are most striking at the beginning of the little book, where love-songs in the older style are treated according to the symbolic and allegorical norm of the new.

In order to introduce unity into the parts and destiny into chance events, the symbolism of numbers was the most convenient, but also the most superficial, of means. The prose text creates a mysterious relation between Beatrice and the number three, and arranges the chief incidents in triple units of time; indeed, the poems themselves are often arranged symmetrically. Six-and-twenty sonnets are, as Pochhammer expresses it, set between five pilasters—that is, the canzoni—into the wall of a temple; that is, into the prose text. To be sure, since the parts were created before the whole, the architectural scheme is not so firm and clear in this case as in the *Commedia.*

Finally, the effort for mathematical arrangement becomes really intrusive in the pedantic commentaries and divisions which are attached to every poem and bring the grammarians' drill into the life of love. The schoolmaster's painful rod is mated with Amor's gentle arrows.

Nowhere is it more clearly visible than here that what young Dante has learned is not yet duly fused with his experience. He already knows his Virgil and quotes him, appeals to Horace, Ovid, Lucan, and Aristotle; but they stand stiffly, like aliens, in his poetry, as authorities and as scientific, not poetic, factors. It has already been shown how laboured the scriptural quotations appear. And yet the value of the *Vita Nuova* consists precisely in the fact that the spirit of the Holy Scriptures takes possession of and saturates the courtly love-service.

Beatrice

To Guinizelli and Cavalcanti, the lady was, in so far as she was regarded as a supersensuous being, rather an Intelligence than an angel, rather an angel than a saint, and love for her was rather luminous than warm, the style of poetry rather brilliant than intense, rather descriptive, rhetorical, and allegorical than narrative, lyric, and symbolic. Guinizelli and Cavalcanti had tarried longer with philosophers, Dominicans and Averroists, than with mystics, Augustinians and Franciscans. How intimately familiar Dante was, even in his youth, with the Franciscan world, has already been shown. In the legend of St. Margareta of Cortona, for example, as it appeared in the circles of the Minorite brethren at the end of the thirteenth century, ideas, eulogies, and descriptions have been pointed out which have many key-notes in common with the youthful Dante's adoration of Beatrice.

In the *Vita Nuova* the courtly homage to women changes, unnoted and as if of its own volition, to saintly worship, and the latter in turn to metaphysical speculation. The poet gradually passes from knightly homage to mystical adoration and philosophic contemplation.

It is not the poet himself, however, but the figure of Beatrice that undergoes this development. It is not his own action, it is Beatrice who, through the intermediary of love, by her apparition in his dreams or wakeful hours, by her radiance, not by deeds, accomplishes the gradual exaltation of her lover. In the *Divine Comedy*, for the first time, Dante was able to make of himself a living figure with a character of its own. In the *Vita Nuova* he is but a tremulous mirror, a quivering vessel, of love. Hence, the tale of this love is a story of passion, and the nature of this suffering is not vividly dramatic, but dreamlike.

The dream of Beatrice's death and ascent to Heaven is the central motif of the *Vita Nuova.* Therefore the canzone, *Donna pietosa e di novella etade*, stands exactly in the centre. And the whole vision of the death and apotheosis of the beloved is packed into two masterly strophes.[1]

> Then saw I many broken, hinted sights
> In the uncertain state I stepp'd into.
> Meseem'd to be I know not in what place,
> Where ladies through the street, like mournful lights,
> Ran with loose hair, and eyes that frighten'd you
> By their own terror, and a pale amaze:
> The while, little by little, as I thought,
> The sun ceased, and the stars began to gather,
> And each wept at the other;
> And birds dropp'd in mid-flight out of the sky;
> And earth shook suddenly;
> And I was 'ware of one, hoarse and tired out,
> Who ask'd of me: "Hast thou not heard it said? . . .
> Thy lady, she that was so fair, is dead."
> Then lifting up mine eyes as the tears came,
> I saw the angels, like a rain of manna,
> In a long flight flying back heavenward;
> Having a little cloud in front of them,

[1] Translation of Dante Gabriel Rossetti. Compare also the famous and inspiring picture of this scene by Rossetti.

After the which they went and said, "Hosanna";
And if they had said more, you should have heard.
Then Love said, "Now shall all things be made clear:
Come and behold our lady where she lies."
These 'wildering fantasies
Then carried me to see my lady dead.
Even as I there was led,
Her ladies with a veil were covering her;
And with her was such very humbleness
That she appeared to say, "I am at peace."

Here the whole description has become narration. The brilliant and decorative picture, such as Guinizelli and Cavalcanti loved, has been intensified into a spiritual impression. These strophes would have delighted the author of *Laokoön*. For what the eye beholds, the poet has transformed into movement and action. Beatrice is not delineated but felt. The reader's power of vision is not sated, but excited, and by a few swift hints he is forced to complete the picture for himself. He who thus, instead of the complete and clarified residuum of his feelings, knows how to offer their inmost fleeting and eternally vibrating effect, is a poet capable of grasping what is evanescent, transcendent, and inexpressible. The entire *Vita Nuova* is, in this sense, the poem of transcendent love.

In order to express in its movement the passing of the beloved image, Dante, with masterly art, introduced an abundance of intervening motifs and created a counter-movement, so that the chief movement, the ascent of this lovely creature to Heaven, might be expressed more splendidly and harmoniously. Though many of these motifs, such as the apparent and disguised homage to other ladies, the learned excursus concerning the nature of love, the solemn exaggeration of trivial and chance incidents into experiences, may appear somewhat laboured and artificial; though they may, step by step, prove to us how uncertain the relation is between the poetic Beatrice and reality; yet within the frame of the whole picture they accomplish their artistic purpose: they veil and carry on like a shining aureole of light and mist the distant glorified figure of the blessed lady. Beside the ingenious poet stands already a gifted, even if an as yet awkward, painter.

But is this Beatrice, whom we have seen thus far only in transcendent movement, a living poetic creation? Are not the lines and colours of her figure blurred amid this aura? Is she a Florentine or an angel; a maiden, a wife, a beloved, or an invention, a dream, a concept?

Attempts have been made to clear away these æsthetic doubts by means of biographical investigation. Documentary evidence has been discovered of the existence, in the Florence of that day, of a Beatrice, or rather a Bice, daughter of the magnate Folco Portinari, and married before 1288 to Simone de' Bardi. That Dante should have paid his homage to a married lady would be quite in the spirit of the love-service, and in accordance with the ideas of the day, would hardly imply any moral impropriety. Bice Portinari is favoured also by an old Florentine tradition recorded by Boccaccio, as well as by the fact that the death of Portinari the father agrees in date (1289) with that of Beatrice's father as related in the *Vita Nuova;* and finally, by the consideration that Dante, with his reverence for the symbolic value of baptismal names, would hardly have invented the name Beatrice, but found it in the familiar form Bice. The historical Beatrice cannot, however, be determined with certainty.

Still, what is there to refute it? We have neither in the *Vita Nuova* nor in the *Commedia* a portrait, but only the poetical apotheosis of a beloved woman who passed from earth smiling and left no trace. "Beatrice died as an angel even before she became a woman, and the poet's love for her has no time to become passion: she remains a dream, a sigh. Just because Beatrice has so little reality or personality, she lives rather in Dante's soul than among actual things. But there she is interfused with the troubadour's ideal, the Christian ideal, the philosopher's ideal—a fusion which is made in profound good faith, and so may indeed be grotesque, but surely not false or conventional." [1]

As an ideal, Beatrice acquires her true life in the soul of her lover only by her death, and her reality only in the Hereafter. Indeed the poet's imagination anticipates her death, and Dante dreams it before it occurs. While she lives he is too shy to approach her. In her life's surroundings, amid her woman friends, in the traces which she leaves behind her, in the city where she dwelt, she is revered. Her immediate presence, her touch, her kiss, would be deadly, like that of a divinity.

A feminine creature that may not be possessed in love, nor gazed at familiarly, nor tortured with jealousy, nor teased in

[1] Francesco de Sanctis, *Storia della letteratura italiana,* I, 59.

banter, nor wooed, and, in lieu of response, offers but a fleeting smile, greets, passes by, and dies—is a meagre motif for a poet: one to be exhausted with three or four sincere poetic utterances. All further details must be devised, learnedly, laboriously, after the fashion of the love-service; and this Dante did.

Nevertheless, he could not part with the motif. He, the lover, was dimly conscious of possible further development which the keenest critic would not have seen. If Beatrice here below was not at home, could not be alive and happy, that was for the lover a sign that she was desired in the next world, that the blessed in Heaven needed her for their happiness, the damned in Hell for their consolation. When Dante contemplated this pure being, he could not but feel himself condemned as a sinner, destined to Hell, and yet in darkest gloom, with her picture in his heart, happy. In this religious experience lay the germ of a poetic world of Christian mythology. Expressed and stated for the first time, but not yet developed, nor mingled with alien ideas, this experience is found in the *Vita Nuova's* first canzone, *Donne ch'avete intelletto d'amore* (second strophe).

> An angel, of his blessed knowledge, saith
> To God: "Lord, in the world that Thou hast made,
> A miracle in action is display'd,
> By reason of a soul whose splendours fare
> Even hither: and since Heaven requireth
> Nought saving her, for her it prayeth Thee,
> Thy saints crying aloud continually.
> Yet pity still defends our earthly share
> In that sweet soul." God answereth thus the prayer:
> "My well-belovèd, suffer that in peace
> Your hope remain, while so My pleasure is,
> There where one dwells who dreads the loss of her:
> And who in Hell unto the doomed shall say,
> 'I have looked on that for which God's chosen pray.'" [1]

This is a *Divine Comedy* in miniature, somewhat like Goethe's "Prologue in Heaven," still cramped within that conventional form in which the mediæval theologians, preachers and poets, loved to set forth the Christian idea of the Atonement. Giulio Salvadori has shown how general the dramatic representation of the dogma of the Atonement was. Sympathy and Truth, Justice and Peace, and a gradual, ever-increasing assemblage of allegorical and sym-

[1] Rossetti's translation.

bolic heavenly hosts consult with God, question and take thought how sinful man is to be redeemed. Finally the incarnation of Christ and the sending of the Angel of the Annunciation to Mary are decided upon. In a sermon of St. Bernard, in a gloss of Hugo of St. Victor, in a song of Jacopone, and in various other passages of mystical literature, we find this scheme. How could Dante have been ignorant of it?

He himself assures us that his poetic originality begins with the canzone *Donne ch'avete intelletto d'amore*, and that the experience of love lies at the foundation of this poem.[1] So the Beatrice motif of the *Commedia* stands at the opening of his career.

Nevertheless, along with the possibility of development of a mythical Christian poetry of Hell and Heaven, the Beatrice-motif contains serious artistic perils of its own. For this love of the new life is too timid, too shy, and too passive to develop ethical motifs of adequate strength; and the figure of the adored one is too hazy for picturesque, firm delineation.

To speak figuratively, the Beatrice of the *Vita Nuova* has forsaken Florence, hovers above the earth, but cannot find her assured place in Heaven until her lover as an ethical, philosophical, and æsthetic man has squarely faced the reality that lies before him. For the time being, he is all dreams, longing, foreboding, desire, and aspirations, without as yet a definite goal.

PEGASUS UNDER THE YOKE

Bad company, reckless friends, sensual or coquettish women, Cecco, Forese, Pietra, Pargoletta, or whatever their names may be, with their seductions awakened in Dante the sting of conscience, and so, moral manhood. An artistic enrichment, a conversion to more objective poetry, they might not have brought him directly. People confuse content with form when they seek or find in moral bewilderment an artistic enrichment of the poet.

If Dante had been an Ovid, a Boccaccio, or a Wieland, then indeed his moral aberration would have guided him to the discovery of his poetic capacity. But Dante is no voluptuary. With lily-white arms, with coral lips, with more or less veiled charms of the feminine body, with voluptuous or shameless pictures, his imagination, even in its sensuous moods, will have nothing to do. His muse accepts neither the open and happy sensuous de-

[1] *Purgatorio*, XXIV, 49 sqq.

light of the ancients, nor the tortured and extravagant passion of the moderns. He is no heathen and no *cérébral*. His imagination remains as pure as Beatrice. Sensuousness stirs in his blood, not in his brain or in his art. For even in the so-called "stone sonnets" we have a transcendence of love: a desire, however wild it may be, which does not hang upon nor cling to its object, but pierces it as a bull would the red rag. So this Pietra, despite her blond locks and sparkling eyes, is no more definite in form and presence than Beatrice, and may quite possibly be a mere symbol, a sign, and a goad to passion, perchance the fondly hated and longed-for native city of the banished poet. Feeling here is everything, the name is but empty sound. Corresponding to the heightened and savage feeling, the expression is now livelier, more energetic, rougher, but also more forced and violent, and along with the force and directness of the style, its artificiality is also heightened. Arnaut Daniel, the master of voluptuous rhetoric, becomes, as we saw, his model. But what with him was style, is with Dante laborious effort. The lyric of this second period grows ornate and overwhelming, over-elaborate and heavy. Our present-day language is quite too smooth to imitate its violent antitheses. The difficult and intricate rhymes, also, are lost in translation. So what follows is only a pallid shadow of the original text.

And stronger throbs my heart whene'er I think
Of her, in places where I meet mankind,
And fears it may betray
Its wish, so that it will be visible.
So much I'd not fear death, that with the pangs
Of longing love my senses doth devour:
That from my spirit gnaws
The force away and cripples every task.
He cast me to the earth and on me trod,
The god of love, and holds the sword wherewith
Of old he Dido slew.
I beg for mercy, while I humbly cry,
But he appears contemptuous of all grace.

Again and yet again he lifts his hand
And mercilessly with my life he plays.
Prostrate I lie supine,
So weak I cannot even quiver more.
Then in my spirit there is heard a cry;
From my remotest veins the blood doth run

Backward unto the heart
That cried to it, and deadly pale am I.
Then under my left arm he smiteth me
So deep that from the blow my heart resounds.
Then say I to myself:
"If once again he strikes me, I am dead
Ere yet the thrust of death befalleth me."

Oh, if I could but see that cruel one
That now my heart devoureth, with her own
So rent! Then gladly I
Would flee before her beauty unto death.
Because this sly and thievish murderess
Even in sunlight is but as in shade.
Alas! that she shrieks not
For me as I for her in the hot gulf.
Then I would cry: "I come to give thee aid!"
And glad as any man so would I do,
And into her blond hair
That Amor craftily doth curl and gild,
I'd plunge my hand and satisfy me so.

As soon as those blond tresses I had grasped,
Tresses which are to me a lash and scourge,
Though 'twere at early morn,
I'd hold them fast beyond the vesper bell.
No pity, no, nor courtesy I'd show,
No, sharp as bears at play I'd be!
And I by Amor scourged,
A thousandfold still would I wreak revenge.
In that bright eye, wherein the sparks abound
That set ablaze in me my tortured heart,
I'd stare at closest range,
Avenging me on her who from me fled.
Then peace would come upon her from my love.[1]

There are, among the canzoni and ballads which have been declared by Dante himself to be allegorical, verses and expressions so glowing, so passionate, so fiery, so fresh, so graceful, and so direct, that it is difficult to apply them to an ideal concept instead of to a living woman. This springs from the essentially lyrical character of Dante's poetry. Feeling is its very life; it does not describe but is intensely conscious of its object; and in this consciousness it permeates its most stubborn subject, conquers and enlivens alike what is beneath or above our earth;

[1] Stanzas 3–6 of the canzone, *Cosi nel mio parlar voglio esser aspro.*

descends to the passions of the flesh, and rises to concepts and eternal values. In the one as in the other direction this Dantesque poetry rushes so excitedly, so swiftly, and, often, with such rude rhetorical overflow, that one may well err as to the goal of its fury. In its very force lies its weakness. As it has the power to ennoble alike sexuality or metaphysics, it is in danger of becoming unruly and of confusing with each other, in magnificent figures of speech, what is highest and what is most vulgar, and, finally, of becoming a super-poetical monstrosity, "half filth, half fire." Imagine a wild fantasy like Dante's, reaching out in every direction, implanted in the brain of a man untrained morally or intellectually—the uttermost self-destruction would be inevitable. To escape such disorder Dante harnessed his wingéd steed to the plough of science and morality.

But this process was completed only gradually and slowly. The Beatrice-motif was not abandoned but extended. In the second year after her death, and in the last lines of the *Vita Nuova*, Beatrice acquires a rival, the *gentil donna*, a lady who consoles the forsaken Dante at first with her sympathy, finally with her love. So thoroughly does she console him that he soon must reproach himself with unfaithfulness to her who is dead and glorified.

But there can be no true jealousy between the two, for while the one is still a living woman, the other dwells among the blessed. Yet if the *gentil donna* is to maintain herself beside the heavenly height of Beatrice, she, too, must be glorified. So she uplifts herself in Beatrice's footsteps, puts off, like her, her carnal nature, and ventures to appear radiantly as a second ideal beside the first. "But if it is nevertheless necessary to follow the one and desert the other, then one must follow the better and, with some courteous regrets, abandon the other." [1] This better one was, for the time being, the *gentil donna*, elevated to a symbol of philosophy. The *Convivio* is devoted to her glorification, as the *Vita Nuova* was to that of Beatrice. If the sonnet, "Two ladies at the summit of my mind," [2] is really Dante's, then there was a time when the poet hoped to unite peacefully the two ideals: the first as visible beauty, the second as active virtue: Beatrice as a supersensuous *Bellezza*, *Leggiadria*, and *Gentilezza*, and the *gentil donna* as mistress of *Cortesia*, *Valore*, *Prudenza*, and *Onestà*.

[1] *Convivio*, II, 15.

[2] *Due donne in cima della mente mia.*

It is at any rate certain that the two motifs enriched and clarified each other. Were it not for Beatrice's example, the *gentil donna* would not have become a symbol, and but for the allegorical interpretation of the *gentil donna* as Philosophy, preferably moral philosophy, Beatrice would not have attained to the clarity and importance which she lacks in the *Vita Nuova* and which became hers in the *Commedia.* After the *gentil donna* had revealed herself as moral philosophy, it was natural to assign to Beatrice the offices of mystical philosophy or theology and to set the heavenly representative of revelation over against the earthly type of wisdom.

While the *Convivio* shows a preference for an essentially prosaic, allegorical, scientifically enlightened rival of the vanished Beatrice, who is lost in blessedness, the latter is forced to unfold her mysterious nature and is made ready for the part which she is to play in the *Divine Comedy.*

It is as a silent and indirect preparation for the *Commedia* that the *Convivio* assumes historical value. The Dante of the *Convivio* turns his attention away from Beatrice, but is not untrue to her; harnesses his Pegasus under the yoke, but does not slay him; becomes a philosopher, but with his eye still on poetry.

THE PHILOSOPHER, PROSE WRITER, AND RHETORICIAN

Unfortunately, the biographical foundation for the *gentil donna* is even more completely covered and lost than Beatrice's. Indeed there may lie concealed under the anonymous term of the "gentle lady" no single person, but a group of ladies who were so fortunate as to become agreeable to the poet; the "coy one" (Pietra), "little one" (Pargoletta), Lisetta, "or other vanity of such brief use."

The period of "moral aberration," if the weakness for feminine beauty must be so called, coincides, at least in part, with the composition of the *Convivio.* Its first canzone is to be assigned to the year 1293, and its completion to 1308. The *Convivio,* however, is by no means to be regarded as a memorial of such aberrations, but as a monument of victory over the errors and misfortunes of those years.

The moral purification is not described in the course of this work, but is emphatically indicated to the reader as completed and ended by means of a practical and austere training. The author desires to rehabilitate himself in the world's eyes. With scholastic keenness he makes a deep rift in his life. The time of youth, he says, ends at fifteen; manhood at forty-five. To the latter belongs moderation of that sensuous love which in early years was doubtless natural.

He who peruses the love-songs of Dante published after the *Vita Nuova* might regard him as a sensual man. The *Convivio*, however, is intended to prove, by allegorical interpretation, that "virtue, not passion, is the mainspring of these poems." The love felt for the *gentil donna*, which was originally, no doubt, sensuous, is interpreted or distorted, for considerations of propriety, to mean philosophic study. Perhaps somewhat the same result was to be attained with various other love-affairs. But the *Convivio* was left uncompleted. The purely personal aim of the work, which was, in its essence, neither artistic nor scientific, is the fundamental error, which wreaked its own revenge.

For Dante's artistic development it was primarily fortunate that the allegorizing of the *gentil donna* was accomplished *post festum;* that is, after the arrows of Amor had burnt out. For, thanks to the tenacity with which the poet clung to the traditional form of love-song, he assured for himself unified and unbroken progress. In our day, when artistic traditions have become seriously disintegrated, and often violate each other, youthful talents are generally rushed from one style into another, from contradiction to contradiction: precocious virtuosos in external form, who, before they have anything original to say, are masters of all the poetic technique of the past and of the present. But for Dante, there was only the one fully elaborated technique; that of the courtly love-song. This, as we have seen, had become even in the *Vita Nuova* too narrow for his spirit. Prose, therefore, was relied on to instruct, inform, justify, and complete the task of the hampered singer. It was a half-scientific, half-poetic form of prose, a mixture of commentary and narration.

In the *Convivio* the same technique is retained externally; but the inner relation between prose and poetry has grown clearer. The prose has become a mere commentary, criticism and science, and no longer intrudes, as in the *Vita Nuova*, into the growth of the poetic feeling; it follows, like a faithful, attentive maid, its lyric mistress; it is, as Dante expresses it, "an intelligent and obedient servant" of the canzoni of the *Convivio*.[1]

[1] *Convivio*, I, 5–7.

But scientific prose should appear, according to the ideas of Dante's time, strictly speaking, only in Latin dress; for Latin was the appropriate language of science. If Dante, nevertheless, wrote his scientific commentary in Italian, he did it because the canzoni which that commentary was to serve were likewise in Italian.

Accordingly it might be expected that all the scientific and prosaic elements of the *Convivio* would be uplifted, controlled, and moulded by a great poetic and lyrical inspiration. The opposite is the case. Learned, scientific, but not artistic preoccupations control, as far as we can see, the composition of the entire fragment of the *Convivio*. The "intelligent and obedient servant" is in truth a pedagogical tyrant, and the canzoni, for their part, are in their lyric nature so little "sovereign," so abstract and analytical, that we actually do not know whether the commentary was written for their sake, or vice versa.

Presumably both suppositions are true. When at the close of the first canzone he says:

> My song, I do believe there are but few
> Who perfectly shall understand thy meaning,
> So darkly and laboriously thou speakest!—

the need, and therefore the intention, of offering further explanation is intimated. In other words, the artist has entered the stage of self-analysis and self-criticism; the mystic has awakened to become a philosopher, the dreamer to be a thinker. But in such a condition of self-analysis, or of awakening, a poet should abstain from singing; for when critical and lyrical adjustments meet, they are likely to jostle each other.

Therefore the *Convivio*, which we must characterize as an essay in critical self-analysis by the poet, can claim no important place in the evolution either of his art or of his science. We have seen already how scientific interpretations in prose, which are in themselves disconnected, are here appended to allegorical poems which in and by themselves are incomprehensible; how the verses are explained by criticism, while the prose in its turn achieves connection only by the aid of the verses. Even if the *Convivio* had been completed we could discover in it, I believe, neither philosophic nor poetic unity. For the condition of the soul that it mirrors is discontinuous and incomplete. Externally a fragment, the *Convivio*, internally also, marks a fragmentary portion of our poet's development.

We stand at a point where the path of the Dantesque spirit divides. On the critical side the *Convivio* points toward Dante's prose works: to his theory of poetry (*De vulgari Eloquentia*), to his political ethics (*De Monarchia*), and to his natural philosophy (*Quaestio de Aqua et Terra*); on the artistic side it leads on to the *Commedia*. The chief line of Dante's development is, of course, the latter. The relation between the two is determined by two essential facts. First: in his scientific works Dante returns, immediately after the *Convivio*, to Latin and to pure prose. Second: the entire content of these scientific investigations is taken up into the Italian art-form of the *Commedia*, and there utilized. The *Commedia*, therefore, takes previous scientific work and prose for granted, while Dante's prose works could exist without the *Commedia*. This relation cannot be overthrown by chronological difficulties. It may be that the composition of the *De Monarchia* and of the *Quaestio* is later than that of the *Commedia*; [1] but the actual composition is something quite independent of the ideas contained. For us, at this point the scientific and prosaic thought is only content, and as such the presupposition of the poetic form. The art of the Latin and Latinizing prosaist has only an indirect interest for the stylistic mystery of the *Commedia*. And precisely in the *Convivio* it frees itself and diverges from the art of the Italian poet. Everything in the domain of the critic and philosopher that cannot become art and poetry is now rejected, and this prosaic remainder finds in the Latin compositions its appropriate, that is, systematic, form. System is the form of abstract thinking.

In the *Convivio* we already have philosophic clarity and assertiveness, but still in a mixed form. In the *De vulgari Eloquentia* the system begins to crystallize; in the *De Monarchia* it has hardened into complete logical order.

So far as regards its form, accordingly, the *Convivio* contains on the one hand the beginnings of the systematic crystallization of philosophy, and on the other, germs of a poetic essence of life. It is, so to speak, a breeding-place of spiritual advancement where the progress of conceptual thinking is about to separate itself from that of poetic blossoming.

[1] As is well known, the *Quaestio* grew out of a geodetic discussion in the chapel of St. Helena in Verona on Jan. 20, 1320.

The progress of the separation may be observed within the *Convivio* itself. Already in the third canzone the allegorizing of the *gentil donna* as Philosophia, and with it, the intellectualistic analysis of the love-poem, are given up:

> The dulcet rhymes of love which I was wont
> To seek out in my thoughts
> I must renounce. . . .

Philosophy, which was the concealed subject of the love-song, becomes the inmost mainspring, becomes practically active in the poet's heart. He no longer sings of philosophy like a servant of love, but philosophically, in the spirit and sense of philosophy. His canzone becomes a sirventes. By the side of the poem above quoted on the nature of nobility, the canzone on the nature of loveliness (*Poscia ch' Amor del tutto m'ha lasciato*) and the one on the nature of liberality (*Doglia mi reca nello core ardire*) should find their place in the *Convivio.* It is easy to see how in these poems the scientific exposition becomes enlivened oratorically, how the didactic treatise passes over into a satirical poem, and the logical form of the systematizer glides into the oratorical manner of the preacher and satirist.

In this direction as well a parting of the ways appears in the *Convivio.* The pathos, the tirades and invectives which are found here dispersed incidentally, and often disconnectedly, in prose and verse, are collected in Dante's Latin letters, and there worked over into purely personal and ethico-political rhetoric. Like the systematizing of the scientific writings, so, too, the rhetoric of these letters interests us only indirectly; that is, only in so far as it was rejected and, to a certain extent, removed to make way for the coming of the *Divine Comedy.*

Nowhere better than in the *Convivio* do we see how dangerous the complicated many-sidedness and restless wealth of Dante's spirit might have proved for the construction of his *Commedia.* The thinker in him awakened and strove toward systematic expression; the moral and active man in him was also aroused, and sought to make himself felt in didactic, condemnatory, admonitory invectives and pleadings. Both threatened to crowd out the pious poet. Perhaps they would have stifled him, and destroyed the *Commedia* in the germ, or eventually burst the finished form of the Christian work of art, if they had not come to their rights elsewhere in Latin prose and eloquence.

So, the mingling of the various elements proved only a moment, a crisis soon overcome. That which in the *Convivio* strives to diverge in all directions, submits later, in the *Commedia*, to order and unity.

THE CRITICAL AND ETHICAL VICTORY OVER MYSTICISM

If one imagines those elements removed from the *Convivio* which were afterwards taken out, that is, elaborated separately—if one excludes the intellectualistic forms of allegory and systematization, as well as the rhetorical forms of satire, admonition, and self-defence—what then remains? The motif of the *gentil donna* has been dissolved by criticism; Beatrice seems forgotten, the pious longing of the youth appears to have died away. Instead of the lovable and wistful poet of the *Vita Nuova*, we see an instructive and eager pedant. Is it still the same man? Is not the entire inner unity torn asunder?

The visions and dreams are ended, Beatrice has vanished; even the rôle of her successor and imitator, the rôle of the *gentil donna*, has played itself out.[1] Still, this rôle was but a mask, a temporary veil. That veil falls—and as the true and genuine bearer of the philosophic burden and problem, a powerful man stands revealed, and a poet as well: Virgil! The transformation of philosophy into a male, the overthrow of feminine mysticism and of the feminine disguise for the thought, the substitution of Virgil for the *gentil donna*—that is the most valuable result of the evolution of the *Convivio*. It is, to be sure, not yet perfected into a work of art, but is contained in the *Convivio* merely as an adjustment of the soul, as a tendency and as a more or less firm conviction. Its transformation into poetry may be followed step by step.

We recall how clearly and firmly the autonomy of reason is proclaimed in the prose commentary of the *Convivio*, and how closely connected with the reverence for natural reason is the reverence for natural morality; how decided is the abandonment of theoretical for practical philosophy, and how the pale *gentil donna* of the first treatise is succeeded in the fourth essay by the mighty representative of freedom of the will, Stoicism and "yon glorious Cato." Cato at first appears merely as an historical personage, but the supermundane rôle which he is to acquire in

[1] Unless one chooses to recognize the *gentil donna* once more in the Matelda of the *Purgatorio*—a most uncertain and arbitrary identification.

the *Commedia*, as the divinely favoured hero of free will, is already foreshadowed in the words of the *Convivio:* "And what earthly man was more worthy to represent God than Cato? Surely none! "[1]

The Cato-symbol may well be earlier in the evolution of the *Commedia* than the Virgil-symbol. Without the Stoic spirit, without the reverence for the masculine and defiant morality of the ancient world, without the experience of self-discipline, Philosophy would doubtless have remained for Dante a woman, a beloved lady, a *gentil donna;* it could hardly have become a man, a friend, a guide and master, Virgil. How weighty this simple and imperative consideration may become for the chronology of the *Divine Comedy* has been overlooked, so far as I can see, by many scholars.

An intellectualistic and naturalistic conception of philosophy, such as we find, for example, in Cavalcanti or among the Averroists, would have led our poet into religious doubt and to the rift between faith and knowledge. Then hostility and jealousy would have flamed up between Beatrice and Lady Philosophy—and it is hard to see how the two could ever have been reconciled again. For such a drama of jealousy, however, only a faint suggestion is to be found in the *Vita Nuova.* This is disposed of in the *Convivio.* The imperious bearing, the "disdainful and dauntless behaviour," of Lady Philosophy frightened the poet. The lady who was at first so amiable and sympathetic became a haughty virago. The lover turns from her, yet hopes hereafter to woo her with renewed power:

> But not because I have not hopes that yet
> To love's sweet rhymes I shall again return.

Yet, after he strengthened his powers by participation in active life, after Fate moulded him to manhood, the mannish woman Philosophy became, for him, a man. And of a man Beatrice no longer has reason to be jealous. Now Virgil and Beatrice can exert themselves, in harmony and mutual helpfulness, for Dante, their friend and protégé. Thanks to the transition from intellectual to moral philosophy, the unity of faith and knowledge is preserved. The Virgil-symbol rests upon the Cato-symbol.

But the Virgil-symbol is, so far as I can see, only critically, not

[1] *Convivio,* IV, 28.

artistically, foreshadowed in the *Convivio*. In the twenty-fourth chapter of the fourth treatise of the *Convivio*, Dante betrays to us a conception of Aeneas that had been familiar to the Middle Ages ever since the allegorical interpretation of Virgil by Fulgentius. It is the conception that the actions and destiny of Aeneas depict for us in typical and figurative fashion the course of man's moral development through the various stages of life. The twenty-sixth chapter of the same treatise contains some trifling specimens of this moral and philosophical interpretation. The fourth, fifth, and sixth books of the *Aeneid*, says Dante, include the second age of man; that is to say, that time in which we should exert manly self-control, moderation, and energy, just as Aeneas did in his renunciation of Dido, in his descent to the underworld, etc.

In short, Virgil, "our greatest poet," is conceived and interpreted by Dante as a teacher of practical moral wisdom, and the *Aeneid* as an ethical and philosophical poem on the successive moral ideals of the four ages of man. In another passage of the *Convivio*, however,[1] even a sort of divine and prophetic utterance is ascribed to a phrase of Virgil. It is the decree of Jupiter which announces the eternal world-rule of the Romans:

> His ego nec metas rerum, nec tempora pono:
> Imperium sine fine dedi.[2]

Here the ethical counsellor, Virgil, appears as a political authority. We see that the high esteem in which Dante holds the Latin poet is primarily practical and political. His æsthetic reverence for him is only secondary. Thus our argument, stated above, of the ethico-mystical origin of humanism, is strengthened, so far as concerns Dante.

The objection will be raised that Virgil appears as an æsthetic model as early as the twenty-fifth paragraph of the *Vita Nuova*, long before the time of the *Convivio*. Certainly; but it must be noted for what purpose and in what sense this æsthetic model is set up. "Furthermore it is a fact that greater licence is permitted to poets than to prose writers." For the poet of the *Vita Nuova*, Virgil is an example of poetic licence, not of norms. As long as we admire in an artist only the liberty that he permits himself, we fail to appreciate his poetic quality.

A profounder artistic understanding of Virgil and of the ancient

[1] *Convivio*, IV, 4.

[2] *Aeneid*, I, 283–284.

classics in general is first attained by Dante in the *De vulgari Eloquentia.* The *Convivio* is still much too fully controlled by personal, practical, and ethical aims to mark any great artistic progress. But this progress is being impelled from many directions.

PURIFICATION OF TASTE AND STUDY OF ANTIQUITY

One of the most powerful and mysterious canzoni, the poem on justice, "Three women gathered close about my heart," was, as we know from Dante himself, to stand in the next to the last place in the *Convivio,* and there to be commented upon. It is a milestone on the road of the poet's development; it closes the cycle of moral canzoni and opens up a new vista toward the *Commedia.* The moral teaching is here no longer an essay on the nature of justice, nor a damnatory sermon, nor in any other manner an oratorical performance; it has become a personal experience, full of lyric and elegiac material: the experience of one unjustly exiled. The banished poet tarries lonely in a strange land, but love for all things good and beautiful reigns unshaken in his heart. Three goddesses come seeking a refuge and a home. As if at the hearth of a friend, they find repose near the poet's loving heart. They, too, the beautiful and noble, are banished. The eldest among them begins to lament. She resembles a drooping rose. In weariness she leans upon her hand. Her naked arm, "a pillar of sorrow," is wet with hot tears. The other hand covers her weeping eyes. She is barefoot, with broken girdle, but royal in her rags. Love, sympathetic, inquisitive, scans her naked charms and inquires about her suffering. When she makes herself known as *Drittura,* Justice, sorrow and shame overcome him. He asks about the other two, and whence they come. She replies: "Yonder where the Nile rises, a tiny streamlet, where willows round about shadow the place, at the edge of the virgin spring, I bore her who is here beside me and with her blond tresses dries her eyes; and when my lovely daughter was mirrored in the limpid spring, she gave life to her who is farther from me." To all three Love utters words of comfort:

> Uplift your heads!
> Here both mine arrows,
> Behold, are rusted in long idleness.
> Largesse and Moderation, all the children
> Sprung of our race, perforce are beggars now.

If that be a misfortune,
Then let men weep for it, let them lament
Whom it befalls,
Whom such a heaven holdeth in its sway—
Not we! Our race is from the eternal city!
If we are today maltreated,
Yet do we live, and men we yet shall find
With whom this shaft of love no rust doth gather.

And now the poet himself begins to speak:

And as I in their heavenly language hear
The homeless powers
Console and pity each other,
Then I account my exile as an honour!
And if by will of fate, or higher judgment
The lily must from white
To dark be stained with blood—
Laudable it is to fall among the valiant.
And if the lovely object of my longing
Were not by distance far removed from me,
That kindled my desire,
Then easy were all burdens laid upon me!
But even now this fire
Devours already both my flesh and marrow.
Death lays his key even now upon my breast.
So if I was guilty,
Full many a moon have I therefor atoned,
So far as penitence effaces guilt.

Like a modest woman—runs the envoi—so shouldst thou, my song, hide the secret of thine inmost meaning. Only to noble natures shalt thou reveal thyself.

And for the blossom that so charming seems,
Awaken thou in loving hearts desire!

This blossom, this drooping rose, is *Drittura:* eternal justice. It is usual to interpret her offspring as "human justice" and "law": that is to say, as natural and legal justice. But of how little importance is interpretation here! The whole poem is thrilled and warmed by throbs of feeling, as if by an electric current. And are they not all feelings that come from the ethical world of justice and love? Smitten by injustice, all the chords of conscience vibrate and resound. A noble, moral suffering is expressed in the figure of the wronged woman. Sympathy, at first amorous and inquisitive, grows pure, rises to moral wrath, to indignation, to conscious power, and finally to proud faith in the victory of right.

Then pain seizes once more the soul that utters tender words of longing. The final wish is for love and forgiveness.

The outward state of things from which these feelings seem to arise is, in part at least, a subsequent, allegorical creation. It would seem strange to us if it were not that feeling, with its natural turns, accompanies and illuminates it. Out of this penetration of innermost personal feeling by oratorical fiction arises the impression of mystery, of marvel, of strangeness. What have the shadowy, remote, virginal sources of the Nile to do with justice? We do not understand; we surmise and are conscious of consecration and solemnity. Along with the ethical impulses the theoretical feelings of curiosity, love of the unknown, eagerness for truth, are also awakened. Within the frame of a troubadour sirventes we have an immeasurable, universal poem: a first sketch for a world-picture.

The effort after universality is characteristic of the entire *Convivio.* At the beginning it seems prosaic, like a compilation and an encyclopædia. In this canzone it takes a poetic turn, but the means with which the poet works are not yet adequate for universal inspiration. Quantitatively they might perhaps suffice, for a poetic spirit can make the briefest poem contain infinity. The lack is rather qualitative.

What diminishes our enjoyment of the poem on justice is the feeling that the mystery which rouses our curiosity exists, in many respects, only for us, not for the poet. Dante conceals from us something that he knows, treats us like children, and plays with his readers. "Let the parts laid bare suffice." A schoolmaster may talk thus, but not a poet. A poet, if he wishes to be universal, must reveal and offer to us his whole soul. His entire subjectivity must become visibly objective. From the educational point of view, it may be appropriate to conceal something, for a time at least; from the artistic viewpoint, every gap in the inner connection, every sudden jump of the imagination, is felt to be an interruption.

From such faults of style and pedantry our poet was liberated by his study of antiquity, above all by Virgil—"Virgil whose taste is genius," as the Abbé Delille says.

Classical Prose

Like most mediæval scholars, it is probable that Dante approached ancient literature first through the later authors. The artificial syntax of Orosius, the stirring rhetoric of Augustine, the mixed lyric-didactic style of Boëthius and other more or less baroque late-comers in classic art, were perhaps the first to captivate Dante's sense of form, and they certainly were not ideal models for the purification of taste. Other writers of historical or scientific prose who are recommended in the *De vulgari Eloquentia* as models of form, Pliny, Frontinus, and presumably also Livy, were known to our poet only in quotations and extracts. Cicero and Seneca, several of whose philosophical works he read connectedly, are omitted, to our astonishment, from his list of great prose writers. The name Tullius is first inserted in the passage referred to [1] by Trissino in the Italian translation of the *De vulgari Eloquentia.*

The prose of the *Vita Nuova* has been studiously compared with that of the *Convivio,* and a number of notable changes have been discovered. In the former the syntax is comparatively simple, the forced arrangement of the words is rare and discreet; a full, resonant emphasis and an occasional approach to verse are noticeable. We are sometimes reminded of the simple French narrative manner, sometimes of the ringing artistic prose of the middle and late Latin literature. In short, mediæval taste is still dominant. Quite otherwise in the *Convivio.* The so-called cursus, the rhythmical close of the sentence, is rarer, but the periods become longer, less natural, bolder and richer in their construction. The artistic ideal of classical prose has come into notice as compared with that of mediæval prose. What has been lost in grace and musical charm is gained in firmness, directness, and clearness. The peculiar qualities of prose have purified themselves.

Should not a similar approach to classical taste be evident in poetry also? Even in the manner in which the troubadours of Provence influenced Dante, we were able to trace a progress from the romantic to the classical style.

Lucan

Already in the *Vita Nuova,* the canon of Dante's taste is anticipated. Virgil, Horace, Ovid, and Lucan are cited as models. Homer, the Greek whom Dante never knew, stands beside them merely as a decorative greatness. The *bella scuola* of the great poets in Elysium (*Inferno,* IV) is already made up. The acquaintance with Statius and Juvenal appears to have been first made in the *Convivio.*

[1] II, 6.

Curiously enough, the most forcible of them all, Juvenal, has left the slightest trace. Dante does not seem to have made any direct and intensive study of his satires.

Much more important was the influence of Lucan, the poet who stands closest to prose writers. He possessed what Dante had to acquire with toil: objectivity and a tranquil eye for external reality. He has nothing of the stirring and transcendent imagination which enlivens whatever is hard, sets in motion things rigid, and makes the superficial profound. He stands helpless in the presence of things; he is not granted the power to transform them poetically. He must be satisfied to delineate them, to analyze them, and to pass judgment on them as a critical historian, or to distort and combine them like an eloquent advocate, or to reproduce them in plaster casts like a descriptive geographer, or again, if he is determined to be an artist, to exaggerate them in dramatic fashion, to decorate them, to compose them, and in every way to adorn and beautify them. All these processes are employed with amazing cleverness, with trained taste, and with dazzling energy in Lucan's *Pharsalia.*

In him Dante may well have admired the easy elegance, the solemn brevity, the learned compactness of his topographical, geographical, astronomical and meteorological delineations, descriptions, and explanations. From Lucan he may well have discovered how a learned excursus, a mythical or historical allusion, or notions of natural history, may be gracefully interwoven with the story to give the cultivated reader an opportunity to revive and enjoy his own knowledge; or how interest is awakened and thirst for information aroused by a series of strange names.

So, for instance, in the very first book of the *Pharsalia,* the description of the various barracks from which Caesar assembles his army made a lasting impression upon Dante.

> Deseruere cavo tentoria fixa Lemanno,
> Castraque, quae, Vogesi curvam super ardua rupem,
> Pugnaces pictis cohibebant Lingonas armis.
> Hi vada liquerunt Isarae, qui, gurgite ductus
> Per tam multa suo, famae majoris in amnem
> Lapsus, ad aequoreas nomen non pertulit undas.[1]

[1] The passage may be freely translated:

> "They left their tents beside Lake Leman pitched
> And camps that high above the ridge of Vosges
> Quelled the fierce, gaily armoured Lingones,
> And these the Iser left, that, rushing down
> Through many a dale to a more famous stream,
> Bears not its own name to the billowy sea."

And so on and on. Through some seventy verses this geographical review runs along, which Dante evidently recalled in the *Paradiso*, VI, 58 sqq. Similarly in the second book (verses 392–438), the description of the Apennine range with its rivers, and that of the Syrtes and the Lybian desert in the ninth book, may have influenced our poet. Especially after the long journeys and wanderings which led the exiled Florentine throughout Central and Upper Italy, and perchance had further sharpened his eye for lands and people, Lucan's accurate landscape pictures could not but invite imitation or even rivalry.

We shall come fairly near the truth if we assume that splendid masterpieces like the story of the founding of Mantua (*Inferno*, XX, 55–99), or the polemical politico-geographical description of the Arno's course (*Purgatorio*, XIV, 29–54), or the emphatic topography of Assisi (*Paradiso*, XI, 43–54), or the astronomico-historical indication of the home of Folquet de Marseille (*Paradiso*, IX, 82–93), and others like them, were suggested, at least in part, by passages in the *Pharsalia*. Compare, for example, the effective excursus on the geographical, climatic, and legendary character of the seat of war in Thessaly (VI, 333–412), or the mysterious information concerning the origin of the Nile, the banks of the holy stream, and the causes of its overflow (X, 194–331).

In youth, Dante's imagination was veiled in dreams and tears. In the school of Lucan he became objective and exact. He equipped himself with an abundance of realities. He is indebted to Lucan for the serpents' names: *chelidri*, *iaculi*, *farée*, *cencri*, and *amfisibena;* [1] from Lucan comes the observation of the figures in the flight of birds,[2] as well as a series of astronomical definitions and, finally, an abundance of anecdotic, mythical, and historical notions.

Such borrowings, chiefly of material facts, would be artistically insignificant were it not that, along with the learned motifs, something of Lucan's style has passed over into the *Commedia*. Mediævalism had no lack of didactic motifs elsewhere, but the corresponding style was dry, pedantic, wearisome, obscure, and irritating. The oratorical elegance of manner, the sententious brevity in emphasizing what is essential, the playful indication of what is familiar, the emotional elaboration of what is novel

[1] *Inferno*, XXIV, 86–87, and *Pharsalia*, IX, 700 sqq.
[2] *Paradiso*, XVIII, 73 sqq., and *Pharsalia*, VII, 711 sqq.

and interesting, the pedagogical circuitous mastering of difficulties, the emphasis and pathos in judging, evaluating, and appreciating, in short, the whole rhetorical art of didacticism, was something unfamiliar to mediæval man. For to him knowledge and instruction were partly a sin, partly a hard and joyless duty; to antiquity they were a necessity, an enjoyment, a diversion, a luxury. Hence the æsthetic pleasure in description, in the playful, dramatic, sophistical and oratorical conquest of difficulties. The charm of the solution is more highly valued than its accuracy. In this spirit the whole of the *Pharsalia* was written. It has an ethical and political purpose: condemnation of civil war and tyranny, and an historical one: an objective account of actual events. Both problems, however, are complicated by the constant effort for rhetorical effect. The poet is determined to be brilliant at any cost. Behind his objectivity there is a measureless self-consciousness, behind his pathos, vanity.

Dante had the wisdom to make his own just so much of Lucan's elegance, brilliancy, and dignity as befitted the sacred seriousness of his subject and the profundity of his own nature; just so much as was necessary to soften the crudity of mediæval didacticism. Rarely, only very rarely, does it seem to us as if he were beguiled into rhetorical ornamentation by his desire to be brilliant. It is as if he wished, by this bit of coquetry, only to show us the peril and the reef past which his genius carried him calmly and safely.

Ovid

To a poet with less weight of character than Dante, the influence of Ovid would have been perilous. For he, too, as well as Lucan, understands the art of filling in the hollow places of his poetry with the tinsel of phrases. Ovid has, to be sure, creative imagination, genuine and rich talent. But he has no roots in reality; he is at home in pleasant invention, delights in illusion and joyous fable. Life and poetry were for him two distinct compartments. So it came to pass that he destroyed his life-happiness through his poems, and on the other hand, did not experience all that he told in verse.

The best that he has to give us is legends, fables, myths. What interests him in these phantoms is not their eternal content of truth, but merely the marvellous. And even in the marvel he beholds not the mysterious action of the divinity; he observes only the effect, the external course of events, the magic or the transformation. The real purpose of his chief work, the *Metamorphoses*, is to present picturesquely, to make credible and attractive, in a purely æsthetic sense, a fantastic world in which no one any longer sincerely believed. Enjoyment of art as an end in itself; a labyrinth of pictures. That which assures to the entire mass its unity is the purpose to give pleasure, a joyous sense of beauty which is spread over it all. The effort to unite historically the various motifs in a mythical history of the world and to apply it all to the glorification of the Roman empire is made, to be sure, but the various parts are not permeated by this idea; the various myths are neither built upon nor developed one from the other. A carefree hand has woven them lightheartedly into a graceful garland. Religious, philosophic, moral, or political aims are to be found only in rhetorical digressions, not in the poet's soul. They only interrupt, but do not change, the keynote of sensuous levity. By roguish exaggeration, witty remarks, and ironical side glances, the teller of tales betrays to us that he himself is not in earnest. To a master like Ariosto, who trifled with all things, the artistic form at least is sacred. Ovid jests even with his muse. With laboured ingenuity, with negligences that sin against style, with every sort of cheap trivialities, he cheats himself out of the approval of the artistic connoisseur. Because he is infatuated with the shortcomings and perversities of his own mind, his artistic love for the creatures of his dreams can never become pure.

One can hardly imagine a greater contrast than that existing between Dante and Ovid, between the *Divine Comedy*, the poem of Truth, and the *Metamorphoses*, a comedy of errors. And yet Dante in one of the most famous cantos of his poem entered into a formal contest with Ovid. In depicting the marvellous, the incredible, the unnatural, he attempts to surpass both him and Lucan, and in fact excelled them both. He took as his model two of the finest episodes respectively from the *Pharsalia* and the *Metamorphoses*. Lucan describes, in gruesome detail, the effect from the bites of venomous serpents, to which the soldiers of Pompey fell victims in the Libyan desert:

> Parva modo serpens; sed qua non ulla cruentae
> Tantum morbis habet; nam plagae proxima circum
> Fugit rupta cutis, pallentiaque ossa retexit.

Jamque sinu laxo nudum est sine corpore vulnus:
Membra natant sanie: surae fluxere: sine ullo
Tegmine poples erat: femorum quoque musculus omnis
Liquitur, et nigrâ destillant inguina tabe.
Dissiluit stringens uterum membrana, fluuntque
Viscera; nec, quantum, toto de corpore debet,
Effluit in terras; saevum sed membra venenum
Decoquit: in minimum mors contrahit omnia virus.
Vincula nervorum, et laterum textura, cavumque
Pectus, et abstrusum fibris vitalibus omne,
Quidquid homo est, asperit pestis: natura profana
Morte patet: manant humeri fortesque lacerti;
Colla caputque fluunt: calido non ocius Austro
Nix resoluta cadit, nec solem cera sequetur.
Parva loquor; corpus sanie stillasse perustum:
Hoc et flamma potest. Sed quis rogus abstulit ossa?
Haec quoque discedunt, putresque secuta medullas
Nulla manere sinunt rapidi vestigia fati.
Cinyphias inter pestes tibi palma nocendi est:
Eripiunt omnes animam, tu sola cadaver.[1]

That is distorted naturalism, violently exaggerated reality, neither truth nor poetry, but an artificial brew of the twain. "One feels the purpose and is disenchanted."

Certainly Ovid is also a practiced and deliberate, calculating story-teller, but at the same time a fresh and naïve fabulist. How gracefully, how suddenly and how naturally he transforms Cadmus into a serpent:

"Ipse precor serpens in longam porrigar alvum!"
Dixit: et, ut serpens, in longam tenditur alvum;
Durataeque cuti squamas increscere sentit,
Nigraque caeruleis variari corpora guttis:
In pectusque cadit pronus: commissaque in unum
Paulatim tereti sinuantur acumine crura.
Brachia iam restant: quae restant, brachia tendit:
Et lacrimis per adhuc humana fluentibus ora,
"Accede, O! coniux, accede, miserrima," dixit.[2]

The surprising beginning and progress of the marvel are capitally described; but then the poet spoils his conception because he spins out the cry of the startled Cadmus for help into an untimely reflection upon a minor detail:

"Dumque aliquid superest de me, me tange: manumque
Accipe, dum manus est; dum non totum occupat anguis."

[1] *Pharsalia*, IX, 763 sqq. and 790 sqq.

[2] *Metamorphoses*, IV, 574 sqq.

Then follow some picturesque verses on the progress of the transformation:

> Ille quidem vult plura loqui: sed lingua repente
> In partes est fissa duas. Nec verba volenti
> Sufficiunt: quotiesque aliquos parat edere questus,
> Sibilat: hanc illi vocem Natura relinquit.

The impression made by the terrible scene upon Cadmus's wife is also spoiled; for in her lament over the occurrence, the poet has dragged in the description of the event so that a confused mingling of tragedy and comedy, of horror and curiosity, of subjective and objective feelings, is the result. It begins with delicious naïveté. The wife cries:

> "Cadme, mane: teque his, infelix, exue monstris!"

As if poor Cadmus could help himself! But just afterward the good woman falls into silly rhetoric:

> "Cadme, quid hoc? ubi pes? ubi sunt humerique manusque?
> Et color, et facies, et, dum loquor, omnia?"

One gets the impression that the poet does not take his description seriously—nor the characters their transformation.

And now let us read in Dante of the awful serpents' bites and the transformations,[1] and observe how the naturalism of Lucan and the picturesque fantasy of Ovid affect and purify each other, and how over the objectivity, clarity, and picturesqueness of the Latin models instead of cold rhetoric, there lies a heavy, unutterable horror.

To be sure, without the most detailed study of the *Metamorphoses*, Dante with his inclination merely to indicate everything, and to hurry from picture to picture, would hardly have learned the art of miniature painting. As he always has the whole in sight, he is ashamed to linger over detail.

> "And here be my excuse
> The novelty, if aught my pen transgress."[2]

So it may have been of great benefit to him to have inherited a few drops of blood from the amiable, communicative lover of words and colours, the fluent, airy, and elegant sensualist Ovid. Fabulous Ovidian pictures, such as the Golden Age, the hermaph-

[1] *Inferno*, XXIV, 97 sqq., and XXV, 46–144.

[2] *Inferno*, XXV, 143–144.

rodite, the madness of Athamas, Erysichthon's agony of hunger, the death of Nessus the centaur, and some warm tones of Ovid's landscape painting, lingered in Dante's memory. Of the humour and wit, or the lasciviousness, of the degenerate Roman he has no trace. The *Heroides*, the *Ars Amatoria*, and the *Remedia Amoris* he can hardly have read entire. His interest and profounder knowledge are limited to the *Metamorphoses*.

This book, however, in accordance with mediæval ideas, he considered, as he did the *Aeneid*, a moral and didactic poem, that is, a collection of examples to be imitated or avoided. One of them, the fable of Aeacus, he has interpreted elaborately in his *Convivio*.[1] A series of others he has utilized in the *Purgatorio* as pendants to biblical examples. By allegorical interpretation, he actually finds philosophical and historical truths in the *Metamorphoses*;[2] in short, frivolous Ovid seems to him a thought-laden, profound poet, a philosopher, and even a theologian.

Horace

In Horace, finally, Dante saw the teacher, to a less extent the artist—but the lyrist not at all. Although he introduces him in Elysium as "Horace the satirist," he cannot have known the satires any better than the odes. Of the Epistles only the *Ad Pisones*, that is, the *Ars Poetica*, left a deep impression upon him. Not much more of Horace than that was known in the Italy of Dante's day.

So we must look for Horace's influence, not in his poetry, but in his theory of poetry, that is, in Dante's scientific works on language and style, in the *De vulgari Eloquentia* and in the dedicatory letter to Can Grande della Scala. Horace there takes his place as a teacher of the means of poetic expression by the side of Cicero and Brunetto Latini, the teachers of oratory, beside Donatus and Priscian, the teachers of linguistic arts, and lastly beside the Provençal poets, who, as we remember, were perhaps the first to arouse and mould Dante's critical sense of form.

Of all these teachers not one preached to the poet with such fine sense, with such noble expression, in so amiable a temper, and with such golden maxims: measure, discretion, the golden mean, taste, fitness in style, naturalness, and unwearying painstaking as to purity of form. No one has so unerringly pierced with his

[1] *Convivio*, IV, 27.

[2] *Convivio*, IV, 15, and *De Monarchia*, II, 8.

gibes the uncouth genius, the affected fop, the indolent botcher, as Horace. "The manner in which he treats the youthful Piso (to whom the *Ars Poetica* is addressed) is the only proper one to employ with a poetical beginner. If he permits himself to be cast down by it, so much the better! If he goes on in spite of it, it is an infallible sign that he is either a fool or a poet born." [1] There is even today no better essay to educate and quicken the conscience of an artist.

Dante read it with the utmost attention. The second book of his *De vulgari Eloquentia* is filled with Horatian spirit. Here, in clear words, Horace's classic ideal of art is set before the poet of the vernacular tongues as the highest aim, and Horace's laws are applied to Italian poetry. "Above all therefore we say that each one ought to suit the weight of the matter to his own shoulders, lest, if the strength of the shoulders be too heavily burdened, he fall perforce in the mire. This is what our master Horace teaches when he says at the beginning of his *Poetics*, 'Choose your subject.' Next, the subjects which are to be treated must be examined with discernment to see whether they are to be sung of in the tragic, comic, or elegiac manner." [2] Dante does indeed understand the words tragic, comic, and elegiac otherwise than Horace. As may be seen from his epistle to Can Grande, § 10, he probably has in his mind the following verses of Horace:

> Versibus exponi tragicis res comica non vult. . . .
> Singula quaeque locum teneant sortita decenter.
> Interdum tamen et vocem comoedia tollit,
> Iratusque Chremes tumido delitigat ore;
> Et tragicus plerumque dolet sermone pedestri.

When, accordingly, he calls his great poem a comedy, he wishes to indicate to us, with Horace in mind, that it belongs neither to the solemn and high nor to the low style, but to the middle one. For the rest, he took his definition of comedy from the *Magnae Derivationes* of Uguccione of Pisa. The choice of the title "Comedy" is, then, an evidence of the artistic modesty and self-knowledge of Dante, an indication of the depth to which Horace's teaching had sunk into Dante's conscience. How this modesty is associated with the highest realization of the difficulty and the magnitude of the poet's artistic mission may be seen from the words: "But to have discretion and caution as is fitting—'that

[1] C. M. Wieland, *Horazens Briefe*, II, 209.

[2] *De vulgari Eloquentia*, II, 4.

is the task, that is the labour;' for it can never come to pass without strenuous mental effort, devotion to art, and mastery of science. . . . So should be refuted the folly of those who, without a trace of art or science, trusting in their natural ability alone, break forth with the highest themes in the highest styles."

To such clarity and purity of art and stylistic consciousness, Dante, with the aid of Horace, had worked his way. At the point where his *De vulgari Eloquentia* breaks off, and his *Convivio* is laid aside, about 1305–1308, he has become by study, will, inclination, and taste a friend and student of the ancient classics.

They and their like, he cries enthusiastically, the poets in whom art and science are united with genius, are the only ones to whom the other world lies open. It was they that the poet of the *Aeneid* had in mind when in his sixth book he speaks through the mouth of his Sibyl:

> Tros Anchisiade, facilis descensus Averni—
> noctes atque dies patet atri ianua Ditis—
> sed revocare gradum superasque evadere ad auras,
> hoc opus, hic labor est. Pauci quos aequus amavit
> Juppiter, aut ardens evexit ad aethera virtus,
> dis geniti potuere.

The circle is about to close. Through the school of pure form and of classic poetry, Dante's spirit struggles back to his Christian subject of the Hereafter.

While he is still busy with Horace over the rules of poetry, the old dream of his youth returns once more: the *descensus Averni*. And a new guide, Virgil, offers himself.

STATIUS, VIRGIL, AND DANTE

Though Dante early became acquainted with Virgil's poetry, yet he first mastered its symbolic value in the *Convivio* and its formal beauty in the *De vulgari Eloquentia*. It was in the mirror of Virgil's imitators, Ovid, Lucan, and Statius, that the art of the master first appeared to him in its serene majesty.

Statius

The closest and most conscientious of those imitators is Papinius Statius. At the close of the *Thebaid*, he says to his own poem:

> Live, I pray: nor yet draw nigh to the holy *Aeneid;*
> Follow her, rather, afar, and always worship her footprints.

And it is also as a follower of Virgil, in the widest sense of the word, that he appears in the *Commedia*.[1]

> "Statius the people name me still on earth;
> I sang of Thebes, and then of great Achilles;
> But on the way fell with my second burden.
> The seeds unto my ardour were the sparks
> Of that celestial flame which heated me,
> Whereby more than a thousand have been fired;
> Of the *Aeneid* speak I, which to me
> A mother was, and was my nurse in song;
> Without this weighed I not a drachma's weight.
> And to have lived upon the earth what time
> Virgilius lived, I would accept one sun
> More than I must ere issuing from my ban."

But the real Statius was not so modest an imitator and faithful shadow of Virgil. It is in his *Silvae*, which were unknown to Dante, that his strength lies. There we have a truly Neapolitan art: effervescent, exuberant, sometimes serious, sometimes gracefully elaborated, essentially decorative, but extremely vivid. Statius is the Cavaliere Marini of antiquity; half baroque, half rococo. He lacks the capacity for great constructive poems. He is a light, lively, quickly heated, quickly chilled, talented improviser, capable of surprising his reader, on a festal occasion, with a lovely jewel of Hellenic quality; full of charming, humorous fancies, and inexhaustible in grotesque and venturesome inventions; a poet born for festivals and pageants, not slowly creative, but bounteously productive.

When he, then, against his nature and in misguided ambition, like Marini, forced himself to year-long labor upon a great mystic epic—what could come of it but a rough, theatrical monstrosity? As no central poetic idea was accorded him, he was compelled to borrow the entire structure of his *Thebaid* from the *Aeneid*, and could only hope to excel his model by terrible exaggerations and through the abundance of bold fanciful details. And, in fact, his details are not lacking in brilliant, exciting, absorbing, moving, grotesque, and powerful episodes.

Such great baroque pageants Dante could utilize excellently in his *Inferno*. There the distorted gigantic shapes and ugly demoniacal faces of the *Thebaid* are in their proper place. Indeed it is

[1] *Purgatorio*, XXI, 91–102.

in a Christian Hell that these massive Michelangelesque limbs and bodies acquire a fitting soul. The entrance into the city of fire, with its lively dramatic swing, is filled with reminiscences of the *Thebaid*. The furies who rise on the battlements are like Statius's Tisiphone.[1]

> Centum illi stantes umbrabant ora cerastae,
> Turba minor diri capitis: sedes intus abactis
> Ferrea lux oculis, qualis per nubila Phoebes
> Atracia rubet arte labor: suffusa veneno
> Tenditur, ac sanie gliscit cutis: igneus atro
> Ore vapor; quo longa sitis, morbique, famesque,
> Et populi mors una venit, riget horrida tergo
> Palla, et cerulei redeunt in pectore nodi.
> Atropos hos, atque ipsa novat Proserpina cultus.
> Tum geminas quatit illa manus. Haec igne rogali
> Fulgurat, haec vivo manus aera verberat hydro.

The manner also in which the heavenly messenger works his way through the thick air of the Inferno reminds us somewhat of Mercury's journey to Hell in Statius' poem.[2]

To be sure, the violent and stirring scenes of Statius have not had a clarifying and purifying influence upon the imagination of our poet, as the calm sensuousness and picturesqueness of Ovid and Lucan did; they matured and enriched much, but changed and determined little. They live on, in their own fashion, in the soul of Dante, as if on kindred soil. So the poet of the *Commedia*, if he does not wish to be a mere copyist, can only use them allusively, and in much abbreviated form. We find the *Thebaid* and the *Achilleid* in the *Commedia* almost solely in the form of reminiscences and allusions, but almost never as a model. In really naïve fashion the poet takes it for granted that his reader can recall Statius's finest scenes, and by this supposition saves himself the task of elaborating his own pictures more completely. Thus, for example, he utilizes Statius as his poetic collaborator in the verses:

> "Who is within that fire, which comes so cleft
> At top, it seems uprising from the pyre
> Where was Eteocles with his brother placed?"[3]

[1] *Inferno*, IX, 37 sqq., and *Thebaid*, I, 103 sqq.
[2] *Inferno*, IX, 82 sqq., and *Thebaid*, II, 2 sqq.
[3] *Inferno*, XXVI, 52–54, and *Thebaid*, XII, 429 sqq.

Or:

> "The same that in the sadness of Lycurgus
> Two sons became, their mother re-beholding,
> Such I became, but rise not to such height." [1]

Or:

> Not in another fashion Tydeus gnawed
> The temples of Menalippus in disdain.[2]

Or:

> Not otherwise Achilles started up,
> Around him turning his awakened eyes,
> And knowing not the place in which he was.[3]

The greatest and most powerful element of the *Thebaid* is the plot. This, however, belongs to the Greeks. Statius gave it a bombastic, circumstantial, and pretentious form. It is only in the powerful abbreviations of Dante that the ancient greatness of the Theban myth is once more revealed. The most brilliant example of this is Capaneus, whose insolence, told in twenty verses of the *Inferno*, makes a deeper impression on us, to put it mildly, than as related in fifty lines of the *Thebaid.*[4]

There is no one of his favourite epic poets with whom Dante took more arbitrary freedom than with Statius. Not one has he so often used as material and so rarely as form, from none has he accepted so many motifs and so little style. How intensely he is interested in the ethical significance of Statius's narratives is to be seen from the citations in the *Convivio* (IV, 25). In fact, the Theban legend is much more ethical and religious than the motley fables of the *Metamorphoses* or the martial scenes of the *Pharsalia.* This eternal content, which consists more in the tale itself than in its rhetorical and fantastic recasting, has naturally been accredited by Dante, not to its original "sources," but to Statius himself. So this thoughtless versifier who more than almost any other exploited pious and popular conceptions for purely ornamental purposes, is regarded by Dante as a profound and orthodox poet. If those spectacular scenes of the *Thebaid* where the powers of Olympus and of the underworld, together with a motley throng of personifications, crowd the stage, were dissolved

[1] *Purgatorio*, XXVI, 94–96, and *Thebaid*, V, 721 sqq.
[2] *Inferno*, XXXII, 130 sqq., and *Thebaid*, VIII, 739 sqq.
[3] *Purgatorio*, IX, 34–36, and *Achilleid*, I, 247 sqq. For similar parallels cf. *Inferno*, XX, 31 sqq., and *Thebaid*, VIII, 84 sqq.; *Purgatorio*, XVIII, 91–93, and *Thebaid*, IX, 434 sqq.
[4] Cf. *Inferno*, XIV, 46–66, and *Thebaid*, X, 897–939.

into allegory, or, in mediæval fashion, interpreted spiritually, then the clever technician could not but be regarded as of a truly religious nature. If the works of Statius had not given Christian readers the impression of piety, Dante would hardly have permitted himself to make Statius a Christian and to assign him a leading rôle in his *Purgatorio*.

The Virgil of Dante

This statement is not intended to deny that the Statius symbol is primarily conditioned and determined by the Virgil symbol. This is expressed clearly enough in the words of the grateful Statius to his master Virgil:

> . . . "Thou first directedst me
> Towards Parnassus, in its grots to drink,
> And first concerning God didst me enlighten.
> Thou didst as he who walketh in the night,
> Who bears his light behind, which helps him not,
> But wary makes the persons after him,
> When thou didst say: 'The age renews itself,
> Justice returns, and man's primæval time,
> And a new progeny descends from heaven.'
> Through thee I Poet was, through thee a Christian." [1]

It is the famous fourth eclogue—to which had been given, even in later antiquity, a Christian interpretation—that is supposed to have guided Statius to Christianity:

> Ultima Cumaei venit jam carminis aetas:
> Magnus ab integro saeclorum nascitur ordo.
> Jam redit et Virgo, redeunt Saturnia regna:
> Jam nova progenies coelo demittitur alto.
> Tu modo nascenti puero, quo ferrea primum
> Desinet ac toto surget gens aurea mundo,
> Casta, fave, Lucina: tuus jam regnat Apollo.

Virgil, however, did not himself know exactly what he was prophesying. Like all great poets, Dante declares, he is as a man who, walking in the twilight of a dream, carries on his back the torch of eternal truth. This most comprehensive and profoundest conception of the value of poetry was founded by Dante upon the historical example of Virgil. Here the quotation from the fourth eclogue becomes associated with the one from the *Aeneid*, VI, 126 sqq.

[1] *Purgatorio*, XXII, 64–73.

This latter passage, as interpreted in the *De vulgari Eloquentia*, would mean that only the complete, artistic, matured poetic genius can find his way securely, because favoured by the Divinity, through the mysteries of the nether world. The former passage, from the way it is treated in the *Purgatorio*, is to signify that in the poet's visionary creation, without his knowing it, eternal Truth is mirrored. This profound, ever-youthful conception of the poet's art is for Dante a desire, not a doctrine; a living faith, not a settled dogma; it is the artist's religion, not his philosophy. And he who fulfills this wish, the confirmer of this faith, the high priest of this religion, is Virgil. He is the complete artist, the exemplar of perfection, God's favourite, the safe guide through the night of Hell, and the unconscious herald of the Christian day. This is in truth the symbolic significance of Virgil, which completely coincides, in Dante's belief, with the historic Virgil. The Virgilio of the *Commedia* is not what he should have been historically, but what he actually was, and to all eternity remains. In his transfer out of history into the *Commedia*, it is not he, but only his environment, that is changed. He lives, moves, and acts, in this new, poetically created world, as he must in accordance with his historical character. He cannot otherwise. This simple fact ends the whole quarrelsome discussion over the allegory of Virgil.

Now since Virgilius and Virgilio are for Dante one and the same, nothing remains save the question: Are they so for us? How far does the present-day conception and valuation of Virgil coincide with Dante's? To what extent is Virgil, for us also, still the embodiment of the perfect poet?

He is no longer that for us. For, in the meantime, we have come to know Homer, Aeschylus, Cervantes, Shakespeare, Goethe, and—Dante: far more lofty poetic peaks, which the growing artist of the *Commedia* had not known. Within that literary horizon, however, which Dante could survey, Virgil does indeed remain, in the judgment of our day, the most gifted, the most nearly perfect, of poets. Accordingly, our different appraisal is due to a change in time, not in principle. Hence the practical side, the motives and purposes of Virgil's poem, are judged by us in an essentially different fashion.

We no longer believe that the fourth eclogue refers to Christ's birth. We know that it announces, in an emphatic form, merely a wish, no supernatural truth. We know, further, that allegorical explanation of the moral and political content of the *Aeneid* is an essentially mediæval and dogmatic practice; that Virgil never, either in science or in actual life, could or did assert authoritative power; that, in short, he is a poet, nothing but a poet. For that very reason he always set forth all human ideals or values as simply feeling, desire, and premonition, never in the compulsory form of a doctrine, a command, or a system. It is dogmatism that distinguishes Dante's Virgil, in science as in poetry, from our Virgil.

Thanks to this conception, it comes to pass that Virgil in the *Commedia* sometimes hardens into embodied authority, and acts not like a human being, but as incarnate, universal Reason. What conceals the real Virgil from us in such passages is, however, no deeply buried mystery, but simply the prejudice of mediæval dogmatism.

Apart from that, the Dantesque Virgil is even today, in all essential points, ours as well. We have, to be sure, more biographical and bibliographical knowledge concerning him, but still if we were to characterize him, our present representation, our picture of his soul and of his mind as we see them, the portrait or monument that we still have before us, coincides in most remarkable fashion with the Dantesque Virgil: an evidence how profoundly, how clearly, how objectively, Dante conceived his rôle, how successfully, in a wholly different world, under imaginative conditions, he restored him to his old self-consistent living form. The Virgil of the *Commedia* is one of the noblest achievements of what we call historical poetry, uniting the utmost freedom in externals with inmost truth and objectivity.

Inner truth and objectivity are always an idealization of the subject, not in the sense of glossing over or concealing what is defective or incidental, but in the sense of developing the incidental into the essential, and the defective and multiform into a unity. In this sense only did Dante, as a poet, idealize Virgil. It is the same sense in which the critical historian also must idealize him—only that the poet proceeded by vision and anticipation, while we as historians must also test analytically and reflectively what is envisaged and imagined.

What Dante so marvellously united in the character of Virgil—the gentle, lovable, feminine, and dreamy traits, with the firm, shrewd, calm, and manly sense of justice and truth—all this we must dissect bit by bit and see how it was put together.

The Historical Virgil

Virgil was by nature a shy, almost maidenly and timid creature, helpless in practical life. He loved books and the quiet landscape of his homeland, suffered severely in the storms of civil war, and could not feel at ease in boisterous society. He was of a contemplative nature, and had only two passions: versifying and philosophic study, dreaming and thinking. But he was granted the privilege of shunning the world without hatred. His incapacity for active life did not embitter him against mankind. On the contrary, he watched that life for which he was so ill fitted with a sort of joyous curiosity. The idyllic, elegiac, and satirical poets of the imperial age are wont to rival each other in railing against Rome, the world-city, and the metropolitan life, while Virgil, who probably found that life harder to endure than they, had an open heart and eye for the greatness of the imperial city. The others with an aristocratic and contemptuous gesture turned away from politics, but Virgil, the most unpolitical of men, became the ardent singer of Roman national feeling. Toward the practical world he is like a child who is taken to the theatre for the first time, and who attentively, seriously, eagerly, and excitedly gives himself up to these new impressions. The most prosaic things are to him picturesque; farming, cattle-raising, bee-culture, all that lives, earth, plants, beasts, humanity and spirit, he embraces with the naïve affection of a Goethe. And as these childlike, primitive friends of Nature are wont to do, Virgil moves from simple observation of all things to scientific inquiry into their causes. The poet becomes of himself a natural philosopher. To comprehend the cosmos in its unity and necessity becomes the need and the employment of his spirit. An intellect that is determined to see things as they really are, and not otherwise, we must characterize as thoroughly masculine. A timid creature in conduct, Virgil is mature and manly in intellect. As he withdrew, so far as possible, from action, as he avoided entanglement in worldly affairs, his most prominent moral quality is innocence, purity; his greatest fault is helplessness, weakness. This Dante also saw, but in an ingenious fashion he made up for this lack of force and initiative. He provided his Virgil, on the dangerous journey through Hell, with supernatural authority, and so released the gentle and peaceful man from the necessity of struggling with monsters and sinners. Behind the pure nature of Virgil he put the Almighty with His power and His victory, long before ordained.

Dante's Virgil needed a strong arm for escape, not for attack.[1] His judgment, however, had to be all the more self-reliant, that he might not be distracted by all the horrors of Hell and might be able to explain to his pupil with calm objectivity even the most terrific storms.

In fact, it is remarkable how the contemplative eye of this gentle character was drawn to the sternest aspects of human life. Can one imagine a more toilsome labour, one of more difficult renunciation, than the crushing world-historical life-task of Aeneas? And how austere and virile is the poet's philosophy of the world! Stoic fatalism, yet not weakened by renunciation and pessimism, full of hearty confidence and unswerving acceptance of life. If one wished to analyze the *Aeneid* philosophically, it would reveal something like a kinship to Spinoza.

No space is left within such a naturalistic and deterministic philosophy for freedom of spirit and for individual action. In such a world, man is but a part of Nature, and passive. There are no heroes, but only instruments, sacrifices and fulfillers of destiny, which is its own purpose and end. That this destiny is kindly disposed toward us mortals can indeed be believed, wished, and hoped for, but not known or proved. So Virgil's intellectualism overleaps itself, and ends in religious mysticism.

This, too, Dante saw. His Virgil yearns for the world of the freed spirit; he hopes for it, he believes in it, but cannot comprehend it, cannot realize it in himself. On account of this inward helplessness, that hope which in life he had, and was justified in having, is blasted in the Christian Hereafter.

> " For such defects, and not for other guilt,
> Lost are we, and are only so far punished,
> That without hope we live on in desire. "[2]

Ill-founded optimism, as soon as the veil is dropped from things, is transformed into elegiac resignation. The mood is changed, but the man and his philosophy of life remain unaltered.

So the historic Virgil is immortalized and glorified, fully appreciated and properly judged, in the *Commedia*.

Dante approached Virgil with boundless love, studied him,

[1] *Inferno*, XXIII, 37 sqq.

[2] *Inferno*, IV, 40–42.

learned his *Aeneid* by heart, came to know the soul of the poet and of the poem, assimilated them—and surpassed them. When he wrote the *Commedia*, he was done with Virgil.[1]

The Influence of Virgil

Whoever follows through the *Commedia* the traces of the *Aeneid* can convince himself of this at every step.

In the *Aeneid* a highly concrete goal is assigned to inscrutable fate, namely, the founding of Roman world-rule. Aeneas is he who fulfills the divine will. At first only an awkward and easily distracted servant of the Divinity, he becomes with time ever more subservient, or if one prefers, ever more resolute: ever weaker in his relation to God, ever stronger toward men. He gradually develops and purifies himself, not as a character, but as an instrument. The true goal is not man, but the Roman empire. Hence the official, nationally religious, impersonal, and solemn style of the entire epic. Dante called this solemn style the tragic. That it was not applicable to his *Commedia* he felt and knew. With him the ultimate goal is the soul of man. Subordinated, and in the service of this soul and its salvation, stand the Roman world-monarchy and the Church. The freer man is, the more superfluous are these educational institutions. Hence the personal, stirring, dramatic style of the *Commedia*, which finally encroaches on all literary types.

The suffering and joy of man are for Dante unique, precious elements of our soul's history; for Virgil they are general, natural phenomena. Hence Dante makes us experience all things potentially and in act, while Virgil describes them neutrally. So the Virgilian expression, "Then first grim terror girt me round about," becomes in Dante: "And I who had my head with horror girt"; and the elaborately depicted feeling:

> Chill horror makes me shake in all my limbs,
> And in my terror curdled is my blood,

or again:

> Then was I stupefied, my hair rose up,
> My voice stuck in my throat,

becomes a brief, intensive impression and experience: "I stood as doth a man that is in fear."

[1] The interchange of eclogues with the grammarian Giovanni del Virgilio is only the epilogue to, not a renewal of, his Virgilian studies.

What a difference between Dido, whose passion, like a disease, runs with all its typical symptoms to the fatal issue, and Francesca, whose love is her whole life, giving her for the first time reality and individuality! That by which Francesca lives destroys Dido.

Even so is it with truth and science. For Virgil the natural need is joy, enjoyment, love-making, splendour, and luxury. After the banquet is over, the beaker yet in hand for the guests' enjoyment, natural science in the garb of poesy is bidden to Dido's royal table:

> Cithara crinitus Iopas
> Personat aurata, docuitque quae maximus Atlas.
> Hic canit errantem Lunam, Solisque labores;
> Unde hominum genus et pecudes; unde imber et ignes;
> Arcturum, pluviasque Hyadas, geminosque Triones;
> Quid tantum Oceano properent se tinguere soles
> Hiberni, vel quae tardis mora noctibus obstet.—
> Ingeminant plausu Tyrii, Troesque sequuntur.

Dante, on impassable paths, at the edge of the abyss, in the Heavenly sea of light, makes scientific inquiries; and in vague, laborious, wearisome words the reply is given. To him knowledge is a necessity, a labour, a struggle. Hence he does not present it in finished speech, but as a drama of thought, as dialectic victory over doubt and error.

It is not true that Aeneas descends to the underworld to seek truth. What, indeed, are all the obstacles which Aeneas has to overcome other than mischances and the caprices of an imperious and angry woman, Juno? The whole plan of the *Aeneid* is essentially irrational; everything that occurs, from the destruction of Troy to the conquest of Latium, is episodic. In order to give an inward connection to these accidents, the most masterful technique was required. It is characteristic, and at the same time decisive, for the relatively small poetic value of the *Aeneid*, that the problem of technique stands in the foreground. Richard Heinze, in his *Virgils epische Technik*, investigated the technique in all its details, and taught us to regard the entire poem as a model example of the finest study in balances. The ethico-political idea of Roman greatness is embodied, he tells us, in a fabulous world whose nature is purely æsthetic. The æsthetic standard is Homer and the natural grace of the Greeks; and the ethical one is the dignity of the Roman. So far as this difficult calculation, this squaring of the circle, could be worked out, Virgil accomplished his task.

In the *Commedia* the technical element does not stand in the foreground, but behind the poetry, like machinery behind the scenes. Dante also has, to be sure, his definite problem, and this is, as we remember, to embody the supersensuous Christian world in physical and worldly forms. But for him this problem is no squaring of the circle, no technical question, but a labour of love. For with all the fibres of his being, he must and will have his Heaven and Hell in flesh and blood, yes, whether he wants to or not, he bears the Hereafter—Eternity—in his mortal breast and already possesses in spirit what he would fain express in words.

Hence all technique is for him a secondary, subordinate consideration.

The careful polishing and adjustment of parts Dante learned from Virgil. Almost everything that he learned in this connection he owes to him. In particular the sixth book of the *Aeneid*, the Nekyia, was constantly before his eyes. It has been shown by careful investigation how many extremely clever and artistic devices he derived from this source and utilized especially at the entrance of the *Inferno* and *Purgatorio*.

Aeneas's journey to Hades, as Virgil relates it, became fundamental not only for the *Commedia*, but for the entire history of the poetry of the Hereafter. Thanks to this intimate relation to the *Commedia*, it may actually be regarded as a stage in the development of apocalyptic literature, the history of which we have briefly related. Here for the first time the purely fabulous character of the ancient journeys into Hades is enriched with new and philosophic elements. The sixth book of the *Aeneid* marks the point where pagan eschatology verges on the Hellenic-Christian beliefs. It gave, on the other hand, an opportunity for Dante to re-introduce classical myths and forms into his Christian Hereafter. Whatever is inconsistent, and only with difficulty united, in Virgil's underworld—Greek fable and Stoic morality, sensuous form and supersensuous ethos—unites easily, in a new spirit, in the *Commedia*. Virgil's nether world attains its purification and revival in the Hereafter of Dante. One is reminded of the verses:

Has omnis, ubi mille rotam volvere per annos,
Lethaeum ad fluvium deus evocat agmine magno,
Scilicet immemores super ut convexa revisant,
Rursus et incipiant in corpora velle reverti.[1]

But if the technical problem was wholly different for Virgil than for Dante, how could the one learn from the other? The journey to Hades in the *Aeneid* is a diverting, adventurous fable which must acquire its value and dignity through its subordination to the divine plan and to the ethico-political purpose of the whole poem. Dante's pilgrimage to the other world is an experience that has its value in itself. Certainly; and yet the two pilgrimages have a large area in common, namely, the practical goal, the ethico-political ideal: Rome and the emperor. Roman hierarchy, the idea of Roman unity and sovereignty, is the common principle in the technical construction.

That Rome which Aeneas had founded in the body, Dante creates in spirit. Only in so far as he wished to write not a Christian and religious, but an ethico-political, Roman Catholic poem did Dante need Virgil's art. Order, harmony, symmetry, are its essence. In Virgil the structure is cleverly concealed and overgrown with the blossoms of legend. Dante set it forth mightily in its constructive nakedness. That which in the *Vita Nuova* was still childish, mystical playing with the symbolism of numbers, is now, in the school of Virgil, serious, artistic thought.

And not only order in the larger sense, not only the feeling for unity and completeness, does Dante owe to Virgil; but the harmony of periods and sentences he also learned from him.

Thou art my master, and my author thou:
Thou art alone the one from whom I took
The beautiful style that has done honour to me.

With all the diversity of their poetic spirit, there is a common ethos in the language of the two: the dignity, the majestic calm and clarity, the mild warmth, the *gravitas romana* and the *pietas romana*.

And all this Dante owes to his intense love and his Latin descent. "Our divine poet! Our seer!" so he calls Virgil in his political

[1] *Aeneid*, VI, 748–751.

question the usefulness and justification of this effort. For the *Commedia* is in some sense a poem of its day. Indeed everything that man creates is cut after a special pattern. Yet I hardly know of a piece of work of which this is less true than of the *Commedia.* In the present stage of our investigation, we have no positive evidence by which to determine absolutely and beyond question the date of composition of the *Commedia* and of its several cantos.[1] As long as we lack definite documentary evidence, I must cling to my subjective chronology.

This is founded, in the last analysis, upon an artistic judgment of values, that is, upon my conviction as to the strict unity of the entire *Commedia.*

The value of a work of art does not offer any conclusive data as to the time of its creation, but the success of a work of art cannot be thought of as independent of its creator's workmanship.

[1] The various attempts contradict and mutually refute each other. It was recently believed that in the *Memoriali* of the Bolognese notaries, in a document of the year 1314, the famous verses of the *Inferno,* III, 94–96, were quoted. But closer study indicates that they are in a different hand, and were probably written in a vacant space at some later date.

V: THE POETRY OF THE "DIVINE COMEDY"

1. The Cultural Value of the "Commedia"

We have now studied Dante's work in its historical conditions, and have traced it to its "sources." To the advancement of piety, of science, and of the life of the intellect in general, the *Commedia* did not contribute, directly, anything of essential importance. We found its significance, not in what it brought, but in what it is; not in the creation of new controlling cultural values, but in a unique personal assimilation of the fundamental ideals of religion, philosophy, and practical life which the Middle Ages had evolved up to that time. The *Commedia* is not a factor but a symptom; not a lever, but a mirror, of culture.

Only indirectly, in so far as the symptom can become a factor and the mirror a tool, only in so far as the exposition of the old is itself something new, and the interpreter of culture is also a leader, may the *Commedia* claim cultural value. This value, which lies in the delineation, in the utterance, in the expression, is essentially æsthetic. As a work of art, and only as a work of art, the *Commedia* is original; only in the evolution of art did it create anything new, namely, the mastery and adjustment of the two imperfect mediæval styles: apocalyptics and allegory.

We must abandon the theory which would fain discover in the *Divine Comedy* a gospel, a program, anything better and more useful than mere poetry. The misguided industry of certain enthusiasts that makes Rembrandt an educator, Goethe the founder of a religion, and Dante an apostle, does its great men a dubious service. For the mightiest works of the human spirit are the pure, not the mongrel—works of *pure* art, of *pure* science, of *pure* will; and it is in their purity that they must be evaluated. The man of genius is never a factotum, but with all his universality, a specialist. Dante is no poet-philosopher, poet-theologian, or poet-moralist, in the sense of vacillation between philosophy, theology, or morality and poetry. He is no poet-philosopher of the incomplete, but of completeness, inasmuch as his whole philosophy, his whole religion, yes, his whole personality, come to their full development only in poetry and only through poetry.

2. The "Commedia" as a Work of Art

It is time, therefore, for us to forget altogether Dante's faith, knowledge, will, and power as we have heretofore depicted them, that is, in their evolution; and to discover them again in a new form, that is, as free, self-determined poetic action. For such action of the poetic spirit, it is not a vital question when, where, or through whom it was actually brought about, whether it is to be accredited to mediævalism or the Renaissance, to Guelfs or Ghibellines, to scholasticism or mysticism, to Dante's middle age or youth, or indeed to that Dante at all; for now everything depends upon this: whether it was accomplished, and whether it has its law, its environment, its fulcrum, within itself, and not merely outside in those circumstances, opinions, events, and models which we have endeavoured, up to this time, to enumerate.

We have already decided the question of the artistic value of the *Commedia* in the affirmative when we discuss its cultural foundations and relations. But an anticipatory decision, based merely upon the general reputation of the *Divine Comedy*, is still far from being a consistent critical appraisal.

Many and contradictory answers have been given to the question of the poetic value of the *Divine Comedy;* these answers we have no space to discuss in detail here. We shall attempt only to classify in convenient form their different points of view.

Some appeal to Dante himself and declare his *Commedia* to be a great ethico-religious and philosophically didactic poem in which the human content is the essential, and the artistic form, with all its force and beauty, the subordinate element. This attitude is taken chiefly by mediæval students and, in modern times, by readers and critics with Catholic or in general Christian leanings, and we are indebted to them in detail for an abundance of objective explanations and opinions, although their point of view cannot be regarded as that of art-criticism in the strictest sense.

It required the victorious assault of modern æsthetics to give us the courage to pass beyond the powerful content, to focus our attention on the artistic form of the great poem of humanity, and to seek the root of its value in the imaginative element. Only now can the question as to the power or effectiveness of this imaginative quality be raised; and two typical views shape themselves with increasing clearness between which, even today, Dante criticism swings: the romantic and the classic view.

According to the first, the supreme beauty is to be found in the wedding and mingling of Dante's fantastic world with real life; and in the union of faith and poetry, of work and personality, of actual experience and future anticipations, that unity is to be discovered which culminates in an infinite harmony of the ego and the non-ego, and which is, therefore, not specifically artistic, but absolutely spiritual. The judgment of romantic criticism is, then, that the *Commedia* does harbour within itself a series of discrepancies or dissonances, yet that these are not to be deplored but rather admired and revered, and are to be understood as deficiencies of Dante's generation, or of human existence in general, and are to find their solution in eternity. Such a solution outside of and beyond the finished work of art implies that the poetic activity, the imagination, can overstep its proper task, and can create poetic associations and harmonies where naked reality holds sway. In fact, romantic æsthetics endeavours to poetize the universe, and takes especial delight in those poets who let their imagination run, so to speak, beyond the edge of their paper. Thus, one of its most important representatives, Francesco de Sanctis, has seen and honoured in Dante the poet *malgré lui*, who, against and in spite of his own plan and theory of art, has been carried away by the guardian angel of poetry.

Classical criticism, on the contrary, keeps in mind the gap between poetry and "reality." It was for a long time unable to assume any helpful attitude toward Dante's *Commedia*, which seemed to it to suffer all too directly from the hardness and narrowness of mediæval life. Even today, after it has given up its formalism and dogmatism in the course of long contests with the romantic theory, and is ready to judge every work of art by its own particular inspiration or idea, it can still have no hearty sympathy with Dante; for it cannot throw overboard nor limit, even in deference to the greatest genius, the general fundamental conception of art as a creative, intuitive activity.

But how, since it is perfectly evident that Dante's cosmic picture, in particular his geography and cosmology, and to a great extent his theory of sin and virtue also, were not created intuitively, but in part logically deduced, in part established empirically, in part accepted and learned scholastically—how can there be any talk here of imagination and poetry? Here there seems to be a discordance between the structure of the poem, which is essentially prosaic, and the free unfolding of Dante's imagination and inspiration, which are essentially poetic and lyrical. The most important representative of classical æsthetics, Benedetto Croce, in his *Poetry of Dante*, sees no escape out of these difficulties, "except to distinguish sharply between construction and poetry in the *Commedia*, to associate closely philosophy and morality, and to regard them consequently as necessities of Dante's mind, but to refrain carefully from assuming any relation of a truly poetic character between them. Only in this fashion," he declares, "can the poetry of the *Commedia* be deeply and perfectly enjoyed, its construction be made acceptable, with some indifference perhaps, but without any aversion, and surely without any scorn."

This mode of escape seems to me impracticable, for if the structure is indeed unpoetic, that is, poetically defective, then criticism, in the presence of a great and austere master like Dante, cannot permit itself to ignore it. It does him higher honour, that is, accords him justice, if it blames or even scoffs. We have no right to gloss it over and to treat the frame of the *Commedia*, of its dogmatic armour, of its philosophic structure, like a "theological romance" or like the libretto of an opera, which is merely the thread that holds together, well or ill, the pearls of resonant poetry.

Nevertheless, I believe that the classical theory of art alone is capable of solving the critical problem in its present-day form. For romantic criticism has given us absolutely all it could. This can be perceived from the fact that it faces the *Commedia* with unfailing approval, indeed with utterly blind reverence and deification, inasmuch as it constructs—as, for example, in H. Hefele's *Dante*—partly from the work, partly from Dante's life, an ideal figure of a poet, and canonizes the master in his work, the work in its master. Before such a process of sanctification, literary criticism has nothing more to say.

3. The Construction

The construction of the *Commedia*, regarded in and for itself, and judged in accordance with present-day ideals, is essentially dogmatic. But for us the question is whether it is so intended within the *Commedia* itself. Dogmatic arrangement and plan characterized the great theologians, from the apostle Paul down to Thomas Aquinas, for they wished to defend, strengthen, and disseminate their Christian belief. The *Divine Comedy*, however, is evidently intended to convert no heathen, to refute no heretic, to convince no doubter, to contend with no scoffer, to carry on no battle for the faith. Here and there polemic and didactic intentions emerge from it, but they run their course, one and all, within the Christian community, and never is there to be noted an assault or sally against the heathen. There is not even a rallying-cry for a crusade against Islam.

In a future life, where every dispute as to belief is fundamentally, finally, and victoriously settled, dogmatism can serve only for exposition, and can have only representative significance. It does actually figure at once as foundation, support, and decoration for the realms of the Hereafter, as background or scenery, and is therefore within the *Commedia*, in its intention, no theological, ecclesiastical, or philosophical, but an essentially æsthetic, element, and cannot, therefore, be ignored or mentally omitted from the poem as something unpoetic, or only half poetic.

To be sure, there may be an unfortunate stiffness, poetic harshness, or technical arbitrariness, in short, a certain incongruity with the impulses of a life and a pilgrimage conducted through the geometric and astronomic realms of fantasy. Let us look more closely.

The poem actually begins with a sort of arbitrary assumption, namely, with the leap from the Here to the Hereafter, or with the dual character of Dante, who is transformed from the born Florentine that he is into the wandering spirit that he would fain be, and, by means of the poem, becomes. This arbitrary assumption, this dualism, is, however, nothing more than the determination to go forth out of himself, to uplift his spirit, to drop everyday tasks, to seize the golden lyre, and to begin this poem.

> Midway upon the journey of our life
> I found myself within a forest dark,
> For the straightforward pathway had been lost.

It is as if in sleep he had gone astray and missed his true path. "Midway upon the journey of life" means, for Dante, as we learn from the *Convivio*, IV, 24, the age of thirty-five years. And the "dark forest," as can be seen from the same passage, betokens the aberrations of our nature, the deviations from the path of virtue and of truth.

The wanderer then, if we take him literally, moves upon two roads at once: upon the natural path of his years, and upon the moral pathway of life. The contradiction is not removed by the fact that the first path is characterized as a route (*cammino*) and the second as a way (*via*): for the road of life does not primarily stand in any visible relation to the way of personality or character. The first runs toward old age or death as its goal, the second toward sin or virtue.

But the further we read and the more we come under the sway of the poetry, the more what seemed to be merely set down and uttered as something foreign reveals itself as the great ethical act of the will, poetically realized: to escape from the dust of earth and rise aloft above self. So, read in the light of the poem as a whole, these opening verses, which, taken by themselves, are not especially effective, become truly "wingéd words."

We must set value on the mighty and, if you will, harsh opening note of the Dantesque *Commedia*, for we are dealing with a poem of the highest ethical and spiritual intensity, not with a pleasant little song. By the upward sweep from the Here to the Hereafter the world of the spirit tears itself loose from earth, and if it is to have a new poetic body of its own, the only connecting links or clamps at the disposal of the architect are at first the abstract aids of numbers, of lines, of mathematics. Out of the dualism brought about by renunciation and flight from the world a new unity must emerge.

So he comes to a divine trinity. The number three is the basic note of his *Commedia*. To the left, Hell; to the right, Paradise; between them, Purgatory; and throughout the whole the chain of the triple rhyme, the *terza rima*, and each of the three chief sections (*cantiche*) is divided into thirty-three cantos, so that the poem consists of ninety-nine cantos, nearly equal in length. An introductory canto, or prologue, completes the tale of one hundred. The fundamental three is connected with the number of the Heavenly spheres: ten. His hundred is made up out of three, ten, and one.

Even if we agree, or concede, that the quantitative units, one, three, and ten, may be derived philosophically or theologically, and, so to speak, are determined *a priori*, that would not suffice to demonstrate that the number of cantos in the *Commedia* must necessarily be one hundred. The poem could just as well consist of ten, three hundred, nine hundred, a thousand, three thousand, or more parts. In short, there remains a certain freedom of choice which it would be hard to eliminate.

Much the same is true as to the construction of the infernal and celestial spaces. We have previously endeavoured to show how Dante could deduce imaginatively the form and arrangement of his *Inferno* and *Purgatorio* from the form and arrangement of the heavens furnished to him by science. In that connection, we did not fail to recall that such a scientific reconstruction of Dante's line of thought can be carried out with only approximate accuracy, never and at no point with absolute certainty.

Within itself, that is, where it is applied, Dante's mathematics is strictly logical. He makes no numerical errors; at least none that are evident. But the application, for instance, the transfer of the symmetry of the heavens to the *Inferno*, is not at all logically imperative; yet it is certainly not capricious. The cause for this arbitrary choice can be sought ultimately only in the mood, in the belief, in the heart, of the poet; "for the heart hath reasons which reason knoweth not," says the pious Pascal. The whole structure stands on the foundation of divine love and justice; the cleverness with which Dante calculates and executes it is not sophistry but reverence. Behind every measurement, every number, we feel a religious conviction of the reality, of the eternal value, sense, and permanence of the spiritual realms so strongly, so consistently, so tenaciously, and so uninterruptedly, that the poet, in the zeal of his visionary faith, hardly distinguishes what was given, taken, and borrowed from Church, dogma, or science from that which was invented by him personally. Not that he permits himself to be deceived by his own fancies, mistakes them for realities, and loses himself in vain imaginings, like those women of Verona who believed that he had been bodily in Hell, but rather that his knowledge becomes vision, his conceptions pictures, and his faith inward sight, and that he, as a naïve, joyous artist, can as little distinguish what he delineates from what he beholds, as the critic who discovers and admires this naïveté of poetic creation.

For that very reason the construction is not to be taken in and for itself, but is intended to be studied and understood in close connection with the action and with the hero of the poem. We cannot any longer concede any independent or hostile juxtaposition of structure and true poetry in the *Commedia*.

4. The Action

If the poet had merely raised an imaginative structure upon a religious foundation, the *Commedia* would have been simply an impressive edifice, and Dante not much more than an ingenious architect and builder—one of the many who could have accomplished the work, which indeed was not original, since the ten heavenly spheres are not his personal invention.

But he actually finds his way through the spaces of this motionless or revolving structure and makes himself the hero of the pilgrimage through the future world, and so the chief, essentially the only, actor. The *Commedia* is in fact a Danteid, although Dante, far from being the sole hero, declares himself dependent, requires a guide and companion, and externally appears rather receptive and passive than active. Inasmuch, however, as all the acts of the various guides, Beatrice, Virgil, Matelda, and Bernard, have reference solely to Dante, he remains, in truth, the chief personage. Where my interests are the primary concern, even though I take no active part, I am the mainspring—that is, under the condition that these interests be actually mine, identical with me. Dante's interest is identical in fact with the most intimate and vital concern of man: the salvation and assertion of his spiritual personality. Therefore, it is he who, through his needs, through his pious desire, through his will for spiritual life, actually endows with existence and activity not only his guides, but indirectly all the minor figures, friends and opponents, devils and angels, indeed even the Divinity itself.

Only the Divinity might be looked upon as the representation of an inner principle independent of Dante. But the God of the *Commedia* is motionless and does not act directly. At any rate, His immediate activity is not evident and reveals itself only as impersonal intervention, as marvel, in thunder, lightning, earthquake, in a form of light, in apparition, vision, and dream. As such marvels come to Dante in every case merely as active aid or as guiding and enlightening revelation, they are actually conditioned and justified by Dante's inmost needs, not by God's. This need which gives to the marvels their justification, their rationality and reality, is Faith. Just because Faith is the favourite child of marvel, therefore Dante, not the Divinity, is its originator, and all the actions of all the characters in the *Commedia* originate in and spring from the inmost activity of the Dante who is the central personage, as poetical figures anticipating the same motif as the whole structure, the entire scenery: that is to say, Dantesque belief, hope, and love, which appear objectively in his vision and its poetic record.

To be sure, the word Dantesque has here a double meaning, and we must not hastily identify Dante the author with Dante the pilgrim or hero. That the author constitutes the unity of his poem is self-evident, and nobody has yet doubted that Dante is the sole creator of the *Commedia.* But this poem can be shown to be a unified piece of work, personal not in the empirical, but in the æsthetic, sense of the word, only if everything else can be understood as being conditioned by the delineation of the hero as the central figure—that is, conditioned poetically and not merely psychologically and historically.

5. The Hero

How is Dante's personality represented in the *Commedia?* It is the only one that remains on the stage from the first to the last verse. All the rest come and go, render service good or bad, essential or incidental, to the central figure. At the close the hero is just as much alone with himself as he was at the beginning. Much has happened, but Dante has still remained Dante. That he has changed essentially, as, for instance, Faust is transformed from a stormy, discontented soul into a deliberate old man and finally into a blessed spirit, no one will seriously assert. If Dante, after he was in Paradise and beheld God, had still had to complete his journey through Hell again, he must have conducted himself there in all respects much as before. And again he must have wept with Francesca, must have been haughty with Farinata, and with the traitors a betrayer.

The objection may be raised that a Dante who has been purified in Purgatory and blest in Paradise could no longer go astray in the forest of sin, fear the wild beasts, or have need of Virgil and Beatrice. That may be philosophically correct. But we move in the world of poesy, and believe, here, only what is poetically evident. Dante's change of feeling is indeed demonstrated in the *Commedia*, even realized, but only externally, only in fable.

This change in Dante's nature is the doctrine, the postulate, the ideal, not the circumstantial and present reality, of the poem. Dante will, should, change; he shows, bit by bit, step by step, how he changes—but he is not changed. He changes, apparently, as a model and example for others; at heart he cannot but remain the same.

In short, the poet has set forth his personality for us monumentally, statically; he has not developed it dynamically. It remains, in the flow of apparitions, an immovable central point. Dante's journey through the other world is a mere show; in reality the other world goes rushing by him, twines about him, enshadows or illuminates him from every side. What moves and develops is not he, but the enshadowing, the illumination, the colouring, the ever new and surprising disclosure of his nature.

Dante's self-knowledge, rather than his alteration, forms the chief subject of the poem. Each part of the *Commedia* reveals a fresh portion of Dante's personality.

It is not true that Dante in the *Inferno* portrays the dark sides, in the *Paradiso* the bright, and in the middle realm, so to speak, the chiaroscuro features, of his true self. No, we have, in each of the three divisions, an entire, undivided Dante. His self-illumination, his self-knowledge, is no analysis, no self-study, which comes gradually, through so and so many fragments, to unity. Were it so, we should have a scientific treatise, or at best, what is called a psychological romance.

The value of Dantesque introspection, however, is not psychological. He who has read the *Inferno* to the end will not be eager for the *Purgatorio* because he hopes to learn something further as to Dante's character, but chiefly in order that he may see what Dante imagines Purgatory to be, what it looks like to him. The interest does not shift from an infernal or heavenly outer world to Dante's ego, but from Dante's ego to the external world.

Now if this were a haphazard, material, and capricious world, for instance, like that external one into which we are born, and to which we must gradually accustom ourselves, then Dante, too, would have changed and developed under its pressure, just as all of us, under the compulsion of life, are ground and polished, made better or worse, wiser or stupider, but never allowed to remain unchanged. The Dante of the *Commedia*, nevertheless, does remain, so it seems to us, like unto himself. This sovereign persistence is possible for him only because the outer world in which he abides is no alien one, but his own inner world, not a fortuitous, but a necessary one; not harsh, but hospitable; not material, but divine; not capricious, but created out of the free spirit of its visitor. To the extent that the Dantesque Hereafter is eternal, changeless, universal, Dante's personality, too, is eternal, unalterable, universal—and vice versa. And just as Dante changes only apparently, as a model and example for others, so the historical, geographical traits and incidents of his Hell, of his Purgatory, of his Paradise, are an apparent, exemplary decoration and background. So closely do construction, action, and hero of the poem harmonize with one another.

Especially in the *Paradiso* it appears that we have to do with two kinds of poetical reality, with an imaginary Heaven, presented picturesquely, as in a dream, and with a real, invisible kingdom of God, existing purely in thought; that is, with a Paradise seen and a Paradise striven for. Whether, and how far, this dualism, or division of the poem into fable and moral, into apparition and aspiration, exists also in the *Purgatorio* and in the *Inferno*, will appear later. First it is all important to point out how this discord is nothing more than a counterpart of the hero himself: Dante as he is, and will be throughout the entire poem, by virtue of his faith, hope, and love. The poem immortalizes, fixes, and glorifies him in his individuality and sets before us at the same time his changed nature, purification, and apotheosis. From the stress of this contradiction the poetic life flows. For how else should a spiritual personality acquire life, in poetry as well as in truth, except through the effort of uniting that which is with that which is to be? Since the whole journey through the next world lasts only for a brief span of earthly time, approximately Easter week, yet runs meantime into Eternity, no space remains for the delineation of an actual, effective change of nature. It is an essential of the whole plot that only an inward spiritual effort, no actual, tangible transformation in the figure of the hero, comes to expression. In short, the temporal as well as the spatial construction is in fundamental harmony with the central motif of the poem, that is, with the self-delineation of Dante as a spiritual personality.

It is only in the execution that inconsistencies might here and there occur. If we wish to be quite clear as to these possibilities, we must go over the entire *Commedia*, step by step, examining and testing each detail. If in so doing we limit ourselves to the study of the inner forms and ignore the Italian linguistic expression, this is merely because we are appealing to readers of an alien speech, not because we regard the externals (which in poetry are among the essentials) as of minor importance. On the contrary, the critical evaluation of Dante's language demands an exhaustive treatment by itself.

6. The "Inferno"

THE STAGE SETTING OF HELL

If in Heaven pure and appropriate form has its abode, no completely lawless unfitness and lack of form rules in Hell; for Hell also is a divinely ordained world. But the aberrations from law and form do attain there their maximum.

The earthly sphere is the incomplete and concrete likeness of the heavenly sphere, a form filled out with matter in a fortuitous fashion, an irregular sphere whose outer surface is determined by Heaven, its content by the material.

Since Heaven is the realm of form, and Hell the realm of matter, Hell has its place in the interior of the earthly sphere, indeed in its inmost centre.

This centre, as the abode of the absolutely material, is just as extreme and abstract as spacelessness, regarded as the abode of absolute form.

The stage of the *Commedia* lies between the outmost limits of the divine and of the infernal world. The Inferno is the most dismembered, but still divinely ordered, landscape, inhabited by devils. This funnel, with its cliffs, abysses, shattered rocks, dilapidated bridges, streams, torrents, lakes, and morasses, with rain, snow, and hail, with firebrands and ice, with wildernesses and forests, in short with all the terrors of wild and hostile Nature, is one of the mightiest creations of poetic imagination.

In the midst of this disordered, unfettered, self-mutilating natural world, there stands a city, resembling human handiwork and enlightened effort. But this city of the Devil is no creation of civilized human hands, but a demoniac construction, a work and an instrument of inhumanity, no barrier nor bulwark against savage nature, but organized savagery itself; a deliberately and intentionally created inhumanity, which, because it is conscious and organized, is far more hellish than the hellish natural world.

The subterranean constructions: the gate of Hell, the city of Dis, graves, fountains, dams, etc., are not in contradiction with subterranean nature, but present themselves as exaggerations and supplements of it, so that there is nothing capricious or unpoetical about them. The order and intent which they reveal are just as devilish and inhuman as the apparent disorder and irrationality of Nature. For, in the last analysis, even the natural phenomena of Hell have in them nothing accidental, but are essentially hostile to man, and torture is the purpose they attain; their cruelty is only less systematic than the hellish constructions. Therefore the poet has placed the infernal city, with its organization and administration, in the lower section of the Inferno, the purely natural transgressions in the upper portion.

Accordingly, the infernal scenery is the poetic expression of an ever-increasing enmity toward man. First we see Nature against man, then man against his neighbour and against himself; after that we behold Nature grown conscious, the city of Dis turned against man until finally, in deepest Hell Nature, man's neighbour, the city, and the ego itself unite in hostility to man so that the drama comes to a standstill.

The scenery is therefore essentially dramatic, is part of the action, and often becomes the action itself. We have in the *Inferno* a drama wherein not only the players but even the scenery actively participate.

Only in poor dramas does the scenery harden into mere useless decoration; in the Inferno, however, furious rain, howling wind, tongues of flame, biting cold, stench, light, gloaming, darkness, and even the motionless stones are things alive that give pain and are malicious. Out of all the shadows of the abysses horrors are grimacing, and behind every rock agony lurks. The earth, the walls of a room, the air, are all spiteful, uncanny, bewitched, enchanted, unaccountable.

To pass through a region so unfathomably strange and hostile would be a perilous venture, and material for a romantic poem. But Dante is no errant knight, and his *Inferno* is no romance.

His intention is not to sing the horrors of Hell, but to comprehend them, to master them with reason.

The *terra infernalis* is to be explored and explained, not to be enjoyed and conquered, as an Alpine peak is by a tourist.

The scenery endowed with life, filled with malice, alive with rage and trickery, has its counterpart in human reason, and especially in Virgil. He, the wanderer's guide, reveals the malice, thwarts the magic, explains and puts to flight the terrors of the infernal world, preserves the order and law which this savagery obeys. His opposition brings Hell's game to a standstill.

Now since Virgil is himself a prisoner in Hell and can offer the How but not the final Why of the mystery, he can calm the action of Hell, indeed, but not destroy it, can show the scenery to be limited, finite, measurable, and purposeful, and strip it of its romantic charm, but must, nevertheless, leave it its actuality and its picturesque reality. He is himself only a part, an inhabitant, even though the wisest, of this kingdom.

Provided Virgil remains true to himself, he still cannot, with the most abstract didacticism and good sense, destroy the poetic life of Hell. He is subject to it.

His character, as we have analyzed it, signifies for the poem no dangerous negative, but one of its most fruitful, liveliest resources.

THE INFERNAL DRAMA

As the scenery of Hell takes part in the infernal drama, it is to be expected that the actors also, on their side, should become part of the scenery and decoration. In fact, a succession of monsters, devils, sinners, and beasts serve as players and supernumeraries at once; and most, if not all, are so merged in the drama that neither the mechanician nor the stage manager can dispense with them.

These minor figures—and all in Hell except Dante and Virgil are minor figures—are yet so fully taken up with their own affairs that the passage of the two wanderers must appear to them a strange, sometimes desirable, sometimes indifferent or unwished-for, interruption of their own toils. So, instead of being the echo, the chorus, or the decorative environment to the chief action, they carry on a variety of independent minor actions.

But in this very multiplicity and diversity of byplay lies a great danger to the unity of the poem. The chief action threatens to become empty and to sink to the level of a mere journey or wandering, the motive of which is but the crossing of the infernal realm, in accordance with a program. Curiosity and haste would then be the only spring of the main action; and in this express-train fashion of travelling, the inhabitants of the land, with all their own peculiar interests, must seem mere fleeting phantoms; somewhat in the manner that human beings, houses, cities, rivers, mountains and forests, signboards, and milestones go whirling by those who sit in a swiftly rushing railroad train.

The danger that the drama may degenerate into tourist sightseeing exists throughout the entire *Commedia.* At the close of the poem the mind of the hasty reader retains no sense of development, but a maze of pictures. The majority of readers of Dante actually remember, not the course and progress of the poem in its entirety, but only certain brilliant episodes. In order to remember the passage, the connection, and the manner in which such meetings, such little dramas, are woven into the chief one, one needs a long and intimate acquaintance with the *Commedia.* It is customary to say that Dante's wealth of pictures and figures is too great for the memory to grasp them all easily. But wealth beyond our powers of enjoyment may become want. So it comes to pass that, at the present day, in most Italian cities where Dante is publicly read and expounded, the poem is cut to pieces, and only single cantos are treated, never the poem as a whole. Such dissection may be due to the scanty capacity of the readers, but to some extent it is a natural result of the construction of the poem.

Just as we plan a long journey, calendar and map in hand, so Dante arranged the successive stops of his pilgrimage through Hell and the hours of the day with such detail and exactness that the expounders find themselves compelled to prepare Dante charts and Dante clocks. To be sure, like all the maps and clocks in the world, they fit only approximately and in a general fashion.

For the comprehension of poetry, which by nature is incommensurable, these attempts at orientation can give no adequate aid. As we do not want to memorize but to understand the poem, we renounce artificial mnemonic aids.

This does not mean that Dante's arrangements and divisions are merely such aids and have a wholly inartistic and pedantic import, or fall outside the poetic action. Since the *Inferno* does describe a pilgrimage or journey, clocks and maps are an essential part of the illusion, and the efforts at orientation by the travellers are, just as much as their most exciting adventures or poetically enlivened action, æsthetically effective, justified, and correct. When Dante, in the eleventh canto of the *Inferno* and in the seventeenth of the *Purgatorio*, makes Virgil explain the moral order of these realms, and when Virgil, at almost every cornice of Hell or Purgatory, inquires for the shortest way, the situation cannot, to an intelligent critic, appear inartistic.

But when Alighieri makes the claim that his divisions and orientations have been fully tested as to their mathematical accuracy and validity, and when his expositors accept this assertion, all this has no longer any relation to poetry and æsthetic criticism. We need not concern ourselves, now that we have left the study of the sources behind us, with the question of the scientific value that is to be accorded to the chronology, astronomy, moral philosophy, and geography of the *Commedia*.

But we shall have to raise the question whether the chronology, astronomy, moral philosophy, and geography within the poem itself, within the limits of the poetic illusion, are consistent with each other; or, in other words, whether this exactitude, after it has once entered into the poetry and has become poetry, is also taken seriously and maintained throughout.

For just by means of this exactitude the poet has overcome the danger that the main and the subordinate actions may fall apart. So it is not that the poet has turned mathematician: it is the mathematician that has become a poet. Chiefly because the divisions and ordering of the journey are taken so seriously by the travellers, the numerous impressions, the many little dramas, acquire their fixed and fitting place, and ceasing to be mere episodes, which might at will be rearranged or even omitted, are built up one upon another, so that the earlier are presupposed and explained by the later. So it is the memory not of the reader, but of the poet and traveller, that holds together the chief and the minor actions. If the reader's memory is unable to follow the poet's, so much the worse for him, so much the better for Dante's glory. For recollection is, in its essence, intellectual will and inward sympathy. Through such sympathy and receptivity on the traveller's part all the scenery and minor action are absorbed into the main theme, all externals become experience, are treasured up and elaborated. The chief action is, accordingly, no hasty trip or mere sightseeing journey, but an orderly, attentive, and profound process of grasping and recasting all minor incidents and scenery.

To be sure, with a companion who forgets nothing, who has the entire past before his eyes and with it the present in all its details, whose spirit keeps pace with each new impression and, like a stream fed by a hundred brooks, widens and grows until at last he becomes superhuman—with such a comrade, travelling is uncomfortable. I know of no other poem that makes larger demands on the reader. The whole *Commedia*, from beginning to end, fully understood and lived through, is an extraordinary task, which only extraordinary people accomplish. Yet even the poet himself as he step by step with scrupulous care, with the strictest inner connection, without digression, without anticipating what is to come, goes on from known to unknown, makes no unjustified demand on his companion.

The division of the infernal region and of the journey through it is therefore no abstract scheme, but a frame that sets off and unites the whole, arrays it and defines it, and permits all the episodes to appear both separately and collectively, a frame which is a part of the picture, because it was planned with it and is viewed with it. It is like the frame of masterly mediæval altarpieces, whose extent and borders were planned by no ordinary artisan, but by the painter himself.

Scenery and plot, main and minor action, are held together by Dante's inmost sympathy and rapt attentiveness. Sometimes he forgets himself so completely in conversation with a sinner, or at the sight of a monster, that this sinner, that monster, becomes the centre of interest and the chief action; sometimes he is so keenly and clearly aware of his own position, so collects himself and becomes so thoroughly absorbed in himself, that the whole of Hell seems drawn and engulfed into this inward swirl. In Dante's *Inferno* there is no definite distinction between chief and subordinate action, chief and minor figures, scenery and drama: for the one passes unceasingly into the other, and this transition is poetic life.

THE GENERAL TONE OF THE "INFERNO"

Such an alternation of outwardness and inwardness, objectivity and subjectivity, self-forgetfulness and self-comprehension, renunciation and appropriation, of individualizing and abstracting, such an exchange between the Ego and the non-Ego, may be more or less violent and abrupt, or natural and regular. It makes a difference whether I am journeying across a plain, where land and people are alike to the point of monotony, or whether I am wandering through a precipitous mountain region where the landscape is varied and inhabitants of diverse race and temperament are thrown together. Both environments, however, the monotonous as well as the varied, offer difficulties to the observer. The former may easily be found monotonous, the latter bewildering. In order that there may be between Nature and its artist lover a rhythmic interchange, a give and take, an easy flow of intercommunication, there is need of a tempered environment, of a region or landscape such as we call congenial.

To be sure, every people, every century, every individual, every instant, finds a different side of the environment especially congenial, and befitting its own nature.

What is the elemental tone and mood of the *Inferno?* And is it possible that a spirit like that of Dante could feel at ease there?

That elemental tone has been recorded powerfully and clearly by the poet himself, in the famous inscription over the Gate of Hell;

> "Through me the way is to the city dolent;
> Through me the way is to eternal dole;
> Through me the way among the people lost.
> Justice incited my sublime Creator;
> Created me divine Omnipotence,
> The highest Wisdom and the primal Love.
> Before me there were no created things,
> Only eterne, and I eternal last.
> All hope abandon, ye who enter in!" [1]

It is the mystery of eternal life, seen from its most agonizing side. For no less eternal and fathomless than life is its most faithful companion, pain. By the force of relentless justice it trickles forth out of the noblest sources of life, out of strength, wisdom, and love.

This divine origin gives Hell its hopeless eternity and unconquerable power. He who thus harbours torture within himself despairs. But he who has the power to draw it forth from his bosom and to gaze on its interminable duration, such a man has conquered it: and nothing of life's sorrow lingers still within

[1] *Inferno,* III, 1–9.

him except the lofty consciousness of dread eternity. An awesome shrinking from an eternity of pain is the keynote of the *Inferno.*

That is why its scenery is conceived as hostile to life, cruel, diabolical, and always on the offensive against mankind: an agony made visible and ennobled by its eternal duration; a fixed threat against the Ego. Therefore the main action of the *Inferno* is a stirring, an appealing and attentive contemplation and inward experience of that scenery.

That Alighieri was never in his life better prepared and emotionally more adapted for such an undertaking and for the full comprehension of hatred, cruelty, and all the agonies of earth than in the days when he had himself undergone his bitterest griefs, the death of Beatrice and of Emperor Henry, and when he could not but doubt his own worth—all this we know full well. The conception of the *Inferno* fits into those years and moods of despair, and every canto bears traces of them.

Not merely external events, however, but his temperament also provided the fitting mood for the *Inferno.* The stuff of which he was made contained more gall than milk. If he did, nevertheless, struggle upward to the hopefulness of the *Purgatorio* and to the cheerfulness of the *Paradiso,* he drew the strength therefor out of the agonized depths of his nature.

In the *Purgatorio,* and especially in the *Paradiso,* the lyrical element as the expression of the poet's mood becomes more and more independent, rises here and there above the narration, action, and scenery, leaves the circumstantial and external, withdraws within itself, so that only the soul and light of those cantos breathes and lives, while the outer features grow pale and fade away.

But in the *Inferno,* the lyric is rarely distinguishable from the epic and the dramatic, and just because it is omnipresent, does not appear as lyrical. The *Inferno* with its tangible realism is like a monster whose soul has no definite organ, and in which not only the limbs but the hair and claws are endowed with life, coiling and writhing like snakes and scorpions.

PRELUDE AND PROLOGUE

Artistically, the true *Inferno* begins with the third, not with the second, canto, as the numerical scheme of the poem might lead us to expect. Dante fittingly prepared his sacred poem, "on which both heaven and earth have laid their hands," with a sort of earthly "prelude" and a "prologue in Heaven."

To be sure, the earthly stage is, for reasons well known to us, a makeshift and not a poetic creation. Hence, all that happens here seems to waver between poetry and purpose.

Dante the wanderer, in the forest of sin, astray from the path of virtue, is a type of mankind in general, and as such cannot at first feel his distress in all its fullness. Instead of a vain, groping search and the hopes and fears of a feverish, toilsome progress toward light, his endeavour is to contrast an allegorical forest with a no less allegorical hill, presumably the mount of Virtue or of Blessedness. If the morning sun which illuminates this hill were the actual sun, with what delight the lost man would have greeted it! But it is, primarily, only the planet "that leadeth men aright on every path," and so something general, probably divine grace or revelation.

But this contrasting of concepts—sin, virtue, blessedness, error, grace or revelation—and the recollection of similar states of mind, suffice to arouse the narrator and to draw from him the poetic spark.

> And even as he who, with distressful breath,
> Forth issued from the sea upon the shore,
> Turns to the water perilous and gazes;
> So did my soul, that still was fleeing onward,
> Turn itself back to re-behold the pass
> Which never yet a living person left.

The assurance that "no living man escapes from the valley of sin" has no longer the mere force of a theological doctrine, but springs out of the anxiety of the emotional crisis.

After a pause, the wanderer undertakes to climb the mountain of virtue. He starts up its lonely slope "so that the firm foot ever was the lower." An obscure description or circumlocution, over which numberless expositors have been puzzled. Strictly speaking, it is only on level ground that the firm foot, that is, that on which one rests his weight, remains always the lower. According to this, Dante would be climbing the slope with the manner of walking suited to level ground: which is hardly possible. The matter becomes intelligible only if we dispose of the slope and treat it as a mere figure (for instance, as the effort toward virtue, which is, alas, rarely attempted by man) or if we interpret the phrase "firm foot," *piè firmo*, in an unusual sense.

But further ascent is halted by a light-footed leopard (or lynx?). The appearance of the animal is disturbing, "never departing from before my face." Did his eye deceive him, or did she prance back and forth before him? "She impeded so my way, that many times I to return had turned." The poet finds time and breath for a play on the words *più volte vôlto,* for this leopard is also merely allegorical, and represents a sin, probably lust of the flesh, sensuality or envy.

> The time was the beginning of the morning,
> And up the sun was mounting with those stars
> That with him were, what time the Love Divine
> At first in motion set those beauteous things;
> So were to me occasion of good hope,
> The variegated skin of that wild beast,
> The hour of time, and the delicious season.

Here there is more to explain than to enjoy. According to mediæval ideas, the sun was in the constellation of the ram at the time of Creation. It was in the spring, the time when Christ was crucified—Good Friday. This significant constellation brings hope even in the presence of sin.

But a lion with uplifted head and ravenous hunger comes to meet the wanderer. And the lion, by whose semblance—note the repeated "seemed," *parea*—the concept of another sin, haughtiness or pride, is revealed, is followed by a she-wolf,

> . . . that with all hungerings
> Seemed to be laden in her meagreness,
> And many folk has caused to live forlorn!

This she-wolf meant to Dante, as is well known, the sin of greed,[1] the most fatal to an orderly state, and to men collectively.

> And as he is who willingly acquires,
> And the time comes that causes him to lose,
> Who weeps in all his thoughts and is despondent,
> E'en such made me that beast withouten peace.

As the creature comes step by step toward him, he draws back, ever deeper into the gloomy valley. With each verse new light streams into the poem.

Against a background mysteriously shadowed with feelings of fright, thwarted hope, anxiety and despair, there rises, at first uncertain and weak "from long silence," but presently more elo-

[1] Cf. *Purgatorio,* XX, 10 sqq.

quent, brighter and more brilliant, the figure of the deliverer: Virgil, the gentle, the wise poet. The allegorical forest, the hill of virtue, the desert slope, the sinful beasts, in short, all that hastily constructed scenery, now disappears and lives again, inwardly only, in the affectionate conversation of the two kindred souls, the poets.

Dante, who but a moment before was mankind in the abstract, and had cried out "Have pity upon me!" suddenly becomes himself in the actual presence of the singer of the *Aeneid.* It is the poet in him that exults and invokes:

> "Now, art thou that Virgilius and that fountain
> Which spreads abroad so wide a river of speech?"
> I made response to him with bashful forehead.
> "O, of the other poets honour and light,
> Avail me the long study and great love
> That have impelled me to explore thy volume!
> Thou art my master, and my author thou,
> Thou art alone the one from whom I took
> The beautiful style that has done honour to me."

Then, after the unbounded love for poetry has expressed itself, the need of the moment comes again to utterance. "Behold," Dante beseeches Virgil—

> "Behold the beast, for which I have turned back;
> Do thou protect me from her, famous sage,
> For she doth make my veins and pulses tremble."

So, since Virgil is a great artist and a wise student of human life, he must have power over the ravening beast. It is upon the foundation of this simple, reverent belief that the authority and absolute power of Virgil rests: a belief which, in our study of the sources, we characterized as dogmatic, but which now, in the sincere faith of the wanderer, becomes poetic truth.

In fact, the poet of the *Aeneid* grows before our eyes to superhuman stature. He becomes a prophet. Solemnly and mysteriously, but truthfully and confidently, he speaks to his pupil and points out to him the path of deliverance.

> "Thee it behoves to take another road,"
> Responded he, when he beheld me weeping,
> "If from this savage place thou wouldst escape;
> Because this beast, at which thou criest out,
> Suffers not any one to pass her way,
> But so doth harass him, that she destroys him;

And has a nature so malign and ruthless,
  That never doth she glut her greedy will,
  And after food is hungrier than before.
Many the animals with whom she weds,
  And more they shall be still, until the Greyhound
  Comes, who shall make her perish in her pain.
He shall not feed on either earth or pelf,
  But upon wisdom, and on love and virtue;
  'Twixt Feltro and Feltro shall his nation be;
Of that low Italy shall he be the saviour,
  On whose account the maid Camilla died,
  Euryalus, Turnus, Nisus, of their wounds;
Through every city shall he hunt her down,
  Until he shall have driven her back to Hell,
  There from whence envy first did let her loose.
Therefore I think and judge it for thy best
  Thou follow me, and I will be thy guide,
  And lead thee hence through the eternal place,
Where thou shalt hear the desperate lamentations,
  Shalt see the ancient spirits disconsolate,
  Who cry out each one for the second death;
And thou shalt see those who contented are
  Within the fire, because they hope to come,
  Whene'er it may be, to the blessed people;
To whom, then, if thou wishest to ascend,
  A soul shall be for that than I more worthy;
  With her at my departure I will leave thee;
Because that Emperor, who reigns above,
  In that I was rebellious to his law,
  Wills that through me none come into his city.
He governs everywhere, and there he reigns;
  There is his city and his lofty throne;
  O happy he whom thereto he elects!"

In these few lines the knot of the poem is tied. All the wishes and impulses of Dante's heart, his own salvation, the future of Italy, the welfare of mankind, and eternal life—all these Virgil has promised him. Only his first and last happiness, Beatrice, the love of his youth, and the resplendent presence of the beneficent God, the truth-loving master must, with wistful resignation, leave to a higher power. In the impatience of his first joy the wanderer does not realize that through this inability to satisfy his first and last need, the competence of Virgil and the success of the whole pilgrimage are put in question.

But, as is wont to happen in a keen and clever mind, the objective uncertainty of the undertaking mirrors itself in him in the form of subjective doubt as to his own power and merit. This is the burden of the second prelude or "Prologue in Heaven." Dante must be lifted out of this questioning and doubt as to himself, which has come upon him suddenly but not without reason, and the adequate power of Virgil must be demonstrated. Both these matters are so closely connected that, as the second is disposed of, the first disappears, and vice versa.

In order to escape his present trouble, Dante is ready to ascend to Peter's gate, though the way be through Hell itself. The pilgrimage begins; but, a presage of discouragement, night falls. This first day has brought to Dante only a morning bereft of hope and a toilsome evening heavy with premonition.

> Day was departing, and the embrownéd air
>   Released the animals that are on earth
>   From their fatigues; and I the only one
> Made myself ready to sustain the war,
>   Both of the way and likewise of the woe. . . .

Again it is the artist and the artistic difficulty that are first discussed. The invocation of the muses and of his own artistic nature is in this mood no academic form; it is the spur that the poet drives into his own flesh.

And now Dante lays before Virgil the doubt which he feels concerning himself. "The path," he says, "along which thou wouldst lead me has been traversed only by epoch-making and chosen personages; by thy Aeneas as the herald and champion of Roman world-rule, and by the apostle Paul, the champion of Christian faith. But who, pray, am I? No Aeneas and no Paul, and I have no universal mission."

This learned and proudly modest exposition of his own task in the evolution of mediæval philosophy would appear to us, humanly speaking, conceited and artistically bad if we did not share with our poet the conviction that such a work of art as the *Divine Comedy* is, in its own way, no less historic and precious than the founding of Rome or the spread of Christianity, and if the justification for this conviction did not ring out clearly from these very verses. The truthfulness and depth of the conviction lies in the very depth of the doubt and in the fundamental thoroughness of his pondering over Aeneas and Paul. Just because these verses are so serious they cannot be graceful and fluent. The mood from which they spring is too strenuous.

> And as he is, who unwills what he willed,
> And by new thoughts doth his intention change,
> So that from his design he quite withdraws,
> Such I became, upon that dark hillside,
> Because, in thinking, I consumed the emprise,
> Which was so very prompt in the beginning.

For so profound a doubt, a yet more fundamental refutation must be offered. The question of historic importance raised by Dante can be disposed of by Virgil only through an appeal to the direct will of God. But since Virgil, a heathen, knows nothing of that will, it must have been communicated to him by a divine messenger. It suffices that he relate faithfully and impersonally the manner in which the divine will was made known to him and the task of guiding Dante through the Hereafter assigned to him. The meaning and content of his tale is as follows:

At about the same time when Hell spat forth the three beasts that blocked the wanderer's way, three blessed ladies in Heaven were making ready to remove this obstacle by their prayers. The Virgin Mary as the supreme Mother of Grace sent St. Lucia as dispenser of illuminating grace, and Lucia betook herself to the blessed Beatrice, that is, to the human intercessor of divine revelation. Beatrice descended into the Limbo of Hell, where Virgil was, and besought him to hasten to the aid of Dante in his distress. By means of this commission Virgil acquired full power to guide Dante on his pilgrimage through Hell and Purgatory.

The three heavenly ladies, then, would seem to be contrasted with the three ravenous beasts of Hell, and as such merely allegorical and devoid of poetic life. But since the last of them, Beatrice, is no other than the glorified beloved of Dante's youth, there streams a warm light of love from her gentle kindly figure, from her personal intercession, from her sympathetic solicitude and anxiety, over Dante's fate upward to Lucia and Mary. The external motive, the practical initiative, comes from Mary; the poetic warmth, the inner action, springs from Beatrice. Lucia stands between them, as Dante's protecting saint. We know from the *Convivio* that Dante suffered in youth from a disease of the eyes, and he may well have had an especial devotion for Lucia, the guardian of the light of the eyes.

Virgil relates this brief heavenly drama in reverse order. So we do not see it as a thing constructed, but actually experience the charming apparition of Beatrice in Limbo:

> "Her eyes were shining brighter than the Star;
> And she began to say, gentle and low,
> With voice angelical, in her own language:
> 'O spirit courteous of Mantua,
> Of whom the fame still in the world endures,
> And shall endure, long-lasting as the world; . . .
> Bestir thee now, and with thy speech ornate,
> And with what needful is for his release,
> Assist him so, that I may be consoled.' "

Out of this loving scene of womanly intercession the rest develops and draws its life from the dialogue between Virgil and Beatrice. We see no allegory; we hear words which indeed, now and then, may seem pale and obscure, but as a whole leave the impression that in Heaven a nameless, all-knowing, devoted love watches over Dante and cares for him as though his welfare were more important than that of Aeneas or Paul.

> "What is it, then? Why, why dost thou delay?
> Why is such baseness bedded in thy heart?
> Daring and hardihood why hast thou not,
> Seeing that three such Ladies benedight
> Are caring for thee in the court of Heaven,
> And so much good my speech doth promise thee?"

Just as chilled blossoms after a cold night raise their heads and unfold in the morning sun, so the wanderer's despondent heart opens to the great decision. The pilgrimage to Eternity begins.

It may be, indeed it is to be assumed with confidence, that these two cantos contain a whole series of mystical, philosophical, moral, and political meanings. First and foremost, however, is their artistic significance; that is, they furnish the motif and outline the plan for its development, so that the reader has a view of the entire poem before reading it.

The prelude on earth, the first canto, left room for serious doubt as to the issue and happy completion of the journey into the nether regions. The prologue in Heaven (second canto) relieves us of all anxiety as to the salvation of the wanderer. We may rest assured that Virgil will bring his charge unharmed through Hell and to the summit of the Purgatorial mountain, whence Beatrice will take him up into Heaven.

Was it not short-sighted thus to dispel all anxiety as to the outcome? Has not Dante deprived himself of an aid to success, available even for the most worthless of tales? Surely, were he a commonplace artist who had to produce his effects by surprises, we should condemn the first two cantos. But the great artists feel themselves most strongly drawn to subjects that are already known to all, which in and of themselves no longer hold us in suspense, and which therefore can arouse interest only through artistic treatment.

Classical and pure art loves what is completed, what has already fully fermented in men's souls. Indeed, a subject-matter can be endowed with the pure life of art only when the practical existence that abode in it has died out or has been destroyed.

This destruction of the subject-matter as such is completed in the two first cantos of the *Commedia.* The whole journey is pushed back out of the imperfect past into the closed period of perfection; it is withdrawn from our practical interest, in order that it may be drawn nearer to our contemplative eye. Before Dante describes Hell to us, we already know that he has overcome it and is in Heaven. So much the better will he tell his tale. He gains thereby that calmness and elevation in the presence of his subject and his experience which he needs in order to draw his lines plainly and accurately. Goethe, when he began his *Faust*, was not yet clear in his own mind as to the fate of the hero and the outcome of the poem. With Dante the experience enshrined in the *Commedia* is decided and closed before the poem begins.

What we characterized as the postulate or ideal of the *Commedia*, the moral ennobling of personality, is, therefore, from the beginning contained and included in what we called the actuality of the *Commedia*, i.e. in the self-knowledge of personality.

Only now, at the close of the second canto, do we know that the poem is to be a comedy and not a tragedy. By "comedy" mediæval men understood any form of poetry which begins in fear, but ends happily. "For, as far as the material is concerned," says Alighieri in his letter to Can Grande, "it begins terribly and repulsively with Hell, and ends prosperously, desirably, and pleasantly in Paradise."

A poem which thus develops into general reconciliation and satisfaction, which bears its ideal not above but within itself—a *Commedia*, in other words—could not, according to mediæval and Dantesque ideas, be composed in lofty language and style, but required an universally intelligible, natural diction. "Therefore," Dante continues, "my poem is to this extent a comedy, that it is not written in Latin, but in the vulgar tongue such as ordinary women of the people use."

In fact, a poem wherein a Florentine woman of the people guarantees a happy issue, and communicates to the greatest master of Latinity divine messages, doctrines, and commands, could not successfully appear in any speech other than the ordinary one of Florence.

In short, in every direction, it is through the first two cantos that the attitude of the poet toward his subject is defined and the prevailing style irrevocably decided upon.

The style will be classical in so far as the material interest is displaced by an artistic one. The language will be popular and natural in so far as the ideal is contained in the reality and the divine idea is communicated through Beatrice, a woman of Florence. The progress will be that of a comedy and will lead from Hell to Heaven, for the world cut off from God has revealed itself to the pilgrim as irremediable sin and to the poet as unimaginable allegory.

After the artistic character of the *Commedia* has been with such completeness set forth in the two introductory cantos, their mystical, philosophical, and practical meanings will become intelligible, not indeed in themselves, but in their connection with the entire poem.

ANTE–HELL AND UPPER HELL

(*Inferno*, III)

In accordance with the Aristotelian division of unjust acts into those prompted by (1) passion and (2) malice, Hell is divided into an upper and a lower part. Passionate iniquities are the outcome of an unbridled temper, acts prompted by lack of moderation (ἀκρασία), and take the form—as the Catholic Church taught, in agreement with the ancient philosophers—of (1) lust, (2) gluttony, (3) avarice or prodigality, (4) sloth, or indolence in well-doing, and (5) anger. The first three are located each in one of three circles of Hell, so that there the geographical divisions coincide perfectly with the conceptual classification. Above and below, however, the poet, fortunately, has planned his Hell independently of mediæval and ancient moral treatises.

His infernal funnel needed an entrance, an ante-room, and was furthermore bound to have, like the beautiful classic Hades, its streams and rivers, and like the popular Hell, its castles and cities.

In order not to leave the vestibule or outer court, into which the infernal gate opens, lifeless and empty, the poet has filled it with the souls of those who were neither good nor bad. We have repeatedly seen how wretched the type of the ethically indifferent appears in a system of ethics. That explains why, so mightily and effectively, the poem rises above this irrationality. If Alighieri had attempted to justify scientifically this section of the indifferent or Laodicean which he created, he would have spoiled his poetry with bad philosophy. If, as a good philosopher, he had devoted no space to this division, if he had let the true Hell with its terrors begin immediately within the gate, had he plunged us at once from the upper surface of life into the depths of eternal woe, then we should have been conscious of a violent leap between the prologue and the Inferno. Instead of this, the vestibule affords a suitable transition.

Between temporal life on the upper surface and eternal death in the depths of the earth, Dante has put apparent death, which is neither true life nor true death: wretched creatures that cannot die, because they never had the force to live: "these wretches that have never been alive," human beings who, without shame or praise, without love and without hatred, passed through life indifferent, worthless, leaving no trace behind, and with them the feeble angels who, when Lucifer rebelled, drew aside in cowardice and held neither to God nor to Satan, masked egoists, too bad for Heaven, too decent for Hell. Such lack of character is more contemptible than all else, and could not but call forth the bitterest scorn, if indeed it was comprehensible at all to such a vigorous character as Dante's. But this colourless lifelessness was to him something unintelligible and uncanny. It is the horror of Hell without its greatness that lies upon the soul like a nightmare, and against it all the spirits of life revolt. Dante weeps as he looks closer; terror seizes his brain. However, after he realizes the utter insignificance of the matter, he must follow the counsel of his guide: "Let us not speak of them, but look, and pass."

By this nothingness, this "darkness without colour, without time," the poet has shut off his Hell hermetically, so to speak, from the upper world.

The rude art of the Middle Ages permitted the flames of Hell to break forth through a hole or maw. Dante put the spirit and temper of all Hell into the inscription at the entrance, and in the very heart of his "All hope abandon" he placed the embodiment of this hopelessness. On this grey, boundless mass of the indifferent, he inflicted no penalty, only a disgusting and ignoble irritation: he has them bitten by gnats and gnawed by worms, and with this the basest form of remorse, helpless envy of all other destinies, even the most terrible. The interest that he as a pilgrim takes in them is the superficial one of momentary curiosity. Not a single shape does he distinguish in their uniformity. Only the ghost of one nameless weakling, "who made, through cowardice, the great refusal," is especially noted, only in order to be the more effectively plunged in oblivion. Even the oldest expositors surmised that this obscurity concealed Pope Celestine V, who by his abdication made room for the ambitious Boniface VIII, Alighieri's bitterest foe.

To linger in the senseless realm of tepid indifference, and with detached irony to colour a thousand vain impulses toward life—the envious and eager struggle upward into form and the downfall once more into nothingness—to depict all this, would be a sadly cheerful task of the imagination, in which a romanticist could spend his whole life, still unsated. To Dante's poetic spirit, eager to reach the heart of life, every moment that he spends here seems wasted. He squanders no colour, no lyric note, on the seemingly dead. He does not portray them, he barely defines them; with epigrammatic keenness he states the formula first of their inward, then of their outward, condition. After he has once beheld them he cannot bear to look at them; so that the fantastic shadowiness of these uncertain ones becomes a disconsolate, empty reality. They have disappointed his thirst for knowledge. With increased eagerness the poet's eye is fixed on more rational scenes. Out of the dreamily stirring and heaving bosom of nothingness, the children of the night struggle up; and the wanderer cannot wait for what they offer. Virgil must censure his impatience. Across the infernal stream Acheron, the skiff of Charon the ferryman draws nigh. His threatening words,

Virgil's reply, the anxiety and despair of the sinners, those who have just died, who press forward for the passage—all is action. With terrific rapidity and accuracy we see divine justice do its work. In a few verses, which need no exposition, the whole Inferno is in action and at work. The earth becomes alive, quakes, and sends forth a crimson light. Dante sinks to earth unconscious and awakens on the farther bank. It seems as if Hell wished to draw him to itself, but in fact it was a heavenly miracle of grace that carried him over.

(*Inferno*, IV)

When he revives and looks about him, trying to orient himself, all is night. From the infernal funnel, swelling and uniting in thunderous sound, there moans, out of the depths upon whose brink he stands, the commingled cry of agony from all the damned. On Virgil's face sympathy shows itself as anxious pallor.

Now, since Hell, so to speak, does not act, but lies like a mighty city in the depths of an abyss, and reveals itself to eye and ear in a single impression as gloomy chasm and rolling thunder, it now, for the first time, unfolds its terrible might, fills and overpowers the consciousness of the wanderer. With murmured words the twain gather courage for the descent. "Let us go on, the long way bids us hasten." But, as is wont to happen, seen at close quarters things appear less terrible than fancy bade us fear. We are in the first circle of Hell. No cry, no torture, no thunder; only a tremulous sigh is audible. Here Virgil is at home, here he grows communicative, conversational. He relates as experience that which the Church teaches as dogma, the tale of the Limbo which is localized in this first circle.

Here, for the second time, the poet overrides with ingenious invention the dogmatic concept of his age. After the Fathers of the Old Testament, through Christ's descent into Hell, were removed out of the Limbo into Paradise, there can remain there, according to Christian dogma, only the unbaptized children, who died before they had time to sin. As a matter of fact, the notion of a sinless personality is as absurd as that of ethical indifference. But Dante has made the one as well as the other what it in essence is: a fantasy. If the Christian concept damns the whole civilized world before and outside of Christianity, then indeed it must endow damnation with some beauty, greatness, and goodness. Just as in the outer court of Hell cowardly abstinence from sin becomes a ghastly image of terror, in the Limbo, on the other hand, heroic innocence takes on the shape of an elegiac elysium. The hero of this elegy is Virgil himself.

As he arrives with his pupil, the noblest, the greatest poets, Homer, Horace, Ovid, and Lucan, come to meet and greet him. "Semblance had they nor sorrowful nor glad." But there is no lack of that fleeting smile that belongs to elegy. As Dante, the Christian poet, is welcomed by the old classical masters as one of their group, Virgil's lips are shadowed by the unenvious smile of the unfortunate at the good fortune of a friend.

To take delight in elegy, to dream oneself nostalgically back into a vanished world, shattered by destiny, a world of beauty and greatness, and "to suffer shipwreck on the sea of infinity" with Hölderlin or Leopardi—what modern poet would have let such a chance go by?

Dante lingers over the elegy of his Elysium as little as he did over the fantasy of the infernal outer court. He does not attempt to restore the past by vain wishes, but desires only to ponder, contemplate, and understand it. His wistful mood does not brood within itself, but urges him to thoughtful observation. His eager eye craves definite objects and hastens from one figure to another.

> There opposite, upon the green enamel,
> Were pointed out to me the mighty spirits,
> Whom to have seen I feel myself exalted.

Heroes and warrior women: Electra, Hector, Aeneas, Caesar, etc.; then the heroes of thought: Aristotle, Socrates, Plato, and many more, a long array of mighty names. The most natural and simplest expression of scholarly enthusiasm is the telling over of names, an eager and direct, but for that very reason a superficial, utterance, which does not permit the poet to indicate the nature of the ancient world in its entirety. So it comes to pass that his Elysium remains somewhat mediæval, and is made visible to us as a castle with seven walls and seven gates girt about by a stream; by which we are presumably to understand the seven virtues, the seven free arts, and that all-embracing discretion [1] without which neither virtue nor science is thinkable. Here is perhaps one of those minor cases where the danger already indi-

Cf. *Convivio*, I, 11. That is, the fearless passing over the moat of the fortress, not the water in and of itself, might be signified by "discretion."

cated, namely, the haste and curiosity of the traveller, prevented a complete poetic development.

(*Inferno*, V)

The moment the elegiac mood is absorbed in self-enjoyment, it becomes idyllic; but if it reaches out with longing into reality, then it becomes tragic. So, after the elegy of the Elysium, there follows inevitably the tragedy of Francesca.

Between elegy and tragedy, parting and uniting them, appears the righteous judge of souls, Minos. Minos stands for justice, on its most unrelenting and terrible side; not the blind, impartial goddess with the scales, to whom we all appeal, but inflexible, avenging justice, whom we would fain escape, but cannot: a grinning monster with eyes that pierce the soul, and a devilish tail, which, by the number of its coils, indicates scornfully the measure of our unrighteousness. In place of the noble and modest majesty of the blind goddess he has a cynical magnificence. Earnest and mighty is his function, cynical and grotesque his ceremonial.

Immediately beyond the tribunal, punishment begins. A storm wind drives and lashes the sinners, whirls them together and rushes them on.

> And as the wings of starlings bear them on
> In the cold season in large band and full,
> So doth that blast the spirits maledict;
> It hither, thither, downward, upward, drives them;
> No hope doth comfort them for evermore,
> Not of repose, but even of lesser pain.
> And as the cranes go chanting forth their lays,
> Making in air a long line of themselves,
> So saw I coming, uttering lamentations,
> Shadows borne onward by the aforesaid stress.

It is the victims of the first deadly sin, the lustful, who suffer here in the second circle. A common misery includes the captives of love from antiquity down; Semiramis, Cleopatra, Helen, Achilles, Paris, Tristan—and the inseparable pair, Francesca da Rimini and Paolo Malatesta.

In order to understand the Francesca episode—which is in truth no episode, but the introductory tragedy of the *Inferno*—we must set clearly before ourselves the circumstances of this tale of adultery, as it was known in Dante's day.

We have the family of the Polentas, lords of Ravenna, and that of the Malatestas of Rimini, whose old feud, as was usual in mediæval times, was one day (about 1275) to be ended by marriage. Francesca, the daughter of the aged Guido da Polenta, was to wed Gianciotto Malatesta, an ugly cripple, it is said, and as such not likely to find favour in the eyes of the beautiful Francesca. Gianciotto's brother, handsome Paolo, must therefore be put forward as the suitor.[1] The plan succeeded. Francesca pledged herself to Paolo. Not until Gianciotto presented himself at the marriage ceremony did she discover the deceit. Meantime Paolo had fallen violently in love with his brother's betrothed, and found it easy to win her love in return. A servant betrayed to Gianciotto their adulterous relations. The husband discovered them and stabbed them to death. This bloody deed is said to have occurred ten years after the marriage, that is, at a time when Alighieri had outgrown his boyhood; so that such a horrible occurrence in the ranks of the higher nobility might well make a lasting impression upon him.

Now inasmuch as the poet could take for granted his readers' knowledge of these events, he could pass over the external facts and was free to throw the whole force of his poetry into the psychological interpretation of the incident. But even this concentration does not satisfy him. Instead of turning the current of his poesy through the inner life of his three chief characters, Paolo, Francesca, and Gianciotto, he concentrates the tragedy upon the central figures, omits action and counter-action, and imparts the quality of profound destiny to that play of chance which, through weakness, passion, adultery, and betrayal, drives its victim to destruction. Thus the vital nerve of conscious freedom, of guilty conscience, and of responsibility, is sundered. Francesca, meant for love, born to love, dying for love, and in her eternal damnation still chained to love, has naught within her or before her save this one passion. It is her sin and her bliss, her Hell and her Heaven, her cruel, joyous fate. This love would be her blessedness if the consciousness of her sin did not poison it. But sin and damnation cannot bring on the pang of conscience, of remorse, because they are just as great, as eternal, and as dear to her as love and Paolo. Therefore Paolo is swept on forever and inseparably at her side: her shadow, her reproach, her punishment, her sin, her recompense, her all.

[1] Paolo was, to be sure, already some six years married.

Of course moralizing weaklings, who know not at all what sin and eternity are, have not neglected this opportunity to cast their reproaches at the greatest of poets. They admonish him how unfitting it is to prolong for all eternity, and to glorify, unhallowed love.

Let us leave these bewildered souls and return to the poet.

> After that I had listened to my Teacher,
> Naming the dames of eld and cavaliers,
> Pity prevailed, and I was nigh bewildered.
> And I began: "O Poet, willingly
> Speak would I to those two, who go together,
> And seem upon the wind to be so light."
> And he to me: "Thou'lt mark, when they shall be
> Nearer to us; and then do thou implore them
> By love which leadeth them, and they will come."
> Soon as the wind in our direction sways them,
> My voice uplift I: "O ye weary souls!
> Come speak to us, if no one interdicts it."
> As turtle-doves, called onward by desire,
> With open and steady wings to the sweet nest
> Fly through the air by their volition borne,
> So came they from the band where Dido is,
> Approaching us athwart the air malign,
> So strong was the affectionate appeal.

Without telling us who speaks, without explanation, the poet lets the soft womanly voice thrill our ears.

> "O living creature gracious and benignant,
> Who visiting goest through the purple air
> Us, who have stained the world incarnadine,
> If were the King of the Universe our friend,
> We would pray unto him to give thee peace,
> Since thou hast pity on our woe perverse.
> Of what it pleases thee to hear and speak,
> That will we hear, and we will speak to you,
> While silent is the wind, as it is now.
> Sitteth the city, wherein I was born,
> Upon the sea-shore where the Po descends
> To rest in peace with all his retinue.
> Love, that on gentle heart doth swiftly seize,
> Seized this man for the person beautiful
> That was ta'en from me, and still the mode offends me.
> Love, that exempts no one beloved from loving,
> Seized me with pleasure of this man so strongly,
> That, as thou seest, it doth not yet desert me;

Love has conducted us unto one death;
 Caïna waiteth him who quenched our life!"
 These words were borne along from them to us.
As soon as I had heard those souls tormented,
 I bowed my face, and so long held it down
 Until the Poet said to me: "What thinkest?"
When I made answer, I began: "Alas!
 How many pleasant thoughts, how much desire,
 Conducted these unto the dolorous pass!"
Then unto them I turned me, and I spake,
 And I began: "Thine agonies, Francesca,
 Sad and compassionate to weeping make me.
But tell me, at the time of those sweet sighs,
 By what and in what manner Love conceded,
 That you should know your dubious desires?"
And she to me: "There is no greater sorrow
 Than to be mindful of the happy time
 In misery, and that thy Teacher knows.
But, if to recognize the earliest root
 Of love in us thou hast so great desire,
 I will do even as he who weeps and speaks.
One day we reading were for our delight
 Of Launcelot, how Love did him enthral.
 Alone we were and without any fear.
Full many a time our eyes together drew
 That reading, and drove the colour from our faces;
 But one point only was it that o'ercame us.
When as we read of the much-longed-for smile
 Being by such a noble lover kissed,
 This one, who ne'er from me shall be divided,
Kissed me upon the mouth all palpitating.
 Galeotto was the book and he who wrote it.
 That day no farther did we read therein."
And all the while one spirit uttered this,
 The other one did weep so, that, for pity,
 I swooned away as if I had been dying,
And fell, even as a dead body falls.

Is this tragedy of love really told purely out of Francesca's mind? Can we expect from a woman, wholly absorbed in her love, such brief, masculine, epigrammatic, profound, and intellectually difficult considerations and such thoroughly Dantesque expressions as "Love, that on gentle heart doth swiftly seize"—"Love, that exempts no one beloved from loving"—"Caïna waiteth him who quenched our life"—"Galeotto was the book and he who wrote it"?

We have yet to see the woman possessed of such a style. And whoso has not the style, cannot have the thought. All this may have been uttered in the name of Francesca, yet not in her character. Francesca's spirit and manner of thinking have become Dante's spirit and manner. It did not satisfy the poet to have gathered from the external circumstances the inward conditions of mind also, and to have constructed out of the various characters that unified feminine spirit which constituted his poesy. He took also the third and final step, drew the gentle, shy woman-soul into his own overpowering spirit; and, through this threefold reflection, from without inward, from the incident to Francesca, and from her to himself, he gives us the event in its fullest and most personal light.

When a public reader or elocutionist chirps out the words of Francesca in a high-pitched feminine falsetto, he misunderstands the untheatrical inner nature of the *Commedia*. The elocutionist should not imitate Francesca's voice, but let the woman's voice be heard through Dante's, like a soulful echo.

The poet does not permit himself to be displaced by his characters. They live in him only so far as he lives in them. Every one else who has tried to appropriate Francesca and to bid her live in epic or drama as an independent being, has paid a heavy price for his rashness. In all the literature of the world there is but one living Francesca: Dante's.

Resurrected for a brief dialogue with the poet, warmed to life by the touch of his soul, she sinks back, as soon as he leaves her, into a darkness that was never again to be pierced.

(*Inferno*, VI)

For an instant the poet, too, sinks as if he would fain accompany his dearest creature into the night of unconsciousness. He is hardly awakened when new impressions master him.

Hell's lust he is to taste no more; now he is to know its bitterness and disgust: "Eternal, maledict, and cold and heavy."

After the howling storm comes filthy rain. The earth reeks. It is Hell's vulgar and repulsive "morning after" debauchery; Cerberus, the foul dog, is rather annoying with his barking, than terrible with claws and bite.

Indolent and deep in the mud lie the souls of the gluttons and wine-bibbers. A Florentine raises himself to a sitting posture:

Ciacco, a parasite and gourmand, of whom the old commentators relate that he made the feasts of rich men merry with his greedy, witty, and foul mouth. His wretched appearance and his enviously malicious speech arouse pity mingled with disgust. When Dante questions this miserable fellow countryman as to the future of their native city, and as to the fate of its illustrious sons, Farinata, Tegghiaio, and Rusticucci, he elicits something of importance from the base mind of this newsmonger. So from a greasy parasite, the political threads wind through the poem.

After Ciacco has given his malignant information and has sunk back, with eyes askance, into the filth, Virgil speaks:

> . . . "He wakes no more
> This side the sound of the angelic trumpet;
> When shall approach the hostile Potentate,
> Each one shall find again his dismal tomb,
> Shall reassume his flesh and his own figure,
> Shall hear what through eternity re-echoes."

Behind the petty figure of the reveller rises the Last Judgment. Three distinct notes are heard together: the misery of the glutton, the evil that overhangs Florence, and the thunder of Judgment Day.

These three sounds unite at once in that harsh sarcasm with which misers and spendthrifts scoff at each other.

(*Inferno*, VII)

Sin, drenched and embittered in disgust, begins to strive against itself in the forms of miserliness and extravagance.

Pluto, who stands guard over these twofold sinners, represents blind, senseless duplicity, the double nature of mismanagement; a purely materialistic rage and frenzy that destroys what it would fain secure, and hungers for what it has destroyed. This monster cannot, must not, be alluring. His speech is something halfway between bestial howl and human utterance. One must be a remarkable philologist to make serious research into the etymology and meaning of Pluto's cry: "Papè Satàn, Papè Satàn, Aleppe!"

Pluto's counterpart as blind madness in giving and taking is Fortuna, who, in accordance with God's decree and in apparent caprice, only seemingly blind, gives and takes: the privileged dispenser of earthly goods, the maker of world-history, "beyond resistance of all human wisdom."

Just between Pluto and Fortuna, between the howling of the monster and Virgil's golden wisdom, the poet has set his description of the misers and the spendthrifts.

Heavy masses of stone or of metal (?) they must roll, with loud outcry, before them, the misers around the one half-circle, the spendthrifts about the other, upon the fourth cornice of Hell. Where the half-circles meet, the twain crash together, scoff at each other, and turn about and repeat their joust on the opposite side. The wanderer strives in vain to recognize one or another among them, so utterly has their sinfulness disfigured them. Only their actions, gestures, utterances, nothing of their form, has the poet portrayed. He has made them quite as shapeless and restless, quite as stirring and as unpicturesque, as Pluto and Fortuna. We see the lustful and the gluttons before us in plastic shape. In this abode of the hoarders and wastrels we hear and see only action and motion; feeling, but no individuality. We have before us an epidemic and materialistic sin. For the miser, all goods are mass and quantity; for the spendthrift, all values are but rags and tatters. They have lost the beautiful world. The poet veils them in loud scorn, which reveals itself in rough rhymes: *chioccia*, *seppe*, *labbia*, *fiacca*, *stipa*, *viddi*, *poppa*, *burli*, *tetro*, *giostra*, *cherci*, *coperchio*, *sozzi*, *appulcro*, *sciocche*, etc.—a hellish orchestra.

(*Inferno*, VII–IX)

After the discord of sin at odds with itself is recognized and portrayed, psychological interest vanishes. From lack of proportion in material things, from bewilderment as to the value of earthly goods, man falls into formal loss of proportion and bewilderment as to his own worth; he tears himself to pieces in anger, loses all desire in his sloth, all aspiration for what is good, or plunges into maddened haughtiness—in short, becomes unrecognizable even to himself. The sins previously noted were indirect disintegration; now the direct disintegration of the self, of personality, is set before us.

The philosophical and theological classification of sins demanded that, after miserliness, *acedia* (unwillingness), and next to it wrathfulness (*ira*), should be treated. But the mettlesome poet was not in a mood to follow this order. To put the indolence of inward deterioration after the hellish strains of materialistic wrath, to let subtle irony or indifferent contempt follow close upon harsh sarcasm—for intellectual indolence and disintegration could hardly be treated save with irony and contempt—that would have meant a falling-off of ethical and poetic energy.

What does the poet do? He changes the vertical order of the scheme into a horizontal one, withdraws the *accidiosi* from our view, and presents to us first the wrathful. Yet even in these he does not become seriously absorbed, but assigns them in part to the scenery, which is to be explained and quickly left behind, and in part to action and assault, which the traveller must actively resist and overcome by force. So just here, where in their pedantry the expositors think they have discovered a series of conceptual incongruities, we have a masterpiece of poetic technique. A degraded and ruined personality is, for Dante, theoretically a thing without interest, but practically something dangerous. His tale grows dramatic, the impressions of his journey fade into the background, and the progress of the pilgrimage demands our attention.

This change is completed even within the seventh canto. Midnight is past; the second day is ended. The second river of Hell, the Styx, comes in sight. The wanderers follow its murky and boiling stream down to the fifth circle, where it forms a morass. Here the wrathful, covered with filth, have their abode in the mud, smite and tear themselves. The *accidiosi*, on the other hand, invisible in the depths, gurgle, and with their complainings make little bubbles on the surface of the stagnant water. We behold humanity, sunk in its own passions, as something sadly meaningless; degraded nature and mere scenery.

But these swamped creatures are unaccountable, and the traveller is destined to experience a sinister surprise among them. At a preconcerted fire-signal, the meaning of which is not understood, because it is as senseless as the utterances of rage, Phlegias comes, swift as an arrow, in his boat, speeding over the water, believing that he detects in the wanderer an enemy, doubtless unknown even to him—but he must submit, disillusioned and incapable of resistance, to Virgil's desire, and serve them as boatman.

Phlegias is not, like Charon, the zealous ferryman of souls. He is the fool of whom the old legend related that he desired to avenge himself on the sun-god Apollo for an insult which was essentially a favour. He represents rebellion which, because made in rage, is its own punishment. "In vain thou shriekest!" A word can master him.

When brutality deems itself wise, it turns arrogant. This bestial arrogance is embodied in Filippo Argenti. Midway across the Styx, he emerges and clutches the boat; but Dante, in bitter anger, casts his curse in the teeth of this stupidly insolent, conceited brutality of his fellow citizen and foe.

Filippo degli Adimari (called Argenti because he in foolish pride had his horses shod with silver) was a Florentine black Guelf, of whose personal feud with Alighieri, of whose wealth, passionate nature, bodily strength, savagery, and assurance, Boccaccio and the other mediæval narrators and Dante-commentators have recorded for us many an incident. The old hatred still quivers in this brief, excited scene. It is a combination of moral detestation and personal hatred so harsh and strong that the reader is horrified:

While we were running through the dead canal,
  Uprose in front of me one full of mire,
  And said, "Who'rt thou that comest ere the hour?"
And I to him: "Although I come, I stay not;
  But who art thou that hast become so squalid?"
  "Thou seest that I am one who weeps," he answered.
And I to him: "With weeping and with wailing,
  Thou spirit maledict, do thou remain;
  For thee I know, though thou art all defiled."
Then stretched he both his hands unto the boat;
  Whereat my wary Master thrust him back,
  Saying, "Away there with the other dogs!"
Thereafter with his arms he clasped my neck;
  He kissed my face and said: "Disdainful soul,
  Blessed be she who bore thee in her bosom.
That was an arrogant person in the world;
  Goodness is none, that decks his memory;
  So likewise here his shade is furious.
How many are esteemed great kings up there,
  Who here shall be like unto swine in mire,
  Leaving behind them horrible dispraises!"
And I: "My Master, much should I be pleased,
  If I could see him soused into this broth,
  Before we issue forth out of the lake."
And he to me: "Ere unto thee the shore
  Reveal itself, thou shalt be satisfied;
  Such a desire 'tis meet thou shouldst enjoy."

A little after that, I saw such havoc
  Made of him by the people of the mire,
  That still I praise and thank my God for it.
They all were shouting, "At Filippo Argenti!"
  And that exasperate spirit Florentine
  Turned round upon himself with his own teeth.

In Filippo Argenti rage and brutality are no longer blind and wild nature, but conscious and malicious. Step by step, without our noticing it, the poet has led us out of the realm of passion and of stupid bestiality to the border of malice (κακία). Here Lower Hell begins, and with it the second and far more extended section of the poem.

But only the conceptual scheme, not the poem, is here divided. On the contrary, the latter continues more stirring, ever tenser; the exchange of words with Argenti was only a prelude to a far greater clash: the contest with the devils, the Furies, and Medusa.

From about the middle of the eighth to the last quarter of the ninth canto the struggle continues over the entrance of the pilgrims into the city of Dis or Lucifer. It is therefore no section by itself, but stands in the midst of the continuous narration: if we study it, however, separately, it can be regarded as a drama in four acts.

Before the wanderers reach the shore, and leave the Styx behind them, they descry the bronze red-hot walls and battlements that enclose the whole lower Inferno. As they arrive, more than a thousand devils appear above the gate. They will permit only Virgil, not the living man Dante, to enter. The latter, a moment previously full of defiance against Filippo Argenti, now humbly and anxiously beseeches his master: "Do not desert me, thus undone!"

He would prefer to turn back. With Dante's defeat the first act ends.

But Virgil does not leave his ward; he parleys with the devils but is rebuffed, and the door of Hell is scornfully shut in his face. Virgil's defeat is the second act.

A pause of expectation follows, filled out by Dante's questions and Virgil's narration of his former descent into Hell, the success of which gives bright hopes. Suddenly the devils turn from defence to attack. The three Furies appear at the summit of the wall and call for Medusa, so that at sight of her the intrusive mortal may be turned to stone.

With both his hands Virgil covers his pupil's eyes to protect him from the awful fate of petrifaction by deadly fright. In this third act the climax is reached. The fourth brings the solution.

What Virgil has hoped and expected comes to pass. A heavenly messenger draws nigh. Tall and mighty as a thunderstorm he strides through the heavy air of Hell and touches the gate with a wand; it opens wide, and the angel thunders his warning to the city. The wanderers enter, "after those holy words all confident."

No simpler or clearer progress of the action can be imagined. In the first two acts the inadequacy of man and of his intellectual powers, in the third the threats of Hell, in the fourth the answer of Heaven; and all most closely interwoven and enlivened by fear, expectancy, hope, and helplessness on the wanderer's part. Nevertheless, the entire passage is regarded as one of the most difficult and least explicable in the *Inferno*. The fault lies with the three verses which the poet inserts between the third and fourth acts of the drama. After he has related how Virgil warns and protects his friend against looking at Medusa, he suddenly turns to the reader:

> O ye who have undistempered intellects,
> Observe the doctrine that conceals itself
> Beneath the veil of the mysterious verses!

Artistically regarded, this brief diversion of our interest, this interruption of the narrative, is a master-stroke; for what now follows, i.e. the intervention of Heaven, required, to so speak, a wholly new tone of voice.

But when we regard these verses as something alien to the poem and as a separate matter, there arises a strife among the learned over the allegorical meaning of Medusa and the Furies. Yes, we even raise the question whether these three fateful verses refer to what precedes or to what follows. So the spectator who, during the pause, has lost the thread, asks his neighbour just where we are; and so disturbs the latter also, who had not lost the connection.

And what special doctrine may be discoverable behind the magic veil? Possibly that, without divine aid, man cannot realize with his natural reason the abysmal malice of the heart? Or perhaps that devilish pride sets itself against self-knowledge? Or that the Furies signify the pangs of conscience, and Medusa doubt or despair?

Are not all these special doctrines paler, narrower, and pettier than the poem? Is the Gorgon that turns men to stone merely doubt, are the Furies merely the sting of conscience? And is Virgil mere natural reason, the city of Hell only the malice of the heart, and the whole mythical struggle only an effort at self-knowledge? Cannot every thinker who becomes absorbed in the poetic view presented draw from it still other doctrines? What ethical observation may not be appended to the single fact that the wrathful have their abode on the same level as a portion of those lost through malice? We must leave it to the pious zeal of Dante worshippers to elaborate such considerations further, for with the super-abundance offered by the *Commedia*, the discussion can have no end.

The drama here noted is characterized above all by the fact that Heaven interferes in Hell, that a religious salvation is effected. But it is not, as in other tales of salvation, an ascent out of night to light. It is a rescue out of darkness into yet darker gloom, a deepening of the consciousness of sin. It is Heaven that drives Hell to the last extremity, forces man, bestialized and disintegrated by passion, into consciousness, moulds out of the beast, under the pressure of the most terrific divine grace, a new man: a negative man, a non-man, who no longer sins from weakness, but willfully. This human horror can come into being only if the divine spirit gives him new clarity and strength of will; that is, gives him clear vision and strength of will to work evil.

The ambassador of God descends into Hell in order to force it to be fully what it is, and to reveal itself in the fullness of its ugliness. Hell opposes this opening up of its inwardness, not from shame, not from weakness or timidity, but from insolence. It fancies that it is Hell by its own handiwork and of its own strength. Threateningly it displays its shapes of terror; for it is a question of concealing its own nature, which is helplessness. The man who lets himself be frightened by such images of terror, and beguiled into belief in the real power of Hell, is lost and turns to stone.

So in this mythical drama, this sham fight of Hell and Heaven's omnipotence, the one with horrible theatrical devices, the other armed with a wand, stand opposed to each other; the one grotesque, the other in majesty unadorned; the one as confusion and uproar, the other as effectiveness and the Word. Man, for whose sake the whole struggle goes on, stands aside, faint-hearted and amazed. It is a drama that leads us out of anxiety to wonderment, from agitation to reflection. It is just this transition that the poet, with these three verses, helps us to make.

The rescuer comes because he was needed. He does not wish to be known or thanked, he has apparently other tasks; and he departs in stormy wind, veiled in his anonymous kindliness. So God appears to anxious children of the world. This messenger of God in Hell, this heavenly one who must make his way through the choking air of night, is a creation of natural belief, but is held and overshadowed by a higher spiritual religion—one of the most remarkable and wondrous creations that ever came forth from the chiaroscuro of pious human imagination.

When a beneficent gift comes from a nameless, alien, kindly divinity, it is not to be discussed, but accepted and utilized. The pilgrims enter. All Dante's amazement, all his curiosity, is naturally centred upon the internal character of the devils' city, which has defended itself so furiously and unsuccessfully. A new world, the kingdom of malice, unfolds itself.

(*Inferno*, X)

After the poet had fully exerted his masterly powers in order to create an artfully natural entrance from upper into lower Hell, he could under no circumstances permit the two realms to fall apart once more. This was the place to treat, with increasing emphasis, the thought of Florence, which Ciacco the glutton had awakened, and which furious Argenti had not permitted to slumber. So, upon the brutality of the Guelf follows the pride of the Ghibelline, Farinata degli Uberti. Ciacco and Argenti are ruled by their passions, and therefore senseless. Farinata, on the other hand, is the most characteristic of Florentines. He is not hidden in filth or slime; he atones his sin in flames.

The first thing that the wanderers see after entering the infernal city is a wide expanse of land dotted with fiery graves. In flaming sepulchres, deep in glowing couches, lie heaps of heretics, or, as we should say, the irreligious. Virgil names the heresiarchs and followers of Epicurus, who have no belief in immortality. But we must not be disturbed by the narrowness of such definitions. We have to do here with a certain psychological presupposition of arrogance and conceit; that is, not with empty and stupid folk, but with strong and evil pride, with personalities that are sufficient unto themselves and recognize nothing higher. Here, too, there is still blindness, lack of moral comprehension, but it is the blindness of strength, the materialism of intellectual aristocrats, of the "enlightened," who here have for their prison the abode of death, a monumental grave, devouring flames as their companions. So the living agony of dead enjoyment, of self-glorification, is made clear. De Sanctis would convince us that the heresiarchs, as a class of sinners, were inserted solely for the sake of Farinata, but that Farinata himself appears not as a sinner, but as a moral hero. It can hardly be that Alighieri, for the sake of an individual, would have destroyed the unity of his poem.

It is true that Farinata does not speak of his sin: but he holds it within him, even as the grave holds him. If he rises for a moment out of his fiery prison, it is but to receive a heavier punishment, and to sink back once more after bitter disillusionment. Farinata's sin or irreligion is as mighty and as powerful as himself. In order to understand the poet's admiration, we must remember that Farinata was one of that savage race of Ghibellines who were one in heart and soul with the greatest mediæval despiser of religion, the Emperor Frederick II. We must set clearly before us how terrible, evil, detestable, and beautiful this mighty example of German knighthood appeared to the imagination of a child of the people, a Guelf and a disciple of Francis. History knows nothing decisive as to Farinata's relation to the Christian religion, but it is natural that the Guelfs should think of their deadly enemy only as a godless man. With this godlessness Farinata is, in Dante's imagination, so wholly unified that the wanderer, as soon as he enters the place of punishment of the heresiarchs, at once in silent thought recalls Farinata. Virgil divines this wish:

> " But in the question thou dost put to me,
> Within here shalt thou soon be satisfied,
> And likewise in the wish thou keepest silent."

Farinata's spirit, even before he becomes visible, dominates the scene: and with him the spirit of Florentine factions.

The chroniclers are wont to trace civic strifes in Florence back to a quarrel between two powerful families (in the year 1215).

And, in fact, the antagonism between Guelf and Ghibelline retained throughout the thirteenth century, and long after, the embittered and personal character of a family feud. Especially for the magnates, the party cause was, to the utmost degree, family interest. How largely political, and especially economic, motives were involved, has been made clear above. In the year 1248, the Emperor Frederick interfered for the first time in the affairs of the city, and Farinata aided him in vanquishing and banishing the Guelfs. With the emperor's death, the tide turned. The Guelfs came back by force, gained the upper hand, and introduced (1251) a comparatively democratic constitution, known as the *Costituzione del primo popolo.* Farinata and his followers were exiled (1258), but found a refuge in Siena and support from King Manfred. On September 4, 1260, Farinata, commander of the Ghibellines, defeated the Florentine Guelfs in a bloody battle at Montaperti, near the river Arbia. The victors, at the close of that month, held a council of war in Empoli to decide the fate of Florence. The general feeling was that this nest of Guelfs should be razed to the ground. Only the "magnanimous, valiant, and wise knight Farinata" opposed this decision, and swore that "so long as a spark of life remained in him, he would with his sword defend the city." [1] The weight of his will turned the scale, and Florence was spared. Farinata died in 1264, one year before Dante was born.

However, the supremacy of the Ghibellines did not long endure. Through the downfall of the Hohenstaufens, in the battle of Benevento (1266), they lost their best supporter, while the Guelfs found an ally in Charles of Anjou. They were soon again in control of the city, and in the year 1267 an effort was made to put an end to party strife by marriages between the most important families. The son of the Guelf, Cavalcante Cavalcanti, Guido, the poet and friend of our Alighieri, was married, though he was still a boy, to Farinata's daughter Beatrice. But as early as Easter of that same year, the most eminent Ghibellines, and among them of course the Uberti family, were forced into banishment. Thereafter they never secured lasting control of the city. Later events—the division of the Guelfs into blacks and whites, the downfall of the latter, their banishment, and Dante's personal misfortune—have been already described.

[1] Villani, VI, 81.

Farinata departed from life in the consciousness of having conquered and assured the supremacy of his party and family. He had a right to regard Florence as the property of himself and his. What wonder that now, when for the first time the speech of Florence reaches his ears, and especially when such a noble utterance as the words addressed by Dante to Virgil is heard—what wonder that he rises in his grave and wishes to know this child of his fatherland: that fatherland "to which I once perchance was too severe." To hear a Florentine speak, to have his thoughts recalled with delight to that beautiful, oft-fought-for Florence, and at the same time to feel the first slight stirring of conscience for his own violence against that dear city—that is the foremost, resistless impulse of this noble and proud spirit.

Dante draws back, affrighted, before the unexpected, mighty voice of this great heart. But Virgil clears his mind. He knows that Dante desired to see Farinata:

> " Behold there Farinata who has risen;
> From the waist upwards wholly thou shalt see him."

With breast free and brow held high, he questions from his fiery grave "e'en as if Hell he had in great despite." Hell grows small compared with his loftiness. Dante, still from a respectful distance, stands eye to eye with him. But as Virgil encourages his pupil and draws him nearer to the imperious man, the latter gazes at his fellow countryman half contemptuously, as one scans a stranger. "Who were thy ancestors?" This he desires to know, and he learns that he has to do with the offspring of a foe, with the son of a Guelf.

> Then said he: "Fiercely adverse have they been
> To me, and to my fathers, and my party;
> So that two several times I scattered them."
> "If they were banished, they returned on all sides,"
> I answered him, "the first time and the second."

The "second time" also! That is for Farinata evil news: the whole work of his life destroyed; his family imperilled, perhaps in misery; his name flouted. Sorrow and anxiety gnaw him within, but he does not let it be seen. He stands immovable and strives for self-control. To relate and analyze, even to dwell on, the spectacle of a humiliation so manfully, proudly, and silently borne, would be unworthy. The discussion is not completed, but so long as the opponent is struggling with the agony of his wound, it cannot go on.

That is why the poet boldly and ingeniously interposed another dramatic scene between the beginning and the end of the first. At Farinata's side a second ghost rises out of the same grave, timorously and cautiously. He wishes to see whether the courageous son of a Guelf who just spoke is alone: whether another, quite as high-hearted, is not with him. It is Guido Cavalcanti's father who, in disappointment and grief, asks after his Guido. Dante answers:

> . . . I come not of myself;
> "He who is waiting yonder leads me here,
> Whom in disdain perhaps your Guido had."

From the expression "*had* in disdain," Cavalcanti cannot but infer that his son has died. For Dante, "had" refers to his vanished youth; for Cavalcanti, it means a vanished lifetime; and, as Dante remains silent, his fear becomes certainty. He falls back with his paternal grief into the grave. Nevertheless, at Easter time of 1300, which is the date of Dante's journey to Hell, Guido was still alive. So Dante, merely because his thoughts were absorbed elsewhere, gave a false impression which he must later recall. Many commentators have taken offence at this mischance. But it is no mischance. The development and tone of the whole scene require it. The second drama must cover the dead-point in the first. For Dante had deliberately driven his arrow into Farinata's heart; to Cavalcanti he had done the same unconsciously. With these irreligious men who wish to suffice unto themselves and to live solely in their own convictions, there can be no successful understanding. Each is bound up in himself. So there is mutual misunderstanding and wounded feeling. Farinata is thinking of his Ghibellines, Cavalcanti of his son. Virgil stands apart, and in Dante's mind also another thought has meantime arisen: the question how it comes to pass that these departed souls no longer have knowledge of their survivors.

The second drama, also, has reached its dead-point. Each one has drawn back and is pondering on a different thought.

Concerning everything that they thus far had to say, each has received only a negative.

But Farinata has meantime mastered his grief. He need no longer conceal the depth of his distress over the defeat and banishment of his partisans: "that tortures me more than this fiery bed." When he now, in sudden enlightenment, prophesies for his opponent Dante the same destiny and, almost in the same words, banishment without return, one tastes still a trace of bitterness in his speech, but no malicious pleasure, no vengeance. He begins to feel himself bound by common misfortune to his political enemy. Why, he asks, all this harshness toward my people? And when Dante reminds him of the blood shed in civic strife at Montaperti, he sighs; but the proud memory of his patriotic action at Empoli holds him erect. He does not excuse or glorify his deeds. He has regained his former balance, his indomitable loftiness of spirit, and can now in brief, calm sentences answer his fellow countryman's successive questions. The drama draws to a close, dissolves in objective conversation, and leads us to a purely theoretical question.

What love is to Francesca, pride, mastered agony, and family loyalty are to Farinata. But neither Francesca nor Farinata is an independent figure; they are great, necessary, passing stages of human nature. Therefore the poet sketched them in powerful words, but did not colour them; summed up their inward greatness, but did not state its details, leaving it to the spectator to think these figures out and forget himself in them. He, however, never forgets himself for an instant. Close to his Farinata, who mightily vanquishes a mighty misfortune, he sets his Cavalcanti, whose force is broken by an imaginary grief; and enfolds them both in a fiery grave which is to hold them forever, after he had summoned them forth for a brief instant. All this time Virgil stands waiting and urges further progress, while Farinata's prophetic words of evil, more persistently gnawing than the prophecy of Ciacco, sink painfully into Dante's soul, and shade off the excitement of the earlier struggles to brooding thoughts. Farinata closes the series of dramatic scenes which began with Filippo Argenti.

Thus a single gigantic poetic wave has carried us over the dam. Only at this point have we time and leisure to think of the new conditions. Poetically considered, the second and lower portion of the Inferno begins here, though the conceptual frontier has long since been crossed.

LOWER HELL

(*Inferno*, XI)

We have passed, without poetic hiatus, out of the realm of the weak will into that of malicious violence. Through an unbroken series of catastrophes the incontinent transgressor becomes the lover of evil. Now that we stand before the first bloody deed, the deadly odour of murder rises out of the depths. Conscience is slain; only disgust remains to be overcome, one need only accustom himself to the stench of crime.

This brief pause in the process that turns a moral man into a savage brute serves to orient the reader. What are all the misdeeds and penalties that yet await us? What relation do they have to that which is already known? The travellers study the plan of the devil's city and its situation for the first time, now that they have entered it and have seen its first inhabitants. Virgil gives his pupil an accurate lecture on the classification and distribution of sinfulness as a whole. The conceptual limitations are here first stated after they have been poetically mastered. Moral philosophy arrives, so to speak, after the feast; for by premature entrance it might have blighted the poetic life of the *Inferno* in the bud; by its belated appearance it will have only a calming and clarifying effect. Just as the life of nature is not destroyed by knowledge of its laws, but rather recognized as order and made helpful and accessible to the practical man, even so the poetic *Inferno*, through the classifications of morality and justice, acquires educational value and general validity. The purely poetical value is certainly not increased thereby, but neither is it harmed or lessened. The eleventh canto is an intermezzo in its proper place, artistically introduced and organized, and, as a link in the poem, indispensable. Imagine it omitted, and the plan of the journey loses its visible unity, Virgil is bereft of a good bit of his wisdom and foresight, the pilgrim is cheated out of his insight and of an opportunity to manifest his thirst for knowledge; and we, the sympathetic readers, are deprived of our restful pause, which we need after so many multicoloured pictures and thrilling impressions.

This eleventh canto is, to be sure, a restful pause only for the imagination, not for the reasoning mind. Dramatic excitement is replaced by didactic tension. Memory and power of abstract thinking are put to a severe test. With austere brevity, in curt, almost impatient language, indicating rather than explaining, the paragraphs of God's criminal code are impressively reviewed. Where Dante believes that he discovers a gap, his guide corrects him almost in tones of reproof.

> "Why wanders so
> Thine intellect from that which is its wont?
> Or, sooth, thy mind where is it elsewhere looking?
> Hast thou no recollection . . .?"

But the pupil thus reproved forgets to be sensitive, in his delight over the subject.

> "O Sun, that healest all distempered vision,
> Thou dost content me so, when thou resolvest,
> That doubting pleases me no less than knowing!"

This delight in questioning and knowing, in learning and teaching, gives poetic life even to the driest science. The treatise becomes a dialogue, the paragraph an epigram, lists turn to watchwords, citations to reminiscences and admonitions, philosophic deductions are transformed into convincing eloquence. The objective poetry of this conceptual system, with its "firstly," "secondly," "thirdly," may fairly be called juridical and theological rhetoric, in the best sense of that word. Without flowers of speech or decorations, brief and bare, in rhythms and rhymes that sound like prose and are repeatedly interrupted by the logical structure of the sentences, the exposition moves forward. The pedantic ingenuity of scholars has made the discovery that this canto is full of ill-made limping lines—as if melodious verses and sonorous rhymes befitted such a subject! If the critic may take exception to anything, it is rather excess than lack of verbal harmony, a surviving remnant of musical quality and effective rhythmic cadence.

(*Inferno*, XII)

Another day of the journey has dawned. It is some three hours after midnight. Down a steep precipice, created by the earthquake on Golgotha at Christ's death, runs the path from the irreligious to the tyrants, murderers, robbers, and slaughterers of mankind. The Minotaur, fruit of unnatural lust between woman and beast—half man, half bull, the monster of Crete that fed on human flesh—is the symbolic guardian of this circle. Other less horrible hybrids, centaurs, stand guard over the sinners.

These mythical creatures are nowise cynical as was Minos, nor are they at all disgusting like Cerberus, nor, in general, in any way grotesque. Despite their twofold nature they are classic, dignified. Their attitudes and movements, their gestures and utterances, are fitting and beautiful. The Minotaur who, smitten by Virgil's consciousness of truth and victory, plunges and tumbles like a fatally wounded bull; the man-horses who, armed with bow and arrows, gallop up and down beside the great boiling river of blood, and, the moment a sinner rises from his crimson bath, wound him with their unerring shafts; Chiron, who stands with head bowed in thought, uplifts it and, with the barb of an arrow, pushes his beard from his mighty mouth and utters vigorous, sonorous, nowise harsh or rasping commands; Nessus, who carries the mortal poet over the river of blood on his broad back, and in quiet, assured speech, with dignified gesture, with serious naturalness, simplicity, and calmness, names the sinners and explains the peculiar nature of the sanguinary stream, and then, having completed his task, goes his way without greeting or farewell—all these are figures of such consummately noble force and style that we imagine ourselves gazing at a Greek frieze.

But how, in the prison of tyrants and bloodthirsty robbers and murderers, is this measured, calm mood comprehensible? Should we not expect the utmost unrest and frenzy? No, for fate has overtaken these brutes and silenced them. They rage no more. Since all their malice was directed outward, so in Hell their inward life is utterly emptied, and without interest. Only their physical pain is uttered in outcries and howls. Of all their deeds naught remains save the trail of blood, "the heart that on the Thames still is worshipped"; of their personality nothing but the name and outer features:

> "That forehead there which has the hair so black
> Is Azzolin; and the other who is blond,
> Obizzo is of Esti."

The poet's eye turns away from the life of a soul grown uneventful and is fixed on the phenomenon of the man-horse. In the atmosphere of pure sensuousness beast and man are alike and can, without becoming grotesque, unite in complete forms and create beautiful, graceful, intelligent, and well-balanced beings, such as are the centaurs.

(*Inferno*, XIII)

On the other bank of the river of blood, tone and scene change radically. Among the violent whose rage was turned against their neighbours, there was no personality and no inward life; more interesting and richer were the outer images that met the eye. Here in the circle of the suicides and squanderers, that is, of the violent whose rage is directed against themselves, all life is again turned inward. The eye of the pilgrim, to be sure, still looks outward, but a desolate, mysterious monotony hedges him in, a gloomy wood without path or trail.

> Not foliage green, but of a dusky colour,
> Not branches smooth, but gnarled and intertangled,
> Not apple-trees were there, but thorns with poison.
> Such tangled thickets have not, nor so dense,
> Those savage wild beasts, that in hatred hold
> Twixt Cecina and Corneto the tilled places.
> There do the hideous Harpies make their nests,
> Who chased the Trojans from the Strophades,
> With sad announcement of impending doom;
> Broad wings have they, and necks and faces human,
> And feet with claws, and their great bellies fledged,
> They make laments upon the wondrous trees.

A subdued lament and weeping swells and quivers through the forest; no human creature is to be seen. It seems as if some one were hidden behind the thicket. Dante, shuddering, stops. But when he, at his guide's bidding, breaks off a tiny twig from a great bush, the plant cries out in human tones and begs for mercy. Gushing, bleeding, articulate sounds stream forth from the broken branch. A burdened human heart, a great tragic doom, struggles forth from the little painful wound and reveals itself. Dante, horrified and sympathetic, hearkens in silence, incapable of uttering a word to the soul within the tree. Virgil must needs intervene and explain.

The imagination of a musician or a painter, set amid the contrasts of this scene, would have gone wild with horror, amazement, and emotion. For Alighieri all that is but a background for the tale of Pier della Vigna.

Pier della Vigna, a Capuan by birth, had risen from humble

surroundings, by discretion and strong-willed ambition, through the hierarchy of courtiers to the rank of imperial chancellor of the Hohenstaufen Frederick II. The unlimited confidence and high favour of his master, which he had won, became his misfortune. Slandered by envious courtiers, and accused—we know not whether rightfully or wrongfully—of high treason, he was imprisoned by the emperor's orders, and his eyes put out. In despair he took his own life (1249).

The poet interpreted these few facts in his own way. He makes Pier della Vigna a suicide "because of his lost honour."

> "My spirit, in disdainful exultation,
> Thinking by dying to escape disdain,
> Made me unjust against myself, the just."

It is the tragedy of the conscientious, passionately proud, ambitious office-holder who has devoted all his powers, all his self-love and conscience, to that office.

> "Fidelity I bore the glorious office
> So great, I lost thereby my sleep and pulses."

These noble and heroic bureaucrats, more familiar to the Germans than to any other people, may become inhuman even toward themselves. If they are overthrown or dismissed, they either kill themselves or become ridiculous. Even in private life their manner of expression recalls the official style. So in the expressions of the Dantesque Pier della Vigna, commentators have found traces of the flowery and elaborate ministerial Latin of that time. This Piero was every inch imperial chancellor. He took his own life because doubt was thrown on his fidelity and competence. In the pride of his official honour he went to his death. Bitterly and desperately hurt, he withdrew within himself as into a tree. Through all eternity he can never forgive, never forget, never recover. Against his emperor who, misled, caused his eyes to be put out, he never for an instant feels resentment. Chance has willed that his mouth, convulsively closed, shall be painfully opened. Now his grievance, set free in blood, gushes agonizingly yet consolingly from his heart: a grievance against all evil report. However curtly, objectively, cleverly he may express himself, however sharp and manly his words sound—there is in them something appealing. We understand Dante's sympathy, and his silence in the presence of this agony.

A painful pause ensues: Virgil breaks the silence, turning the interest to the general condition of suicides in Hell. All of these, to judge from the nature of their punishment, are, like Pier della Vigna, defiant and violently vain. There are no Werther natures among them. They did not kill themselves because weary of the world, but in their rage thought it not worth while to carry through to the end the problem of life. Their souls, which would not endure bravely, knot themselves into thorny brambles. The liberating word that they would not find in life is violently torn from them by the Harpies. Their human bodies against which they sinned will be restored to them on Judgment Day in mockery, and not for a lasting abode. The second suicide with whom the wanderers speak, that unknown Florentine who hanged himself in his own house, actually disdains to tell his story. He mentions his native city in irony. The old destructive god of war, not John the Baptist, he says, is the true guardian spirit of Florence; he will yet give the Florentines more trouble.

The life that has been cast away vegetates in Hell, gnarled, venomous, and motionless. Other sinners who, like the Sienese Lano or Giacomo da Santo Andrea, madly flung away all worldly goods, rush frantically, chased by hungry dogs, howling and shrieking through the thickets, and are torn to pieces. They are the suicides of their own economic life, who in this uproarious fashion keep company with the destroyers of their own physical life. A frenzied, noisy chase sweeps through the horror of the wood and leaves behind the torn and bleeding human bushes.

(*Inferno*, XIV–XVI)

The agony of the hardened and defiant spirit is heightened to frenzy in those who had directed their violence, their rebellion, against God. In the figure of the blasphemer stubbornness and pride attain their peak, Here, it may be said, the ethos of sin and hatred toward God is triumphant. The external torture, the fiery rain which unceasingly and unerringly falls from a hostile heaven upon the sandy desert of the rebels, means nothing to the defiance of Capaneus.

He is a heathen, one of the Seven against Thebes, a mythical rather than a historical figure. The god whom he mocks is called Jupiter, not Christ or Mary, and his blasphemy is veiled in mythological illusions. Were it not thus transferred, this vicious assault against the divinity would have been hardly endurable by Christian ears. But it is only an æsthetic softening, not a moral alleviation, of the blasphemy. All the pride, all the sacrilegious contempt and fury, all the defiance of which the unholy spirit is capable, resound together in the curse of Capaneus. It is a long-winded, eloquently arranged curse, deliberately studied and sharpened, at once passionate and subtle. To offset this harsh note, the deepest tone of Virgil's mighty voice is required: and thereupon the turmoil subsides and calm returns.

The evil-doers that follow after Capaneus, sodomites who have sinned against Nature, despite all the ethos and pathos of their wickedness, are hardly worthy of any especial exertion of poetic power.

Why did the poet put not Capaneus, but the sodomites, at the utmost extreme of sin by violence? And why, since he did put the two together in a single circle, has he not set the sinners against Nature first, and the magnificent blasphemer against God last? Has he not neglected an effective climax?

The best reply is that facile effects and brilliant arrangements are not at all characteristic of the steadfast epic progress of this poem. The passionate climaxes always stand midway, or at any rate never at the end, of the poetic units of the *Commedia.* At the close of a canto, or of certain grouped cantos, the tone usually drops.

It is further to be considered that the soul of a typical sodomite bears but little relation to the normal blasphemer. A natural, evident transition was not practicable. There was, so to speak, a lack of foundation for an ethical and pathetic climax from the one sin to the other. So Dante with delicate art inserted a mythical episode between the blasphemers and sodomites.

Sodomy is something indecent and repulsive, like gluttony or drunkenness, and chiefly physical; it usually does not at once destroy the individual altogether, and leaves the character, to a great extent, intact. Therefore Alighieri, to whom character is always of interest, faces such sins in the *Purgatorio* as well as in the *Inferno* without profound ethical abhorrence. In the realms of gluttony and sensuality he is fond of turning his thoughts to higher things, and of muting in these passages the moral keynote that resounds throughout his entire poem. With the gourmand Ciacco, and with Forese, he talks of political matters; with Bonagiunta, Arnaut Daniel, and Guido Guinizelli, he speaks of poetry; and with the sodomite trio, Guido Guerra, Tegghiaio, and Rusticucci, and with Brunetto Latini, his discourse is once more of politics.

The mythical episode inserted between the two groups of sinners is the mysterious "old man of Crete," an interlude between violence against the spirit and violence against nature, between gigantic and terrible beings and the vilest and basest creatures, between fearful perversion of the heart and unendurable error of the senses. We can admire a rebel against the Deity; in the presence of the debased instincts of nature we stand aghast. Our human self-respect feels itself degraded; the disgust and misery of original sin overcome us. We detect and behold sin as an incomprehensible necessity, as something older and more deep-seated than our nobler will.

Under the impressions of such feelings and thoughts, the excited imagination creates a fatalistic myth of man's original sin.

Before Virgil guides his pupil to the sodomites he shows him a bloody brook. It is the Phlegethon which flows out of the wood of the suicides into the fiery desert of sand, and thence hither by unseen ways.

"In the mid-sea there sits a wasted land,"
 Said he thereafterward, "whose name is Crete,
 Under whose king the world of old was chaste.[1]
There is a mountain there, that once was glad
 With waters and with leaves, which was called Ida;
 Now 'tis deserted, as a thing worn out.
Rhea once chose it for the faithful cradle
 Of her own son; [2] and to conceal him better,
 Whene'er he cried, she there had clamours made.
A grand old man stands in the mount erect,
 Who holds his shoulders turned tow'rds Damietta,
 And looks at Rome as if it were his mirror.
His head is fashioned of refined gold,
 And of pure silver are the arms and breast;
 Then he is brass as far down as the fork.
From that point downward all is chosen iron,
 Save that the right foot is of kiln-baked clay,
 And more he stands on that than on the other.
Each part, except the gold, is by a fissure
 Asunder cleft, that dripping is with tears,
 Which gathered together perforate that cavern.

[1] In the Golden Age Saturn ruled as a King in Crete. [2] Jupiter.

From rock to rock they fall into this valley;
Acheron, Styx, and Phlegethon they form;
Then downward go along this narrow sluice
Unto that point where is no more descending.
They form Cocytus; what that pool may be
Thou shalt behold, so here 'tis not narrated."

This giant, this idol, is the creation of an imagination almost Chinese. Life that degenerates, development that leads to decay, progress that becomes disgrace, power and splendour that turn to weakness, the whole story of civilization and freedom become botchwork—that is the general meaning of this grotesquely impressive figure. Merely for contemplation Virgil sets it before his pupil, who studies in it the geography of Hell.

Meantime that disconsolate melancholy which we feel when we see the profoundest sources of our nature poisoned is imperceptibly and gently dissipated, so that an easy conversation now becomes possible between Dante and the sodomites.

And how cordially Dante speaks to his fellow townsman and old teacher, Brunetto Latini! The confidential exchange of thoughts is in sharp contrast with the inhospitable region in which pupil and teacher meet. Dante walking along on a protected wall or dyke, Brunetto with other sinners beneath the fiery rain and disfigured by burns, with difficulty recognize each other; but at every word that they exchange, something of the barrier between them falls away. Out of the fact that the master finds himself in a humiliating position, the pupil in an honourable one, that the one bends down in all love and reverence, while the other looks up at first shamefaced, then joyous and unenvious, there arises a hearty and charming interplay of feeling. Brunetto is one of those good, unselfish teachers who are glad if their pupils surpass them. Not for his own sake, but for Dante's, he would have wished to live longer. The misfortune of his pupil, which he foresees, he charges not to Dante, but to the malice and wickedness of the Florentines. His invective against Florence becomes a eulogy of Dante. Thou art too good for that people!—thus he consoles him for his impending exile. Our pilgrim faces with cheerful defiance a banishment so lovingly announced. In contact with his old teacher he has regained the courage to live, and now even the tortured soul thinks with some pride of the learned book that bears his name on earth: "Commended unto thee be my *Tesoro*." So each was stimulated by the other. Dante has shown a new side of himself, as a loving pupil and cordial man.

Since Brunetto in his unselfishness could not reveal any well-marked trait of his own, the clearer light falls on Dante, though he does not push himself forward nor give us an occasion to feel the slight turn in the poetic interest.

Among the sodomites are to be found not only great scholars and grammarians, but also notable warriors, statesmen, knights, and magnates. Three eminent Florentines, the battle-tried leader of the Guelfs, Count Guido Guerra, his powerful fellow partisan Tegghiaio Aldobrandi degli Adimari, and the rich, highly respected citizen Jacopo Rusticucci, hastened through the fiery rain to the dike where Dante walked with Virgil. All three belonged to the great generation of the Florentine civil wars. Their deeds were told with reverent admiration in Florence when Dante was a boy. When he first met Ciacco the glutton, he asked concerning these chieftains of the people. Now he sees these dignitaries running after him amid rain and sand, though he is unknown to them—circling about him, unable to stand still under the shower of fire. There is a conversation similar to that between Dante and Brunetto. Eager courtesy, reverence, and sympathetic attraction on the one side; courteous requests, growing admiration, hasty greeting and farewell on the other. A capital picture of the situation. But Dante steps more decisively than at first into the foreground, and the three mighty characters are even more dimly drawn than Brunetto.

What unites the traveller with these less familiar fellow citizens is solely their common interest in their native city. This has become so purely personal and moral that in answering the inquiry about conditions on earth, Dante does not speak to the questioner alone, but to Florence, and in the presence of the entire Inferno:

> "The new inhabitants and the sudden gains,
> Pride and extravagance have in thee engendered,
> Florence, so that thou weep'st thereat already!"
> In this wise I exclaimed with face uplifted;
> And the three, taking that for my reply,
> Looked at each other, as one looks at truth.

We see how the poet, since his meeting with Latini, slowly and gradually builds himself a seat of judgment, from the height of which he flings his curt indictment at Florence in such a fashion that it flies over the heads of his characters into reality.

The middle of the sixteenth canto thus closes the artistic circle which began at the opening of the fourteenth, and holds closely and firmly together two such diverse human types as blasphemers of God and sodomites.

(*Inferno*, XVII)

We forget, however, that in the same circle the usurers are included as a third type of mankind. In accordance with the moral and philosophical division outlined by Virgil, usury, like sodomy, is a form of violence against nature, and, like blasphemy, an insult to divine law.[1] But the typical usurer, regarded psychologically, might be thought as remote from the sodomite as is the latter from the blasphemer.

The poet, to be sure, united the usurers spatially with the sodomites; he thus brought the divisions of Hell into harmony with the sections of his law; but as to time, that is, as to the succession of the experiences that befall the pilgrims, their sensations and reactions, he has separated the usurers as widely as possible from the sodomites. The usurers are accordingly still included in the circle of the violent, but the incident which leads to them is part of another unity, lyrically and also ethically distinct.

Long before Dante has any occasion to think of the usurers, his eager eyes and ears are met by a host of novel impressions. Yonder is the cataract of Phlegethon that falls with a roar into the dizzy depths of the eighth circle, that is, the third of the lower Hell. Dante is reminded of a waterfall seventy-five yards in height which he may have seen in the Apennines of Romagna. Virgil throws the cord, with which Dante had girt himself for the journey to Hell, into the abyss.

At this signal, a strange and terrible monster swims up through the dusky pit and lays himself down on the edge of the rock. Geryon, we are told, has a kindly human face, but an evil-looking pointed tail, hairy paws, and a snakelike body which is painted with all sorts of knots and rings. It is all an image of fraud. Geryon is the messenger of the eighth circle, the realm of deceit and treachery. The cord of the law, i.e. of obedience and loyalty, has had the power to entice him out of the depths and to subject

[1] Cf. *Inferno*, XI, 99 sqq.

him to Virgil's will. Much subtle thought has been expended upon this cord, but its significance should be made tolerably clear by the service which it renders.

To be sure, the casting off of the cord, the appearance of the monster, and even the assurance of the poet that he really did see Geryon, have a surprising effect and seem almost prearranged.

As the wayfarers approach the landing-place of Geryon, Dante catches sight of a group of sinners: the usurers. While Virgil is coming to an understanding with the monster, Dante goes to observe briefly this third type of the violent in the seventh circle. After seeing something so utterly monstrous as Geryon, and afraid to tarry longer, he is not in the mood for deeper sympathy. People who have taken advantage of their neighbours might properly be included among the deceitful. The fiery rain intended for the men of violence affects these merely as an annoyance, hardly as a penalty. So they react to it in comic fashion, shaking off the flakes of fire and behaving like an irritated dog ridding himself of vermin. At the neck of each hangs a purse bearing his coat of arms, and they take advantage of Dante's presence to add the personal irony of their mutual insults to the objective irony of their condition. They utter, brief and shrill, the note which is to resound deeper below.

After the realm of the fraudulent has been thus announced, we are prepared for the descent. And yet it is no descent, but a flight through night and air, a strange ride on Geryon's back. To the wiles of deceit only the arch-deceiver can lead us. The strange situation arises that the craftiest of creatures, half man and half serpent, must help on the journey in quest of knowledge. The friends of truth ride on the dragon of falsehood: a venturesome undertaking that requires utmost foresight, tremulous alertness, and ever-wakeful distrust. With tingling senses, wide-open eyes, suppressed breath, jumping nerves and muscles, Dante clings to his conveyance and to his guide. Every movement of the beast, every turn of its flight, is followed and observed with full consciousness. His anxiety makes it clear as day. From these conditions the poet delineates the flight so vividly that we feel as if we were with him. Under the pressure of fright the mind is wont to exaggerate fantastically, but here everything is reported objectively and with the utmost accuracy. The description is based not solely on Dante's excited mood, but also on the cool equanimity of Virgil, who is assured of his mastery over Geryon. In relating the story this calmness is shared by the narrator; it clarifies and arranges his vision, and we perceive the sequence of events as through a double mirror—of fright and of confidence. By this means the poet enables us to glide, so to speak, free of dizziness, slowly and gracefully into the abyss.

(*Inferno*, XVIII)

We are in the eighth circle. In ten concentric moats, hollowed in the rocks, and uniformly bridged over, the tenfold types of deceit are held and tortured—from the vulgar and base to the crafty, treacherous deceitfulness of the heart, a tenfold crescendo. Procurers and seducers of virgins in the first moat, flatterers and wantons in the second. The former are lashed by devils, the latter are immersed in filth. Debasing and degrading penalties befit a filthy calling.

The poet selects a modern, then an ancient, example of each type. The two moderns, the Bolognese nobleman Venedico Caccianemico as pander, and Signor Alessio Interminei of Lucca as flatterer, he perhaps knew personally. He expresses his contempt for them in conversation. The ancient examples Jason the seducer, and Thaïs the hetaira, are given to Virgil to describe. From far and near he shows us baseness: at first with biting, then with veiled and deeper, irony. In the person of Caccianemico, who acted as go-between for his own sister Ghisolabella and the Marquis of Este, the ignoble action is painted scandalously; all Bologna is compromised; everything is mercilessly uncovered. In the case of Jason we have a magnificent Don Juan with a baseness that contrasts with his knightly figure. "Still what a royal aspect he retains!" His shameful deeds are reported as something noteworthy. Alessio Interminei typifies cowardly flattery that would fain hide, and is unmasked by the mere mention of his name. With Thaïs, flattery becomes shameless, a selfish art which rouses our moral disgust while outwardly amusing us. Therefore Dante presented her in the most revolting situation, but added a little rococo boudoir scene out of her life-story.

(*Inferno*, XIX–XXIII)

As soon as fraud imperils state or Church and ecclesiastical baseness appears as simony—in the third moat of the circle—a new tone is heard. Without transition the nineteenth canto begins in fierce anger:

> O Simon Magus, O forlorn disciples,
> Ye who the things of God, which ought to be
> The brides of holiness, rapaciously
> For silver and for gold do prostitute,
> Now it behoves for you the trumpet sound,
> Because in this third Bolgia ye abide.

Simony is venality and bribery in spiritual and ecclesiastical matters. Akin to it is a form of secular simony, that is, venality in administrative or judicial office: barratry. The questions must arise, why Dante did not put these two forms of deceit directly side by side, and why he let pass so effective a descent as that from secular to ecclesiastical simony would have been. Why has he assigned the third ditch to the simoniacs, the fifth to the barrators, and the fourth to the soothsayers, who have no visible connection with either? Like the nineteenth canto, the twentieth also begins somewhat harshly and abruptly. We receive at first glance the impression of capricious disarrangement of the poet's scenes. It is a case like the previous one, where the order of blasphemers, sodomites, and usurers can be justified only poetically and lyrically.

In the famous edict of banishment, January 27, 1302, Alighieri had been accused by his fellow citizens of venality, and so of secular simony, of graft. In the depths of his heart, however, he feels himself so pure of such guilt that he can contemplate it without bitterness; yes, can even depict it with the cheeriest humour of which his character is capable. The official who takes advantage of a good opportunity to put another man's money into his own pocket is to Dante a clever rogue who could fool the Devil, if God in Heaven were not omniscient. The infernal comedy of Cantos XXI and XXII is inspired by this genuinely Italian conviction.

It stands in sharp contrast to the sternness with which ecclesiastical simony is treated. To the corruption of state officials Dante had adjusted himself, and he could depict it in comic fashion. Ecclesiastical venality, however, and the corruption of the papacy, he detested and fought throughout his life. For him, therefore, the question was one of a full ethical tension here, a loose one there. While simony and barratry are, from the moral and psychological point of view, so closely akin, none the less wide apart are the states of mind which they arouse in our poet's memory. Therefore Alighieri, who is determined to live his poem, requires a means of transition from his first mood to the second. This he finds in the description of the soothsayers in the twentieth canto. In the presence of the false prophets it is primarily Virgil, the poet-seer, whose wrath is roused, while Dante, the foe of the simoniac popes, has time to recover from his moral indignation.

But why do the prophets and sorcerers and not some other class of sinners provide the bridge from spiritual to worldly simony? A closer examination of the canto on simony will make this clear.

The pilgrims come from the ditch of the panders and prostitutes to that of spiritual adultery. The Church is the bride of Christ. Therefore his wrath is hurled directly at the highest responsible office, at the supreme head of the Church, the pope. After the first apostrophe, we expect a thundering explosion. Instead, with a firm and surprising directness, the poet slowly, cautiously, with a cool smile, draws his bow. He calmly describes the locality, even alludes to something apparently personal, but is already aiming at the head of his foe.[1] The rock bottom of the third moat is full of round holes; they are like the holes in which the priest stands as he baptizes.[2] But here the simoniac priests are set head downward in the holes. Only their twitching feet are visible. Tongues of flame play to and fro on the soles, as if on fatty fuel—a cruelly, maliciously, and accurately described torture.

Three popes, still living or fresh in memory, have been put by the poet into one of these holes, in such a fashion that the newcomer, crashing in headlong, pushes his predecessor farther down. This description of the popes, with feet ablaze and thrust into a hole, is inspired by an almost brutal scorn, and threatens a lack of respect for the Holy See as such. Let us imagine Giovanni Gaetano Orsini, who as Nicholas III (1277–1280) had sat in Peter's chair, the powerful Boniface VIII, who died in the year 1303, and Clement V, the first Avignonese pope, whose earthly remains, perhaps only a few months before (1314), had been laid to rest—imagine these highest dignitaries branded in such fashion by a

[1] Undoubtedly verses 19–21 in Canto XIX have a hidden reference to simoniacs, as the defilers of things holy. It is precisely from them that the poet wishes to distinguish himself, who had broken a sacred object in order to save a child.

[2] Such holes are to be seen in the baptistry at Pisa.

poet of their own day! And yet the whole canto is neither ignoble nor irreverent, but austere and noble throughout. It is with the finest and soberest hues that the audacious savagery of the drawing is coloured. The two latest popes, Boniface and Clement, are not yet in Hell at all; for the poet has assigned his journey to the year 1300. The presence of Nicholas III in the hole is indicated, indeed, but only indirectly. The wanderers are obliged to clamber down to him from the edge of the rock above. Dante leans over the hole in a listening attitude, which he describes as rather comic than dignified. He does not know who is tortured there. This man takes him for his own successor Boniface. Dante is bewildered by the pope's words. He remains, uncomprehending, in his stooping posture. In frank and brief words, with manful self-criticism, Nicholas makes all clear to him and confesses his own name, his guilt and punishment, thus rising spiritually above himself, though he remains in the hole; and not only above himself, but above his successors Boniface and Clement, whose misdeeds and fate he announces with prophetic pathos. Even in his degradation this Orsini, who fell into simony not for his own but for his family's sake, retains something of his pride. The reader, however, realizes it later and through his own meditation, not directly from the poet's picture of the pocketed popes. Instead of a cruelly comic and petty scene we have a far-reaching, prophetic, and tragic outlook.

This prophetic tone which Nicholas strikes is taken up by Dante, is continued in a speech of reproof, at first personal, but growing ever loftier and closing with apocalyptic notes which warn of historical and divine judgment.

Virgil, the poet of the empire, stands attentively by and rejoices that his pupil can so forcefully scourge the worldly character of the papacy. In his enthusiasm he encircles him with his arms and carries him up to the bridge that arches over the fifth moat, setting him down gently on the crest of the rock.

Now we understand why the false prophets and sorcerers have their place in the fifth ditch. The father of simony had been a sorcerer, and the previous canto had rung ever louder and deeper of the future and the past so that with absolutely perfect continuity, after the simoniacs, panders, and barterers of the spirit, come the soothsayers and sorcerers, the swindlers and forgers of the spirit.

After his attack on the popes, Dante is exhausted; his hatred of Boniface and Clement was aroused, and he needed to regain self-control. In weariness he begins the twentieth canto: "Of a new pain behoves me to make verses."

The sight of this new anguish he cannot endure. As he beholds the terribly distorted figures of the soothsayers, who carry their faces turned backward on twisted necks, as he sees their tears trickle down their shoulders and backs, he leans against the rock wall and weeps. Virgil reproves him, condemns his weakness, and in strenuous words, with an abundance of special explanations and reminders, points out to him the sinners who silently pass by. The eloquence of the wise and zealous guide is effectively contrasted with the speechless sorrow of the spectacle. Our inward eye, following Virgil's utterances, slowly turns away from the disfigured human frames, and feasts on historical and legendary memories. Amphiaraus, the soothsayer whom the earth of Thebes swallowed, Tiresias, who transforms himself by magic into a woman and then again into a masculine shape, Aruns, the Etruscan interpreter of sacrifices and of the stars, and finally Manto, the virgin seer—a varied, long-banished, romantic world of magic reveals itself. When Virgil comes to speak of Manto and his own native city, he cannot refrain from describing the whole fair land of his home, the lake of Garda with its shores, the course of the Mincio and its meadow lands, and the great swamps about Mantua; and how the wandering prophetess had founded here her city in the midst of the wilderness. With such utterances he lightens his pupil's heart and his own. The tale of Mantua's foundation seems at first irrelevant and appears like a pleasant digression, but doubtless has its deeper significance. Here, in the abode of the mystifiers, Virgil, the conscientious, wishes to dissipate the errors which overlie the past of his fatherland, correct his own statements (*Aeneid*, X, 198 sqq.), and "pay to historical truth its due." His intimate, sincere speech offsets the hocus-pocus of the witches and wizards, who have now been silenced.

While Virgil and Dante proceed, conversing, a new day of their journey through Hell has dawned, with a masterly transition from the twilight of romance to the harsh comic glare of Hell.

We are in the fifth moat of the eighth circle, where corrupt officials and greedy rascals gasp in sticky pitch.

The humour of this canto has been criticized as too elaborate and bitter, the comic element as rude and stiff. But hearty laughter can be heard only where misery is absent. If the poet, in the realm of malice, had found space for free and happy comedy, then the keynote of the *Commedia*, which throughout the hundred cantos is essentially ethical, would have been lost. Just as far as the seriousness of the general tone permits, and to the very limit of what is artistically possible, cheerful and good-natured humour is here in evidence. A single stride further in imaginative indulgence, and the earnestness of the *Inferno* would have been impaired.

In the infernal comedy of the fifth moat, four types of characters appear: first the devils, a tricky, brutal, lying troop, with cynical wit and malicious spirit. Each devil by himself is by no means stupid, but as they appear together, their intelligence is comparatively short-sighted and childish. Secondly, the sinners, the first of whom is passively maltreated and derided by the devils, while another succeeds in outwitting the entire company. By this tricky game, by this undignified brawling of sinners and devils, the rights and power of the demons as guards and dispensers of penalties, and of the sinners as punished criminals, are disturbed and, at least for a moment, put aside to make room for a farce. Such a trick as the Navarrese Ciampolo carries out is certainly not the rule and custom. It is an exceptional incident which would hardly have occurred if Dante, the third character in the comedy, had not given the opportunity for question and answer, proposals and discussions, and if the fourth personage, Virgil, had not undertaken to intervene. The devils promptly recognize Dante and Virgil as the causes of their mishap and attempt to wreak vengeance. So the friends of truth, without intending it, give occasion to errors and deceptions. One may be no less scrupulously a man of honour than Dante, may be equipped with no less assurance and absolute power than Virgil, and yet, in the midst of rascals, may at best bring about mad confusion, and in the end be persecuted and belied. This unintentional mishap has been utilized by the poet as a source of merry humour and keenest ridicule.

That is to say, a particular comic note originates from each of the four types of actors. The sinner, once a councillor of Lucca, and in part also Ciampolo, are treated with bitter scorn and abused with malicious wit. The devils are possessed of a coarse realistic humour which ends, to their discomfiture, in a drastic and comic situation. Dante himself, against his will, appears as an element in the comedy. Virgil, though momentarily deceived by the devils, maintains quietly and discreetly the note of serious dignity. Imagine Virgil absent, and the comedy would degenerate into a wild farce.

A rough and cutting laughter, which gradually grows stronger until it finally becomes uproarious, rings out in this scene—and is silenced in serious thought. The comic element in these cantos bears throughout the character of a passing phase. No one of the four types of personages is in itself comic. Only strange combinations bring laughter to this moat of fluid pitch.

A councillor from Lucca brought hither by the devil is cast into the seething stream. The sudden change from Lucca to Hell is pure comedy of situation, the significance of which is duly emphasized by the devil:

> . . . "Here the Santo Volto has no place!
> Here swims one otherwise than in the Serchio." [1]

While the councillor struggles for breath, the devils drop him in the pitch as a cook might drop meat into a boiling pot.

These same cruel devils next go after the wanderers. The bridge is broken down at this point. They are in need of guidance. Virgil proceeds to negotiate with them, while Dante hides behind a rock. The chief devil orders his uncanny comrades to escort the travellers. At first timidly, then curiously, and at last good-humouredly, Dante observes the grotesque bodyguard assigned to him.

> A savage company! But so 'tis said
> At church with saints, with roisters in the tavern.

The situation is disturbing to him, but amusing. While he still dreads the power and trickiness of the rogues, he cannot but laugh at their droll behaviour and enjoy their wit.

See there! They have fished a sinner out of the pitch and mean to tear him in pieces. But Dante wishes first to learn who he is and whence he comes. The sinner, a cunning fellow, Ciampolo from Navarre, takes advantage of the opportunity, and tells his

[1] The Santo Volto is a miraculous image of Christ in the cathedral at Lucca, by which city the river Serchio flows.

tale as well as he can, as interestingly as he can, and having persuaded the devils to step back from the shore, escapes their claws and plunges into the pitch. Two devils flying at his heels fall in the brew, whence they are with difficulty rescued. With this farcical catastrophe the infernal humour culminates in a clash of bodies. "And in this manner busied did we leave them."

In silence the two go their way. Only the moral of the noisy scene still speaks, softly as though from a fable of Aesop, to Dante's inward ear. Harm to others, harm to self; another's mishap mine own, says he comfortably to himself; then it occurs to him that it was his fault that the devils fell into the pitch. Anxiety possesses him. They are already after him with heels and wings. If Virgil had not taken him in his arms and carried him, as a mother does her child, safely down the rock wall to the bed of the sixth moat, the jest would have been fatal for him.

Perilously pursued by the armed malice of the devils, the poets take refuge among the smooth falsities of the hypocrites.

(*Inferno*, XXIII)

The poet's epic hatred, which, though most bitterly aroused against the simoniacs, was felt in the other moats also, has been dissolved in laughter.

Towards the sinners in the remaining moats, Dante's mood is different. His conscience is not concerned with the horrors of the second half of the eighth circle. Sympathy and anger hardly dim his eye again. His delineation becomes constantly clearer and more objective, until, in the last circle of the *Inferno*, it cools down to a mere formal report, like one on some famous robber or murderer who interests us as a strange phenomenon, but is otherwise too remote to awaken in us a reaction of sentiment. Astonishment, horror, and every sort of imaginative abhorrence are driving out ethical excitement. Picturesqueness increases and finally maintains itself in the calm tones of scientific accuracy.

How did the poet keep the ethical undertone and the conscientious notes of his symphony from being drowned in the din of a remorseless world?

The description of the hypocrites was a difficult problem. A hypocrite is interesting poetically only so long as we have not yet seen through him. But God's Hell contains only unmasked hypocrites. The bland cleverness with which they kept this false nature turned toward the world is gone. Slowly and laboriously, groaning under their heavy burdens of leaden cloaks, they drag themselves along. It is not they who are poetically important; it is their condition, their environment, and this new mantle of gilded lead which has come upon them. The peculiarity of their bearing is the manner in which all their movements are hampered. Caiaphas, the archhypocrite, actually lies firmly nailed on the ground, "crucified with three stakes upon the earth."

This state of things, by its very nature, permits of no dramatic movement. If nevertheless the poet presents to us two hypocrites talking, it is because he wishes to expose two detested political characters out of the most recent history of his native city, Catalano Malavolti and Loderingo Andalò; if he starts to set forth vigorously the details of the betrayal of the Ghibellines by these members of the Bolognese "Joyous Brethren," when they were acting as Podestà of Florence in the year 1266, he does it so that by the sudden change which follows we may feel more clearly how useless it is to discuss right and wrong with hypocrites.

The loss of ethical interest, which we characterized as a hidden danger in these cantos, is recognized and made evident by the poet.

(*Inferno*, XXIV–XXV)

Since now no personality rises above the whole horizon of the poem, Nature becomes the object of ethical attention. The wanderers have lost their way. Their understanding, their will, their muscles, must push on in a fierce struggle through the rocky wilderness.

> Still we arrived at length upon the point
> Wherefrom the last stone breaks itself asunder.
> The breath was from my lungs so milked away,
> When I was up, that I could go no farther,
> Nay, I sat down upon my first arrival.
> "Now it behoves thee thus to put off sloth",
> My Master said; "for sitting upon down,
> Or under quilt, one cometh not to fame,
> Withouten which whoso his life consumes
> Such vestige leaveth of himself on earth,
> As smoke in air or in the water foam."

In the seventh moat, where deceit takes the form of robbery, Dante feasts his eyes with cruel eagerness on the punishment.

His moral hatred, instead of softening into indifference, rises to savagery. He himself, the spectator, grows unnaturally blood-thirsty. "From that time forth the serpents were my friends." But it is not the cold æstheticism of an intellectualist that makes him cruel; rather it is the shocked feelings of a man whose moral consciousness has become unbalanced. For in the presence of thieves, forgers, and traitors, his ethical hatred grows fanatical. From the zealous eagerness of his gaze we divine the force of his moral will. If the mood of the last cantos of the *Inferno* offends the taste of a gentle, well-balanced man like Goethe or Manzoni, the reason is to be sought not in the poetical but in the moral powers of perception. For despite the exaggeration of the elemental moral feeling, the artistic balance is thoroughly and classically maintained. The cruder the motifs, the purer grow the pictures. Nowhere is the rage of an injured conscience described with greater calmness and vividness.

> We from the bridge descended at its head,
>   Where it connects itself with the eighth bank,
>   And then was manifest to me the Bolgia;
> And I beheld therein a terrible throng
>   Of serpents, and of such a monstrous kind,
>   That the remembrance still congeals my blood. . . .
> Among this cruel and most dismal throng
>   People were running naked and affrighted,
>   Without the hope of hole or heliotrope.
> They had their hands with serpents bound behind them;
>   These riveted upon their reins the tail
>   And head, and were in front of them entwined.
> And lo! at one who was upon our side
>   There darted forth a serpent, which transfixed him
>   There where the neck is knotted to the shoulders.
> Nor *O* so quickly e'er, nor *I* was written,
>   As he took fire, and burned; and ashes wholly
>   Behoved it that in falling he became.
> And when he on the ground was thus destroyed,
>   The ashes drew together, and of themselves
>   Into himself they instantly returned.
> Even thus by the great sages 'tis confessed
>   The phœnix dies, and then is born again,
>   When it approaches its five-hundredth year;
> On herb or grain it feeds not in its life,
>   But only on tears of incense and amomum,
>   And nard and myrrh are its last winding-sheet.

And as he is who falls, and knows not how,
By force of demons who to earth down drag him,
Or other oppilation that binds man,
When he arises and around him looks,
Wholly bewildered by the mighty anguish
Which he has suffered, and in looking sighs;
Such was that sinner after he had risen.
Justice of God! O how severe it is,
That blows like these in vengeance poureth down!

These are no ordinary thieves; it is a desperate gang of robbers and kleptomaniacs who are given over to serpents and dragons, the venomous guardians of hidden treasures. The man whom we just saw consumed by fire and reborn is Vanni Fucci, a bestial bastard from Pistoia, a bloodthirsty despoiler of churches. "I saw no soul as insolent toward God." With the delight of a hound he prophesies civil war and destruction for his native city and for Florence. With an indecent gesture he scoffs at God, just as the serpents assail him afresh.

Like Vanni Fucci are the other sinners of this circle: the murderous centaur and cattle-thief Cacus, and the five Florentines of whom we learn hardly anything definite. They are not to be regarded as thieves in the ordinary sense, but as rebels against a holy right of property. It was from a similar point of view that Dante put the wastrels with the suicides. His thieves are godless offenders who steal less from love of wealth than from hatred of all law. They are not accidental thieves, but confirmed kleptomaniacs. As such, they are hardly human; hence their burning to ashes and their transformation into serpents and creatures halfway between serpent and man. Inwardly these half-human, half-bestial natures can hardly be made intelligible. We have before us a mystery of the soul and of boundlessly evil natures. Only externally, by the most exact and painstaking observation and through the vivid description of their transition from man to beast, from beast to man, do they become intelligible. The incomprehensible marvel of their horrible metamorphoses must be revealed to us so visibly that it is logically convincing and almost seems necessary. The burning of Vanni Fucci, the figure of Cacus, and the twofold transformation of the Florentine thieves, are no aimless exploits in the professional art of description; they are more than that, for they are accompanied and enlivened by a succession of sensations which are to be understood not merely from literary parallels, e.g. in Ovid or Lucan, but quite as well from the ethical nature of the subject, which is thoroughly Dantesque.

Terror, amazement, and bewilderment are finally merged in gruesome comprehension and acceptance. Hence the first transformation is presented to us in utter suddenness, without preparation or transition: simple narrative. Cacus, on the other hand, is set before us not by narration but in full description, though again with utmost brevity. The second metamorphosis, however, the transfusion of Agnello Brunelleschi into the dragon-serpent, is presented to us as a drama and is mirrored in the cries of the onlooking sinners and in Dante's words. The wonder grows vivid and clearly impressionistic. The third and last metamorphosis explains itself: a direct cinematographic picture. The poet here is conscious that the whole effect depends on the graphic detail and power of his pen, that it is not so much a question of poetic as of technical dexterity, that it is not truthfulness which is required, but illusion and finish. Here he may boast of having excelled Ovid and Lucan, the virtuosos of vivid and picturesque expression.

Step by step the poet familiarizes us with the marvels of the seventh moat. The incredible and the horrible come closer and closer to us, until we, like doubting Thomas, can almost touch it. From the middle of the twenty-fourth to the end of the twenty-fifth canto, the transition is completed from an impressionistic to a naturalistic method of observation.

(*Inferno*, XXVI–XXVII)

Neither among the hypocrites nor among the thieves is there space for a human figure of any note. The poet felt this, and made up for the lack of familiar faces by passing cities in review: Florence, Pistoia, and yet again Florence—the cradle and abode of hypocrisy and thievery.[1]

The politico-ethical emphasis appears in the following cantos ever more frequently and with increasing force. We have reached a second time a form of political fraud. Simony was selfish deceit in public life. We found it in the third moat. Now, in the eighth moat we meet not selfish and vulgar fraud, but a higher school of plotting and intrigue, enjoyed for its own sake, no mat-

[1] Cf. *Inferno*, XXIII, 107 sqq.; XXV, 10 sqq.; XXVI, 1 sqq.

ter in whose service. It is pure Machiavellism as a fine art, and as a necessity of the evil soul. Morally these master liars stand on a lower plane than those others who are essentially only apprentices in the Devil's service; intellectually, however, they stand higher and are, as villains, to be admired; for every action, if it is to succeed artistically, requires a man fully equipped.

Such a one, from top to toe, is the archdeceiver Ulysses.

To be sure, antiquity saw in him not a criminal but a hero. An heroic epic glorified naïvely the tricks of this clever Greek, and did not ask about the downfall and death, but about the life and victories, of Odysseus. Dante, the Christian poet who was the first to recognize in him the evil-doer, described the triumphant hero on his way to destruction. He set the tragedy over against the epic. It is an especially fine touch when he makes his Virgil, the heathen moralist of antiquity, address to the "hero" the tragic question, "whither, being lost, he went away to die."

So the ancient hero must, in the world of Christian righteousness, relate his own tragedy; and it is revealed that Ulysses does not feel his destruction tragically, as if ordained by fate. He does not know, and does not feel, that it was a divine power that wrecked his proud vessel. Only we, the audience, foresee and know it: "The Lord breathed upon them and they were scattered." Ulysses remains, even in Hell, the natural heathen; but the spirit of the listeners and the air in which his words resound are tragically illumined. Like a faraway breath, the fresh sea-air of the *Odyssey* draws through the breakers' roar of the *Inferno*. But if one listens more attentively, it appears that Ulysses in his new environment is not quite the same. Another higher and remoter longing than homesickness for Ithaca has taken possession of him. The craving for knowledge, the passion for exploration and discovery, draw him out of the Mediterranean to the ocean. Thirst for knowledge and hunger for information are the beginning of evil conscience.

So the Dantesque Ulysses stands, a many-sided figure, at a point where the remotest perspectives in the history of the human spirit meet: Homer, the Fall, Christopher Columbus; Hellenism, mediævalism, and the Renaissance; unbroken natural force, terrible guilt, and the bold spirit of discovery. Meantime strength and courage are infused into the will, abysmal evil into the intellect, of this hero. Flickering lights of divine truth play over his utterance, and the epic tale is illuminated, not merely from without, in tragic firelight. In short, deceit is, in Ulysses, so consistent and intellectually so clear, that he is at the point of discovering the truth.

Among all the frauds of Hell, Ulysses is the greatest, most brilliant, most beautiful, the most like Lucifer.

Clothed in flame, he goes on with his battle-comrade Diomedes, roaring and glowing. The flame is the penalty for all his evil plots and the symbol of his fiery spirit. Not Ulysses, not Diomedes, but the abstract misdeeds of both sigh and weep in the flame: two proud, cold, and indomitable souls veiled by a moving blaze. Only to a great poet like Virgil do they deign to reply, and Ulysses relates the tale of his death:

> Thereafterward, the summit to and fro
>   Moving as if it were the tongue that spake,
>   It uttered forth a voice, and said: "When I
> From Circe had departed, who concealed me
>   More than a year there near unto Gaëta,
>   Or ever yet Aeneas named it so,
> Nor fondness for my son, nor reverence
>   For my old father, nor the due affection
>   Which joyous should have made Penelope,
> Could overcome within me the desire
>   I had to be experienced of the world,
>   And of the vice and virtue of mankind;
> But I put forth on the high open sea
>   With one sole ship, and that small company
>   By which I never had deserted been.
> Both of the shores I saw as far as Spain,
>   Far as Morocco, and the isle of Sardes,
>   And the others which that sea bathes round about.
> I and my company were old and slow
>   When at that narrow passage we arrived
>   Where Hercules his landmarks set as signals,
> That man no farther onward should adventure.
>   On the right hand behind me left I Seville,
>   And on the other already had left Ceuta.
> 'O brothers, who amid a hundred thousand
>   Perils,' I said, 'have come unto the West,
>   To this so inconsiderable vigil
> Which is remaining of your senses still,
>   Be ye unwilling to deny the knowledge,
>   Following the sun, of the unpeopled world.
> Consider ye the seed from which ye sprang;
>   Ye were not made to live like unto brutes,
>   But for pursuit of virtue and of knowledge.'

So eager did I render my companions,
With this brief exhortation, for the voyage,
That then I hardly could have held them back.
And having turned our stern unto the morning,
We of the oars made wings for our mad flight,
Evermore gaining on the larboard side.
Already all the stars of the other pole
The night beheld, and ours so very low
It did not rise above the ocean floor,
Five times rekindled and as many quenched
Had been the splendour underneath the moon
Since we had entered into the deep pass,
When there appeared to us a mountain, dim
From distance, and it seemed to me so high
As I had never any one beheld.
Joyful were we, and soon it turned to weeping;
For out of the new land a whirlwind rose,
And smote upon the fore part of the ship.
Three times it made her whirl with all the waters,
At the fourth time it made the stern uplift,
And the prow downward go, as pleased Another,
Until the sea above us closed again."

With utmost clearness and objectivity Ulysses tells his tale; nevertheless, the powers that swept him to his death remain a mystery to him. He divines them, but he does not understand them. The Christian listener, on the other hand, cannot for an instant doubt that the lofty, dusky mountain from which the whirlwind came forth is the Purgatorial mount. As an unconscious sinner, the weatherbeaten seafarer went to his death in almost joyous pride. Perhaps he could have wished no finer end. Only later in Hell does the insight come to him that a higher power overtook him. But this consciousness is not deep enough to embitter the proud enjoyment of his life's rich experiences. Ulysses is no tragic figure like Farinata, Pier della Vigna, or Francesca. Among all the sinners who have been dashed to pieces by the Deity, he is the cheeriest: too supple and clever to feel the painful delight of defiance, and too hard to feel the sting of conscience. He is one of those crafty world-conquerors on whom neither misfortune nor remorse can have decisive effect.

Such an elastic and double-natured soul is ill-suited for the embodiment of an ethical conception of sin. Therefore the poet has set beside him, for the sake of completeness, Guido da Montefeltro.

The Count of Montefeltro is in fact a sort of mediæval Italian Odysseus. "The most sagacious and subtile soldier who lived in Italy in his time," he is called by Villani the chronicler. At the time of the *Commedia*, his name was still so famous that the poet had no need to name him expressly. A simple characterization sufficed, for every one knew who that warrior of Romagna was who in old age became a Franciscan.

Guido was born in 1223. He belonged to the Ghibelline party and was for the Romagna what Farinata was for Tuscany: the dreaded, victorious field-marshal. In June of 1275, as chief commander of the exiled Ghibellines, he defeated the Bolognese Guelfs in a bloody battle. In the late seventies and early eighties he fought in the service of the city of Forlè and defeated the French who had been called in by the Guelfs. Nevertheless, all Romagna came gradually under the control of the pope and the Guelfs. Guido himself was obliged to submit, in 1286, to Pope Honorius IV. But when Pisa, the old nest of the Ghibellines, appointed him commander, he broke his pact with the Church and fought against Florence. For this he and all his family were excommunicated.

Later, after Florence and Pisa had made peace, he seized upon the city of Urbino. He succeeded in releasing himself a second time from the ban of the Church. At last, weary and craving peace, he entered the monastery where he died in 1298.

In the last years of his life, when he was already a Franciscan monk, he came into contact with Pope Boniface VIII. Boniface was living at that time at perilous odds with the Roman family of the Colonnas. The crafty old warrior, it seems, helped the pope with clever counsels. In violation of a treaty, the fortified town of Palestrina was captured, and the resistance of the Colonnas was definitely broken (1298).

What is most notable in the Count's life, i.e. his wavering, dishonourable relations with the Church, becomes the dominant trait of his characterization in the *Commedia*. In his lifetime he hated, fought, feared the Church, and finally served it with his intrigues; after death, in Hell, he behaves in the same way toward his nobler ego, his conscience. He hates and fears it and appears as a master of deceit, without, however, being able to rejoice in his mastery. He is, like Ulysses, a clever deviser of lies, but, unlike him, he is ashamed and afraid of his craft, and yet unable to give it up. He tries to throw the blame on Boniface, "the great priest," and feels the degradation of his position, is ashamed and would fain be silent, but lacks the necessary greatness even for that. The damnation which he almost escaped irks his soul. He is impelled to tell his tale and show how and wherefore and by what malicious chain of circumstances he came to be in Hell.

To be an archtraitor and afterward, when punishment is nigh, to wish not to have been one, is anything but heroic. The figure of Guido was in danger of making a terrible impression compared with the nobler sinfulness of Ulysses. But in that case he could not serve as a complement to Ulysses. It was essential for the poet that Guido should not appear too petty beside Ulysses. That he in fact regarded the historic Guido as an ethically great man is proved by the *Convivio* (IV, 28). But how has he managed to give the desired impression of his greatness?

He has, to put it briefly, subjected his Guido to the irony of fate, and precisely thereby screened him from the reader's irony. Ulysses is lofty in act and in spirit; Guido becomes so from his doom, by what he has suffered, rather than by what he has done. The poet is deliberately silent as to all the great victories of the Ghibelline chieftain. Instead of the deeds he tells of the stage on which they were wrought, the Romagna and its political status. This Romagna is like a park full of wild beasts which are at all times ready to pounce on one another. Here Guido lived and fought; here he became crafty and famous. That fame was his doom. He had already left that stage to live in penitence and meditation with God; but his acts were on his trail. Pope Boniface had him summoned, that he might acquire wisdom from the old fox. That was the beginning of the end. But that end is what the poet chose to show us. Boniface, with the spiritual authority of the supreme shepherd of souls; Boniface, whom we know as the covetous and ambitious simoniac (*Inferno*, XIX), demands the commission of a sin from the Count, and grants him absolution as a reward. The Count obeys—and now events rush upon him. The second act of his doom, death and damnation, follows hard upon the first. The Devil and St. Francis, the founder of the Count's religious order, are at strife for his soul. It is an embodiment of the opposition between good intentions and evil deeds. Here it is made clear that right and truth are based on actual deeds, and not on virtues desired or longed for.

With grotesque and dignified irony the Devil appears as a logician who keeps his accounts better than man. He seizes his victim by the hair and says:

> "For who repents not cannot be absolved,
> Nor can one both repent and will at once,
> Because of the contradiction which consents not.
> . . . 'Peradventure
> Thou didst not think that I was a logician!'"

Not a penny's worth of the Count's guilt is forgiven him. Minos with a furious gesture shows him the total amount of his insolvency.

What Ulysses only feels and divines but understands not, the relentlessness of the voice within, Guido experienced in all its terrors and can recount with wondrous clearness of vision. By the extent of this insight he is richer and greater than Ulysses; but so much the deeper is his agony. His voice shrills like the Sicilian bull, while Ulysses's murmurs and moans "like a wind-whipped fire."

(*Inferno*, XXVIII–XXIX)

Workers of discord also are the sinners in the ninth moat, Mohammed, Pier da Medicina, Bertran de Born, and others. But while Ulysses and Guido devise their tricks out of artistic delight in lying, and have loved and practised not the mischief itself but only the means to that end, the lie, the occupants of the ninth ditch go at their work directly; they seek results. Mischief and discord, war and devastation, are their delight. They are the fabricators and Joyous Brethren of all dissent. Wheresoever an orderly community, founded on obedience, faith, love, and lawful conduct, is flourishing, there they dig and undermine until it all falls apart in hatred, distrust, and anarchy. To destroy all good order in social life is their business. Therefore the organism of their own body is hewn to pieces, sliced, cut into tatters by the devils' swords.

> "Because I parted persons so united,
> Parted do I now bear my brain, alas!
> From its beginning, which is in this trunk.
> Thus is observed in me the counterpoise."

Justice is represented here as a gruesome field of battle. Bloody limbs, pierced bodies, a host of terrible and disgusting pictures.

Even the words, rhythms, and rhymes clash as if living flesh were being slashed.

But these cleft bodies move, go their way, speak, and point with a sort of shameless pleasure to their horrible wounds and strips of quivering flesh. Their own wretchedness is not enough; an irresistible need drives them to relate to the wanderers as much as possible of alien, neighbouring, present, past, and future trouble and strife. Mohammed calls attention to his kinsman Ali's slashed face and prophesies the death of the Christian sectary, Fra Dolcino. He takes delight in depicting the hard-beset heretic and worker of discord as he gasps, half starving, in the Alpine snows. With gory throat Pier da Medicina talks of a terrible double murder on the open sea. In the reader of Dante's day such allusions, which we hardly understand, aroused moral horror and physical repulsion. Here Medicina opens the mouth of Curio, who was said to have incited Julius Caesar to civil war, so that Dante may see the sinner's slit tongue. Mosca dei Lamberti, the instigator of the Florentine civil war, pushes forward and lifts the bleeding stumps of his arms, until Dante hurls a curse at his head.

The most terrible and beautiful figure in this moat, however, is Bertran de Born, the minstrel of discord. He carries his own head before him like a lantern, pushes it forward, holds it before the poet of the empire and of world-peace, and makes himself known.

In all these sinners, the consciousness of their guilt is combined with a sort of pleasure—shamelessness or cruelty toward themselves.

Dante becomes aroused and cannot turn his eyes away, but at the instant when his attention threatens to degenerate into mere curiosity, the thought of his own flesh and blood shoots through his brain. His father's cousin, Geri del Bello, was of a nature like Bertran de Born's, a man who sowed the seeds of discord and fell by a murderer's hand, and whose blood still cries for vengeance. While he must learn from his own family history how feud and murder in turn beget more murder and feud, while he feels how he himself, purely by birth and kinship, might be urged on to vengeance and bloodshed, while he devotes a sympathetic thought to his uncle, who, himself a murderer and murdered man, lashed by devils, still continues to thirst for the blood of his slayer—a mild tone of cordiality warms the cruel pageant of the ninth moat.

(*Inferno*, XXIX–XXX)

But sympathy, according to Dante's sincerest conviction, is out of place among the sinners of lowest Hell. "Here pity is alive when it is wholly dead."

After he had let himself be softened by a personal remembrance, without realizing it, his sympathy drew him nearer than was wise to the most desperate of these sinners. In the tenth and last moat of the eighth circle, the moral tension of the pilgrim, not of the poet, slackens. He falls into all too intimate converse with the sinners, jests with them over the foolishness of the Sienese folk, grows inquisitive, and takes pleasure in their wretched chatter and quarrelling. In short, he runs the risk of being contaminated by the polluted breath of a pest-house, for the tenth moat is one great abhorrent home of disease.

All sorts of falsifiers, smitten with every kind of illness, lie, run, writhe, and drag themselves to and fro. A stench of sweat and purulence, a roar of heart-rending groans and cries!

One is tempted to believe that the poet has brought together here, as if in a refuse-dump, all the deceivers that did not fit into the previous moats. In fact, we find, side by side, the most diverse types of sinners: alchemists, counterfeiters, forgers of wills; Myrrha the incestuous, Potiphar's wife, and Sinon, who by his lies induced the Trojans to receive the wooden horse into their city.

In all of them the poet sees a common trait, a misuse of economic and moral credit, things which are condemned as contemptible by the mercantile and civic conscience. So this last moat, like the first, bears the label of a meanness which is rather cowardly and base than malicious.

From its instability, however, it may prove malicious also, but it is a malice without intelligence or greatness, merely the malice of vileness. The thoroughly false, bad soul may show itself at times good-humoured and agreeable, at other times furious. But its good humour is venomous, its fury swinish. Myrrha and Gianni Schicchi bite, run, and scream like swine let loose.

These vulgar souls do not become chastened, nor are they tortured; they are diseased. Their degradation is its own punishment. The degenerate spirit creates in the body fever, madly raging hydrophobia, and lurking big-bellied dropsy.

After the penalty has become so immanent and the sting of conscience an unendurable twitching and itching of the skin and disgusting scurf, the danger arises that the sinner, wholly occupied with his disease, may forget the chief concern, namely, the consciousness of his guilt. To keep this consciousness awake, the sinners rail, insult, assail, and trick one another. They are witty, sarcastic, ironical, have sharp tongues and a no less keen sense for the ridiculous side of their neighbours. Their garrulity takes on all tones from good-humoured chat to repulsive squabbling. Occasionally they cuff and pound each other. "Cads' strife ended, quickly mended."

What wonder that a student of humanity and an artist, like our pilgrim, is interested in these petty evil-minded folk, and lingers and listens more attentively than is seemly? But as soon as Virgil chides him, he is sincerely ashamed. Only for a moment does psychological curiosity get the better of morality, and thus again Alighieri saw and overcame the peril that threatened his poem.

(*Inferno*, XXXI–XXXV)

We now descend to the last circle. The song of justice nears its close: the most terrible writhings and convulsions of sin, and finally its petrifaction into inert stolidity. The lowest level of moral degradation coincides with the death of the soul, and the benumbing of nature. This dead-point is marked by Lucifer, whose life is only apparent, a crying, self-detesting mockery, and a parody of real existence.

At the end of the ninth circle stands Lucifer; at its beginning, that is, about its circumference, the giants; from their posts to his, all is ice—a circular, frozen well which descends like a funnel toward the centre of the earth. There are four concentric zones which merge imperceptibly into each other: Caina, Antenora, Tolomea, Giudecca. The first takes its name from Cain, the traitor to his own clan, the second from the Trojan Antenor, the betrayer of his native city, the third from Ptolemy, the betrayer of guests, and the last from Judas, the betrayer of his benefactor and master. The farther we descend, the deeper are the sinners buried in ice. At first the upper part of the body emerges from the ice, then only the head; then the expression of pain becomes rigid, the tear congeals and forms a "crystalline visor" over the face, and finally the whole body is frozen in, expressing torture only through its form, attitude, and position, which are visible through the ice. "And they appear only as straws in glass." In the fourth zone soul-life is no longer external. In the second, however, the poet set the awful final tragedy of the *Inferno*, that of Ugolino.

Ugolino is the last real man, the last personality, of the nether world. Directly behind him stand devil-men, men who have the Devil as a second self. Directly before him are villains that shun the light, in whom all inward greatness is lacking. Their significance is chiefly historical or anecdotic; they are passing apparitions and make poetic life without coming to life themselves; they interest the pilgrim directly and strongly, but his readers only indirectly and weakly. They are of the environment.

Aside from Dante, the final circle has but three chief figures: the giants, Ugolino, and Lucifer. The giants and Lucifer are effective chiefly by their external appearance, by their physical size; Ugolino by the greatness of his suffering and his hate.

Ugolino's tale, with its stormy passion, stands between two calm descriptions.

Such, in large outlines, are the last cantos of the *Inferno*. Life is congealed; the lyric warmth retreats; pain and gloomy hatred alone persist in this field of ice.

At the end of the eighth circle with its ten moats, the murky air is rent by a note of trouble like that of Roland's horn at Roncesvalles, and what seems to be a city of lofty towers appears in the distance. It is the giants, whose feet are deep in the ninth circle, while their motionless bodies rise high above the level of the eighth. They are mysterious, uncanny. Their presence is first revealed by sound, then by the outline of their shadows; gradually the face, shoulders, breast, a part of the chest, and the arms of one and another of them become visible. The traveller cannot get a clear general impression. Even from below, in the ninth circle, he sees only their height and their movements—and grows dizzy. On account of their height, the giants extend into two fields of vision: those of the eighth and ninth circles. There is no point of view from which to see their figures entire. The imagination is excited and must create a whole out of visible fragments and from measurements. It is the impossibility of seeing them that makes the giants impressive. And not only their bodies, but their souls—yes, their entire significance—are, so to speak, unintelligible and mysterious. They do not reveal themselves, but must be explained and interpreted.

Mythical figures, sons of the earth and the sea, children of darkness, monstrous creations of Nature are they. They have rebelled against God, that is, Jupiter, and have been defeated and overthrown. The myth of the Tower of Babel is brought into connection with the Greek legend of the Battle of the Giants. As far back as Augustine and Orosius, Nimrod is described as a giant and as the builder of the Tower of Babel. Accordingly we see him here grouped with Ephialtes, Briareus, Tityus, Typhoeus, and others. They have all been subdued, and the fiercest of them are in chains. Their heroic age lies behind them. They now stand as monumental figures, dismal memorials of their own past. Only a convulsive tremor, like an earthquake, shakes, from time to time, their fettered bodies, a last memory and throb of their mythical life. But because of their motionlessness, their attitudes and distinctive marks, they take on an allegorical character. Their significance varies between myth and allegory. They seem to us partly the foremost champions and victims of pride, partly the exemplars of rebellious insolence, and affect the feelings much as they do the intellect, now with dread, now with curiosity. "My error fled, and fear came over me."

The pride of the giant Antaeus is stupid and vain. With the hollowest of compliments Virgil is able to win him over and make him useful. The meaning of Virgil's words, in plain prose, is: "It seems that even at the present day there is an opinion, Antaeus, according to which you would have helped your brother giants to victory over Jupiter, if you had been able, in your time, to take part in the Titans' war. And consider also the great merit of having captured a thousand lions, in a region which was later famous through the deeds of Scipio Africanus!" The childish giant makes much of such matters. Intensely flattered, without suspecting the scoff hidden in the poet's artful speech, Antaeus readily and good-naturedly extends his broad hand. The two wayfarers take their places on it, and he carefully sets the clever little human beings down on the surface of the ninth circle.

As for the touch of comedy in this incident, Alighieri has been careful not to elaborate it. His giants have nothing in common with Number Nip or our other giants of romance. The romantic giant is the good-humoured child of a nature that lives and works, not in opposition to the spirit, but in indissoluble union with it. The stupidity of the romantic giants is therefore no real lack, no absence of the spirit, but the dull spirit of a good, practical, comfortable, and droll stupidity.

But the Dantesque giant is stupid because the source of intelligence, God, has departed from him. He is stupid and evil at once and can be regarded and treated only ironically, satirically, or tragically, but by no means humorously.

Where feeling no longer speaks, facts must talk. We have, therefore, in the ninth circle, pure delineation or description, with heavy shadows of satire, of irony, and of tragedy.

> Whereat I turned me round, and saw before me
> And underfoot a lake, that from the frost
> The semblance had of glass, and not of water.
> So thick a veil ne'er made upon its current
> In winter-time Danube in Austria,
> Nor there beneath the frigid sky the Don,
> As there was here; so that if Tambernich
> Had fallen upon it, or Pietrapana,
> E'en at the edge 'twould not have given a creak.
> And as to croak the frog doth place himself
> With muzzle out of water—when is dreaming
> Of gleaning oftentimes the peasant-girl—
> Livid, as far down as where shame appears,
> Were the disconsolate shades within the ice,
> Setting their teeth unto the note of storks.
> Each one his countenance held downward bent;
> From mouth the cold, from eyes the doleful heart
> Among them witness of itself procures.

The sinners befit the locality. Behold the two sons of Count Alberto di Magona. They betrayed and slew each other. Side by side they now are frozen in. Dante asks their names. They lift their heads; tears come to their eyes, freeze, and veil their sight. They dash their heads furiously against each other. All this without uttering a word. A felon near by, however, relates with downcast face the story of the treacherous brothers, the shame of other men about whom he had not been asked, and his own disgrace.

Dante now is interested only in the names of the sinners, not in their life-story. A traitor is sufficiently identified by a label. For that very reason the damned of the ninth circle strive in every way to evade inquiries. Dante's desire to recognize the traitors and their wish to remain unknown result in a conflict at the very outset. Dante strikes his foot—"I know not whether by intent or chance"—against the face of one of the frozen tribe. He shrieks and in his pain utters the word *Montaperti*—a word that was then stamped in the memory of every Florentine in large crimson letters. It is the name of the terrible battle in which the Guelfs were vanquished by the Ghibellines (1260). Dante pauses; his curiosity is aroused; he seeks information, which the sinner, however, refuses. He then seizes and tears his hair, but can only extract shrieks of pain from the traitor. Meantime, another of this evil fraternity reveals the name of the betrayer of Montaperti: Bocca degli Abati, who in turn, to avenge himself, straightway tells the other's name, and adds four more for good measure. Such are the ignoble conflicts of this base brood.

Then unexpectedly Ugolino's figure arises.

"But how can the most eloquent form of the entire *Commedia* find its place here, among these petrified beings?" The ablest interpreter of Ugolino, Francesco de Sanctis, asked this question and fitly answered it:

"Ugolino is not the traitor, but he who is betrayed. To be sure, Count Ugolino had been in his time a traitor, and as such has his place in the ninth circle. But, just as Paolo is eternally bound to Francesca, so, by a most ingenious complication, Ugolino is eternally bound to Ruggieri, who has betrayed him—bound not by love but by hatred." [1]

The many plots which were in reality devised by these two traitors cannot be fully verified at the present day. The little which is known, and which may aid the better understanding of the poem, is somewhat as follows.

Ruggieri degli Ubaldini was archbishop of Pisa during the years 1278–1295, and held to the Ghibelline party. Count Ugolino della Gherardesca, one of the most powerful nobles of Pisa, was also originally a Ghibelline, but, after the downfall of the Hohenstaufens, had passed over to the Guelfs. As such he was ban-

[1] *Nuovi saggi critici*, 21st ed., Naples, 1906, p. 55.

ished from the city in 1275. He summoned the Guelfs of Florence and Lucca to aid him against his native city, defeated his fellow citizens, and forced his way back into the city. It may have been on account of this behaviour that our poet regarded the Count as a traitor. During the years 1276–1285, Ugolino was the most powerful and most honoured lord of Pisa, and controlled, more or less absolutely, its internal and external relations. Thereafter, however, a dangerous rival appeared in the person of his own grandson, Nino Visconti. Discontent with the rule of the Count—who had not always been fortunate in his war against the Genoese—came to the surface. The old Ghibelline party, to which the powerful families of the Gualandi, Sismondi, and Lanfranchi belonged, worked against him. Archbishop Ruggieri managed to flatter the Count cleverly and hypocritically while undermining the ground beneath his feet. In June, 1288, Ugolino was surprised by a sudden attack of the Ghibellines and taken prisoner. Two of his sons, Gaddo and Uguccione, and two of his grandsons, Brigata and Anselmuccio, were with him, were captured with him, and in February, 1289, suffered with him death by starvation.

The contemporary chroniclers leave us in no doubt that the Bishop and the Count were, in trickery and cunning, worthy of each other. "And so the traitor was by the traitor betrayed;" thus Giovanni Villani closes his account. He may well have been influenced by Dante's *Inferno*.

Dante has not at first done anything to make the Count seem less guilty than the Bishop. The two are frozen into the same hole as sinners of the same type. The one lies with his head over the other's, like a hat upon the head. Ugolino is the hat, Ruggieri the head. But the hat presses itself furiously against the head and gnaws greedily at it.

> And even as bread through hunger is devoured,
> The uppermost on the other set his teeth,
> There where the brain is to the nape united.
> Not in another fashion Tydeus gnawed
> The temples of Menalippus in disdain,
> Than that one did the skull and the other things.

This sight, viewed with calm eyes, awakens the poet's curiosity. He wishes to learn the cause of this strange cruelty. Interested heretofore only in names and personalities, he now comes upon an extraordinary case, the origin and cause of which he is eager to learn. His inquiry brings out a most accurate and awful answer:

His mouth uplifted from his grim repast
  That sinner, wiping it upon the hair
  Of the same head that he behind had wasted.
Then he began: "Thou wilt that I renew
  The desperate grief, which wrings my heart already
  To think of only, ere I speak of it;
But if my words be seed that may bear fruit
  Of infamy to the traitor whom I gnaw,
  Speaking and weeping shalt thou see together.
I know not who thou art, nor by what mode
  Thou hast come down here; but a Florentine
  Thou seemest to me truly, when I hear thee.
Thou hast to know I was Count Ugolino,
  And this one was Ruggieri the Archbishop;
  Now I will tell thee why I am such a neighbour.
That, by effect of his malicious thoughts,
  Trusting in him I was made prisoner,
  And after put to death, I need not say;
But ne'ertheless what thou canst not have heard,
  That is to say, how cruel was my death.
  Hear shalt thou, and shalt know if he has wronged me.
A narrow perforation in the mew,
  Which bears because of me the title of Famine,
  And in which others still must be locked up,
Had shown me through its opening many moons
  Already, when I dreamed the evil dream
  Which of the future rent for me the veil.
This one appeared to me as lord and master,
  Hunting the wolf and whelps upon the mountain
  For which the Pisans cannot Lucca see.
With sleuth-hounds gaunt, and eager, and well trained,
  Gualandi with Sismondi and Lanfranchi
  He had sent out before him to the front.
After brief course seemed unto me forespent
  The father and the sons, and with sharp tushes
  It seemed to me I saw their flanks ripped open.
When I before the morrow was awake,
  Moaning amid their sleep I heard my sons
  Who with me were, and asking after bread.
Cruel indeed art thou, if yet thou grieve not,
  Thinking of what my heart foreboded me,
  And weep'st thou not, what art thou wont to weep at?
They were awake now, and the hour drew nigh
  At which our food used to be brought to us,
  And through his dream was each one apprehensive;

And I heard locking up the under door
  Of the horrible tower; whereat without a word
  I gazed into the faces of my sons.
I wept not, I within so turned to stone;
  They wept; and darling little Anselm mine
  Said: 'Thou dost gaze so, father, what doth ail thee?'
Still not a tear I shed, nor answer made
  All of that day, nor yet the night thereafter,
  Until another sun rose on the world.
As now a little glimmer made its way
  Into the dolorous prison, and I saw
  Upon four faces my own very aspect,
Both of my hands in agony I bit;
  And thinking that I did it from desire
  Of eating, on a sudden they uprose,
And said they: 'Father, much less pain 'twill give us
  If thou do eat of us; thyself didst clothe us
  With this poor flesh, and do thou strip it off.'
I calmed me then, not to make them more sad.
  That day we all were silent, and the next.
  Ah! obdurate earth, wherefore didst thou not open?
When we had come unto the fourth day, Gaddo
  Threw himself down outstretched before my feet,
  Saying, 'My father, why dost thou not help me?'
And there he died; and, as thou seest me,
  I saw the three fall, one by one, between
  The fifth day and the sixth; whence I betook me,
Already blind, to groping over each,
  And three days called them after they were dead;
  Then hunger did what sorrow could not do."
When he had said this, with his eyes distorted,
  The wretched skull resumed he with his teeth,
  Which, as a dog's, upon the bone were strong.

The intensity of this agony and hatred overshadows all else. Ugolino is great through his inexhaustible capacity for feeling and giving torture. The ordinary man, after a few hours of hunger, becomes comfortably stupid, indifferent, benumbed. Ugolino throughout eight days has endured and fully tasted all the phases of agony. In the first days, so long as suffering was a novelty, speech, weeping, lamentation, would have been a relief. Therefore it was denied him. In the last days, when exhaustion should set in and silence become a necessity, he must shriek and cry out with the strength of all his failing vitality. Companions and friends in misfortune are the greatest consolation; here they are the cause of utmost distress. Through the companionship of his children and children's children the suffering is multiplied in Ugolino, instead of divided. The poet has made these children younger, more helpless, more tender, and more innocent than they could really have been. The hardened and wicked Ugolino is smitten on his gentlest and noblest side—in his paternal love. The beings who are most precious and dearest to him must torture him to death. To be unable to help them is the most terrible pang of all. He feels so intensely within him the force of helpless parental love that even thereafter he cannot reveal it in words. Many a year after his death he is still exiled and imprisoned in this pain. It is granted to the other sinners of Hell to pour out their suffering in full, clear utterance. Francesca knows and names the word of her doom: Love! Ugolino feels it and cannot speak it. He relates the external conditions of his own and his children's death by starvation, he repeats it day by day, almost hour by hour, he experiences it once again, perhaps a thousand times, but in his soul it goes on forever. And the innocent tear shed for his kin is still mingled with the inhuman rage felt against his foe; the father's love is still shut within the hatred of the traitor; and the noblest need of his heart, to be helpful, is still mixed with and defiled by greed for his bestial food. This man's last words—"Then hunger did what sorrow could not do"—as he bites into the Bishop's skull, awaken a terrible doubt. With a shudder the reader imagines that this tender father would have been capable of devouring the dead bodies of his children. Because Ugolino's agony is not pure, that is, not spiritually felt, since not merely the helpful father-heart, but with it the beast with its hot hunger, was crucified, no resurrection out of this suffering is possible.

Ugolino's physical hunger takes on spiritual dimensions, grows to ravenous, furious rancour, and in this fashion becomes eternal. Paternal love grown measureless serves only to heighten hate. Hate draws its strength from love, and hunger from hatred. So Ugolino is the human and bestial type of an eternal, indestructible agony and hatred.

The eternal and infinite measure of Ugolino's hatred is brought out tragically by the fact that the most guiltless, tenderest beings, just the same as the transgressors, fall victims to agony and injustice.

But the sight of undeserved suffering threatens to confuse our moral sense. So, at this point in the poem, the ethical keynote rises to a curse.

"A curse upon Pisa!" cries the poet. "May the penalty be as unheard of, as unnatural as the sin against Ugolino's children! May the Arno be dammed at its mouth, and drown all Pisa, man and mouse, beneath its raging waters!" This curse is the counterstroke of outraged conscience.

In the presence of the next traitor, Fra Alberigo dei Manfredi of Faenza, the poet's lack of conscience is felt. Dante promises the sinner that he will clear the ice from his eyes if he will only tell his name. Alberigo not only does so but gives all the information that Dante could wish. But Dante refuses him the favour he had promised him, and even claims credit for his broken promise. "To be rude to him was courtesy."

Quite as surprising as the wanderer's breaking of his word is the condition of the traitor. Fra Alberigo had caused his cousin and his cousin's child to be assassinated, at a banquet of reconciliation where they were his guests (May 2, 1285). Henceforth his body, down to the date of his natural death, is taken in charge by a devil. It is no longer Alberigo but the devil who up above in the world wears his clothes and shows his features. The soul's death occurred immediately after the crime. The same fate of double life, on earth and in Hell, has befallen Branca d'Oria, who treacherously slew Michel Zanche in the year 1275, but did not, in fact, die until four years after Alighieri (1325). This violent separation of soul and body, this miracle, is not explained, developed or related, but simply asserted, and confirmed by the statement of Alberigo himself. The reader doubts and wonders; by serious thought, not through direct vision and feeling, he is brought to the realization of the horrible nature of these sinners; and the canto draws to a close.

The last canto, the finale, is a descriptive report.

The canto begins, grotesquely and solemnly, with a parody of the church hymn, *Vexilla Regis prodeunt Inferni* ("The banners of the infernal king advance"). But in reality there is no further progress and no more movement.

Lucifer is the immovable and crushed devil: conquered and petrified like the giants into an allegory and memorial of himself:

a marked contrast to Milton's fighting, lively, and dramatic Devil. Round about him is ice, rigidity, silence. Down to the navel he is eternally held fast at the dead-point of gravity. Once so mighty, the ghastly distortion of the spirit is now an inert natural phenomenon. As the absolute spirit is thought of as a divine trinity, so Lucifer is its negative parody. As such he has three ugly faces. The one in front is red and betokens original hate, the very opposite of divine beneficence; the face to the right is yellowish white and may well betoken helplessness contrasted with omnipotence; that to the left is black and represents absolute ignorance, the opposite of omniscience. Beneath each face there is a pair of bat-like wings, with which the fettered monster, however, cannot fly, but only start a breeze. These wings, swaying to and fro, make Lucifer the ironic pendant to God, the source of motion and warmth. The wind made by these wings is cold, and hardens all things to ice. Each of the three mouths of Lucifer devours a sinner. They are the three greatest malefactors in the world: Judas Iscariot, the betrayer of the heavenly King, and Brutus and Cassius, the traitors to the first earthly emperor, the murderers of Julius Caesar. Mute, incapable of word or thought, mere quivering, gory lumps of flesh, they endure their torture and survive only as reminders or symbols of uttermost sinfulness.

The wanderer gazes on the entire spectacle *sine ira et studio.* His excitement is purely intellectual—fear, which is gradually transformed into fright, disgust, amazement, curiosity, thirst for knowledge, and reflective understanding.

Hence the size of Lucifer is not stated, but indicated by three standards of measurement in a sort of geometrical proportion:

> And better with a giant I compare
> Than do the giants with those arms of his;
> Consider now how great must be that whole,
> Which unto such a part conforms itself.

The poetic object, now become essentially material, appears before our eyes as quantity; and its immensity, its colossal nature, is its poetry. The artist lets massiveness produce its own effect and refrains with masterly moderation from any lyric treatment which could here only be weak oratorical decoration. Hence, the profoundly significant myth of Lucifer's fall to the centre of the earth, into the frozen lake, which a less reticent poet would have expanded to excess, is disposed of as naked fact in six close-packed lines. After the lure of infernal magic has been fully experienced, our feelings can only marvel at its originality, at the admirable structure of the Inferno, and so we withdraw behind the scenes—which in their own fashion are now once again to be enjoyed as a spectacle, but this time summarily and in barest outlines.

Indeed in no other canto do notable matters so abound as in this. While the two poets are standing in front of Lucifer, the day ends. It is evening in the world of living men. They then cross the centre of the earth, working their way between Lucifer's hairy side and the ice-crust. The moment they reach the farther side, it is morning. Without knowing it, in an instant Dante has gone over to the antipodes. Another notable detail is the passing of the world's centre of gravity, where Virgil and Dante have to turn their heads where their feet had previously been, going upward instead of downward. From Lucifer's legs up to the surface of the Southern Hemisphere, they follow a dark path beside which a brooklet rushes. What does this brook signify? It may well be the river of Lethe which carries down to Lucifer, from the top of the Purgatorial mount, the memory of sin, the last remnant of human wickedness and weakness.

Only just before morning do the pilgrims reach the upper surface of the Southern Hemisphere, at the foot of the mountain of Purgatory. An uninterrupted way has brought them out of punishment to purification.

RETROSPECT AND PROSPECT

But Hell and Purgatory are not merely connected by the itinerary.

We shall see how often from the heights of Purgatory the travellers have occasion to point backward to their upward progress out of the depths of Hell. It is by such retrospect that they must justify their presence in Purgatory. On the other hand, if we except the introductory cantos, the *Inferno* contains no allusions to Purgatory. The former describes an eternal and independent world, while the latter is an intermediate realm connecting Hell and Heaven. Accordingly the *Inferno* presents itself as a poem more complete and closed than the *Purgatorio*. It is intelligible by itself, and has its principle of poetic unity in an ethico-lyrical keynote which runs almost unbroken, in its variations, through thirty-three cantos. Where it seems lost, and replaced by impulses of sightseeing, craving for knowledge, curiosity, we really have no gaps or poetic defects, but merely that alternation of the dialectic of feelings in accordance with which the inmost impulse of the voyager appears as need not only of purification, but of knowledge and self-knowledge as well. Only if we materialize and dogmatize the structure, arrangement, and landscape of Hell as something existing for itself alone, instead of regarding it as the dreamland of the poet's soul, does the arrangement interfere with the life of the *Inferno*, and the poem falls apart into disjointed, arbitrary poetic episodes. But instead we have shown that it is an unbroken stream of poetry which may have its windings, rapids, and dams, but never loses itself.

We have seen also how from about the middle of the eighth circle downward, that is, after the comic descriptions of the twenty-first and twenty-second cantos, Dante's mood gradually changes, and how more and more his ethical hatred rises, and how he takes delight in beholding terrific penalties. This poetic enjoyment of devilish rage and power weighs on the wanderer's soul and makes him not evil, certainly, but hard and stern.

Hence the profound silent need, of the pilgrim, of the poet, of the reader, for other and milder tones. The *Inferno* lacks a conclusion reconcilable with human mercy.

The awakened but unsated longing for such a conclusion leads us, under the escort of the poet and pilgrim, to the *Purgatorio*.

7. The "Purgatorio"

MOOD, SCENE, AND ACTION

The fundamental mood of the *Purgatorio* is thus determined: need of atoning mercy, hope of blessedness. The *Inferno* echoed utter despair; here hope runs its entire course, from weary, almost indifferent waiting to burning impatience.

All hopefulness is, however, reminiscent; every onward glance presupposes a retrospect. The rosy dawn of the soul's peace is still darkened by shadows of pain and discord.

More distinctly than either the *Inferno* or the *Paradiso*, the *Purgatorio* has the divided, elegiac atmosphere of transition, of a middle kingdom, where salvation is won, where freedom is striven for, where men struggle upward. The upward struggle from inadequacy to perfection is the innermost action of the *Purgatorio*.

How does this mood, this inner action, express itself outwardly in the scene and structure of the *Purgatorio?*

In its construction the poet was no longer wholly free. The demand for symmetrical relation to the *Inferno* fettered him. As the one is a hollow funnel, so the other is a mountainous cone; the nine circles are matched here by nine terraces. In both realms, at every transition there is a guardian, in each realm its symbolic representative, and at each stage a special class of sinners. Hence the necessity to put life into the fixed plan, to diversify it, and to keep it from becoming rigid.

The poet has amply met this need. A new feeling, a loftier inspiration, a religious fervour growing out of ethical enthusiasm, transform the fixed frame into a new structure. If we observe this frame, however, in and by itself, that is, apart from its poetic enlivenment, it does appear stony, and the complete theological inadequacy of the Catholic doctrine of Purgatory with its magical and political ecclesiasticism, as we have found it in our study of the sources, returns afresh to our consciousness. One need only regard Dante's *Purgatorio* not as that which it really is, poetry, but as something actually existent by itself, to discover a petty asylum of mercy, whose rules and ceremonial show a strong resemblance to a sanatorium. If, for example, not only in Dante's delineation, but in eternal reality, the serpent of temptation glides every evening into the Ante-Purgatory, and if it is invariably driven away by two guardian angels, then this significant vision is transformed into a mere fantasy, and reminds us of those clocks on German churches or town halls, where at noon the cock, Death, the twelve apostles, and other puppets go nodding past us. The speaking trees and voices in the air, the rushes that grow ever anew, the inevitable earthquake, and similar magical signs of divine grace lose their vitality, if they are taken literally, and become mere childish automata. We must not confuse the holy semblance with the person that bears it nor regard what is emblematic in the *Purgatorio* as its poetic essence, nor yet as an external addition which may be stripped off or disregarded.

Between the spirit and its representation there is in this part of the *Commedia* a different relation from that existing in the *Inferno*. Here the two forces are so far apart and of such different intensity that it might sometimes seem as if the one were about to tear itself loose from the other, and as if the critic had to remove the outer illusion of the ghostly world in order to save the content of the poetry. In truth, however, an increased inspiration corresponds to the heightened tension and profounder mood; for now the pious faith of the pilgrim and poet comes into play and fuses the diverging forces into unity.

Just how this tension between plan and action, form and content, illusion and reality, gives vitality to the poem, may best be shown by a glance at the inhabitants of Purgatory. Man finds himself, on the Purgatorial mount, in a condition psychologically far more significant than in Hell or in Heaven. The damned and the blest have reached their goal; they bestir and develop themselves no more. It is only as warnings or models that they stand at the wayside as the living pilgrim passes. The human souls in Purgatory have indeed departed this life, but continue, even after death, their progress and development. They must make up for what they have neglected, atone for the evil they have done, but this atonement is under totally changed conditions—outside of life, without any special activity, and far from their earthly environment. They must win freedom by wearing fetters, grow strong by chastening, and perfect themselves by passive endurance. The figure of the palm tree pressed down with stones, so that it may struggle aloft more vigorously, would be a good frontispiece for the *Purgatorio.* For in the contrast between outward force and inner impulse lies the peculiarity of the condition of the souls in Purgatory. In Paradise and in Hell the outward form of the souls is a likeness of their inner nature. Francesca without her Paolo, Farinata without his fiery grave, Ugolino without the archbishop's skull—is unimaginable. In the attitude, the position, the habitation, the environment, of the damned, their inmost character is expressed. They are so vivid as to be tangible.

The souls of Purgatory become intelligible only through their speech. There is something abstract about them; they must explain and express themselves, for they are disfigured by the penalties they endure. In the Ante-Purgatory their bearing is still free and natural; in the true Purgatory it is checked and controlled. So much the more touchingly and vividly does their utterance pour forth. The contrast between their outward and inward condition becomes the mightiest mainspring of the poetry.

While their bodies appear more and more shadowy, the visibility of their souls increases. These people become truly objective to us, not from their outward features, but because of their utterances. It is their spiritual activity that conditions the visibility of external things. The more completely we penetrate them, the more intelligible does the paradox of their outward semblance become. Their torture, their penance, their disfigurement, reveals itself as something which they themselves have approved, desired, willed, and even created. Compulsion becomes their desire, and the desire is the expression of their free will. The transparency of the soul among these pilgrims of hope grows proportionately with their moral purification. The better we come to know them, the more highly do we value them and sympathize with them. The longer we live with them in their abode, the more completely does the institutional character of this abode vanish.

The living pilgrim, too, undergoes a sort of religious conversion. Not that he had entered Purgatory a doubter or a heretic; but he came from the spectacle of Hell, his breast swelling with moral indignation and ethical zeal. He came in the exaltation of a consciousness that had maintained and asserted itself in the very presence of the Devil. Now the need of a spectacle of penance, of self-abnegation and devotion, of obedience and humility, is urgently felt by him. He must now learn the moral value of suffering and the liberating power of patient endurance. Not all, but only religious, suffering makes us free.

Since the pains of Purgatory are now revealed and felt as a religious penance, they no longer impress us as an institutional and ecclesiastical cure, but become profound Christian poetry.

Therefore man on his way through Purgatory shares outwardly and inwardly the sufferings of the souls in quite a different fashion from what he did during his descent into Hell. While he submits to the laws and requirements of this new realm, they are transformed into experiences of his own. In the *Purgatorio* Dante begins to feel himself a sinner. He leaves his elevation and descends, like Goethe's Mahadöh, as a sympathetic companion to these insufficient ones.

> He among them makes his dwelling,
> All their burdens beareth he.
> Would he learn to spare or punish?
> He as man mankind must see.

Now sin is not merely embodied objectively and externally: he begins to feel its sting in his own breast also. But while making himself accessible to sin and penance, he comes to share in Heaven's grace. Out of these ethical depths of human sympathy the poem wings its religious flight.

This process of overcoming dogmatic institutionalism is depicted in the poem itself. We recognize it, for example, in the fact that the ascent of the mountain at first costs the utmost exertion, but the higher we go, the easier it becomes, and it ends by demanding no effort at all.

Furthermore, the ascent of the mountain can be accomplished by day only; that is, so long as the sun of divine grace is shining.[1] Bereft of heavenly illumination, man can only slip downward. This ordinance reveals the religious character of the journey of redemption.

At the entrance into the real Purgatory, the angel carves with his sword seven P's (*Peccata*), emblematic of the seven mortal sins, on the wanderer's brow, and directs him to free himself, step by step, from these seven brands. Such ceremonies make it clear that the pilgrim is here, not merely with his understanding, as a spectator, but in his full capacity as a man of feeling and of will.

The three chief types of inward sympathy—human or psychological interest, moral loyalty, and religious devotion—are the three powers with which the poet enlivens the external world of his Purgatory.

The harmony of these three modes must be heard again from canto to canto in detail.

ANTE-PURGATORY

(*Purgatorio*, I)

On the lowest level of Hell, the poem had dropped to a mere objective report. The wanderers worked their way laboriously out of the abyss to the upper surface of the earth. "Let dead Poesy here rise again." True poetry, ever victorious, is here invoked. Like a sigh of relief resounds here the appeal to the muses, which at the beginning of the *Inferno* had sounded like a sharp rallying-cry to all the poet's powers.

It is dawn, and there is a blue light in the sky; Venus heralds

[1] *Purgatorio*, VII, 49 sqq.

the approach of the sun and outshines the spring constellation of the Fishes. Over the Southern pole four new stars appear, unknown, large, brilliant lights that no mortal eye has yet seen. A fresh, resplendent, mysterious world reveals itself. Suddenly a venerable old man, Cato, stands beside the rapt poet: a puzzling figure, and yet so gentle and kind that one might revere in him one's own father. No less puzzling in its kindliness is the order which the enigmatic man gives to the wayfarer: Dante is to wash the grime of Hell from his face at the water's edge and bind his brow with pliant rushes.

Surprise follows on surprise, marvel on marvel. No sooner had Virgil plucked a rush than another sprang up in its place. The eastern sky grows red, the sea glimmers, the sun rises, a new day is begun.

This first canto is fragrant as a mild morning breeze, and it shines like a brightening dawn. But the colour is still faint with grey shadows, the music is still subdued. Yet beyond the first muffled tones, we divine a resounding harmony; and it is with unquenchable thirst for new and clearer impressions, with renewed interest, that the two begin the journey out of darkness.

> Sweet colour of the Oriental sapphire . . .
> Unto mine eyes renewed delight did bring.

It is but beheld, and what is beheld is related and described in a sort of joyous haste. But as an abundance of lovely and incomprehensible objects meet the eye, the reader becomes ill at ease, curious, and knows not whether to brood over the first riddle or to hasten on at once to a second, a third, a fourth. What is the significance of the four stars, of Cato whom they illumine, of the rush, and of the numerous astronomical data?

The last canto of the *Inferno*, too, was full of such riddles, and it, also, awakened curiosity, but those were the last riddles of a world already traversed and explored. Here we have enigmas and mysteries full of hope that bid us hasten on. We divine their meaning, and therefore the poet does not explain them. At the sight of the four stars he neither ponders nor questions; he is enthusiastic:

> Rejoicing in their flamelets seemed the heaven.
> O thou septentrional and widowed site,
> Because thou art deprived of seeing these!

The reader shares this joyous excitement and is satisfied to feel that these stars have an extraordinary value. Later comes the expounder who tells us that in Dante's symbolism these stars signify the four cardinal virtues. With Cato it is much the same. We suddenly have his dignified figure lifelike before us, see the expression of his austere yet kindly face, and understand his words even before we know whence he comes and who he is. In conversation with Virgil his character is revealed to us, his strict righteousness, his pious unity with divine law. His character makes his symbolic function clear to every thoughtful reader.

The historical Cato Uticensis was an inflexible, rigid Stoic and republican. When the course of destiny put him and his principles in the wrong, he voluntarily quitted life. This characteristic suicide has been interpreted by Dante as a religious sacrifice, as an act of submission to fate as the divinely human natural law—a conception especially suggested by Lucan's *Pharsalia:*

> Hi mores, haec duri immota Catonis
> Secta fuit, servare modum, finemque tenere,
> Naturamque sequi, patriaeque impendere vitam,
> Nec sibi, sed toti genitum se credere mundo.[1]

In the other world where the law lies open to the day and rules without contradiction or doubt, the unflinching champion of law naturally becomes a harmonious character. His earthly hate and love are overcome.

> Marcia . . .
> . . . can no longer move me, by that law
> Which, when I issued forth from there, was made.

The Dantesque Cato still retains the manly strength and virtue of the historic Cato, but the hardness, the inflexibility, the pose of virtue, have disappeared. What formerly was effort, has become nature. The man who once represented moral and po-

[1] *Pharsalia,* II, 380–383:
> "These were the stricter manners of the man,
> And this the stubborn course in which they ran;
> The golden mean unchanging to pursue,
> Constant to keep the purpos'd end in view;
> Religiously to follow Nature's laws,
> And die with pleasure in his country's cause,
> To think he was not for himself designed,
> But born to be of use to all mankind."
> —Rowe's translation (1718).

litical law by his deeds now represents it through the mere presence of his personality. He is the symbol of what he strove for and attained: political, moral, rational, natural order, and freedom of active life.

Cato's Stoicism makes his injunction to Virgil and Dante intelligible. Dante is to cleanse himself from the grime of Hell, from the stains of lawlessness, and is to gird himself with the pliant rush, the emblem of humble obedience to the law.

As this universal law further reveals itself figuratively in the course of the stars, the poet's eye is directed ever more frequently and reverently toward the sky. Astronomical observations become needful.

The mightiest of all stars is the sun. It is no accident that it rises over us as the journey begins. While the natural law rules among the stars, divine grace shines forth from the sun. The meaning of the journey through Purgatory is none other than the restoration of degenerate nature by divine grace. All astronomical and scientific observations which we meet have their place within Purgatory somewhat as natural religion does within natural morality.

The return of sinful man to perfect nature is, however, no natural process, but a miracle of grace. Therefore the miracle stands beside natural philosophy; and the stars, which move in accordance with manifest law, act in conjunction with the rushes and many other phenomena, which move in accordance with mysterious commands. Scientific observations go hand in hand with pious wonderment.

The first canto leads at once into a new world, with a yearning anticipation of all its elements and of all it stands for.

(*Purgatorio*, II)

Without repose the journey is continued. The impressions accumulate, are intertwined, while the shadows of night still mingle with the beams of day.

From afar there comes a gleam of rosy light across the waves. Swift as lightning it approaches, and flecks of white become visible. A pious song floats shoreward. It is a ship full of departed souls, guided over the sea by an angel of God. Every motion and feature of this phenomenon is noted. Even Virgil is full of curiosity and astonishment. He seems about to offer an explanation, but in reality he, too, must wait to see, and his words only heighten his pupil's suspense. The passengers leap in throngs to land, gaze about them, realize that they are strangers, and inquire the way to the mountain. Then they become aware of the two pilgrims, who are no less strangers and newcomers. They exchange questions and utter cries of amazement. Dante the inquirer becomes in turn an object of inquiry. None knows any other, none knows the country. The situation is on the point of becoming comic when a dear friend of Dante's youth, Casella, steps forth. But even he, in this new environment, is no longer the same, and his friend's attempt to embrace him is vain. A smile flits over Casella's lips. Just as between Cato and Virgil, so now between Dante and Casella, mutual astonishment is felt, questions are asked and answered. But Dante, not yet equal to the manifold impressions of this new world, asks for a reminder of the old days. He begs his friend for music, and Casella begins to sing a stanza from one of Dante's canzoni:

> Love, that within my mind with me discourses
> Wistfully of my lady,
> Discusses things with me concerning her
> Such that my reason is bewildered quite.
> So sweet the words of love resound,
> So that my soul that hears and feels them
> Cries: "Woe is me! that I have not the power
> To tell what of this lady I did hear!" [1]

It is the song of longing for truth and wisdom. While all the souls hearken, enchanted, to the sweet tones, and Dante stands overcome and "melts at his own fire," Cato, the ancient warden, scatters the attentive throng of listeners and drives them upward to the mountain. They flutter thither like startled doves. In shame the poets hasten after them.

These curious souls, who, but just arrived in the next world, would fain satisfy their sensuous craving to see and to hear, instead of going straight to their tasks of purification, seem to us lovely indeed, yet with a touch of the comic. A trace of earthly weakness and worldly levity clings to them still. They have been released from the agonies of death, and do not yet feel the pangs

[1] *Convivio*, second canzone.

of remorse. It befits their condition of kindly lightheartedness that Casella should find the time and disposition to sing, and the rest to listen. They are dear children of the world, and it is quite in the order of things that the ordinances of the Church up yonder in the living world should still be their guide. Even the year of jubilee (which began in January, 1300) and the plenary indulgence granted by so worldly a pope as Boniface VIII helped them on and hastened their passage overseas. As with children, attitudes and gestures are more interesting than the inward life; and they are sufficiently characterized by their outward semblance. Hence the poet devoted to them verses vividly picturesque and full of idyllic reminiscences.

(*Purgatorio*, III)

Cato interrupts the idyll and summons the sluggards to duty. Even Virgil had allowed himself to be diverted by his enjoyment of musical art, and must needs feel ashamed. In silence he hastens with his disciple toward the mountain, but does not know the way. Luckily, souls approach who are familiar with the country, and they give him information.

Here, for the first time, Virgil's inadequacy becomes evident. In the *Inferno* he had a ready answer for every question; in the kingdom of Grace his knowledge becomes fragmentary, and his hesitant voice betrays the consciousness of failing powers: in his tone we hear at times a hopeless wistfulness. The *Purgatorio* might also be called Virgil's tragedy: a long, gentle tragedy, full of subdued melancholy. The pupil's thirst for knowledge begins to outrun the master's wisdom. The bond between them is gently loosening. But, in the same measure that they part company objectively, they draw closer together as human beings. The place of their pedagogical interests is filled by friendship and love.

> I pressed me close unto my faithful comrade,
> And how without him had I kept my course?
> Who would have led me up along the mountain? . .
>
> "And thou be steadfast in thy hope, sweet son."

The pupil fears he is losing his master, as he does not see his shadow beside him. Virgil calms his anxiety by an explanation of the shadowy and therefore shadowless corporeality of the departed. But as this condition is supernatural and miraculous, he is himself unable to solve the riddle, and can only commend to his young friend pious reverence and acceptance of the mystery.

> . . . Here [he] bowed his head,
> And more he said not, and remained disturbed.

The painful melancholy of Virgil is followed, in the same canto, by the sweet melancholy of the youthful king, Manfred. He is one of a group of souls who have dwelt for some time at the foot of the Purgatorial mountain and must await permission to enter on the task of purification. In fact, the entire Ante-Purgatory is intended for the lax who for any reason postponed their repentance until death.

Manfred, an illegitimate son of Frederick II of Hohenstaufen, assumed, after his father's death, rule over the kingdom of Sicily, in place of the rightful heir, Conrad IV, and after the latter's death in 1254, in place of the youthful Conradin. In 1258 he ascended the throne, although his nephew, Conradin, was alive. The pope, who regarded the kingdom of Sicily as a papal fief, and who wished to create in Southern Italy a Guelfic state in place of the Ghibelline kingdom of the Hohenstaufens, put Manfred under the ban of the Church. Urban IV offered the Sicilian crown to Charles of Anjou and preached a crusade against the excommunicated Manfred. At the battle of Benevento in 1266, the youthful, highly gifted prince was overwhelmed by the French and by the fanaticism of the Guelfs. He met his death heroically on the battlefield. But religious animus pursued the memory and the corpse of the dead. Guelfic writers accused him, without a trace of proof, of parricide and fratricide. The Archbishop of Cosenza had the remains of the excommunicated king disinterred and scattered over unconsecrated ground.

Dante, though of Guelf descent, contrasts the glorified, beautiful figure of his Manfred with the petty, irreconcilable rage of the Guelfs. As Cato had cast aside his earthly love, so has Manfred his earthly hatred. Without a shadow of resentment he tells of the injustice done to his dead body.

If the priests knew the boundless mercy of God, they would not be so ready with their curse. Yet Manfred is far from questioning the power of the Church; on the contrary, he knows its importance and reveres it. He strives no longer; he has forgiven. Only the memory of the mutual hatred of himself and his foes persists and throws a shadow of melancholy on his soul. With a smile the blond youth points to the death-wound dealt him at Benevento. But, becoming as it is to his face, he does not coquet with it. He makes himself known to the pilgrim from the world only because he still has, yonder among the living, an anxious and loving daughter, Costanza, the pious wife of Peter III of Aragon. How happy she will be to hear that her father, though he died under the ban of the Church, has won his salvation, and that she may, with good hope, pray for him! The downfall of the house of Hohenstaufen in Italy is one of the bloodiest and most savage tragedies of the Middle Ages. The poet, however, paints a pious picture of love out of the memories of this irreconcilable hatred. Our meeting with this first character blest by divine mercy tells our hearts that the horrors of Hell have vanished.

(*Purgatorio*, IV)

The toil of the ascent begins. Dry, didactic verses follow on the gentle tones of affection. The attention and mental exertion that Dante devoted to Manfred is gone. The sun has risen high. Through a narrow, steep, rocky gorge the poets clamber up. As they come into the open again, the ascent grows yet more precipitous. A brief pause for rest, which the gasping Dante fills out with topographical, geographical, and astronomical questions, and the unwearied Virgil with corresponding information. The exertion of the muscles is followed by the effort after abstract and mathematical comprehension.

When all has been explained and the weary pedestrians have again caught their breath, a merry laugh is heard. At the wayside Belacqua is lounging, the witty lazy-bones, a Florentine craftsman who lived in Dante's youth and was famous for his indolence and nonchalance. Doubtless merely from laziness, he has postponed his repentance and contrition till the very end. So now he must wait, bowed down with heavy weariness. Their energetic climbing seems to him useless and ridiculous, as do also the scientific queries of his fellow countryman; he is sunk in a pious, comfortable fatalism. As the lazy man throws his gibe at the energetic ones, the strenuous pilgrim answers with a laugh at his friend's amusing indolence.

But the guide urges him on:

> . . . "Come now; see, the sun has touched
> Meridian, and from the shore the night
> Covers already with her foot Morocco."

How magnificently these verses, after the ignoble indolence of man, set forth the untiring march of the sun!

(*Purgatorio*, V)

Again and again the poets are blocked in their upward struggle. New bands of negligent and inquisitive folk crowd upon them and strive to detain them with chat and questioning. Virgil indeed cries:

> "What matters it to thee what here is whispered?
> Come after me, and let the people talk;
> Stand like a steadfast tower, that never wags
> Its top for all the blowing of the winds."

After all, however, man's will is barred by God's will; and Belacqua was not so ill-informed. Innumerable souls who have felt in their own persons the superior power of destiny, press on the wanderer's heels, ask through him to be remembered in the prayers of their living and loving relatives, and relate the tale of their death.

> "O soul that goest to beatitude
> With the same members wherewith thou wast born,"
> Shouting they came, "a little stay thy steps."

All these shades died a violent and sudden death and crave the prayers of their survivors. Here first of all is a Guelf captain and Podestà, Jacopo del Càssero da Fano, who, pursued by the hirelings of his foe, Azzo VIII of Este, was overtaken and murdered (1298). By a hair—since on his flight he fell into a morass—he failed to escape his doom. There, again, is Count Buonconte of Montefeltro, the son of Guido the traitor, whom we know from *Inferno*, XXVII. He was in command of the Aretine Ghibellines at the battle of Campaldino—that battle in which our poet himself fought on the winning side (1289); and there he fell. His corpse, despite a careful search, could not be found. Even with the lifeless body a capricious destiny played, a blind destiny, a foolishly malicious power. An angel of God rescued the Count's soul, a stupid devil wreaked his rage on his body. The dead man tells, with mingled horror and pleasure, how it came about. He is still wholly under the influence of his dying hour, which in reality was not at all extraordinary. An invocation to the Virgin Mary saved his soul, but his body was washed into a brook by a furious storm, and thence into the Arno. In the memory of him whose corpse underwent such a fate, in the heart of the Count who so narrowly escaped the deadly enemy, this ordinary event takes on a fantastic, terrible colouring. It seems to him that, even after death, he is forced to follow his corpse. He cannot take his eyes from the peril undergone; he lingers by his remains, and sees with dread and amazement how storm gathers over them, how they become the prey of Nature, the booty of the Devil; and he follows his own semblance as it is rolled and tossed by the waters and finally buried beneath the mud of the river.

Even so a man who has been terrified by the wraith or foreboding of sudden death follows long, in his thoughts, behind his bier, and wanders in a waking dream about his open grave.

The third soul that speaks to Dante is a gracious, quiet lady: Pia dei Tolomei of Siena. She had been one day secretly done away with (1295) by her husband, Count Nello Pannocchieschi—no one knew why, she least of all. Passively, with closed eyes, she met her doom. After the excited and imaginative fatalism of Buonconte, the brief, calm words of Pia have the sound of defenceless, touching submissiveness.

> "Do thou remember me, who am the Pia;
> Siena made me, unmade me Maremma;
> He knoweth it, who had encircled first,
> Espousing me, my finger with his gem."

(*Purgatorio*, VI)

The first half of the sixth canto carries to its end this drama of chance and destiny. As though about a winning gambler, the shades crowd about Dante and beg for the prayers of the living. When he is finally alone with his guide, he is desirous to know whether mortal prayer really has the power to bend the divine will. Virgil gives him only incomplete information, and lets his utterance end in pious hope:

"Verily, in so deep a questioning
  Do not decide, unless she tell it thee,
  Who light 'twixt truth and intellect shall be.
I know not if thou understand; I speak
  Of Beatrice; her shalt thou see above,
  Smiling and happy, on this mountain's top."

With fresh vigour they clamber higher, while the sun sinks. Serious and proud, a soul stands beside the way: the troubadour Sordello from Mantua. When, on his curt inquiry, Virgil names his own city, Mantua, the two fellow countrymen fall into each other's arms at the beloved name.

The thought of their native city has united, with its magic power, two men who had stood far apart. At this point, Dante cuts short the beautiful web of his tale, and inveighs in a voice that is altered by deep emotion:

Ah! servile Italy, grief's hostelry!
  A ship without a pilot in great tempest!
  No Lady thou of Provinces, but brothel!
That noble soul was so impatient, only
  At the sweet sound of his own native land,
  To make its citizen glad welcome there;
And now within thee are not without war
  Thy living ones, and one doth gnaw the other
  Of those whom one wall and one fosse shut in!
Search, wretched one, all round about the shores
  Thy seaboard, and then look within thy bosom,
  If any part of thee enjoyeth peace!
What boots it, that for thee Justinian
  The bridle mend, if empty be the saddle?
  Withouten this the shame would be the less.
Ah! people, thou that oughtest to be devout,
  And to let Caesar sit upon the saddle,
  If well thou hearest what God teacheth thee,
Behold how fell this wild beast has become,
  Being no longer by the spur corrected,
  Since thou hast laid thy hand upon the bridle.
O German Albert! who abandonest
  Her that has grown recalcitrant and savage,
  And oughtest to bestride her saddle-bow,
May a just judgment from the stars down fall
  Upon thy blood, and be it new and open,
  That thy successor may have fear thereof;
Because thy father and thyself have suffered,
  By greed of those transalpine lands distrained,
  The garden of the empire to be waste.

Through thirteen more terzets a song of rebuke rolls on: majestic, threatening, scornful, and with terrific insistence exposing the political wretchedness of Florence. Then, as if nothing had happened, the next canto resumes the interrupted tale.

Is that not an offence against good style? Does not this surprising digression, as the poet himself calls it, bear the marks of a personal, unobjective outbreak? But the more closely we study the following cantos, VII and VIII, that is, the close of Ante-Purgatory, the more clearly we shall see how deep this invective, which seems so violent an interruption, is rooted in the natural soil of the poem.

(*Purgatorio*, VII–VIII)

Before the sun goes down Sordello guides our poets to the edge of a dale hollowed out in the mountainside. It is a charming valley, beautified with blossoms of jewel-like brilliancy and sweet odours—a fairy scene. We are reminded of Elysium in the Limbo. So, before we see the dale, Virgil, in making himself known to his fellow countryman, tells him about Elysium.

In this valley a chosen band of emperors, kings, and princes watch and wait for permission to proceed.

There is a certain kinship between Virgil and Sordello, similar to that existing between the valley of the princes and the Elysium of the great souls. Virgil glorified the ethico-political ideal of the Roman empire; he is the epic herald of the advent of that rule and beheld with joyous eye the splendour of the Augustan age. Sordello, on the contrary, lived in a degenerate period of the empire, and branded with wrathful contempt the decay of imperial rule. He is the lyrical satirist of political degeneration. Proudly he seeks a place of rest apart from the princes. But as soon as he recognizes Virgil, the singer of the Ideal, he bends low, embraces the knees of his great fellow citizen, grows eloquent, and eagerly points out, describes, and characterizes, from a height, the various sovereign rulers. Calmly now, objectively and without scorn, he gives a rapid sketch of each. The satirist in him is neutralized, so to speak, by contact with Virgil, and he is transformed into a narrator. The satirist denies with subjective passion and blames; the narrator sees only the negation of reality made actual by reality; that is, the downfall of an institution. Therefore Sordello's objective speech is crossed, as it were, by a crimson thread, the idea of decadence.

It is not, however, on the mood of the troubadour but on that of the rulers that this thought weighs heavily and with melancholy. They are great princes who, absorbed in lesser cares, have neglected their duty. The Emperor Rudolph of Hapsburg, who cared more for his dynastic power than for the empire and Italy, the "garden of the empire"; Ottocar II of Bohemia, Philip III of France, Henry I of Navarre, Peter III of Aragon, Charles of Anjou, Henry III of England, and William VII, Marquis of Montferrat. Several of them—for example, Rudolph and Ottocar, or Peter and Charles—had fought against each other on earth. Now they sit together, united by sorrow, and consoling one another. Most of them have been succeeded by worthless sons and grandsons, of whom they must be ashamed. It is as if their own neglect were to avenge itself on their children. Only in the sure hope of heavenly bliss do they find consolation. Therefore they send ardent songs of prayer heavenward: *Salve Regina, Mater misericordiae . . . ad te clamamus exsules, filii Evae. Ad te suspiramus, gementes et flentes in hac lacrymarum valle.* As the sun vanishes, one of the band rises, and with clasped hands, his face turned toward the East, begins to sing the evening hymn:

Te lucis ante terminum
Rerum Creator, poscimus,
Ut tua pro clementia
Sis praesul et custodia.
Procul recedant somnia
Et noctium phantasmata. . . .

In the weary attitudes and gestures of the princes, in the evening shadows that are falling, in the mysterious glow and fragrance of the flowers, in the pious choral song of male voices, in the thoughts that fill the pilgrims gazing at them from afar: decay and fall of princely power, fate forever omnipotent—in all this, the departure from earth's misery and the longing for Heaven are merged in melting harmony. Who does not know the verses in which the homesickness of this evening mood is expressed as if in a noble solo:

'Twas now the hour that turneth back desire
  In those who sail the sea, and melts the heart,
  The day they've said to their sweet friends farewell,
And the new pilgrim penetrates with love,
  If he doth hear from far away a bell
  That seemeth to deplore the dying day.

When the night rises and the home of light is veiled, the exiled souls who feel themselves strangers on earth, and cannot yet ascend the heights, must be dismayed. They have prayed, for they are in fear of the spirits of darkness, and wait "pale and pious" for a consolatory sign. Two angels fly down, protect the valley, and put to flight the serpent of temptation. At the same time at the southern pole, where before sunrise four stars had been, three new stars appear in flaming light. They represent the counterpart of the natural virtues: faith, hope, and love.

The poets have descended from the height, and mingle in the princely gathering. Here Dante, despite the darkness, meets with a companion in arms and friend of his youth, Nino Visconti of Pisa, judge of Gallura, and makes the acquaintance of a young count of the Malaspina family.

Both these figures the poet introduced chiefly for personal reasons. He had doubtless become acquainted with Nino Visconti as a young man and a soldier, probably during a campaign of the Florentines against Pisa (August, 1289), and had acquired a warm sense of comradeship toward him. At the court of the Malaspinas, on the other hand, he, as an unhappy exile, was to find a hospitable refuge and a cordial welcome (autumn of 1306). The name of Visconti, we may assume, was associated with happy memories; the name of Malaspina was connected with painful experiences by the bond of gratitude. When the poet puts into the mouth of Visconti sorrowful words against his faithless wife, while with Malaspina he speaks only of the fame and splendour of the noble house and finds a hopeful sign for himself therein, it would appear that he wished to impress on his own and the reader's mind, through these contrasted glimpses of his life, the diversity and uncertainty of human destiny.

Soothed by these intimate feelings, which did not rise fully to the surface of consciousness, cradled in memories and hopes—while the souls of the departed remain wakeful—the pilgrim falls asleep. The first day in the new world, the passage through the Ante-Purgatory, is ended.

It is a truly musical and yet simple art with which, in this final canto, all the previous modes are gently united and brought to a close. The external action—the setting of the sun, the coming of the angels, the apparition of the three stars, the attack of the serpent and his flight—is spiritualized by the inner action: prayer, conversation, thoughts, and feelings of the departed souls and of the pilgrim. While Visconti, distressed by painful thoughts, is suffering from the disloyalty of his wife, the stars of faith, hope, and love shine forth in the sky; while the serpent is repelled by the angels, the child of the noble Malaspina family comes to the poet's side. The picture of humanity, as it bids farewell to earth and in sad, pious longing awaits its eternal freedom, blends into the picture of Alighieri who, expelled from his native city, awaits consolation by a noble, princely house.

The departure of the Christian from earth is accomplished without bitterness of spirit: a gentle transition. But it was with violence that Alighieri was removed from his native city. It was a departure in hatred and anger. Hence, at this point in the poem, that is, at the beginning of this political section, the vale of the sovereign rulers, a profound, irreconcilable dissonance was felt between the poetic and the personal tone. The banished Florentine, whose political conscience had been exasperated by misfortune, could not be expected, at once and with full sincerity, to give a mild and hopeful picture of an assemblage of rulers who had been neglectful of their political duties. He must first—it was a matter of personal necessity—thunder out the righteous indignation that was in his heart. But after the tempestuous outbreak, "O servile Italy," had cleared the poetic atmosphere, a cloudless evening sky appeared in the closing cantos.

PURGATORY PROPER

(*Purgatorio*, IX)

The ninth canto of the *Purgatorio* corresponds to the eighth and ninth of the *Inferno*. There, a lively struggle, at the entrance into lower Hell; here, a calm, solemn ascent to the place of penitential purification. The resistance which the home of mercy offers to those who stand without is no violent opposition by an evil conscience, but a lawful one that can be overcome only by submission and obedience. The purpose of the institution is revealed from without by a ceremonial which the newcomer must undergo.

Under the influence of divine Grace, Dante in a dream feels himself seized by Jupiter's eagle and borne up into the heaven of fire; at the same time his sleeping body is carried by Lucia, the dispenser of illuminating grace, and Dante's protecting saint, to the very gate of Purgatory. Both events have the same significance and a certain parallelism. Three times, always at the beginning of a new task, the poet has felt it necessary to venture on this division of life. He desires to emphasize, at the decisive turning-points, that variance between the external and inner events which we have characterized, and also to set forth the correspondence between them.

The ceremony of entrance follows, also, with a solemnity to which our especial attention is called (verses 70–72), that of admission or entrance. The angel at the gate, the sword with which he inscribes seven P's (*Peccata*) on Dante's forehead, the silver and the golden keys with which he unlocks the gate, the three steps by which the gate is reached, the diamond threshold, the thundering sound of the hinges of the portal, the command not to look backward—all these are formalities behind which a dogmatic sequence of ideas, presumably the Church's doctrine of penitence, confession, penance, absolution, or the like, lies hidden, which can no longer be recognized with certainty, but only more or less successfully surmised.

But the poetical effectiveness lies precisely in the fact that these symbols are mysteries—in the last analysis, the mystery of God. Their significance is the veil that enfolds them Hence the entire canto is composed in a style of lofty ambiguity: inwardly obscure, but picturesque and brilliant in language and figures.

(*Purgatorio*, X–XII)

The nature of the mountain of Purgatory is now to be described step by step. It is logically worked out from the spiritual conditions of the dwellers in this realm, and through them made visible.

These conditions vary: transitional states, transformation from sinful individuals to a perfect ideal, something halfway between the damned soul and the blissful, between materialism and spirituality. Sin is, for the souls in Purgatory, only a memory, and virtue only a hope. They hover between their past and their future, and have practically no present. Instead of living, they dream; instead of acting, they suffer; instead of willing, they remember and they hope.

What they lack, in order to be adequate personalities, is set over against them by the poet's ingenuity as an external, half-known, half-strange, and half-hostile, half-helpful environment. The souls are fainting under their terrible experiences. Their individuality is blurred. They are very much alike and unite in groups. Inasmuch as they must struggle with the unknown and difficult nature of the mountain, they have to bestir themselves and cannot be mere contemplative beings. They are contending, unconsciously, against a part of their own ego. Their problem is to acquire again, in a new sense, the scattered fragments of their personality, and to become whole once more. When, through struggle and suffering, they have made themselves at home in this environment that had been alien to them, and have adjusted themselves to its divine harmony, then of itself there is established within them a feeling of completeness, and they rise jubilantly heavenward as victors.

This, in rough outline, is approximately the ingenious manner by which Alighieri has constructed out of purely contemplative mental states a remarkable type of moral activity and ethical effort.

Since in the depths of his soul he is convinced that the supernatural mountain rests not merely on his own poetic invention but on God's omnipotence, goodness, and wisdom, he is in a position to endow the figments of his imagination with the life of piety.

(*Pride*)

The first terrace of Purgatory proper is occupied, as we already know, by the penitent proud. The lesson here is twofold: first, the reliefs on the wall and on the pavement representing historical acts of exemplary humility and of deterrent pride; second, the punishment of the souls themselves, who move about, each bending and groaning under the weight of a massive stone.

But how profoundly and piously this ordinance is felt in the poem! At first we have pure description, clear, objective pictures. We are in the kingdom of Grace, where all is bright and pure, and where the moral command is set before us as reality, as historical fact, where the divine will speaks unmistakably out of the plastic forms that live humbly in the hardness and pride of marble. The more these are studied, the more lifelike they become, the more clearly does the stone reveal the movement and the will to act. The first picture, the Annunciation, shows us humility in absolute passivity; the second, David dancing before the Ark of the Covenant, depicts a humility which has become religious service; the third, the well-known scene of the Emperor Trajan and the widow, develops with dramatic vividness the practical helpful humility of civic daily life. This crescendo of speaking pictures arouses the emotions of the gazing poet so that presently he breaks into eloquent admonitions. At the same time the action begins, as the bands of penitents draw nigh.

The children of pride are notably changed. Their necks bent under their burden of stones, their assertiveness bowed under a weight as of a nightmare, they struggle onward. In the most familiar and most comprehensive prayer of Christendom, in the Paternoster, their individuality is lost, and their voices, once so sharp and defiant, pray softly and in unison for their own and their fellows' weal. All individuality seems extinguished in this world where the sculptures are eloquent and the earth speaks of divine wisdom. Slowly, however, and laboriously, some individuals become distinguishable. Omberto Aldobrandeschi is nothing but a chance example of the whole band enfeebled by the sin of pride. All the artists, all the famous painters and poets, Oderisi d'Agobbio, Franco Bolognese, Cimabue, Giotto, Guido Guinizelli, Guido Cavalcanti, are mentioned here without merit of their own, dropped to the level of moralizing illustrations. That which lasts and endures is not the artists, but the art. The cause is greater than the individuals.

So two motifs are intertwined in this canto: foolish pride, crushed by penance, human glory outshone by the splendour of its source. The first motif in its epic execution produces an effect of tension and oppression; the second in lyric enthusiasm liberates us. Hence, at the close, the conciliatory figure of Provenzan Salvani, a man of pride who, even in his lifetime, humbled himself.

But the tale of this abasement casts a threatening shadow over the future, when Alighieri, also abased, will even have to beg. Bent and oppressed, the pilgrim walks beside Salvani. Through his sympathy for him he purifies himself.

The parting comes quickly. Dante, again straightening his body, but with a spirit that is forever bent, proceeds with his guide. The examples of pride punished which he sees at his feet pass easily and in numbers beneath him. As he feels himself free, it is no longer the pictures that speak to him; he himself speaks of them and ever more vigorously to them. As he finally breaks out admonishingly,

> Now wax ye proud, and on with looks uplifted,
> Ye sons of Eve,

his voice sounds no longer, as in the tenth canto (121 sqq.), didactic and chiding, but ironical. One laughs at a weakness that has been overcome.

But facing the angel who guards the ascent to the second terrace, Virgil once again warns his temperamental pupil to be humble—for the work of purification may not be accomplished a second time.

> "Remember that this day no more returns."

(*Envy*)

(*Purgatorio*, XIII–XIV)

The ascent to the second terrace is bright and almost cheerful, less mysterious and solemn than the entrance into the first circle. Our pilgrim feels relieved. The angel has removed the heaviest of the seven P's from his forehead. As Dante in joyous doubt, fingering his forehead, traces with his hands this miracle of Grace, Virgil smiles.

The new region seems at first deserted; only the sun marks the way. Invisible voices in the air bid man love his neighbour. Virgil explains the things that Dante does not understand, for, in the circle of the envious, the sympathy, the community of feeling on Dante's part which we observed in regard to the proud, is lacking. He knows himself to be relatively free from envy. The more objectively does his outward sense comprehend the figures. The penitents are sitting before him in plastic attitudes like beggars. They who in life grudged each other everything now lean wearily on one another.

> And one sustained the other with his shoulder,
> And all of them were by the bank sustained.

Their eyes, which looked askance at others, are now sewn and closed with iron wire. A penitential robe, pale as envy, cold as stone, covers them. Their sightless, upturned faces beg for pity. As Dante gazes at them, he silently reproaches himself that he, seeing, stands before the blind. He is anxious not to pass them by, and he addresses them. He is answered by a woman of Siena, Sapia by name, a remarkable being. She tells how she revelled in the misery of others, exulted in the bloody defeat of her countrymen at Colle di Valdelsa (1269). A last trace of this wild malice still lingers in her soul. With a sort of weary irony she speaks of herself and of the foolishness of the Sienese.

The others have listened. The conversation grows lively and passes on along the rows of the envious. They wish to make the acquaintance of the divinely favoured pilgrim. He, however, conceals his identity from the eyes of justifiable envy. Instead of naming himself, he mentions in veiled words the river of his home city. But this very reserve makes the others talkative. In particular, one, Guido del Duca, pours out his burdened heart in bitter, passionate, and, at the last, touching words and tears.

Guido, who must have died about the middle of the thirteenth century, had lived a brilliant, knightly, and festive youth-time in the circle of the Romagnole nobility. But his envious eye darkened his happiest hours. Only now, in the Hereafter, has his inward eye been opened. Too late! Now this lofty spirit sees in the smiling landscapes of Tuscany and the Romagna nothing but decadence and destruction. He hears the Arno mentioned, and the whole river valley, with its inhabitants, seems to him transformed as if by evil magic. In the Casentino, swine abide; the Aretines have become howling whelps; the Florentines have transformed themselves into wolves, the Pisans into foxes. And all this is saddest truth! For close beside Guido sits a nobleman, Renier da Calboli, whose nephew, Fulcieri, is destined to slaughter like a cruel, shameless butcher the wild Florentine wolves (an allusion to the massacres of the Florentine white Guelfs and Ghibellines in the year 1303, by the Podestà Fulcieri da Calboli). With sarcastic wrath, poor Guido must smite the posterity of his own friends. In his holy zeal he must accuse himself and the others. How pitifully have all the haughty noble families of his home degenerated, what poor creatures have the children of the noblest fathers come to be, the Manardi, Traversari, Carpignas! Unbounded bitterness rises from his heart, and horror and disgust spread over the present and the future, so far as the poor blind man can behold it. Rage, hatred, repentance, melancholy, and homesickness, mingle in his words. Now he no longer envies any one. The boundless misery of humanity chokes him. He, to whom the condition of others had seemed so rosy and enviable, must now account those men happy who have remained childless. Amid the general decadence, continuity of the family is a curse. Such is the bitter aftertaste of envy. Sobbing like a child, the stern, strong man collapses:

> " But go now, Tuscan, for it now delights me
> To weep far better than it does to speak,
> So much has our discourse my mind distressed."

Silently, without a farewell, the pilgrim leaves these "dear souls."

In the air, terrible words against envy roar like thunder; but it is with a gentle voice that Virgil explains their meaning, so that once again, at the close, the two undertones of the canto, punitive satire and sad penitence, are blended.

(*Anger*)

(*Purgatorio*, XV–XVI)

In Hell, the poet had set the wrathful close beside, in fact among, the slothful. In the *Purgatorio* he does his best to keep them apart. Pride, envy, wrath, compose the lower section of Purgatory; but *acedia* belongs with avarice, gluttony, and lust in the upper division. The boundary-line runs between anger and sloth. That line is not concealed but emphasized broadly by the insertion of several didactic passages. Why?

Because, to put it briefly, the *Purgatorio* is a sort of inverted *Inferno*. There below, man appears as a prisoner, clamped down and held fast by his sinful past, and it matters not whether he lacerates himself in rage or stifles in sullen sloth. Here above, however, he struggles out of the fetters of his sinful state and grows to moral activity and freedom. Hence, the conquest of indolence marks a decisive turning-point. To bridle one's pride, envy, and anger, is positive training; it is the exercise of humility, pity, and gentleness. In upper Purgatory, however, a higher, negative discipline is required: a struggle against greed, gluttony, and lust; that is, renunciation of worldly enjoyment. As it cannot be renunciation through weakness or dullness, one must will strongly before renouncing. Hence the central mediating and separating position of *acedia* in Purgatory.

The boundary which runs between wrath and *acedia* and parts

Upper from Lower Purgatory corresponds to the boundary between Lower and Upper Hell. As the latter is made prominent by the red-hot walls of the infernal city, so it would be expected that the former would be clearly marked by a material barrier, by an especially lofty parapet or a chasm, a leap or a flight, or something of the sort. Instead, the ascent from the third to the fourth terrace is as simple as possible.

Indeed, the ascent from the second to the third level is notable in this respect. During the climb, Virgil explains to his pupil the distinction between the effort to acquire earthly and heavenly goods; that is, he distinguishes the economic from the moral will. Just afterward, in the circle of the wrathful, Marco Lombardo develops the doctrine of the freedom of the will. Hardly have the travellers arrived in the circle of the indolent, when they devote themselves to a detailed survey of the moral gradations of all Purgatory, and Virgil demonstrates how every level corresponds to a special error of human desire. This desire is called love, and like desire, it also rises from the practical to the moral, inasmuch as, above the sensuous, natural, and fettered love, there exists a love moral, supernatural, and free.

One sees that all these explanations form a circle, and Virgil's final argument (XVIII, 73 sqq.) comes back to the first (XV, 73 sqq.). At the beginning as at the end we have the reference to Beatrice. The entire cycle embraces Dante's moral philosophy.

Instead of the struggle under the walls of Dis we have a cycle of ethical discussions. These begin at the end of the second, and close at the beginning of the fourth, terrace, thus both uniting and separating the third from the fourth, wrath from *acedia.*

The passionate speech of Guido del Duca made our poet thoughtful, and on the terrace of the wrathful he falls into a reverie. Like an intoxication there comes over him a gentle dulling of the senses, a drugging of the irascible will, together with clearness of inner sight. In the form of dreams and visions he beholds the examples of gentleness: Mary in the Temple, Pisistratus, Stephen the martyr; pictures which bring peace to his soul. Wrath, a furious frenzy, requires, for its cure, to be calmed by a sleeping-potion.

The wrathful suffer their penalty in a thick smoke which clouds and irritates the eyes. But this external night leads to light within.

Through the deep darkness resound the luminous words of Marco Lombardo.

Marco was a nobleman who enjoyed a high reputation in Upper Italy in the second half of the thirteenth century. Among the souls in Purgatory he still has an authoritative position. His words sound zealous, instructive, admonitory. Remarkably enough, he does not speak of his own passion, or of anger in general. But with honest and holy wrath he preaches against all debasement, lawlessness, or distortion of the will in moral, legal, and political life. "The laws exist, but who lays hand upon them?"

His philosophy, enlivened by noble enthusiasm, glides at once into admonition, but has neither a querulous nor a sanctimonious tone. The practical, virile, intelligent, benevolent, by no means gentle spirit of this zealous censor expresses itself in a sharp, concise, and cutting, almost harsh style. It is as if enlightened anger, become practical reason, were speaking *ex cathedra*. While Guido del Duca spoke in veiled figures and with bitterness, Marco talks clearly, frankly, freely, and without hatred. He blames not individuals but conditions: the legal relations between state and Church. When he names persons, he does it only in an appreciative sense. Becoming quite objective, he says almost nothing of himself. The passionate subjectivity of the wrathful man has been purified in him to holy zeal. He has almost attained perfection. His opinions, his forms of expression, his peculiarities, are coming to coincide with Alighieri's character and style. At most it is a certain didactic tone that betrays his former irritable self.

For the second time a gentle current of dreams lays hold on the wayfarer. It is spontaneous illumination, less rapt, more definite than before. The clouds are dispelled, the last shadow of passion vanishes before the splendour of the angel who stands at the gate of exit.

The ascent is accomplished without effort, but they are hardly on the level of the fourth terrace when the sun sets and they can go no farther.

(*Sloth*)

(*Purgatorio*, XVII–XVIII)

Virgil explains the divisions of Purgatory. His calm explanation is in harmony as to its content, but contrasted in style to the eager instruction which Marco Lombardo had given.

Whence I, who reason manifest and plain
In answer to my questions had received,
Stood like a man in drowsy reverie.

Nevertheless, the chief problem, the freedom of the will, is by no means satisfactorily solved by Virgil; and it seems as if the pilgrims, too, were attacked by the indolence which broods over this circle.

Breathless, bustling, urging themselves to haste, like a band of Bacchantes, the ghosts of the slothful rush through the night, dimly outlined, fleeting figures. The words of the Veronese abbot of San Zeno are enigmatic, prophetic, and personal allusions; for he has not time to express himself more clearly. As his shade vanishes, his speech dies away, leaving no echo in Dante's mind.

If more he said, or silent was, I know not,
He had already passed so far beyond us;
But this I heard, and to retain it pleased me.

Perhaps a modern poet would have elaborated to greater effect the significant contrast of the weary man, who is falling asleep, with the running, shouting ghosts. For Alighieri the beauty of the scene is limited by its didactic purposes. The symmetry of the poem required historical examples of promptness worthy of imitation, and of slothfulness punished.

Such examples inspire not speed, but thought. But a race accelerated not with the whip but with historical memories, or a troop of Bacchantes rushing on for logical reasons, is a paradox. So these slothful folk cannot be made quite vivid. They remain, even in poetry, what the conditions make them: fleeting shades.

(*Avarice*)

(*Purgatorio*, XIX–XXII)

Dante has fallen asleep, and as was to be expected, has a symbolic vision. The charms of the sensuous world, by which the penitents of upper Purgatory have allowed themselves to be beguiled, appear to him in the form of a siren. Her song rises meltingly, alluring as a South Italian folk-song:

"I am," she sang, "I am the Siren sweet
Who mariners amid the main unman,
So full am I of pleasantness to hear."

The more eagerly the sensuous, dreamy eye gazes at her, the more beautiful and full of life she grows. But Virgil, the eye of reason, summoned hither by an honourable lady, that is, Grace or Revelation, lays bare the malodorous ugliness of the seductive creature. Dante awakes.

The details of this little drama stand out as if under the spotlight, and while the reader ponders on the meaning of what he sees, it fades quite away. Desire, temptation, disgust, pursue and follow each other in the dreamer's thought like hurrying ghosts.

The sun is high in Heaven, Virgil puts to flight his pupil's nightly thoughts, and, with strengthened will, they climb upward.

Three figures, two misers and one spendthrift, characterize the path of purification through the realm of material greed: each in a different moral state, and each on a higher level than the one preceding. Their condition and the corresponding temperament, not the actions or particular convictions, make these people important. They are lyric figures, not characters. The dramatic quality which attached to the proud under their burden, to the envious in their discourse, to the wrathful in their sermon, and to the slothful in their furious race, has fallen away.

The condition of Pope Hadrian V is one of entire renunciation and devotion. In life he was the covetous son of Count Fieschi of Lavagna, greedy for wealth. But when, in the year 1276, he was elevated to the papal throne, disillusionment came, and presently death:

> " I saw that there the heart was not at rest,
> Nor farther in that life could one ascend;
> Whereby the love of this was kindled in me.
> Until that time a wretched soul and parted
> From God was I, and wholly avaricious;
> Now, as thou seest, I here am punished for it.
> What avarice does is here made manifest
> In the purgation of these souls converted,
> And no more bitter pain the Mountain has.
> Even as our eye did not uplift itself
> Aloft, being fastened upon earthly things,
> So justice here has merged it in the earth.
> As avarice had extinguished our affection
> For every good, whereby was action lost,
> So justice here doth hold us in restraint,
> Bound and imprisoned by the feet and hands;
> And so long as it pleases the just Lord
> Shall we remain immovable and prostrate."

This pope is living wholly in his penance. Nothing else concerns him. He has become calm, peaceful, almost gentle, and expects nothing more from mankind. There is a sad clarity and devotion in his words; no hatred, no reproach for others. He thinks of his papal dignity as of a remote, impersonal, wholly official matter, in terms couched in the Latin of the Papal Chancery: *Scias quod ego fui successor Petri.* Dante's reverential manner, even his presence, oppresses him. "Depart thou now . . . seeing thy presence interrupts my weeping." He has still a kindly thought for his pious niece Alagia, but this last earthly tie shows how lonely and silent his heart has grown.

Through this contact with Hadrian's sorrowful yet peaceful soul, even Dante, the bitterest foe of all the covetous, has become elegiac.

His curse, "Accursèd be thou, ancient wolf," dies away in a pious sigh: "When will he come through whom she shall depart?"

Wistful and touching is the praying lament of the sinners: "Sweet Mary! . . . O good Fabricius!"

Above this rises the second figure: Hugh Capet, the founder of the French royal line. He, too, is dead to the world; but his memories of earth are neither quieted, nor softened, nor paled by renunciation. He is a stronger, keener temperament than the pope. To his own penance, to his own suffering, which held Hadrian captive, he hardly gives a thought. It is the sins of others, the crimes of his children and his children's children, that absorb him. In his sons and grandsons, however, he hates and detests only his own sins.

> "I was the root of that malignant plant
> Which overshadows all the Christian world,
> So that good fruit is seldom gathered from it."

With wild delight, the founder of the Capetian royal house announces the disgrace of his line. With merciless frankness he unveils their self-wrought shame:

> "From me were born the Louises and Philips,
> By whom in later years has France been governed.
> I was the son of a Parisian butcher." [1]

The language in which Hugh relates, or prophesies, the deeds of Charles of Anjou, Charles of Valois, and Philip the Fair, re-

[1] This mediæval legend as to the Capets' origin naturally suited Dante's desire to brand his deadliest enemies.

calls the grotesque, sarcastic style of a monkish exhorter to penitence. This fierce arraignment of his offspring, this delight in the thought that God would wreak a wrathful vengeance on his descendants, show that he must have renounced his own kin and become hardened almost to inhumanity.

Through this implacable hatred toward himself and his own kin, the last sinful stain that no tear, no love, effaces, must be gnawed and cut away. Therefore Hugh, in the wildness of his desire for penance, stands a grade higher than Hadrian. One step farther, and his cold hatred will be transformed into heavenly love, and his soul, pure and free, will soar aloft. Of all human temperaments in the *Purgatorio*, that of Hugh Capet is the most exaggerated, the least human.

In fact, hardly had he uttered his last cruel word—

> " O Crassus, tell us,
> For thou dost know, what is the taste of gold? "—

when the mountain quakes with the divine shudder of love. "Glory to God in the highest!" A soul has set itself free.

It is the soul of Statius. He illustrates the third and last stage: the condition of purity regained.

Statius was not, in his sinful days, a miser, but a spendthrift. Here, too, as in Hell, avarice and prodigality stand on the same footing. As the proper mean between these extremes, Statius is now the harmonious and moderate man. And not only between greed and waste, but between the various forces which are to be found in Purgatory, he holds the middle ground: between pagan reason and Christian revelation, between moral will and pious devotion, between repentance and hope.

Such balance in the spiritual life is impossible. Here there can be no dead-point, just as there is no human being absolutely clear of sin. From this viewpoint, Statius appears to us as the representative of an extreme concept, as the white raven which may be imagined, but in actual experience never found. He represents a transitional stage in the moral and intellectual development of man. Much in him becomes intelligible only if we consider this abstract side of his nature.

He is midway between Virgil and Beatrice, between rationalism and mysticism, and hence is appointed to explain the natural philosophy of Purgatory; that is, the nature of a supernatural world.[1] We have already seen that the doctrine of the soul which our poet puts into his mouth is neither science nor myth, and that the style of these passages is the prophetic expression of a half-rationalistic, half-mystical form of thought.

The moral indecision of Statius accords with his twofold intellectual nature. It is no accident that he tarried more than four hundred years on that middle terrace of Purgatory, among the slothful. Four is the number of that circle, and one hundred stands for completion. It is not an accident that his final release occurs not among the slothful, but in the next circle. For only here does virtue appear as the proper mean, as the boundary-line between two extremes. Statius accordingly, to put it figuratively, stands with each of his feet in a special transitional circle; on the borderline between evil and good, and on that between the false and the true will. The two imaginable perversions, according to Dante's theory, of love (the moral will), namely, the qualitative and the quantitative, cannot, according to the plan of Purgatory, be overcome earlier than at the end of the fifth circle. Here release as a fact is for the first time possible, and at this point Statius appears.

If he now, as one purified, escorts our pilgrims to the summit of the mountain, he does it—and therein he reveals his twofold nature—partly as guide, partly on his own account. At first he strides on ahead, then walks between Virgil and Dante, and finally lingers behind Dante. By this order the passing of leadership from Virgil through Statius to Beatrice is foreshadowed.

According to this, the figure of Statius should have a half-philosophic, half-symbolic significance, so that his intermediate rôle might be compared to a mathematical function.

But the Dantesque Statius has also an historical side. He is the poet of the *Thebaid* and of the *Achilleid*—the imitator of Virgil. Unfortunately Dante was not particularly well informed as to the life, the works, or the character of the historical Statius. He has therefore pieced together his scant and faint historical date with inventive details in accordance with the symbolic requirements of his poem. History informed him that Statius lived in the latter half of the first century after Christ and con-

[1] *Purgatorio*, XXV, 37–108, and XXI, 40–60.

tinued Virgil's school of pagan poetry. But Dante's poem required a Christian, and he therefore invented or constructed the legend of the secret conversion of Statius. Out of this arose a host of questions which likewise could only be solved fictitiously. How, why, through whom was Statius converted? What sins brought him to Purgatory?

What now becomes interesting as to Statius is not so much the man himself as his destiny, his relation to heathenism, Christianity, Purgatory, Virgil, and Dante. It was for his sake that the whole mountain quaked. In the first as in the second life, the most remarkable strokes of fate have befallen him. This man is an event, or, as the physicians would say, a typical case. The significance of the case lies in the fact that he, through his abnormality, makes the norm intelligible. We see the ordinary destiny, which Nature has in store for us, in an extraordinary light. By means of Statius's case, we see in a new light the mysterious laws of Purgatory. As a personality he tells us little, but he is a focus wherein the most diversified rays of the poem meet.

He explains the earthquake in order that the two may tell him whence they come and for what purpose; he informs them of his earthly life and his stay in Purgatory, while Dante reveals Virgil's name to him and Virgil describes to him the Limbo of the great heathen souls. A lively, tense, joyous, and in part even merry exchange of information among the three poets ensues. What speaks and lives therein is things, events, circumstances, facts, rather than persons. An earnest tone of mutual respect, admiration, joyful surprise and curiosity, pervades and spices the conversation—the proper tone for the realm of the gluttons, to which the three have in the meantime ascended.

(*The Gluttons*)

(*Purgatorio*, XXIII–XXIV)

Gluttony is a material and revolting vice. The penance of the gluttons is that in unsated desire they must waste away and like Tantalus have before their eyes, yet beyond their reach, fragrant fruits and clear water. The Greek myth of Tantalus displays a tragic irony. But the Christian poet, to whom eating and drinking seem less important, removed the tragic element from Tantalus's condition and softened its irony to humour. "Foolish and greedy children" is what these famished folk appear to him, as they go hurrying by, stretching forth their hands to a living tree, which offers food and drink to them, but withdraws it from them, giving them instead austere instruction.

The sinners submit good-naturedly to this game. Though emaciated and wasted away to skeletons, they strive to forget their hunger and to think of higher things. In that they make themselves known instead of hiding their hateful vice in defiance and shame, they rise above their instincts, renounce their past, and accept their sorry state. Hence their cordial, communicative, almost inquisitive nature. Here Dante finds a friend of his youth with whom he had wasted many a wild night in revelry—Forese Donati. As before between Virgil and Statius, here again we have a lively give and take of question and answer. Memories, hopes, and news are exchanged. They act as two good comrades, aged and sobered by error and misfortune, are wont to do when they meet again under wholly different conditions and in strange surroundings: they mingle joyful and painful, merry and remorseful, personal and general reminiscences.

Forese Donati, like Statius, is of importance rather because of his meeting Dante than in himself. He is more of an event than a personality, and the poet is concerned with the changed condition of his friend rather than with his character. He is of course no longer the old Donati; he has lost his levity and jesting manner. The spirit which broke forth of old in wit and ribaldry, out of a body unwieldy from gluttony and gorging, gazes at us out of sunken eye-sockets: clear and prophetic.

Thanks to their suffering, the gluttons have acquired that keen glance which we see in the big eyes of wasted and sickly mortals. Like Forese, Bonagiunta da Lucca (Bonagiunta Orbicciani) has the gift of prophecy. He recognizes in Dante the founder of a new and loftier poetry, by which his own verses are thrown into the shade. Gladly and unenviously he announces to his great rival a joyful event, the further details of which we unfortunately do not know. Bonagiunta also has become objective. "O brother, now I see the knot!" These painfully cheerful words of belated insight may be read as a typical expression on the brows of all these gluttons.

Yet despite their enlightenment and prophetic wisdom, they are not remarkably profound. In this world the confirmed glutton is usually a commonplace fellow, and never a fiery spirit. His thoughts, so far as they do not circle about the kitchen and the wine cellar, relate to objects in his immediate environment. Accordingly, even the purified and reformed gluttons of the *Purgatorio* have a relatively narrow field of vision. Forese speaks of his wife, his sister, his relatives, of party politics and of public morals in Florence. Bonagiunta thinks of his Lucca and of his verses. These lighter, personal questions are, to be sure, grasped and discussed by them with deep and sound understanding; but it is a bourgeois sort of wisdom, without much passion, that flows from the parched lips of these people.

Their disfigured countenances, their terrible emaciation, make a deeper impression than their words. How is it possible, Dante asks, that disembodied souls suffer from hunger and thirst and waste away?

This significant doubt is removed by Statius with a no less remarkable display of biology, physiology, and psychology. The excursus on the relation between body and soul, the content and style of which are already familiar to us, comes in exactly at the right place, in the interval between the gluttons and the lustful.

(*The Lustful*)

(*Purgatorio*, XXV–XXVII)

The victims of erotic sinfulness are especially the artistic, imaginative, amiable, romantic, and weak natures; by which we do not deny that lust has also its baser and more vulgar side. Alighieri, however, a true Italian and true artist, has not here, any more than in the *Inferno*, depicted the disgusting side of the matter. His lustful transgressors, even the homosexual ones, are invariably talented, agreeable, sensitive, almost appealing characters. The reader will recall Francesca and Brunetto Latini. In the *Purgatorio* we meet important lyric poets and pioneers of the Dantesque love-poetry, Guido Guinizelli and Arnaut Daniel, as examples of lust. At the mere sound of their names, soft, artistic stanzas rang in the ears of the mediæval reader. It is hardly needful to characterize these illustrious troubadours. The situation in which the pilgrim of eternity meets them is in and of itself sufficiently effective.

For just as their names are resonant and musical, so their

penance, in spite of pain and agony, is spectacular, colourful, sonorous. In a valley of flames they pass to and fro. They sing:

> Summae parens clementiae,
> Lumbos jecurque morbidum
> Flammis adure congruis,
> Accincti ut artus excubent
> Luxu remoto pessimo.

They call out to each other examples of chastity, and of punished lust. With hasty loving greetings, full of fine courtesy, they pass each other by. Like diligent ants that meet each other, like cranes when they part, they gather and hover away. Courtly, picturesque, melodious, and distinct, flows Guinizelli's utterance. Without an ignoble word it touches on the most delicate matters. Of the old sensuousness nothing is left save curiosity and a touching desire for love and intercession, perhaps also a dainty remnant of artistic vanity. As Dante approaches Arnaut Daniel and gives him the flattering assurance,

> How gladly I would wish to know his name
> And hold it kindly in my memory,

the troubadour, well pleased with himself, cannot refrain from uttering, together with his name, melodious words of Provençal:

> Tan m'abelis vostre cortes deman,
> Qu'ieu no me puesc, ni voill a vos cobrire.
> Ieu sui Arnaut, que plor e vau cantan.[1]

(*Ascent and Farewell*)

Still, however attractive the matter sounds and looks, it has its evil side; for Dante, if he would attain the height, must pass through the midst of the crackling forest of flame. Here, at the exit of Purgatory proper, the hardest test is before him. His sensuous nature must be purified by fire. He draws back and fears the worst for his own physical Adam. It is a charming scene in which the anxious pilgrim has to be reassured.

> Upon my claspéd hands I straightened me,
> Scanning the fire, and vividly recalling
> The human bodies I had once seen burned.

[1] "So pleases me your courteous demand,
I cannot and I will not hide me from you.
I am Arnaut, who weep and singing go."

Towards me turned themselves my good Conductors,
And unto me Virgilius said: "My son,
Here may indeed be torment, but not death.
Remember thee, remember! and if I
On Geryon have safely guided thee,
What shall I do now I am nearer God?
Believe for certain, shouldst thou stand a full
Millennium in the bosom of this flame,
It could not make thee bald a single hair.
And if perchance thou think that I deceive thee,
Draw near to it, and put it to the proof
With thine own hands upon thy garment's hem.
Now lay aside, now lay aside all fear,
Turn hitherward, and onward come securely;"
And I still motionless, and 'gainst my conscience!
Seeing me stand still motionless and stubborn,
Somewhat disturbed he said: "Now look thou, Son,
'Twixt Beatrice and thee there is this wall."
As at the name of Thisbe oped his lids
The dying Pyramus, and gazed upon her,
What time the mulberry became vermilion,
Even thus, my obduracy being softened,
I turned to my wise Guide, hearing the name
That in my memory evermore is welling,
Whereat he wagged his head, and said: "How now?
Shall we stay on this side?" then smiled as one
Does at a child who's vanquished by an apple.
Then into the fire in front of me he entered.

Just at the moment when Dante is about to dispense with his guide, he seems to feel more strongly than ever the need for help. Like a child he must be led between Virgil and Statius and be sustained as he crosses the blazing forest.

When, after the agony of fire is past, he lays himself down nigh to the summit for the last night's sleep, the mood of homesickness steals over him, a foreboding of parting and farewell, and that feeling of his own inadequacy, that mixture of despondency and confidence, of thankful tenderness and hopeful anxiety, with which the youth leaves his father's house to take his first step as a free man. He is overcome by these feelings, so that he cannot utter or analyze them. His inward state is confused with the external situation: and both express themselves in charming pastoral pictures.

Even as in ruminating passive grow
The goats, who have been swift and venturesome
Upon the mountain-tops ere they were fed,

Hushed in the shadow, while the sun is hot,
  Watched by the herdsman, who upon his staff
  Is leaning, and in leaning tendeth them;
And as the shepherd, lodging out of doors,
  Passes the night beside his quiet flock,
  Watching that no wild beast may scatter it,
Such at that hour were we, all three of us,
  I like the goat, and like the herdsmen they,
  Begirt on this side and on that by rocks.

Yet nowhere is there danger, nowhere a wolf to fear. On the contrary, upon this divine height, the stars appear brighter, larger, nearer; calmer and clearer than yonder on earth glimmers the night. But an inner anxiety, an awe of eternal happiness, at whose threshold the wanderer lies down for this last sleep, hovers about his resting-place.

A lovely dream reveals to the pilgrim his future happiness; his longing, which at eventide grew despondent, becomes impatient and strong-winged at early morn.

Such longing upon longing came upon me
  To be above, that at each step thereafter
  For flight I felt in me the pinions growing.

He rushes upward. On the summit Virgil appears before him, looks him in the eye,

And said: "The temporal fire and the eternal,
  Son, thou hast seen, and to a place art come
  Where of myself no farther I discern.
By intellect and art I here have brought thee;
  Take thine own pleasure for thy guide henceforth;
  Beyond the steep ways and the narrow art thou.
Behold the sun, that shines upon thy forehead;
  Behold the grass, the flowerets, and the shrubs
  Which of itself alone this land produces.
Until rejoicing come the beauteous eyes
  Which weeping caused me to come unto thee,
  Thou canst sit down, and thou canst walk among them.
Expect no more or word or sign from me;
  Free and upright and sound is thy free-will,
  And error were it not to do its bidding;
Thee o'er thyself I therefore crown and mitre!"

It is Dante's coming of age and Virgil's farewell. Virgil wishes no thanks, no tear, no backward look. He sees only the mighty goal. After he has cast a glance upon the Earthly Paradise, upon the Golden Age of which he had dreamed as a poet, he draws back in silence, rewarded by the thought that his greatest, dearest pupil now enjoys this bliss.

THE EARTHLY PARADISE

(*Purgatorio*, XXVIII–XXXIII)

With Virgil the most beautiful and most human figure has departed. Statius stands aside.

Here, on the height of human perfection, in the old and magically beautiful garden of deserted happiness—here was the place for the pilgrim, in a solemn hour, alone twixt Heaven and earth, to give thought to himself. Here he must have felt how heavily the painless, peaceful, sinless condition of Paradise weighs on the mortal's soul. In despair amid this peace, for which we all long, but for which not one is fit, he must have collapsed.

Bright-coloured birds with chirping song, fearless companionable beasts, great fragrant flowers, all Nature with her charming but innocent allurements, the magic of an uninterrupted life, would have striven in vain to console him. He would even long again and fervently pray for release from his lonely happiness, for absorption into the infinity of God. Then Beatrice, the heavenly maiden, would have descended to him gently, with affectionate chiding, with loving reproof, and would have carried him safely from the void of earthly pleasure into divine bliss.

In some such way would the Earthly Paradise have taken shape in the mind of a modern poet. Alighieri constructed it otherwise: not only because he was thoroughly mediæval, Catholic, and dogmatic, but above all because the plan of the poem, with its cleavage between spiritual and scenic events, would hardly have permitted such a Protestant inwardness, such absorption of the conflict into the isolated conscience of the individual. But it must not be overlooked that the brilliant pageants, tableaux, allegories, and fancies with which the poet adorned his picture of Paradise, are essentially nothing but the colourful glow and magic reflection of that wistful and reminiscent entanglement in earthly things which takes possession of the purified, but as yet unredeemed, pilgrim once again, in a final assault, at the very height of his happiness. As far as concerns their psychological and lyrical content, the cantos of the Earthly Paradise, with their brilliant and stirring symbolism, carry on the same melody that we have indicated as the inner voice of the poem, but with so rich, varied, and learned an instrumentation that they seem, to our modern ear, almost forced. But why, if he were going to render audible the inmost and faintest repinings and doubts of the human heart, should not so introspective a poet as Dante employ the most resonant artistic means which his age put at his disposal? Dante neither exaggerated nor falsified the inner experience of the pilgrim; he only projected it on the gigantic screen of the history of Christian redemption, raised it above his individual isolation, and so catholicized it.

This process begins with Matelda. The solemn calm of the forest is made beautiful by her feminine grace and cordiality; an ineffable charm attends her. For a painter like Botticelli one could imagine no better subject than this singing, garland-weaving creature, as she suddenly appears, in all her mysterious loveliness, before the pensive poet. The sweetest names that grow on Helicon we would fain lay at her feet: eternal Spring, bewitching innocence, unspoiled Nature, light-hearted grace, playful freedom, faultless emotion, unity of art and Nature, dance and blessedness incarnate—all this is Matelda. She has been rightly called the soul of the Earthly Paradise. With equal reason she might be called *Natura integra*, or the priestess of *lex naturalis sive divina.* The action of this perfect being is an effortless and balanced play of the powers of the will and the powers of life: active life in its perfection without struggle or aim, active life as delight and play, as the weaving of flower wreaths, as dancing, as the self-sufficing joy of divine Nature. As such things can only be dreamed, wished for, or imagined, but not realized, Matelda's charm is elusive and mystical, her character hedonistic, her whole appearance a *fata morgana.* She is alive only so long as our sensuousness fondly weaves pictures. In fact, before the wayfarer beheld her in the forest, he had seen her, in his restful slumber, as Leah weaving blossoms into garlands (*Purgatorio*, XXVII, 97 sqq.). Now she is called Matelda; the dream has taken on the name and features, we know not whether of a German nun, or of a Florentine friend of Beatrice, or of yet another person.[1] Only

[1] That behind Matelda lies hid the Countess Matilda of Tuscany, that "grim, ascetic virago" (Bassermann), is unthinkable.

Beatrice recognizes and utters her Italian name (*Purgatorio*, XIII, 119).

But the poet could not leave her a mere illusion or picturesque decoration. He must assign her a definite rôle in the moral and religious growth of man. And now Matelda becomes instructive. The child of *Natura integra*, who cannot properly know anything about good and evil, of the fall of man and its penalty, delivers a lecture on "the highest good" and "our fall." Through her contact with the sinner's need, she becomes helpful, speaks of Lethe, and sees to it that the souls are bathed therein. The flower-girl becomes the attendant of souls, somewhat as from a happy dream may spring the impulse to a good action. We can raise no objection to such metamorphoses, in the realm of the wanderings and transformations of souls.

Heaven opens, and the whole hierarchy of divine and natural, ecclesiastic and lay, cosmic and human, ideal and historic, revealed and rational Law, descends in a festal procession, to display itself before the marvelling wanderer. The several figures of this mystical procession can be identified with some probability, but not with certainty. The central group consists of the Church's triumphal chariot, drawn by the divine and human Griffin (Christ). The Church is the fundamental mediator between God-given natural law and man-made positive institutes. Seven lights, the seven gifts of the spirits, four-and-twenty elders, the twenty-four books of the Old Testament, four apocalyptic beasts, that is, the four evangelists, in short, the pillars of Church authority, march in the van; on the right of the chariot, three nymphs, on the left, four: that is, the seven virtues as active executors of the Church's commands; behind the chariot the authors of the Acts, the biblical Epistles and Revelation: that is, the followers of Christ.

But the Church as a legal body, as a corporation and ideal organization, or, allegorically speaking, the chariot, is a practical construction, which requires an idea or theoretical content. At the prayer of all the intercessors for salvation, this Church idea, the spirit of Catholic dogma, this revealed divine truth, now descends in the form of Beatrice to take its place on the chariot.

So it is not the despairing cry of a lonely wanderer, but the official invocation of a consistory of ecclesiastical authorities, that causes Beatrice to descend. Her arrival is imposing, solemn, but essentially theatrical. It is no immediate experience of the heart, but rather a pageant, which we first witness, and to which the pilgrim yields as a natural experience of his soul that is no less in him than above him, and into the current of which he is presently drawn. We have to do, so to speak, with an *auto sacramental*, which reaches beyond the stage, seizes the wanderer, and makes of him the involuntary sacrifice and hero of the action. Hence the dramatic quality is to be sought not in the splendour of the performance nor in its theological significance, but in the awesome threat, terror, and nightmare of the human conscience, where the glory of Heaven and the need of the sinner's heart are brought closely face to face.

Distant, almost hostile, like a lofty suzerain and commander, Beatrice, the glorified love of Dante's youth, appears to her abashed friend.

> E'en as an admiral, who on poop and prow
> Comes to behold the people that are working
> In other ships, and cheers them to well-doing.

Beatrice appears as the accuser and the judge of her beloved. The profoundest matters of conscience are dragged forth and mercilessly treated until the sinner in the confessional turns red for shame, weeps, and breaks down. The cruelly exaggerated ethical rigor of Alighieri, who in Hell assailed the sinners, here cuts into his own flesh.

Beatrice's words cut like lashes, and like a punished schoolboy he is pointed out and exposed to the eyes of the compassionate representatives of the ecclesiastical authorities. It is one of the boldest and most pathetic of self-accusations.

Remorse, humiliation, and shame overwhelm the proud man in the midst of the festive splendour of the Church and shake him as though in a fever.

Readers of the *Commedia* have felt, even before this, that the pageant was a glorification of the Catholic Church which could not imaginably be more magnificent or more sincere. Numberless later allegorical Christian pageants and triumphal marches in poetry and painting were inspired by Dante's *Paradiso terrestre*.

Whoever fancies that he senses in Alighieri a Protestant temperament must be referred expressly to this passage. A Protestant would not have let slip the opportunity to make the pilgrim, here at least, stand on his own feet. But Dante is never, and least of all here, where he is about to take his flight heavenward, bereft of the Church's aid. Here he learns that the Church's authority, which presents itself in such splendour and so impersonally, is at the decisive moment his most considerate and tenderest advocate. The allegorical representatives, the angels and the Virtues, intercede in this drama of conscience. It is their pity, and not Beatrice's reproaches, that move the proud man. It is the compassionate aid of the Church that brings tears to his eyes, and with them his salvation. Herein the profoundest and most beautiful idea of the Catholic Church is to be found, namely, that man, if he faces alone, without aid, the spirit of divine truth and the terrible voice of his conscience, must founder on the rock of his own pride. Even in the feminine form of Beatrice, the truth is of such austerity that man cannot endure it. As the voice of God, that is, our conscience, judges and condemns us with absolute logic, there is need of a church which takes us under its protection against ourselves.

After renouncing his past errors and drinking oblivion from Lethe, the pilgrim's sight is widened to a vision of world-history. Beside the allegory of the invisible Church there appears its earthly image, beside the *ideal*, the drama of its decadence. Before the wanderer departs from this earth, from which he has inwardly set himself free, he sees once more, but dimmed through the veil of symbolism, and in shadowy outlines, the utmost wretchedness of this earth, the degeneracy of Christ's Church.

An "unsubstantial semblance," a discoloured parody of the glorious revelation of the ideal, an ugly metamorphosis of beauty, mirror, upon these heights, the worldliness of the Church.

The chariot of the ideal Church has come in contact with the withered tree of world-rule; the *lex divina* has wedded with the *lex naturalis;* the *civitas Dei* has breathed a new life into the *civitas terrena;* the Christian conscience has regenerated the pagan conceptions of good and evil. The God-man, the Griffin, his work accomplished, has departed heavenward, leaving behind him revealed truth, Beatrice, and the active principle of goodness embodied in the seven nymphs. But the man, Dante, out of his profound satisfaction over the solution of his problem, has fallen asleep, under the protection of his complete happiness, beside Matelda. Suddenly he is awakened. Before his eyes begins the pitiful drama of the Church's history. Jupiter's eagle swoops down through the tree of world-empire and mutilates both chariot and branches in hostile rage. That is the persecutions of the Christians and the division of the empire into the Eastern and the Western branches. A lean, ugly fox approaches, to defile the chariot, but Beatrice drives the limping beast away. That is the heretical sects which are refuted by the Church Fathers. The eagle descends a second time, bestrews and soils the chariot with his plumage. That is the Donation of Constantine. Out of the earth rises a dragon and shatters the body of the chariot with his pointed tail. That is Satan, who tears humility and modesty out of the hearts of the princes of the Church. Now all the parts of the chariot are completely covered with eagle feathers. That is the peak of worldly power in ecclesiastical hands. Now the chariot is transformed into an apocalyptic monster. Instead of the seven virtues, it has seven bestial heads: the seven deadly sins. Instead of Beatrice a harlot sits in pride upon it, the spirit of lies, the false clerical authority. This harlot mates with a giant, i.e. with false worldly authority: a disgusting union of papal and imperial despotism. But the intimacy does not last long. The giant beats the woman and carries her off into the forest. That is the final condition of Church politics, the age of Dante, the Avignon exile of the popes, the friendship and enmity with Philip the Fair of France.

The poet has refrained from giving the historical interpretation of this spectacle.

In and of itself, what we see is neither magnificent enough to overwhelm us, nor petty enough to amuse us. The artistic impression produced by the transformation of the chariot is a mixed one. The scene as a whole is effective through its enigmatic ingenuity, and is a spectacle not for men but for higher beings. Only the Ideals themselves, the Virtues and Beatrice, comprehend it, grieving and angry at it, while the pilgrim is left in a state of timid curiosity and bewildered amazement.

He is criticized by Beatrice for this dull half-hearted interest. To put it crudely, she makes it a reproach that he is not also an Ideal. Instead of sating his curiosity, she heightens his craving for knowledge by her solemn and obscure prophecies, and turns his thoughts from the past to the future. He can only surmise and in humility record the words of her apocalyptic utterance; he can only accept God's decree, and hopefully look forward to an early betterment of earthly conditions.

From his own past the pilgrim is freed. He has forgotten it. But with the memory of his sins he has also lost the comprehension of his rescue. He is handed over, helpless, to a Beatrice grown superhuman. His good, helpless, confident, inadequate condition, which demands guidance from the Ideals even in the clear light of noon, reminds us of Hölderlin's blind minstrel:

> Where art thou, light of youth, that evermore
> Still at the morning hour dost waken me?
> My heart awakes: yet with her holy charm
> Night still doth hold and overmaster me.

Out of this twilight rises the fiery shape of the Future.

The pilgrim is led to the river Eunoë. A draught of this water restores to him the memory of all the good that he has ever wrought or experienced. Within him all grows clear. Suddenly the poem breaks off. So at death, in an instant, the earth falls away beneath us. The poet has felt this break so profoundly that the slightest outward pretext suffices to bring it about. It is the natural end of an outlived experience.

> But inasmuch as full are all the leaves
> Made ready for this second canticle,
> The curb of art no farther lets me go.

8. The "Paradiso"

ITS ALLEGED INCONSISTENCY

The enlightenment, purification, and conversion of the pilgrim, or, if you will, of the reader, considered as an educational process, may be looked on as completed when the summit of Purgatory is reached, so that the only theme left for treatment in the *Paradiso* is the joyful bliss felt in the sight of the Godhead. Enough material perhaps for rapturous, fragmentary utterances and lyrical outpourings, hymns, sequences, or lauds, but hardly sufficient for three-and-thirty descriptive cantos. For how can that be made visible which is in its very essence supersensuous, and accessible at most by the tones of feeling, certainly not by the figures of human speech?

Considering all this, literary criticism held long to the belief that it must see in Dante's *Paradiso* a poetic absurdity. The poet himself seems to agree with this view in all those passages which emphasize the inexpressible, incomparable, invisible, incomprehensible nature of heavenly revelations, visions, and experiences.[1]

Indeed, toward the close of the poem the artist's renunciation of any attempt to depict the Divinity becomes more and more the leading motif.

> Even as he is who seeth in a dream,
> And after dreaming the imprinted passion
> Remains, and to his mind the rest returns not,
> Even such am I, for almost utterly
> Ceases my vision, and distilleth yet
> Within my heart the sweetness born of it;
> Even thus the snow is in the sun unsealed,
> Even thus upon the wind in the light leaves
> Were the soothsayings of the Sibyl lost.[2]

But it is only as a pious wish, and not in reality, that the artist made his renunciation; and when finally he falls upon his knees humbly before his lofty task, he does so in order that the reader may once more recognize in him as the poet that universal human inadequacy and religious need of help which the pilgrim, even before his entrance into Hell, had felt so profoundly. All the doubts uttered by Alighieri as to the inadequacy of his imagination, and of human language in general, mean essentially only that we have to do here with a supernatural, transcendent subject, and that his work is essentially a religious poem. That such a poem is in itself impossible or absurd was by no means his opinion, and cannot be ours.

Fairly viewed, the *Paradiso* is in fact not diverse in nature from the *Inferno* and *Purgatorio*, which it continues and completes. Why should the infernal Hereafter be less unsubstantial and paradoxical, less incomprehensible and inexpressible, than the heavenly one? All the three realms are in their essence equally marvellous, mythical, remote from our experience, unapproachable by the senses, accessible only through spiritual contempla-

[1] Cf. *Paradiso*, I, 4–9; I, 70 sqq.; X, 46 sqq.; X, 74 sqq.; XIII, 22 sqq.; XIV, 79 sqq.; XIV, 103; XVIII, 8–12; XXIII, 23 sqq.; XXIII, 61 sqq.; XXIV, 23–27; XXX, 22 sqq.; XXX, 31 sqq.; XXXIII, 55 sqq.; XXXIII, 121 sqq.

[2] *Paradiso*, XXXIII, 58–66.

tion. Though the poet may delude us into accepting certain differences, the critic will, with approximate certainty, distinguish, even in the *Paradiso*, the scene from the action, the outer from the inner occurrences, the form from the content that permeates and vivifies all; and he will have to raise, and endeavour to answer, the old question as to the completeness and poetic unity of the poem as a whole.

THE SCENE

The stage-setting within which the transcendency of the spirit, or the passing over of man to God, occurs, was, for the mediæval thinker, mathematically defined and exact; it could be reckoned, measured, and clearly grasped. It was the nine concentric heavenly spheres which contained all space, and were bounded by eternal spacelessness. These spheres were thought of as spatial, but not as corporeal, masses. They were inhabited by immaterial Intelligences and were impelled by a force physically unlimited, by a sort of spiritual dynamics, or sympathy and telepathy. All movement in Heaven is spiritual magnetism, supersensuous love, will that seeks after God. Everything corporeal in Heaven is to be thought of in similar terms: as pure form, as a bodiless figure, luminous, transparent, shadowless, regular, complete, rounded, intangible appearances. There remains of the colour of the body only light, of its extent only the point, the line, or the curve, of its thickness only the outline, of its weight only motion, of its contacts, sounds, and vibrations only the musical harmony; in short, of the whole, only a law-bound abstract configuration, objective to the eyes and ears, and in the last analysis, merely the idea. The senses of touch, taste, smell, are all but extinct. Only the noblest senses, which approach nearest to thought, that is, hearing and sight, are active. But even these do not function in the proper sense of the word. The angels and the blessed in Paradise need neither gaze at nor listen to each other. They think, understand, and love each other directly; that is, not through the senses, but through God. Only for the mortal wanderer's sake do they shape words, songs, and dances. Here everything that is still perceived as visible and natural is in reality reflection, emblem, formula, and symbol of an ineffable essence. This appears and disappears, flashes and vanishes, has and has not a local habitation, takes on shape and disintegrates, speaks audibly and turns dumb, embodies and disembodies itself, comes and goes. The whole scenery of Paradise whirls, sways, and changes its tints on the verge between appearance and vanishing. What distinguishes it from the stone funnel and the quaking mountain is motion. But heavenly events proceed so harmoniously and smoothly that the spectacle of things there reveals eternal permanence, amid the dance of change.

THE ACTION

The organization of the *Inferno* and *Purgatorio* had to be devised by the inventive art of the poet and shaped into artistic reality. But the heavenly spheres of the *Paradiso* were presented to him by mediæval astronomy as a scientifically determined reality. Here his inventive art had the converse problem, namely, the dissolution of the all too fixed empirical reality into symbolic semblance.

The symbolism of the Heavens and of their several planets he did not have to create. They were known and familiar to mediæval man. But the representation of the journey from earth to Heaven, and from one Heaven to another, demanded original treatment. Any wandering, even if it be a hovering flight, has its temporal and spatial conditions. Some hindrances and oppositions, even if it be merely distances, have to be overcome. The poet succeeded, with masterly art, in portraying the marvel of a timeless, spaceless, unhindered, heavenly journey. Uplifted and carried along by the divine light which is mirrored in Beatrice's eyes, he rises upward. He moves, without consciousness of motion. He does not know whether it is his spirit only, or whether the body goes with it. He feels no exertion, has no sense of time and space. He recognizes the Heavens and keeps his sense of direction in them only from their conceptual succession. He rushes from star to star and seems to be at rest. The local distribution of the heaven-dwellers among the different spheres exists only for him, for his mortal eye: in reality there is, he is told, but one Paradise everywhere and for all. In fact, after he has traversed Heaven after Heaven, and become acquainted with all sorts of blessed souls, all Paradise presents itself to him, in the spaceless Heaven of the Empyrean, in a new form, uniting all the blessed spirits as in an immense rose. The first arrangement is denied and asserted, removed and explained, by the second.

We no longer know whether the pilgrim has gone to Heaven or whether Heaven has come to him. Is it Dante who is the acting subject, or rather the heavenly powers? There are situations in the poem where he appears as a chance spectator of heavenly rejoicings, and others where it becomes clear that it is only for him, little man though he is, that the eternal spirits in bliss, and yes, even the Divinity, are revealed as light, motion, sound, in luminous figures and triumphal processions. It is not clear whether man moves about the universe or the universe about him; whether we have before us personal action, that is, a journey, or something that has occurred, that is, an experience. If an action requires subject and object, active and passive, an inner and an outer side, then the *Paradiso* has no action, for here the one is always the other as well. As the stage-setting sways back and forth between what is and what seems, so does the action between the ego and the universe.

Between the ego and the universe there can be room only for an action which in reality is no action, that is, thinking. I think in all things, or all things think in me—the result is quite the same. In this sense the *Paradiso* may be defined as the poem of pure thought, or of pure contemplation.

In the *Inferno* and the *Purgatorio*, thought was usually in the service of action, the true in the service of the good. In the *Paradiso* the relation is reversed, so that will, sentiment, and love pass into the observant quest after knowledge, strengthening and deepening it.

STYLE AND MOOD

The fundamentally contemplative character determines the colouring of the poem. Precisely because so much light and starry splendour is to shine in Paradise, a dull grey or pallid background must be created, against which the gold and silver can stand out. For pure blessedness does not live in varied tints, but finds its natural element where there is no joy in the living and blooming products of earth.

The demand which, in the *Paradiso*, is made on the reader with repeated and increasing urgency, namely, to imagine the light of the Heavens as always brighter, a thousandfold stronger than sunlight; the light in Beatrice's eyes as ever more radiant, more divine; and from sphere to sphere, the harmony of the songs ever more perfect—this demand leaves our imagination no power of contemplation, gives it no wings, leaves it empty and crippled, and to that extent, seems to miss its aim. But it has—and this is the essential—the negative result that all the phenomena of earthly life become petty and worthless in comparison with those of Paradise. Thus arises that dull grey of pallid thought to which we have referred and which the poet will and must create in us, so that the holy mood of transcendence and apotheosis may work within us.

The mere fading and vanishing of sensuous observation is, to be sure, no ascent to eternal bliss, but merely the indispensable prerequisite thereto. The positive element must be added, which can be nothing other than the heightening and satisfying of the supersensuous desire, effort, and deliverance of the knowing and loving faculties of our nature and of our soul. Hence, in the *Paradiso*, the progressive extenuation of sensuousness is accompanied by an increasing demand for speculative comprehension and loving acceptance of things eternal. Metaphysical, theological, mystical discourses, dramas, visions, and revelations, are here so appropriate and essential to the entire mood and tone and to the vividness of the poem, that the leading lyrical motifs arise from them, so that it would be very ill advised indeed to consider them as irrelevant or even wearisome digressions, or as unbecoming flourishes. Like a theme which has its own dialectic movement, Christian belief is so treated throughout the entire poem that what gives power and guidance is not the order of scholastic and dogmatic concepts, but the needs of the pilgrim's soul. The heavenly journey is, in its inner action, a contemplation of faith. Even the spiritual examination which Dante passes at the close of his heavenly voyage is to be regarded as a blissful survey of truth attained, as the assured confidence of the religious man, not as a painful school test.

If, accordingly, these theoretical, speculative, contemplative, and visionary processes make up the backbone of the poem, one might characterize the threatening, scornful, warning utterances and retrospective allusions to political, ecclesiastical, and moral evils on earth, especially in Italy, as interruptions. This in a general way is true. Strictly speaking, however, the conditions are not such that the entrance of the mortal Florentine into the abodes of Heaven disturbs the untroubled calm of the blessed.

The mere presence of the premature guest reminds the glorified spirits of human misery and sin: so that the damnatory and admonitory, blessing and cursing passages of the poem are, so to speak, the dust which the vehicle of the traveller cannot but stir up wherever it traverses the plain of eternal peace. Satire and innuendo are no more out of place in Paradise than in Hell or Purgatory; rather do they indicate, like a ship's wake, the course which the poet steers.

LOWER PARADISE

(*Paradiso*, I–IV. *The Moon*)

The poem begins with nine or ten abrupt strokes. It sounds like the first strokes of the wings of a mighty creature lifting itself up from earth; brief and vigorous, then growing longer and lighter, finally hovering and calm. By the forty-sixth verse the narrative is running freely. The thought goes hand in hand with the rhythmic progress. Almost every one of the first ten or fifteen terzets brings a change of tone and a new motif.

Throughout the whole God-filled universe, then upward to the source of light and down to his own human spirit, roves the poet's glance. The magnitude of his experience in Paradise and the inadequacy of his art stand in clear and lofty contrast to each other.

> Because in drawing near to its desire
> Our intellect ingulfs itself so far,
> That after it the memory cannot go.

So the artist, if he wishes to portray even the shadow of his visions, must beseech divine aid. The artist's prayer is natural religion and Christianity as well, it is mythic and mystical, humanistic and evangelical. It is impelled by the earthly thought of fame and the hope of the rewarding laurel, and by the expectation of heavenly bliss; it has two peaks, like the Dantesque Parnassus. The spirit of Apollo is, then, a holy power, the poet-philosopher is a poet-theologian, and like a biblical psalm resounds the epic proëmium: "The glory of Him who moveth everything."

A bright morning has dawned. Beatrice gazes at the sun. Dante forces hmself to do the same. There is a splendour as of white-hot iron on its disk, which here on the summit of the mountain appears larger and nearer than on earth. Dante's eye, dazzled, turns aside. Now Beatrice gazes heavenward. Dante hangs on her glance. Something indescribable is going on within him. The light grows ever greater. Harmonious tones sound all about him. Without being aware of it, he rises from the earth and knows not whether his impressions are sensuous or spiritual. Beatrice has to explain to him what has befallen him. They are in the first sphere, floating through the mass of the moon.

Transfiguration and flight, a disembodied materiality, a physical problem with a theological solution, is the theme of the first Heaven.

In fact, the first thought of a living man, coming from earth to Heaven, would be an inquiry into physical laws. How does it happen that I am flying without exertion and that I pass through visible bodies without displacing their mass? The reason is—so runs the answer—that here the laws of Nature coincide with those of the spirit. Gravity and magnetism are divine will. The centre of attraction is no longer the earth, but God; so that now the same natural law that brings a stone to earth makes the spirit rise. Mass and density are spiritual qualities or graded differentiations of intelligible force; so that the harder body represents a lower stage, the soft and transparent body a higher stage, of spiritual nature.

This principle is explained by Beatrice and illustrated by the spots on the moon.

The canto on the moon's spots (*Paradiso*, II) is generally condemned as scholastic, unpoetic, and wooden. It is, however, for us especially instructive, because Dante was himself conscious that here was the parting of the ways between prose and poetry. He had already treated this question in the *Convivio* (II, 14). The spots or shadows on the moon, he then thought, came from thin or hollow zones in the mass of the moon, places which reflect the sun's rays from deeper cavities and therefore more weakly than the rest of the smooth and thicker surface of the moon. This purely physical explanation is here retracted. If the refutation was to be effective, it also must proceed by physical examples and be carried out in an essentially prosaic spirit—which the poet has done, at length, and without shrinking from experimental illustration (verses 67–105). No marvel that art-criticism thought it saw here only rhymed prose, and utter absence of poetry. To be sure, if one considers the incriminated verses in and by themselves, that is quite true. But the poet's purpose is by no means fully attained with the refutation of the *Convivio* and the abandonment of the physical theory; it is, indeed, only introduced. His aim, even if we wish to limit it to mere instruction, extends much further. Not only is it an error, which, as Beatrice says, must melt away as though in the rays of the sun; but a more comprehensive and vital truth is to supplant it,

> " such a living light
> That it shall tremble in its aspect to thee."

The special question of the moon's spots is brought into connection with the whole theory of the heavenly spheres, their movements and action, and opens an immense vista on the cosmos and its laws. The physical refutation widens out into astronomical and theological speculations. These are, to be sure, according to Dante's conception, still science, indeed the purest science; according to our present-day ideas they are mythical. The critic of a work of art, however, must not concern himself with this question, but with the conviction on which these assertions, be they science or stellar myths, are upborne, and by which they are coloured. If now one reads again the impressive verses (112-148) and hears how Dante calls the Empyrean "the Heaven of peace divine," and the Heaven of the fixed stars "the Heaven that has so many sights," or "the Heaven that so many stars make fair," and how he characterizes the spheres in general as "organs of the world" and "holy orbs," and every star as "a body precious and endowed with life," and the power that moves the universe as "joyous Nature," and how the connection of that power with the heavenly bodies is thought of as endowing them with a soul and is compared with the joy that shines from the pupil of a human eye—then there can no longer be a doubt that here science, or, if you will, myth, is inspired by the pious feelings of a fervent spirit. This feeling is the lyric current that endows the stubborn material with poetic movement.

But all this might be passing excitement and oratorical decoration of the didactic material, and would be indeed nothing more, if the question of the moon's spots stood alone and had a separate interest in itself. But not only is it interwoven in the mythical plan of the universe, and, as we have seen, made theoretically inseparable from it; but it has also a practical connection with the action, that is, primarily, with the heavenly journey. The problem of the moon's spots is brought up again in the Heaven of fixed stars. As the traveller looks down from the height of the eighth sphere and back at the seven planets, he sees that the spots have vanished from the moon.

> I saw the daughter of Latona shining
> Without that shadow, which to me was cause
> That once I had believed her rare and dense.[1]

He accepts this remarkable fact as something quite natural. The commentators usually explain it by the assumption that the spots are only on the side of the moon turned toward the earth. But they are taking something quite doubtful for granted, namely, that Dante knew that the moon turns toward us always one and the same side. The explanation must be sought rather in the voyager's eye than in the movements and position of the moon. "I saw," not "it was," stands in the text, and immediately thereafter, it is said that he was now able to face the light of the sun which he had before found unendurable. Throughout all Paradise the vision of the voyager grows stronger through dazzling and blinding experiences. The moon's spots, regarded as a condition caused by the influence of the superior spheres, and especially of the Heaven of fixed stars, are quite unsubstantial, a mere accident which must vanish as the eye, turned heavenward, grows clear. From the point of view of the upper regions the moon is regarded as just as spotless, pure, and eternal as the souls of Piccarda and Costanza, who denote the moon on the moral side. The theoretical problem of the order of the stars is intimately connected with the ethical and mystical progress of glorification and apotheosis.

From this new side, it is given a fresh example. In the moon he meets souls who had been prevented by external compulsion, in fact by man's violence, from fulfilling their Christian vows. Piccarda speaks for them; she is Forese Donati's sister. She had entered the Minorite convent of Santa Clara, but was forced into marriage, presumably for political reasons, by Corso Donati. For the poet this Piccarda whom he formerly knew and who now

[1] *Paradiso*, XXII, 139 sqq.

appears to him here as a silvery light, with human countenance, unrecognizably recognizable, is a delicate, glorified being. Everything incidental is effaced. What is said of Piccarda applies to the others who have suffered a similar fate, for example, the Empress Costanza of Hohenstaufen, mother of Frederick II.[1] "What of myself I say applies to her."

How this case is treated by Beatrice, with the aid of Thomistic casuistry, we have already heard. A distinction is made between an absolute and a relative will—an apparent distinction which has its visible counterpart in spatial relations. Only apparently, only as an external sign, are the souls of Piccarda and her companions connected with the moon. Actually they dwell in no sphere of the movable Heaven, but in God. So the problem has not only a physical, moral, and theological side, but also a sort of topographical one: the relation of earth to Heaven, or of Nature to the spirit, is pursued in all directions.

It is the persistence of that relation which gives unity to the first four cantos; lyric tones and images envelop and enfold the sturdy religious texture of these elements. But one must not be diverted by this masterly poetic ornamentation. Behind all the decoration there stands a single experience of faith.

Regarded poetically, the chief effect of this consists in the unveiling of an extended, magnificent perspective, which stretches from the finite into the infinite, and arouses in us feelings now of dizziness, now of eager longing. We believe that we behold the universe, we feel lost and exhausted, when we hear such mysterious, magnificent verses as:

> The con-created and perpetual thirst
> For the realm deiform did bear us on,
> As swift almost as ye the heavens behold.

Or:

> Within the heaven of the divine repose
> Revolves a body, in whose virtue lies
> The being of whatever it contains.

Or:

> Therefore springs up, in fashion of a shoot,
> Doubt at the foot of truth; and this is nature,
> Which to the top from height to height impels us.

[1] As a matter of fact, Costanza, so far as we know, had never become a nun. The poet seems here to be following a Guelf legend.

(*Paradiso*, V–VII. *Mercury*)

While those souls abide in the first Heaven whose pious will was hindered by compulsion from without, the second is the dwelling place of those who have too much rather than too little to show in the development of their practical activity. It is the Heaven of the planet Mercury, which takes its name from the god of trade, of contracts, and of legal proceedings.

The great organizers of law, of social life, who, wholly contented with their earthly task, wrought good on this earth, and who were more intent on honour among men than on pious devotion, have here their home. Their prominent representative is the creator of the *corpus juris civilis*, the Emperor Justinian.

Before Beatrice uplifts her friend to this second class of spirits, she gives, as is fitting, a special juridical turn to the religious theme which she had already treated from the point of view of moral philosophy, and instructs him on the validity of vows. Just as in the moral will there is an absolute and a relative side, so in the vow there is a distinction to be made between the unchangeable form and the alterable content. The form is absolute: namely, that something is to be done; but that "something" is subject to change. But only the Church, as the sole intercessor between God and man, can determine the limits within which one action of a pious man may be substituted for another. An urgent warning against foolish and extravagant vows ends the discourse. This serves as an introduction to the extended political and legal development of this topic in the Heaven of Mercury.

The logical connection of the speculations in the first Heaven with those of the second is not outwardly visible, but inwardly it is so close and firm that the epic link seems, by comparison, a poetic intermezzo. It is the religious thought with its inner necessity that summons the characters and brings them to the fore.

The smile of Beatrice, the brightening of the star, the heavenly joy of the traveller at his arrival in the second sphere, are loving marvels which, masterfully varied at their recurrence in each sphere, become familiar and awaken a feeling of intimacy even on the remotest heights.

Out of a briefly outlined history of the empire, symbolically and mystically coloured, Justinian evolves the universal, secular, and religious tendency of that empire and of its legal nature. The thought as well as the style of this splendid and stirring utterance, which effectively closes with political satire, is already known to us.

> "In order that thou see with how great reason
> Men move against the standard sacrosanct,
> Both who appropriate and who oppose it.
> Behold how great a power has made it worthy
> Of reverence."

The demonstration becomes, on Justinian's lips, a mystical eulogy and a lofty sermon. The poet has made out of the treatise a brilliant masterpiece of oratory, for here he is himself most passionately concerned.

After this bright flame, a subdued image appears. Beside the lofty imperial figure of Justinian, he sets as a modest human contrast the good, loyal Romeo. This man, whose name was Romieu de Villeneuve, was chamberlain and seneschal of Count Raimund Berengar IV of Provence (ob. 1245). A legend grew around his name, Romieu, meaning "pilgrim." It is said that while on a pilgrimage he visited and remained with Raimund. By unselfish services he increased the wealth of the count, and succeeded in securing four kings as husbands for the four daughters of the house. When he was maligned to his master by envious courtiers, he left the prince whose splendour he had created, of his own accord and without ill-will.

> "Then he departed poor and stricken in years,
> And if the world could know the heart he had,
> In begging bit by bit his livelihood,
> Though much it laud him, it would laud him more."

It was a happy thought to grant a place beside the great legal-minded benefactors of mankind to the quiet and faithful servant, and to let the pathos of worldly justice die away in an elegiac note. For "ingratitude is the world's reward."

At once, however, faith and its requirements are again emphasized. The imperial principle of worldly justice must be followed by the treatment of divine Grace and salvation, especially from its lawful side; that is, the influence of divine Grace in the world's history, Christ's assumption of humanity and his death for our redemption, must be derived from the disturbed relation between God and man caused by Adam's fall, and must be treated as a lawful atonement, which had become imperative and could be made by Love alone.

The subtle ecclesiastical spirit, the Pauline mingling of legalism and love, and the correspondingly scholastic style of these discussions, are already known to us. True Roman Catholic theology now speaks from Beatrice's lips. Its logical proofs develop the idea of love from that of law, and thus present the speculative prologue to the third Heaven.

(*Paradiso*, VIII–IX. *Venus*)

This belongs to the loving spirits and is characterized by the planet Venus. It completes Lower Paradise, whose inhabitants are still to some extent human. Middle Paradise, which includes the spheres of the other planets, that is, the fourth, fifth, sixth, and seventh Heavens, belongs to a higher class of spirits. While the souls of Lower Paradise are chiefly regarded as examples or opportunities for instructive discourses on the fundamental religious problem of nature and spirit, the souls of Upper Paradise have a significance of their own. They are exemplars and authorities, while the souls in Lower Paradise were, for the most part, so situated that Dante viewed them as illustrations, not as teachers. The rôle of instructor was undertaken usually by Beatrice, and only exceptionally by the souls. In Middle Paradise this arrangement ends. Beatrice has little more to say, for now the spirits themselves instruct the wanderer.

In Lower Paradise, pure faith is in the foreground; in Middle Paradise, the application of it. The principles developed at the beginning are employed by the authorities of Middle Paradise in criticism of existing earthly conditions. In fact, the essentially metaphysical speculation gives way to an essentially negative group of ideas applied empirically and polemically.

Similarly in the *Purgatorio* we were able to distinguish first a positive, and later a negative, discipline. The parallelism is evident, only that in Paradise, as in a completely unified realm, permeated uniformly with divine love, the borderlines are drawn less sharply, and the transitions are correspondingly more gradual and longer.

Such a transition is especially noticeable in the third Heaven.

The religious theme, as will be remembered, has now reached the point where the realization of love and of grace arises out of the idea of justice. We have, then, to put it schematically, worked out the following equalities in the fundamental subject of Nature and spirit:

1. Natural heavenly power = God's will
2. God's will = Justice
3. Divine justice = Grace or love

There remains, to close the circle of concept, only one final equality, namely:

4. Divine love = Natural power.

The third Heaven brings this conclusion. It does not, however, bring it in the purely abstract form of the previous cantos, but as a consequence of a criticism of actual conditions. Nor is it the symbolic Beatrice, but a historical personality, Charles Martel, who leads us, apparently by chance, to this final conclusion. Charles explains to the pilgrim the natural influence of the stars on human destiny as essentially beneficent, providential, helpful, good in and of itself, and willed by God.

But these ideas of natural philosophy are developed by Charles independently of the previous dialectic chain of ideas. To be sure, at the beginning of the eighth canto, before he introduced Charles Martel, the poet had indicated briefly the natural religion of the ethical influence of the heavenly bodies on man; but Charles Martel is significant for other reasons than a discourse on the stars. He has known Dante personally and, above all, he has a political past and possesses experience by the aid of which he, like many other figures of the later cantos, is fitted and competent to rebuke and to prophesy. Although his announcements are cut short by the poet, he is the first prophetic nature in the *Paradiso*. Prophecy is essentially nothing other than an emotional form of reproof, of praise, of correction; in short, of pious desire.

As a result of this speculative style, a personal turning toward oratory and lyricism takes place. The scene is enlivened; the characters grow more numerous, until they finally unite in great choirs. Their utterance becomes more insistent, their attitude authoritative and representative.

With fascinating directness, this exaltation is accomplished at the entrance of the traveller into the Heaven of love.

And as within a flame a spark is seen,
  And as within a voice a voice discerned,
  When one is steadfast, and one comes and goes,
Within that light beheld I other lamps
  Move in a circle; speeding more and less,
  Methinks, in measure of their inward vision.
From a cold cloud descended never winds,
  Or visible or not, so rapidly
  They would not laggard and impeded seem
To any one who had those lights divine
  Seen come towards us, leaving the gyration
  Begun at first in the high Seraphim.
And behind those that most in front appeared
  Sounded "Osanna!" so that never since
  To hear again was I without desire.
Then unto us more nearly one approached,
  And it alone began: "We all are ready
  Unto thy pleasure, that thou joy in us.
We turn around with the celestial Princes,
  One gyre and one gyration and one thirst,
  To whom thou in the world of old didst say,
'Ye who, intelligent, the third heaven are moving';
  And are so full of love, to pleasure thee
  A little quiet will not be less sweet."

All Heaven comes to meet the mortal. He is greeted with a song of his own composition. The speaker is a personal acquaintance, Charles Martel, the oldest son of Charles II of Naples and Anjou, who, as son-in-law of the Emperor Rudolph I and as grandson of Stephan V of Hungary, in the year 1292 was crowned King of Hungary, and could have become also King of Naples and Provence if he had not died, a youth of twenty-four years, in 1295. In the spring of 1294 he spent three joyous and happy weeks in Florence. It is to be assumed that the lovable young prince conversed in those days with the poet of the *Vita Nuova* on devotion to women, on the love-song and Provençal art, perhaps on politics and law. The political hopes which Alighieri may well have built on him were shattered and the Angevin power passed into the hands of his younger brother Robert. Our poet's sympathies were on the side of the elder line, which was excluded from the throne by Robert's accession, while the latter is heartily hated by Dante as the perverse and greedy opponent of the emperor.

Based on this high personal and political regard, Dante puts to Charles Martel the question, how it is possible for a degenerate offshoot to spring from a noble line.

The answer is objectively and smoothly connected with the principles already developed, as their spontaneous continuation and completion.

Beatrice's doctrine of religious redemption and the resurrection of the body had culminated, at the end of the seventh canto, in the statement that the human spirit is a direct and therefore indestructible creation of God, while the human body is an indirect production, through the medium of the heavenly spheres, and therefore changeable and destructible. Here Charles Martel takes up the thread of discourse and carries it on somewhat as follows:

I. The influence of the heavenly spheres extends not only to the bodily life of individual creatures, but also conditions their social existence; that is to say, their political organizations.

II. Organized social life is only possible because men have by nature diverse capacities, and therefore are dependent on each other.

III. Our earthly nature, in and of itself, in its regularity would not be able to generate individual differences; so far as nature goes, the son must be like the father.

IV. So there emanates from the heavenly spheres not only an earthly and natural impulse to generation and reproduction, but also a celestial and natural or providential impulse toward differentiation and individualization.

Hence the conclusion, which we cannot but expect, is reached; namely:

4. Divine love (Providence) = Natural power (in the heavenly, not in the earthly, sense).

If one pays close attention to the speculative side of the poetry, the connection will be found to be somewhat as we have reconstructed it; but if attention be paid to the forms instead of to the thought, we have a scene that has grown out of the poet's memories, disappointments, hopes, inclinations, and disinclinations.

The master who has intertwined the fervent and worldly motif with the heavenly one in such artistic fashion cannot be sufficiently admired.

Indeed, for the modern eye it is almost impossible to trace such combinations of what is temporal, accidental, and personal with what is eternal. How great is the need of historical investigation for the proper understanding of the position, the attitude, the phrasing, and the style of the troubadour Folquet de Marseille, has already been stated. Many interpreters have struggled vainly to discover the reason which may have impelled the poet to translate to Paradise such a disreputable and shameless woman as Cunizza, the sister of the tyrant Ezzelino III da Romano. All these spirits with their veiled, prophetic words of reproof have something about them that is mysterious and inexplicable. The shadow of the earth, which, according to mediæval astronomy, extended precisely to the heavenly sphere of Venus, does not indeed darken them, since they are glorified, but certainly makes them somewhat obscure and unintelligible. They reflect the divine idea in their detailed, ambiguous, sibylline utterances. But they see with the utmost clearness and assail the misdeeds and evil conditions of our earth. How ambiguously Cunizza, for instance, speaks of herself!

> "Cunizza was I called, and here I shine
> Because the splendour of this star o'ercame me.
> But gladly to myself the cause I pardon
> Of my allotment, and it does not grieve me;
> Which would perhaps seem strong unto your vulgar."

But how striking and unmistakable is Folquet's attack on the greedy short-sightedness of the popes!

But, as has been said, the poem required such transitions from speculation to polemic and from a pallid to a colourful style.

MID-PARADISE

(*Paradiso*, X–XIII. *The Sun*)

In the cantos which deal with the fourth Heaven, the poet makes perhaps his greatest and most ingenious effort to avoid the worldly style of narrative. And yet one might have expected to find him here yielding to the natural current of his tale. The speculative theme had come to a pause in the third Heaven. The dwellers therein had attained more and more their own personal significance.

Now, in the Heaven of the Sun, which belongs to the great religious thinkers, to the philosophical and theological authorities, the doctrine of faith needed no further development, for it could now be viewed directly, described, and glorified in its exemplars. Was not the spiritual development of St. Francis of Assisi, of St. Dominic, of Thomas Aquinas, epic material of the most perfect sort?

It is true that a heavenly splendour and a divine loftiness passed over from the purity and elevation of the subject into these cantos. But it is, as the poet well knew, and with modest sincerity confessed, the excellence of the content, not of the poetic form, that insured this success.

There is something touching in the pious simplicity of the mighty artist who would gladly conceal himself behind the yet mightier subject. "Observe for yourselves," says he to his readers; "admire and absorb yourselves in the divine ordering of the sun's path as it with beneficent change brings to us spring, summer, autumn, and winter." How Dante rose to the sun, and how, within that light, the yet brighter light of the spirits shone, he is unable to tell us.

> I, though I call on genius, art, and practice,
> Cannot so tell that it can be imagined;
> Believe one can, and let him long to see it.

He, whom this had befallen, thanks his God so earnestly that he forgets Beatrice, his guide, who had admonished him to be thankful. As the epic poet vanished behind his subject, so did Beatrice, for the moment, vanish behind the Creator.

But finally the subject forces the artist to his task. The tale begins. Only it is no longer a tale, but a comparison; no longer a description, but a symbol. By his apparent retreat the artist has attained what he desired. He has awakened in the reader a consciousness of the inadequacy of all words and figures of speech, has separated the form from its material, and now can wind it again in statelier folds about that material, and can substitute for a close-fitting and transparent style an imaginative and laudatory ornamentation. The heavenly sun-illumined movements of the dignified masters of theology, philosophers, scholars, and saints may now be set forth as a dance of gracious maidens, or even as the striking of a clock. There is left to the reader only the charming picture; for the reality, veiled in its majesty and untouched, remains beyond the sight in the poet's faith and feeling, and in its own holy worth.

As now St. Thomas greets the traveller and names for him the lofty spirits about him, his words fall from an unattainable spiritual height slowly and weightily. They form, for the human ear, strangely distorted hieroglyphic figures. Painstaking, amazed, surmising, as one solving riddles, with the aid of the noble and familiar names which he hears—Albertus Magnus, Gratian, Peter Lombard—with the aid of his scholastic training and reading, with the help of a whole theological library, the mortal must make rhyme and reason of the saint's mystical words. And with the best of wills, even a listener like Dante would not be safe from misunderstanding, were it not that the saint from time to time grants him a plain word or two of guidance. This saint does not wish to be understood, but to be attentively studied. The obscurity in his speech is only in the expression, not in the sense.

The meaning is clear. Divine wisdom is no longer to come before the pilgrim in general concepts, but in its greatest human examples; that is, historically. Now, since the entire history of Christian thought cannot possibly be unrolled, a selection is necessary. At first only the most important epochs are mentioned: Francis of Assisi with his school, and St. Dominic with his. Each draws light and worth from the other, since the Dominican Thomas relates the life-story, or, if we will, the divine mission, of St. Francis, while the Franciscan Bonaventura tells the tale of St. Dominic.

Here in Paradise a man's life-work is identical with his divine mission. Like natural law and spiritual law, so human merit and heavenly mission are now shown to be one and the same. Hence the life of the saints is represented not under its human, but under its divine, conditions; and instead of a historically coloured account, we have a prophetic narration. If we make the test and set the life-story of the two saints (*Paradiso*—XI, 28–121, and XII, 37–105) from the past over into the future, we shall see how through the mere change of grammatical tense-forms the twofold style, which is contrary to our modern taste, transforms itself into a faultless prophecy. We shall understand how and why the poet made the effort to substitute the prophetic for the epic manner. Precisely that which in historical perspective appears to be clearest and closest at hand, namely, the statements as to the time and place of events, this reveals itself in prophetic perspective as the remotest, least distinct and obscurest. Hence the detailed, laborious circumlocutions for the birthplaces of the saints; hence the constant inclination to obscure what is historically clear, and vice versa. This procedure must not be hastily condemned as perverse ingenuity or child's play, for the spirit is serious and the play is earnest; it is a spirit more like that of Hegel than that of Voltaire.

Together with the historical high-lights, the lowest points are also to be indicated. Critically objective, Thomas and Bonaventura contrast the merit of the founders of their orders with the degeneracy of their disciples. That degeneracy, viewed from Heaven, no longer appears as something incurable, nor as the diabolical destruction of the divine plans, but merely as a partial loss. Hence it is portrayed without special excitement, in a sober light, with modest, belittling metaphors (sheep, cowls, mould, cards), and on a reduced scale.

The last triumphs of Christian thought—the joyous renunciation characteristic of Franciscan mysticism, and the critical theology of Dominican scholasticism—would be unintelligible without a glance at the sources of these ideas. These principles are half human, and are called reason and practical wisdom, the other half divine, and their names are revelation and speculative wisdom. The first principle found its highest historical embodiment in the Old Testament king, Solomon, the second in the first man, Adam, who was created and enlightened directly by God, and in God's Son, Jesus Christ.

Both categories of wisdom are explained by Thomas Aquinas; the diversity between merely human and divinely human knowledge is traced back to the difference between depraved nature and perfect nature; the natural and supernatural origins of religious thought are indicated.

So the discourses and narratives of the saints in the fourth Heaven, seemingly connected by mere chance, have an objective, that is, a dialectic, connection. Externally they are called forth by the silent questions and misunderstandings of Dante. Artistically they are interrupted and connected by apostrophes to the reader and by the dances and songs of the spirits in the sun. We have thus, in the fourth Heaven, a scene extraordinarily rich in ideas and pictures, with firm structure, lively dialogue, and highly ornate language.

(*Paradiso*, XIV–XVII. *Mars*)

But in the fifth Heaven, where the religious idea becomes deed and action, in the Heaven of the planet Mars, where God's warriors, the martyrs and the crusaders, dwell, a purely epic style is appropriate; and here the poet has had recourse to all his resources. Nowhere in the *Paradiso* does the narrative run on so naturally.

Still, this Heaven has and must have its speculative prologue. For the character of the poem must needs be continuous. It was necessary to show how, even in the higher perfection of Paradise, the pure idea requires to be translated into deeds; in other words, how the souls of the blessed crave a heavenly body, and how they are to receive it at the Last Judgment, by God's grace not only without sacrifice of their ideal clarity, but even with advantage to their radiant splendour.

Beatrice knows that her friend cannot ascend to the fifth Heaven until he is familiar with this state of things. The explanation is given, at the suggestion of Beatrice, by that spirit who knows better than the rest how to appreciate the eternal value of the worldly, practical, physical element. That is, beyond question, King Solomon.

Prepared and instructed by Solomon, the pilgrim may venture to forget at his entrance into the fifth Heaven the usual contemplative gaze into the face of his guide.

So much the more sensuously and directly does the pageant present itself to him. The light from the disk of Mars is warm and red. Out of its dusky glow a mighty cross shines, and out of the cross the figure of the Saviour: a living radiant picture which is made up of thousands and thousands of glittering and chanting spirits: a splendour of colours, of lights, and of tones more brilliant and sublime than any the traveller had yet seen.

At his arrival the resonant hymns are hushed. All Heaven is silent that the mortal may speak. Like a falling star a spirit of light descends from the cross and addresses him:

> "O sanguis meus, O super infusa
> Gratia Dei."

It is the poet's own progenitor, his great-great-grandfather Cacciaguida. He speaks to his descendant so profoundly, so loftily, so nobly, that he is not understood.

Out of unfathomable spiritual distance comes the ancestor's voice; it descends, draws nigh, grows intelligible and ever clearer, more personal, more familiar and paternally intimate. Over boundless expanses, swift as lightning, naturally and easily, the grandsire reaches his offspring, the chosen scion of his house, whom he has been awaiting for centuries. And now they converse together and understand each other as if they had always been together. It seems as though before our very eyes pure thought became action, the word became flesh, and the eternal became a daily event.

All Paradise is an approach of man to God. Here within transcendence we have in contrast, at least for an instant, a descent of the spirit to mankind, a sort of incarnation. In his human form on the cross appears the figure of Jesus Christ; the spirit of the glorified Cacciaguida speaks in absolutely personal fashion to his own flesh and blood. Although he reads all thoughts and wishes in God's mirror and has no need of words, he yet desires to hear the utterance of his descendant.

> " But that the sacred love, in which I watch
> With sight perpetual, and which makes me thirst
> With sweet desire, may better be fulfilled,
> Now let thy voice secure and frank and glad
> Proclaim the wishes, the desire proclaim,
> To which my answer is decreed already."

The answer is family history and home memories.

Cacciaguida was born about the end of the eleventh century in the Porta San Piero quarter of Florence, and baptized in the Chapel of St. John. He had two brothers, Moronto and Eliseo, and belonged to an old knightly family. He married a noble lady of Lombardy. From her came the name Alighieri. The Emperor Conrad knighted him. He followed the Emperor to the Crusades, and in the war against Islam he died a martyr's death.[1] All this he relates in grandfatherly tones.

> " Florence, within the ancient boundary
> From which she taketh still her tierce and nones,
> Abode in quiet, temperate and chaste.
> No golden chain she had, nor coronal,
> Nor ladies shod with sandal shoon, nor girdle
> That caught the eye more than the person did.
> Not yet the daughter at her birth struck fear
> Into the father, for the time and dower
> Did not o'errun this side or that the measure.
> No houses had she void of families,
> Not yet had thither come Sardanapalus
> To show what in a chamber can be done;

[1] Probably in the second crusade, A.D. 1147.

Not yet surpassed had Montemalo been
 By your Uccellatojo, which surpassed
 Shall in its downfall be as in its rise.
Bellincion Berti saw I go begirt
 With leather and with bone, and from the mirror
 His dame depart without a painted face;
And him of Nerli saw, and him of Vecchio,
 Contented with their simple suits of buff,
 And with the spindle and the flax their dames.
O fortunate women! and each one was certain
 Of her own burial-place, and none as yet
 For sake of France was in her bed deserted.
One o'er the cradle kept her studious watch,
 And in her lullaby the language used
 That first delights the fathers and the mothers;
Another, drawing tresses from her distaff,
 Told o'er among her family the tales
 Of Trojans and of Fesole and Rome.
As great a marvel then would have been held
 A Lapo Salterello, a Cianghella,
 As Cincinnatus or Cornelia now.
To such a quiet, such a beautiful
 Life of the citizen, to such a safe
 Community, and to so sweet an inn,
Did Mary give me, with loud cries invoked,
 And in your ancient Baptistery at once
 Christian and Cacciaguida I became."

But what is this old Florentine idyll doing in Paradise? In the Heaven of God's warriors, was not a triumphant procession of all the martyrs and heroes of the faith to be expected? Why does not the voyager question his grandfather as to that historic Crusade rather than as to the civic and social history of an uneventful time? Why not the Emperor Conrad rather than an obscure Alighieri? Why not the Holy Sepulchre, rather than the narrow streets of Florence?

The personal reason is self-evident. Dante exults in his high descent and beautiful home.

O thou our poor nobility of blood,
 If thou dost make the people glory in thee
 Down here where our affection languishes,
A marvellous thing it ne'er will be to me;
 For there where appetite is not perverted,
 I say in Heaven, of thee I made a boast!

But behind this vanity, to which the poet alludes as if smiling at himself, there is an objective motive, namely, the fact that the great religious idea cannot become action that moves the world except through self-depreciation. Even God's son must lie in the cradle, a weeping and laughing infant, and all great victories are preceded by an idyll: the childhood of heroes.

In the realm of perfection, where every earthly thing presents itself in inverse order, death appears in the kindly guise of birth, strife as the game of childhood, and martyrdom as a smiling birth-gift of destiny. Therefore Cacciaguida, instead of lingering over the clash of arms at his baptism in blood, can dwell on the simple peaceful days of his baptism in water, and therefore his reminiscences abide, not merely for their own sake, but as the first important elements of an individual life and as a tragic outlook on the degeneracy, feud, civil war, and downfall of the beautiful city.

Just as fast as an alien population floods the city, the good stock and good morals are perverted.

> " Ever the intermingling of the people
> Has been the source of malady in cities,
> As in the body food it surfeits on."

The old nobleman knows this. Out of this civic evil, however, there arises personal misfortune for his remote descendant. Therefore Cacciaguida's tale turns to a review of the Florentine families and ends with a prophecy for his descendant.

In this descendant the ancestor loves his family, all the Alighieri. So, at the very beginning, he had admonished him that he should pray for his great-grandfather, the first Alighieri, who was still in Purgatory. At the close he bids him scourge the sins of men with courage and without cowardly caution. In this contact with his ancestor the poet steels himself for the combat. Here is the spring, so to speak, out of which the sacred poison of satire flows throughout the whole *Commedia*.

> . . . "A conscience overcast
> Or with its own or with another's shame,
> Will taste forsooth the tartness of thy word;
> But ne'ertheless, all falsehood laid aside,
> Make manifest thy vision utterly,
> And let them scratch wherever is the itch;

For if thine utterance shall offensive be
At the first taste, a vital nutriment
'Twill leave thereafter, when it is digested.
This cry of thine shall do as doth the wind,
Which smiteth most the most exalted summits,
And that is no slight argument of honour;
Therefore are shown to thee within these wheels,
Upon the mount and in the dolorous valley,
Only the souls that unto fame are known;
Because the spirit of the hearer rests not,
Nor doth confirm its faith by an example
Which has the root of it unknown and hidden,
Or other reason that is not apparent."

This prophecy clears up all the more or less obscure hints which the traveller had heard, gathered up and stored in his memory concerning his earthly future, his impending banishment, his hospitable reception at princely courts, and the like. For Cacciaguida's utterance is not, like that of the others, obscure or half-illumined. It announces misfortune and, at the same time, consolation, foretells misery and fame. Thanks to this two-sidedness, it is objective, complete, and truthful, yet emotionally vivid; a complete picture of the subsequent years of our poet's life: complete not through the recital of all details, but because of its varying colours and moods behind which the large outlines of the events glimmer. He who undertakes to tell the tale of Alighieri's life, finds here in Cacciaguida's prophecy the proper tones and shades. There is hardly a modern Dante biography in which, at the proper place, one does not find the famous verses:

"Thou shalt abandon everything beloved
Most tenderly. . . .
Thou shalt have proof how savoureth of salt
The bread of others, and how hard a road
The going down and up another's stairs."

Nowhere does the poet express more purely the spirit of his life than here, in the Heaven of martyrs and of God's warriors, showing thereby how fully he had accustomed himself to live his earthly life as endurance and struggle in the name of the Lord.

After viewing his own work and life from the heights of eternity, our traveller hears the names and sees the gleaming lights of the warring champions of truth: Joshua, Maccabaeus, Charlemagne,

Count Orlando, William of Orange, Renouard, Godfrey of Bouillon, Robert Guiscard; when named by Cacciaguida, with soldierly brevity, each in turn flashes brightly.

(*Paradiso*, XVIII–XX. *Jupiter*)

The warriors are followed by the conquerers and rulers; the fighters, by the princes of peace. They, with wise gentleness and justice, introduced the religious idea into the turmoil of this world. Here amid many other kings, David, the Emperors Trajan and Constantine, the good William II of Sicily, shine forth—and Trojan Ripheus,

> the one most just
> Among the Teucrians, and most upright.[1]

Since other such just and upright ones, including the Emperor Justinian, have already appeared in the second Heaven, there seems here to be a repetition.

In fact, the three upper planetary Heavens repeat the motifs of the three lower ones. The martyrs of the fifth Heaven bear the same relation to the patient sufferers of the first that the God-intoxicated spirits of the seventh bear to His lovers in the third, and that the righteous of the sixth sphere bear to those of the second. It is, however, no mere repetition, but a resumption and completion of the motifs. Let us recall how the three lower Heavens were still traversed by the earth's shadow, and we shall understand why the poet desired to show us those lower stages once more in a higher order and in a purer light.

The imperial eagle whose history was related by Justinian in the second Heaven is at home here in the sixth, lives, moves, and triumphs. Here it is no longer a symbol in the human sense, but a supernatural reality, a unit made up of thousands on thousands of righteous spirits, a heavenly existential form of the *civitas Dei*.

The principle of this form of life is the will for righteousness, its final goal the contemplation and adoration of God as the infinitely righteous One.

These simple and lofty thoughts are represented somewhat as follows. The voyager at his entrance into the sixth Heaven beholds within the luminous disk of Jupiter a flutter and whirl of

[1] Virgil, *Aeneid*, II, 426–427.

lights and hears their song. Like water-birds that circle to and fro, rejoicing, they form by their groupings a series of Latin letters. As often as they have represented one, they pause an instant and are mute. Dante, listening intensely and reverently, combines the letters into the sentence: *Diligite justitiam, qui judicatis terram* (Love justice, ye who judge the earth). After the spirits of light have formed the final M, countless other spirits come floating down to them and gather about the tip of the M. Then they flit about and by each other like myriads of sparks and form, as they come to rest, the head and neck of an eagle; while the lower portions of the M move slowly to form the body of the eagle.

The description of this spectacle is followed, as if it were Dante's personal solution of the riddle, by a passionate outbreak.

This passes in three waves. *O dolce stella*, that is, the praise of Heavenly justice; *O milizia del ciel*, the prayer for earthly justice; *Ma tu che sol per cancellare scrive*, arraignment of the representative of Heaven on earth, or an attack against the injustice of the contemporary pope, John XXII.

The fundamental thought has been made into doctrinal pictures of light and into passionate speech.

The imperial eagle, the ideal emblem of the *civitas Dei*, which has been shaped out of multiplicity by the power of will, of justice and love, into unity, must be made useful to the traveller by the instructive presentation of speculative concepts. A thousand heads with one will, with one feeling: that is found often enough on earth. But here we have the marvel of a thousand spirits with a single concept, with a single utterance and a single voice.

> So doth a single heat from many embers
> Make itself felt, even as from many loves
> Issued a single sound from out that image.

Not only moral and natural law, not only will and destiny, but will and intellect, feeling and knowledge, belief and thought, melt into unity in God's realm.

This unity extends even to the grammatical forms of the eagle's speech, in which "I" and "mine" have replaced "we" and "our."

The subject-matter of the utterance is determined by the position of the sixth Heaven in the theological system of Paradise. After the legal principle of the Imperium and the rule of divine justice have been set forth by Justinian and Beatrice in the second Heaven, we find ourselves on a level where Imperium and righteousness appear no longer harsh and relentless, but wise, gentle, and infinite: as a Mystery.

Therefore the imperial eagle must, above all, show how divine justice lies beyond the reach of human knowledge, and how therefore it cannot be understood, but must be accepted, revered, loved, believed. To doubters it appears like something arbitrary, to the pious as gracious choice, to the sinner as unexpected punishment. Accordingly the eagle first describes the surprise that awaits all the evil princes at Doomsday, those princes who now sit self-satisfied on their thrones. With heavy monotony, like the unerring blows of a skilful smith, threatening words fall on the crowned heads of Europe: *Li si vedrà . . . li si vedrà . . . vedrassi . . . vedrassi.*

With increased light and sonority and yet again with solemn repetition: *Ora conosce . . . ora conosce . . .* the eagle next describes the happy surprise of the pious princes who by divine election are uplifted to this sixth Heaven. David, for the seemingly scant merit of his song; Trajan, although originally a pagan and already damned; King Hezekiah, saved only by a miracle from a sinner's death; the Emperor Constantine, despite his fatal weakness toward the Roman pope; William II, in reward for his just and gentle reign over Sicily; and Trojan Ripheus, against all human expectation: each one has received the grace of the Lord with thankful joy.

Instead of being satisfied in the pious contemplation of these dispensations, our poet, a clever pupil of scholasticism, considers a justification and explanation indispensable. Now, for the first time, the utterance of his eagle is able to rise to lyrical glorification of election by grace.

(*Paradiso*, XXI–XXII. *Saturn*)

Such details vanish in the seventh Heaven, the highest and last of the planetary system.

The planet Saturn, which once brought the Golden Age to earth, belongs to the hermits and monks. These have lived already on earth as pure citizens of Heaven, hostile to all sensuality, removed from all worldly impulses, absorbed in love and contemplation of God. Thanks to their renunciation, penance, and mortification, they have won for themselves in spirit that Eden that lies on the crest of the Purgatorial mount. On desolate mountain-tops, where horrible worship of idols was once indulged in by the heathen, they created their Christian Paradise as a hermitage, a place to torture the flesh and to house the spirit. On the rock wall of Catria, a peak of the Apennines, Peter Damian, and on the crest of Monte Cassino, St. Benedict, found places of refuge for themselves and their disciples. Now these penitents sway effortlessly, as dancing lights, on the golden Jacob's ladder of mystical contemplation, from their planet up into the boundless Empyrean and back again, from themselves to God, from God to themselves, a blessed, speechless undulation. Here there is no festival, no pageant, only an ascent and descent, a silent, luminous breathing of the spirits in God. Their jubilation, if it wished to break forth in audible tones, could be endured by no human ear; and Beatrice's smile, if it were to reveal itself, would annihilate the traveller. The splendour of the description is lost in the poetry of the thought. As earth casts its shadow on the lower Heavens, so the Empyrean throws its light on this highest planetary sphere. Beatrice's admonition befits the reader also: "Fix in direction of thine eyes the mind."

Accordingly, the description is almost completely broken up into conversation, and the conversation veiled in brilliant suggestions. The words of Peter Damian are not, perhaps, obscure, but mysterious; not unintelligible, but ambiguous; outwardly simple and clear, they open up a multiplicity of wavering outlooks.

The wanderer, still filled and moved by the thought of election through grace, is eager to behold the original cause of these marvels. But the happy soul replies to him:

> "On me directed is a light divine,
> Piercing through this in which I am embosomed,
> Of which the virtue with my sight conjoined
> Lifts me above myself so far, I see
> The supreme essence from which this is drawn.
> Hence comes the joyfulness with which I flame,
> For to my sight, as far as it is clear,
> The clearness of the flame I equal make.
> But that soul in the heaven which is most pure,
> That seraph which his eye on God most fixes,
> Could this demand of thine not satisfy;
> Because so deeply sinks in the abyss
> Of the eternal statute what thou askest,
> From all created sight it is cut off."

Damian sees and sees not, perceives and perceives not. Actually, he has solved the question by recognizing predestination as the ultimate and absolutely accepted fact; and again has not solved it, since he suggests, behind this fact, another mystery.

Facing this profound and by no means sophistical ambiguity, we may perhaps surmise a double meaning in Damian's second speech also. He relates how he led a pious, contemplative, solitary life on the summit of Mount Catria.

> "I in that place was Peter Damiano;
> And Peter the Sinner was I in the house
> Of Our Lady on the Adriatic shore."

It is not impossible that these much-discussed verses indicate a doubling or splitting of the ego. Then the sense would be: I, Peter Damian, that is, my spiritual ego, abode in the happy hermitage on the heights of Catria, and that, too, at the very time when my bodily ego remained in the temple of the Holy Virgin at Ravenna. Such duplications are familiar in mediæval legend and especially as miracles of Mary. If our interpretation is correct, we would have here on the heights of human blessedness a counterpart to the Satanic duplication of the ego, as the poet depicted it in the deepest abyss of the Inferno, in the persons of Fra Alberigo and Branca d'Oria (*Inferno*, XXXIII). Just as there a devil, so here the Virgin, or some other divine power, would have represented in human society him who had departed from the world. Certainly such a double meaning of the words would not be unsuited to the poetic style of the seventh Heaven.

Even in the short, vivid description of the worldly-minded priests who have become physically fat, ostentatious, and grasping, and intellectually so dull, the same illuminating double sense is to be discovered: the portly prelate who covers, with his costly mantle, himself and the whole body of his steed, two beasts under one skin. We fancy we have a picture-puzzle before us, but what seems a jest is grimmest earnest. When Damian utters a witty word, Heaven thunders with holy anger, so that the traveller turns in anxiety to his guide.

What wonder that in this remarkable realm where love appears as anger, wit as earnestness, the image as concept, and deepest obscurity as light, the mortal feels a craving to look on the picture unveiled (*imagine scoperta*)? He would fain be permitted to behold in his true form St. Benedict, who stands before him as a vision of light. But such a favour can be granted him only in the Empyrean, where the spirit, so to speak, shows its naked self. Only at the top of Jacob's ladder, where space ends, does the symbolic veil fall.

While the essence of the Deity and of the blessed remains veiled behind gleaming light, the hardest mystery of our earth, on the other hand, is unveiled and solved. The degeneracy and destruction of the highest ideals, the evil on earth, appears as a brief, divinely appointed trial, as something conquerable, almost petty:

" In verity the Jordan backward turned,
And the sea's fleeing, when God willed, were more
A wonder to behold, than succour here."

The rescue, the Golden Age, is near at hand.

" The sword above here smiteth not in haste
Nor tardily, howe'er it seem to him
Who fearing or desiring waits for it."

"O'er all the tree tops is calm." Above the planets the fixed stars shine; and over earthly misery a deliverer stands guard. Upborne by the feeling of the pettiness of our pains and the greatness of the universe, the poet floats out of the planetary realm.

His passage from Middle to Upper Paradise is one of the greatest movements of the poem. Hurried on with the speed of thought, the pilgrim enters the constellation of Gemini. It is the sign under which he was born, so that he sees himself here, in the heavenly home of his spirit, at the source of his genius.

Whom thou forsakest not, O Genius,
Thou'lt uplift above the slime
On thy fiery pinions;
He shall wander
As with flowery feet
O'er Deucalion's muddy flood,
Slaying easily the Python,
Mighty Pythian Apollo.

Like Goethe's wanderer, so the wanderer Dante draws, out of pious reverence for his genius, Apollo-like power for the loftiest flight.

To you devoutly at this hour my soul
Is sighing, that it virtue may acquire
For the stern pass that draws it to itself.

A last glance downward. Below lies Earth, ridiculously small, but encircled by the sure pathways of the moon, the sun and all the planets: a spectacle of smallness within greatness. Lost in starry space, far from his earthly abode, he wins his spiritual home, and seeks the way to it in Beatrice's glance.

> The threshing-floor that maketh us so proud,
> To me revolving with the eternal Twins,
> Was all apparent made from hill to harbour!
> Then to the beauteous eyes mine eyes I turned.

UPPER PARADISE

(*Paradiso*, XXIII–XXVII. *Heaven of the Fixed Stars*)

We are in the Heaven of the fixed stars. This creates by its slow movement the individual variations from the regular natural course and is therefore the individuating principle of all life. From this Heaven we receive the peculiarities of our body, spirit, and character, the germ and kernel of our personality. Now since our spiritual personality is forfeit to Hell by Adam's fall, therefore the God-man who has wrested from the Devil his prize appears in this Heaven as the Victor. Here also the paladins of the Saviour, Peter and the other apostles, who have, so to speak, secured the conquest, appear as guards at the entrance to Upper Paradise. Here is seen finally, the prize *par excellence*, the first human lost and won again in the battle for the salvation of souls—our progenitor Adam.

The triumphal procession of Christ is unrolled as a gigantic, stormy, endless natural phenomenon, which passes with the solemnity of a holy drama. A host of lights, the ransomed souls, whirl on before Him who triumphs. He Himself is incomprehensible: a sun, a God, a man, supreme wisdom, supreme power. Silently He moves on, while the rapt wanderer loses consciousness.

The Mother of God follows, crowned with a circle of light and with the song of the Angel of the Annunciation: a rose among lilies, a star, a sapphire, a woman; eager as little children, behind her, the heavenly hosts singing *Regina coeli*—the whole a blessed, shapeless, that is, ever-changing, whirl of lights, voices, melodies figures, and thoughts.

This rapture which words can only hint at, not really communicate or create, is a revel of clarity and holy sobriety, a mindful and comprehensive fantasy, a mythical thought and song, through which we learn the names, the embodiments, appearances, movements, and gestures which the Divinity assumes in our consciousness, and realize the significance which, at a favourable opportunity, it acquires for us.

What will the Christian pilgrim have to do now, if he comes to this point where the mythical guardians surround and watch over the divinely natural source of his personality? He will have to recognize and acknowledge that his full spiritual welfare, his faith, hope and love, is a gift from God. He will have to express this insight in the form of a confession. His confession acquires, through the presence of the theological Beatrice, the scholastic semblance of an examination. It is not, however, an examination that one can fail to pass; it is a joyously excited intellectual game of question and answer, by means of which a realization that we possess in the inward form of a certainty is elaborated into the external form of doctrine and proof. Accordingly the examination passes through three stages, the inmost of which is a personal certainty, its outermost a formal definition of the idea, and the middle stage a process of demonstration. The order may be varied at will. In faith, the definition of the idea stands first and the confession last. In hope, the confession, which in Dante's mouth must take the form of self-praise, will be taken for granted by Beatrice, so that the candidate has only to carry out the development of the concept and of the proof. But the concept of love is, in the strict sense of the word, neither defined nor deduced; for the essence of heavenly love is sufficiently defined when he who loves states and confesses the direction and impulse of his love. The final success of the examination consists, of course, in the fact that confession and realization reunite, and that the personal feeling takes on the character of the most universal validity. This union, however, can only come to pass if the student-candidate expels from his intellectual life all irrelevant curiosity, all dilettantism, and becomes an absolutely transparent vessel of the truth.

The poet has indicated, in an intermezzo, this purification of his craving for knowledge. As John, the examiner on the subject of love, appears, Dante is seized with curiosity, and desires to attain certainty directly through his own eyesight concerning the question disputed in the Middle Ages, whether the apostle went to Heaven bodily or in spirit. Meantime he gazes at the luminous figure of John until he is blinded. Only when the examination is completed does he receive again through Beatrice's miraculous glance his increased power of vision.

Furthermore, the poet does not wish to have the disputed question of John's ascension regarded as one in and of itself out of place, for he makes John himself decide it in the sense of an incorporeal spirituality. It was only Dante's curiosity that was out of place. Similar disputed questions—How long was Adam in the Earthly Paradise? At what time was he there? What language did he speak? What was his sin?—questions which for us today have become meaningless, are answered in authoritative fashion. Adam furnishes Dante the answers as a voluntary gift.

To us, however, he offers at the same time fresh evidence of the fact that in the eighth Heaven, in the realm of personality, the union of inner with outer, classroom knowledge is made clear. All forms of cognition meet in this sphere: the ecstatic and fantastic form of the vision, the authoritative and dogmatic one of revelation, the scholastic one of conceptual definition, and the inept one of curiosity. The artist runs through all the grades of inner comprehension, from dazzling gold to dull grey.

Then in a sudden oratorical outbreak he lets the suppressed ethical forces find utterance again. Red anger was necessary, so that the white light of the sphere of fixed stars might not pale. The apostle Peter thunders forth a denunciation against the degenerate representatives of Christ on earth. But as a too direct expression of passion would ill befit the lofty dignity of the speaker, his words must be coloured harmoniously and his figure illuminated. The sounds roll and resound as in an enormous megaphone, and at the sound Heaven grows dark.

> ". . . my place,
> My place, my place, which vacant has become . . .
> . . . of my cemetery made a sewer
> Of blood and stench, whereby the Perverse One,
> Who fell from here, below there is appeased!"

While the blessed ones whirl like a snowstorm on high, Dante looks once more earthward. Our globe is turned, and offers to the eye the remotest western confines of its inhabited side. It becomes night for mankind, and the wanderer rises to the crystalline Heaven.

(*Paradiso*, XXVII–XXIX. *The Crystalline Heaven*)

This Heaven, the ninth and last limited one, bears no stars. Here is pure immaterial space and pure timeless, infinitely swift motion. From here everything is moved, limited, and measured. It is the Heaven of abstract conformity to law, the source of all temporal and spatial conditions, of all regularity and permanence amid change. As from the eighth Heaven comes what is individual, so from this comes whatever is general, whether it be mathematical, natural, spiritual, or historical uniformity and necessity.

This Heaven is the eternally regulative, divinely natural movement of the universe about the motionless centre of our earth; it signifies, to put it exactly, the static dynamism of things, the combination of boundless speed with infinite permanence, of progress with rest. After Beatrice has developed this idea, she sets over against it, as a picture of humanity, the persistence of inertia, the everyday routine, habit, a principle of movement which wastes instead of preserving.

> " Full fairly blossoms in mankind the will;
> But the uninterrupted rain converts
> Into abortive wildings the true plums."

As the ceaseless movement is wasted through inertia, so law-abiding permanent truth is distorted by capricious inventions. Therefore, in this Heaven, Beatrice is strenuous, not only against vulgar habits, but against the fantastic chatter which is devised and haughtily uttered by theologians and preachers.

The vision which, in the bodiless sphere of space, meets the eyes of the traveller—for each of the three upper Heavens has its special vision of the Godhead—shows nothing plastic, picturesque, or musical. It is a mathematical, systematic, accurate model of rest and motion: of motionless point and circling line. God appears as the fixed point at an infinite distance, infinitely small, but with utmost illuminating power.

About that point nine concentric circles revolve in such a fashion that the inmost shine and rotate more clearly and swiftly, the outer ones less brightly and more slowly: the inverted scheme of the astronomic world. While the nine heavenly spheres circle about the hidden point in our earth in such a manner that the remotest are fullest of divine light and the nearest are most incomplete, the wanderer notes that here all force and all light are drawn toward the centre.

The nine circles of light are the nine orders of angels, that is, of pure Intelligences. Their names are Seraphim, Cherubim, Thrones, Dominions, Virtues, Powers, Principalities, Archangels, Angels. In this order they gaze upward; in reversed order they exert influence downward, so that the ninth Heaven, farthest from the earth, receives its motion from the order of the Seraphim, which circles closest to God.

The number of angels is infinite. But a portion of them rebelled against God immediately after their creation, and were transformed into devils.

In this graphic description, mathematical and astronomical arrangement, and theological and mythical deduction of the angels that move the Heavens and intervene between God and man, we have the final outmost encircling frame of our natural and spiritual world. It is mythical, that is, religious, imagination and poetry, in which the scientific and dogmatic element appears only as applied, elaborated, and poetically glorified material.

(*Paradiso*, XXX–XXXIII. *The Empyrean*)

In the highest Heaven, in the Empyrean, where everything temporal and spatial vanishes, the indescribable event of complete absorption into God occurs.

The poet, with wise and conscious moderation, has postponed this event to the last stanza of the *Commedia*. The very ones who are nearest to God are not drawn by Him into Himself; on the contrary, the more violently they struggle toward Him, the more steadfastly does He hold them off. So it comes to pass that the Seraphim do not vanish in Him, but circle about Him, and that the spirits of the blessed, compressed, as it were, between the repelling force with which He resists and the centripetal force with which they press toward Him, must be crowded together into fixed groups and forms and moulded into earthly, even human, shapes.

The poet clung to a profound thought in the transcendent

concept of God, namely, that the Absolute does not give itself fully and wholly even to the thirstiest human soul, and does not become wholly immanent in any one of its creatures. He made this thought artistically vivid by showing that precisely in the highest and most supersensuous Heaven the blessed spirits appear in bodily form. By a marvellously imaginative change of form, they gradually arrange themselves in the gigantic shape of the living Rose of Heaven.

First all the lights and faces that the spatial spheres brought are extinguished. The vision of the angelic choirs vanishes, as do the stars before the dawn. For a brief instant there is nothing round about but empty pallor. But Beatrice smiles ineffably, and announces the bliss of the Heaven of light. The eye of the traveller feels itself exalted by a sudden ray:

> And light I saw in fashion of a river
> Fulvid with its effulgence, 'twixt two banks
> Depicted with an admirable Spring.
> Out of this river issued living sparks,
> And on all sides sank down into the flowers,
> Like unto rubies that are set in gold;
> And then, as if inebriate with the odours,
> They plunged again into the wondrous torrent,
> And as one entered issued forth another.

They are the souls and the pure Intelligences, the human beings and the angels, who, in a sort of spiritual wedlock, create for themselves new forms.

This supersensuous revelry of light dazzles the pilgrim's eye. Then the stream becomes a lake and so remains.

> Then as a folk who have been under masks
> Seem other than before, if they divest
> The semblance not their own they disappeared in,
> Thus into greater pomp were changed for me
> The flowerets and the sparks, so that I saw
> Both of the Courts of Heaven made manifest.

Assembled into an enormous amphitheatre, all the souls appear in glorified and illuminated bodily shape and with human faces. This harmonious Heavenly Rose, odorous with blessedness, is in direct contrast with Hell's funnel permeated with discord. The picture cannot be understood through any earthly comparison. It seems to be at rest, and is alive; its outmost circles, wider than the circumference of our sun, seem to vanish into infinite distance, but here the remotest is no less clear to the eye than the nearest; it mirrors itself in itself, receives its light from the Godhead, and sends it down to the Heavens of the spheres. It is full, but a few places are still vacant—and there the great seat, on which rests a crown, awaits the Emperor Henry—

> . . . noble Henry, who shall come
> To redress Italy ere she be ready.

His opponent, Pope Clement V, will presently thrust Boniface VIII into the flaming grave of the simoniacs.

This message is Beatrice's last word. Before she forsakes her friend, and finds her place in the Rose, she, the glorified lady, has become woman again for a moment, loving and beloved, and shares hate and hope with her poet.

Everywhere in this highest Paradise human nature breaks through the heavenly veil of light, to come and go like something intimately connected with it, throbbing and breathing. This earthly element, also, is to be grasped only as a vision, as the reverse side of the divine vision. For him who has become wholly absorbed in the contemplation of the supersensuous world, it suddenly flashes before the eyes as a new sensuousness. The emptiest and most general of signs, a number, a circle, a triangle, a point; and the most expressive picture which we know, the human countenance—both are indispensable and essential in the world of Paradise. In the lowest Heaven the human face was still present, as a physical remainder; in the highest Heaven it appears as spiritual completeness. The two types of vision heighten and supplement each other in progressive mutual helpfulness, until in the contemplation of the absolute Godhead the likeness of man, framed within a tricoloured light, stands radiantly forth.

In this dialectic of reality and symbol is the true reality of the spirit—the metaphysical being. But this escapes the artist's shaping hands, and in pious modesty he renounces the attempt to capture it, to materialize it. This renunciation of the artist is not merely a religious act, but as a proper sense of measure, limit, and form, it is even artistic, and in the closing cantos of the *Paradiso*, it actually becomes the motif of the poetry and gives to the entire *Divine Comedy* roundness and completeness: while the poet realizes that he is as inadequate, as mortal, as much in need of help, as the pilgrim had been from the first.

The picture passes, but admiration and longing abide in him who sees.

Like bees thirsting for flowers, the angels flit from the Rose to God from God to the Rose. The pilgrim who, in boundless eternity, realizes these little intimate events in the life of the flower, stands and gazes in reverence and tenderness. He seems to himself like the Northern barbarian at his entrance into the capital of the Christian world.

> I who to the divine had from the human,
> From time unto eternity, had come,
> From Florence to a people just and sane,
> With what amazement must I have been filled!

While his eye, entranced, traverses the circle, his thirst for knowledge becomes prayer—and, unperceived, in Beatrice's stead, St. Bernard has come to his side.

Why Bernard takes Beatrice's place is not immediately evident. Only after many-sided studies in the history of religion have we, in due time, felt ourselves able to explain in some degree the leading rôle played by this saint in the *Commedia.*[1] Only from the unassuming naturalness and obviousness with which Beatrice goes as Bernard arrives do we conclude that a long-prepared, significant revolution has come about in the pilgrim's mental state. In its complete extent and value, however, this shifting of the inmost centre of gravity becomes comprehensible only at the end of the poem. The entrance of St. Bernard begins the final decisive struggle, which ends when the pilgrim awakens from his vision of Paradise.

> Here vigour failed the lofty fantasy:
> But now was turning my desire and will,
> Even as a wheel that equally is moved,
> The Love which moves the sun and the other stars.

So from contemplation to desire and to volition, all the way over and back, Bernard is to guide the pilgrim.[2] Beatrice has supplied grace, strength, and freedom, which were necessary to the understanding of heavenly thoughts and visions (*Paradiso,*

[1] Cf. the discussion of St. Bernard in Vol. I.

[2] Cf. Vol. I, *loc. cit.*

XXXI, 82–87). But Bernard helps to bring home the results of this entire quest after knowledge, the moral harvest. For such up-gathering there is need of cheery confidence and consistent reverence. Therefore Bernard, as a pious old man full of cheerful goodness, presents himself. Like a tender father he speaks to Dante. The latter, meanwhile, is just about to lay hold on the last mystery of the Godhead by the boldest and firmest effort of his feeling and thought. We surmise that Dante's impetuosity might overleap itself and miss its mark if the gentle father were not at his side calming him and praying for him.

Unfortunately the contrast between the young, zealous seeker after God and the calm piety of the old man is not developed to its full effect. It is indeed indicated, but is somewhat obscured by the long explanation of the hierarchic arrangement of the souls in the Heavenly Rose. Instead of sating at once the craving for knowledge, the saint first plunges into churchly didacticism and shows how wisely and justly the places are distributed among the children of the Old and the New Covenants, among the contemplative souls like Rachel and Beatrice, among deserving personalities and innocent babes. He holds the impatience of the wanderer and of the reader in check with kindly deliberation, and bids rise before us once more the mystery of salvation by Grace.

Not until after this doctrinal problem is disposed of, and to use Bernard's words, the good tailor has stitched the coat according to the amount of his cloth, does poetry rise to its profoundest strain.

In the adoration of the Holy Virgin, in the picture of Mary and in the hymn to Mary, Catholic piety from the earliest date down to the present day has found its purest artistic expression. Peace enters into Dante's heart—"The ardour of desire in me was ended"—while he prays silently in the words of the saint:

"Thou Virgin Mother, daughter of thy Son,
  Humble and high beyond all other creature,
  The limit fixed of the eternal counsel,
Thou art the one who such nobility
  To human nature gave, that its Creator
  Did not disdain to make himself its creature.
Within thy womb rekindled was the love,
  By heat of which in the eternal peace
  After such wise this flower has germinated.

Here unto us thou art a noonday torch
  Of charity, and below there among mortals
  Thou art the living fountain-head of hope.
Lady, thou art so great, and so prevailing,
  That he who wishes grace, nor runs to thee,
  His aspirations without wings would fly.
Not only thy benignity gives succour
  To him who asketh it, but oftentimes
  Forerunneth of its own accord the asking.
In thee compassion is, in thee is pity,
  In thee magnificence; in thee unites
  Whate'er of goodness is in any creature.
Now doth this man, who from the lowest depth
  Of the universe as far as here has seen
  One after one the spiritual lives,
Supplicate thee through grace for so much power
  That with his eyes he may uplift himself
  Higher towards the uttermost salvation.
And I, who never burned for my own seeing
  More than I do for his, all of my prayers
  Proffer to thee, and pray they come not short,
That thou wouldst scatter from him every cloud
  Of his mortality so with thy prayers,
  That the Chief Pleasure be to him displayed.
Still farther do I pray thee, Queen, who canst
  What'er thou wilt, that sound thou mayst preserve
  After so great a vision his affections.
Let thy protection conquer human movements;
  See Beatrice and all the blessed ones
  My prayers to second clasp their hands to thee!"

Now Dante uplifts his face to the Divine Trinity. The bliss of the universe fills and overflows the mortal man.

As the geometrician, who endeavours
  To square the circle, and discovers not,
  By taking thought, the principle he wants,
Even such was I at that new apparition;
  I wished to see how the image to the circle
  Conformed itself, and how it there finds place;
But my own wings were not enough for this,
  Had it not been that then my mind there smote
  A flash of lightning, wherein came its wish.
Here vigour failed the lofty fantasy:
  But now was turning my desire and will,
  Even as a wheel that equally is moved,
The Love which moves the sun and the other stars.

BIBLIOGRAPHICAL NOTE

By J. E. Spingarn

I. GENERAL WORKS

II. MEDIÆVAL RELIGION

III. MEDIÆVAL THOUGHT

IV. MEDIÆVAL LITERATURE

V. DANTE

BIBLIOGRAPHICAL NOTE

On the Literature Available in English

I. General Works

The *Cambridge Mediæval History*, in eight volumes, with full bibliographies (vols. i–v, Cambridge, 1911–26), is not a history but a storehouse of historical information. There are numerous briefer surveys of the mediæval period, for the most part textbooks and compilations, from E. Emerton's *Mediæval Europe* (Boston, 1894) to D. C. Munro's *The Middle Ages* (New York, 1921). But Gibbon's *Decline and Fall of the Roman Empire* (best edition by J. B. Bury, 7 vols., London, 1896–1900) remains unrivalled for the unfolding of the drama of mediæval life, despite its Voltairean bias, though less satisfactory for the later than for the earlier centuries; and to this should be added two other classics, Bryce's *Holy Roman Empire* (1862; new ed., London and New York, 1904) and Gregorovius's *History of the City of Rome in the Middle Ages* (transl., 13 vols., London, 1894–1919). For mediæval Italy, H. D. Sedgwick's *Italy in the Thirteenth Century* (2 vols., Boston, 1912), H. B. Cottrell's *Mediæval Italy during a Thousand Years* (London, 1915), and P. Villari's *Mediæval Italy from Charlemagne to Henry VII* (transl., London and New York, 1910) may be consulted; and for a vivid contemporary account of thirteenth century life, the chronicle of the Franciscan Salimbene as translated in G. G. Coulton's *From St. Francis to Dante* (2nd ed., London, 1907). For Dante's own city, E. G. Gardner's *Story of Florence* (London, 1901), P. Villari's *The First Two Centuries of Florentine History* (transl., 2 vols., London, 1894–95), and especially the selections from Villani's *Chronicle* translated by Selfe and Wicksteed (London, 1906), may suffice. And not to forget that vital element in history which some have mistaken for history itself, all of these works may be supplemented by P. Boissonnade's *Life and Work in the Middle Ages* (transl., London and New York, 1927), a rapid sketch of economic and social history from the fifth to the fifteenth century, with a useful bibliography, and W. Cunningham's *Essay on Western Civilization in its Economic Aspects: Mediæval and Modern Times* (Cambridge, 1910), as well as by the works referred to below at the end of the section on Political Theory.

H. O. Taylor's *The Mediæval Mind* (3rd ed., 2 vols., New York, 1919; 1st ed., 1911, not recommended) and his earlier book, *The Classical Heritage of the Middle Ages* (New York, 1901; 3rd ed., 1911), are interesting and valuable compilations, touching almost every phase of mediæval culture, though seldom wholly adequate in their presentation of philosophic and religious ideas. C. H. Haskins's *Renaissance of the Twelfth Century* (Cambridge, Mass., and London, 1927) is a brief but highly competent survey of twelfth century culture. *The Legacy of the Middle Ages*, edited by Crump and Jacob (Oxford, 1926), and *Mediæval Contributions to Modern Civilization*, edited by F. J. C. Hearnshaw (London, 1921), contain essays by various scholars on the most important aspects of the period. L. J. Paetow's *Guide to the Study of Mediæval History* (Berkeley, Cal., 1917) is a very useful bibliography, with a section on "Mediæval Culture," and may be consulted with advantage as a first step in the study of any historical question; the *Guide to Historical Literature*, which is being prepared by a committee of the American Historical Association, will also doubtless be most helpful. The problem as to the origin and validity of the conception of a "middle age" is discussed from various points of view in G. Gordon's brief notes on *Medium Aevum and the Middle Age* (Oxford, 1925), J. T. Shotwell's article on the "Middle Ages" in the *Encyclopaedia Britannica*, 11th edition, O. Spengler's *Decline of the West* (transl., New York, 1926), and B. Croce's *History: Its Theory and Practice* (transl., New York and London, 1921); the last contains a brief but penetrating chapter on mediæval historiography.

II. Mediæval Religion

The history of Christianity, as well as of the religions that influenced it directly or indirectly, may be studied in the general histories of religion, of which G. F. Moore's sober and able *History of Religions* (2 vols., New York, 1913–19) and S. Reinach's brief and Voltairean *Orpheus* (transl., London and New York, 1909) represent opposing types; the latter, in Giovanni Gentile's words, "forever moves round about religion but never enters inside it," and to some extent this is true of all histories of religion, even those that are worlds apart from Reinach's shallow oversimplification of history. Of the briefer histories of the Christian Church, Williston Walker's *History of the Christian Church* (New York, 1918), written from the Protestant point of view, and F. X. Funk's *Manual of Church History* (transl., 2 vols., London, 1910), written from the Catholic point of view, supplement each other admirably; of the longer histories, J. Alzog's *Manual of Church History* (transl., 4 vols., Dublin, 1895–1900) is Catholic, and W. Moeller's *History of the Christian Church* (transl., 3 vols., London, 1893–1900) is Protestant. The latest sketch of the history of Christianity, C. Guignebert's *Christianity, Past and Present* (transl., New York and London, 1927), is by a competent French scholar who aims at "objective historical science," and proves his objectivity by a strong anti-Catholic bias. All of these books, except Guignebert's, contain more or less useful bibliographies.

The doctrinal development of the Church may be studied in G. P. Fisher's *History of Christian Doctrine* (New York, 1896), or more fully in R. Seeberg's *Textbook of the History of Doctrines* (transl., 2 vols., Philadelphia, 1905), a solid work with numerous translations of texts, or in A. Harnack's more brilliant but more opinionated *History of Dogma* (transl., 7 vols., London, 1894–99); to these may be added H. B. Workman's *Development of Christian Thought to the Reformation* (London, 1911), F. W. Bussell's *Religious Thought and Heresy in the Middle Ages* (London, 1918), and R. L. Poole's *Illustrations of the History of Mediæval Thought in the Departments of Theology and Ecclesiastical Politics* (London, 1884; 2nd ed., with briefer title, 1920), which shed light on both philosophy and theology; but perhaps the most convenient textbook of all for the student of Dante is the Jesuit B. J. Otten's *Manual of the History of Dogma* (2 vols., St. Louis and London, 1917–18), compiled chiefly from the Catholic histories of Schwane and Tixeront. For the history of the Eastern Church, whose later development is largely ignored in most of the above works, W. F. Adeney's *Greek and Eastern Churches* (Edinburgh, 1908) or B. J. Kidd's *Churches of Eastern Christendom from A. D. 451 to the Present Time* (London, 1927) may be consulted. The fifth, sixth, and seventh chapters of G. Santayana's *Life of Reason: Reason in Religion* (New York, 1905) constitute a brief history and criticism of Christianity which are at least distinctly different in tone from the work of the specialists.

The *Catholic Encyclopedia* (15 vols. and index, New York, 1907–14) and J. Hastings's *Encyclopaedia of Religion and Ethics* (12 vols. and index, Edinburgh and New York, 1912–27) are useful works of reference in connection with religious studies, but the articles in the former are of very unequal merit and the latter is characterized by some extraordinary omissions. Too many Protestant works on religion, in other respects admirable—for example, the *Guide to the Study of the Christian Religion*, edited by G. B. Smith (Chicago, 1916) and even the *New Schaff-Herzog Encyclopedia of Religious Knowledge* (12 vols., New York, 1908–12)—are weak and often even useless in the mediæval field. All four of these works contain good bibliographies.

ORIENTAL SOURCES

For more extended treatment of the ancient religions of Egypt, Babylonia, Assyria, and Persia than can be found in the general histories of religion, A. Erman's *Handbook of Egyptian Religion* (transl., London, 1907), J. H. Breasted's *Development of Religion and Thought in Ancient Egypt* (New York, 1912), M. Jastrow's *Aspects of Religious Belief in Babylonia and Assyria* (New York, 1911), which for most readers will be found more satisfactory than his earlier and more exhaustive work on the *Religion of Babylonia and Assyria* (Boston, 1898), J. H. Moulton's *Early Zoroastrianism* (London, 1913), and M. N. Dhalla's *Zoroastrian Theology* (New York, 1914) may be consulted, but no single work in English covers the ancient Persian field as adequately as A. V. W. Jackson's "Die iranische Religion" in the second volume of the *Grundriss der iranischen Philologie* (2 vols., Strassburg, 1896–1904). There is a vast literature on the Jewish antecedents of Christianity, from which the following may be selected: for the Old Testament period, J. P. Peters's *Religion of the Hebrews* (Boston and London, 1914), K. Budde's *Religion of Israel to the Exile* (transl., London and New York, 1899), A. B. Davidson's *Old Testament Prophecy* (Edinburgh, 1903) and his *Old Testament Theology* (Edinburgh, 1904), and A. Bertholet's *History of Hebrew Civilization* (transl., London, 1926); for the period between the Old and the New Testaments, W. Fairweather's *Background of the Gospels, or Judaism in the Period between the Old and New Testaments* (Edinburgh, 1908), G. F. Moore's *Judaism in the First Centuries of the Christian Era* (2 vols., Cambridge, Mass., 1927), E. Schürer's *History of the Jewish People in the Time of Jesus Christ* (transl., 5 vols., London, 1885–91), J. Klausner's *Jesus of Nazareth* (transl., London and New York, 1925), R. T. Herford's *Pharisaism* (London, 1912), and J. Drummond's *Philo Judaeus, or the Jewish Alexandrian Philosophy* (2 vols., London, 1888); and for an elementary survey of both periods, G. A. Barton's *Religion of Israel* (New York, 1918). Two volumes of studies by various scholars, *The People and the Book*, edited by A. S. Peake (Oxford, 1925), and *The Legacy of Israel*, edited by E. R. Bevan and C. Singer (Oxford, 1927), sum up the ancient and mediæval contributions of Israel to religion and thought. The influence of these and other Oriental religions in the Roman Empire is dealt with in the next section.

There is no better introduction to the history of the ancient world, Oriental as well as Greek and Roman, than J. H. Breasted's elementary but highly competent textbook on *Ancient Times* (Boston, 1914); M. Rostovtzeff's ampler *History of the Ancient World* (transl., 2 vols., Oxford, 1926–27) covers somewhat the same ground from another point of view and with greater interpretative insight; for fuller information the *Cambridge Ancient History* (8 vols., vols. i–vii, Cambridge, 1923–28) should be consulted.

GREEK AND ROMAN SOURCES

The chapter on "Religion" in G. L. Dickinson's *Greek View of Life* (London and New York, 1906), a brief survey like L. R. Farnell's article on "Greek Religion" in Hastings's *Encyclopaedia of Religion and Ethics* or A. Fairbanks's *Handbook of Greek Religion* (New York, 1910), and especially C. H. Moore's *Religious Thought of the Greeks* (2nd ed., Cambridge, Mass., 1925), may serve as introductions to a large literature, which includes, for the general temper of Greek religion, G. Murray's *Five Stages of Greek Religion* (new ed., Oxford, 1925), in which the growth of mysticism is explained by the facile formula of "failure of nerve," and L. R. Farnell's *Higher Aspects of Greek Religion* (London, 1912); for worship and belief, E. Rohde's *Psyche: The Cult of Souls and Belief in Immortality among the Greeks* (transl., London and New York, 1925), J. E. Harrison's *Prolegomena to the Study of Greek Religion* (3rd ed., Cambridge, 1922), and L. R. Farnell's *Cults of the Greek States* (5 vols., Oxford, 1896–1909); and for religious ideas, J. Adam's *Religious Teachers of Greece* (Edinburgh, 1908), E. Caird's *Evolution of Theology in the Greek Philosophers* (2 vols., Glasgow, 1904), and P. E. Moore's *Religion of Plato* (Princeton and London, 1921). Two recent histories of Greek religion by foreign scholars, M. P. Nilsson's (transl., Oxford, 1925) and P. Zielinski's (transl., Oxford, 1927), give a somewhat different, though in the second case hardly wiser, treatment to the subject. The most important texts are translated in F. M. Cornford's *Greek Religious Thought from Homer to the Age of Alexander* (London, 1923) and E. Bevan's *Later Greek Religion* (London, 1927), which together furnish an excellent bird's-eye view of the whole field from the beginnings to the triumph of Christianity.

For Roman religion, W. W. Fowler's *Religious Experience of the Roman People* (London, 1911), with the possible addition of S. Dill's *Roman Society from Nero to Marcus Aurelius* (London, 1904) and J. B. Carter's *Religious Life of Ancient Rome* (Boston, 1911), will probably suffice; for the Oriental and other influences in the Empire at the time of the expansion of Christianity, F. Cumont's *Oriental Religions in Roman Paganism* (transl., Chicago, 1911), T. R. Glover's *Conflict of Religions in the Roman Empire* (London, 1909), and J. Oakesmith's *Religion of Plutarch* (London, 1902); for Mithraism and Manichaeism, F. Cumont's *Mysteries of Mithra* (transl., 2nd ed., Chicago, 1910), F. C. Burkitt's *Religion of the Manichees*

(Cambridge, 1925), F. Legge's *Forerunners and Rivals of Christianity* (2 vols., Cambridge, 1915), the articles on "Mithraism," "Manichaeism," and "Mandaeans" in Hastings's *Encyclopaedia of Religion and Ethics*, and especially A. V. W. Jackson's forthcoming book on the history of Manichaeism. For the pagan "mysteries," Rohde's *Psyche*, Harrison's *Prolegomena*, and as a general introduction to the subject, F. M. Cornford's chapter on "The Mystery Religions and Pre-Socratic Philosophy" in the *Cambridge Ancient History* or the articles on "Mysteries" in Hastings's *Encyclopaedia of Religion and Ethics*, may be consulted; for recent statements of their influence on Christianity, S. Angus's *The Mystery Religions and Christianity* (London, 1925) and A. D. Nock's article on "Early Gentile Christianity" in *Essays on the Trinity and the Incarnation*, edited by A. E. J. Rawlinson (London, 1928).

A systematic treatment of classical mythology will be found in W. S. Fox's *Greek and Roman Mythology* (Boston, 1916; useful bibliography), the first volume of a valuable series, *The Mythology of All Races*, edited by L. H. Gray, which is to extend to thirteen volumes, and already includes Egypt, Persia, India, etc. The mediæval survival of the goddess Fortuna and of the concept of chance is dealt with in H. R. Patch's *The Goddess Fortuna in Mediæval Literature* (Cambridge, Mass., 1927). The religious and philosophic writings ascribed to Hermes Trismegistus may be read in English in W. Scott's *Hermetica* (4 vols., Oxford, 1924 sq.) or in G. R. S. Mead's *Thrice-Greatest Hermes* (3 vols., London, 1906). The closing days of the pagan world are described with more charm and insight, though with no more learning, in G. Boissier's *La fin du paganisme* (2 vols., Paris, 1891; 6th ed., 1909) than in S. Dill's *Roman Society in the Last Century of the Western Empire* (2nd ed., London and New York, 1899).

EARLY CHRISTIANITY

P. Wernle's *Beginnings of Christianity* (transl., 2 vols., London and New York, 1903–04), which has been largely followed in the present work, and A. C. McGiffert's *History of Christianity in the Apostolic Age* (2nd ed., New York, 1910) are good surveys of the origins of Christianity; a briefer treatment, with special emphasis on the historical environment, will be found in S. J. Case's *Evolution of Early Christianity* (Chicago, 1914) and F. J. F. Jackson's *Studies in the Life of the Early Church* (New York, 1924). L. Duchesne's *Early History of the Christian Church* (transl., 3 vols., London and New York, 1909–24) is one of the best histories of the early church; B. J. Kidd's *History of the Church to A. D. 461* (3 vols., Oxford, 1922) and H. M. Gwatkin's *Church History to A. D. 313* (2 vols., London, 1909) deal with the subject from other points of view. Probably the simplest introduction to the historical problems of the New Testament is B. W. Bacon's *Making of the New Testament* (Home University Library, 1912); A. Jülicher's *Introduction to the New Testament* (transl., London and New York, 1904) and A. H. McNeile's *Introduction to the Study of the New Testament* (Oxford, 1927) are more detailed, while J. Moffatt's *Introduction to the Literature of the New Testament* (3rd ed., Edinburgh,

1918) is exhaustive, but more particularly for the specialist. H. H. Wendt's *The Teachings of Jesus* (transl., 2 vols., Edinburgh, 1892) may be supplemented by J. Moffatt's *Theology of the Gospels* (London, 1912) and E. F. Scott's *The Fourth Gospel: Its Purpose and Theology* (Edinburgh, 1908). Matthew Arnold's *St. Paul and Protestantism* (1870) and the essay on "St. Paul" in W. R. Inge's *Outspoken Essays* (London and New York, 1919) are excellent introductions to the study of St. Paul's character and thought; to these may be added P. Gardner's *Religious Experience of St. Paul* (London, 1911) and A. Deissmann's *Paul, A Study in Social and Religious History* (transl., 2nd ed., London, 1926); and for the influence of the pagan mysteries, perhaps the ablest and most moderate statement of the case is H. A. A. Kennedy's *St. Paul and the Mystery Religions* (London and New York, 1913). E. von Dobschütz's *Christian Life in the Primitive Church* (transl., London, 1904) studies the life of the early converts; for an understanding of the spirit of early Christianity and the actual means by which it arrived at its commanding position in the Roman Empire A. Harnack's *Mission and Expansion of Christianity in the First Three Centuries* (transl., 2nd ed., 2 vols., London, 1908) is indispensable. E. Hatch's *Influence of Greek Ideas and Usages upon the Christian Church* (7th ed., London, 1898) is still the best account of Greek influences on early Christianity; C. Bigg's *Christian Platonists of Alexandria* (2nd ed., London, 1913) describes the influence of Neo-Platonism and the origin of the doctrine of the Logos, in Philo, Origen, and Clement of Alexandria. The first volume of P. Batiffol's important work on the constitution of the early Catholic Church has been translated under the title of *Primitive Catholicism* (London, 1911).

G. Krüger's *History of Early Christian Literature* (transl., London and New York, 1897) is a concise handbook of the literature of the first three centuries; C. T. Cruttwell's *Literary History of Early Christianity* (2 vols., London and New York, 1893) is more readable but less authoritative. The early non-canonical literature may be read most conveniently in the *Apocryphal New Testament*, translated by M. R. James (Oxford, 1924), and the *Apostolic Fathers*, translated by Kirsopp Lake (2 vols., Loeb Classical Library, 1913); and the chief patristic writers to the time of Gregory the Great have been translated in the *Ante-Nicene Fathers* (10 vols., New York, 1896) and *Nicene and Post-Nicene Fathers* (26 vols., New York, 1886–95). B. J. Kidd's *Documents Illustrative of the History of the Church to A.D. 461* (2 vols., London, 1920–23) and J. C. Ayer's *Source Book for Ancient Church History* (New York, 1913) are convenient collections of translated texts. Useful bibliographical suggestions for the study of the Old and New Testaments and early Christianity in general will be found in Smith's *Guide to the Study of the Christian Religion.*

GNOSTICISM

There is no better introduction to the study of Gnosticism than J. P. Arendzen's article on "Gnosticism" in the *Catholic Encyclopedia;* and some of the most important Gnostic texts may be read in English in G. R. S. Mead's theosophically tinctured *Fragments of a Faith Forgotten*

(London, 1900) and in the translations of the *Pistis Sophia* by G. Horner (London and New York, 1924) and G. R. S. Mead (London, 1896). Fuller treatment of the subject may be found in F. Legge's *Forerunners and Rivals of Christianity*, C. W. King's valuable but somewhat antiquated *Gnostics and their Remains* (2nd ed., London, 1887), Harnack's *History of Dogma*, and J. Watson's *Philosophic Basis of Religion* (Glasgow, 1907), the last a defence of the intellectualistic basis of Gnosticism against Harnack and others. One of the most searching studies of the subject, W. Bousset's *Hauptprobleme der Gnosis* (Göttingen, 1907), has not been translated into English, but its author has summarized its conclusions in his article on "Gnosticism" in the *Encyclopaedia Britannica*, 11th ed. The chief Christian opponents of Gnosticism, Irenaeus, Tertullian, and Hippolytus, may be read in English in the *Ante-Nicene Fathers*.

MONASTICISM

The traditional view of monasticism and its history is presented with scholarly moderation in E. C. Butler's article on "Monasticism" in the first volume of the *Cambridge Mediæval History* and in his *Benedictine Monachism* (London, 1919), and with romantic fervour in Montalembert's *Monks of the Occident from St. Benedict to St. Bernard* (transl., 6 vols., London, 1896). More or less divergent views are expressed in H. B. Workman's *Evolution of the Monastic Ideal* (London, 1913), A. Harnack's lecture on *Monasticism* (transl., London, 1901), and especially G. G. Coulton's *Five Centuries of Religion* (vols. i–ii, Cambridge, 1923–27), a valuable contribution to the social and economic history of monasticism, though one-sided enough in its emphasis on defects to give point to a Catholic reviewer's description of it as "muckraking the monks." [1] All of these works have much to tell us, and O. Zöckler's *Askese und Mönchthum* (2nd ed., Frankfurt, 1901) possibly has something to add to them; but we must agree with a distinguished German historian that a truly philosophical and impartial history of the whole movement still remains to be written. The *Rule of St. Benedict* may be read in Cardinal Gasquet's version (London, 1925). There is a convenient account of all the religious orders in F. Cabrol's article on "Religious Orders, Christian" in Hastings's *Encyclopaedia of Religion and Ethics;* but there is nothing in English to match the exhaustive treatment and full bibliographies of M. Heimbucher's *Die Orden und Kongregationen der katholischen Kirche* (2nd ed., 3 vols., Paderborn, 1907–8). The mediæval arguments on the relative merits of the active and the contemplative life are summed up in the in-

[1] In an appendix on "American Mediævalists" (vol. 1, page 521) Coulton comments rather acidly on Taylor's *Mediæval Mind*, Adams's *Mont-Saint-Michel and Chartres*, and Cram's romantic *Gothic Quest;* but are not the professional mummifiers of mediæval literature, in America at least, quite as fair game as the generalizers and enthusiasts? And are there not historians even in England who are amazed and indignant at finding that human institutions are human, and who need to be reminded of Dr. Johnson's outburst: "Sir, you are so grossly ignorant of human nature as not to know that a man may be very sincere in good principles without having good practice"?

troduction to J. Zeitlin's translation of Petrarch's *Life of Solitude* (University of Illinois Press, 1924) and in the second part of E. C. Butler's *Western Mysticism* (London, 1922).

MEDIÆVAL CHRISTIANITY

The mediæval church may be studied in the general histories already mentioned, or in special works such as A. Lagarde's *Latin Church in the Middle Ages* (transl., New York, 1915), which contains much valuable material, F. J. Foakes Jackson's *Introduction to the History of Christianity, A.D. 590–1314* (New York, 1921), or M. Deansley's briefer *History of the Mediæval Church* (London, 1925). H. H. Milman's *History of Latin Christianity* (2nd ed., 6 vols., London, 1857), though somewhat antiquated, is still valuable. The rapid historical sketch of *The Papacy* by G. Krüger (transl., London, 1909) will serve as an introduction to the larger histories; the Catholic point of view, as stated briefly in G. H. Joyce's article on the "Pope" in the *Catholic Encyclopedia* and A. Fortescue's *Early Papacy* (London, 1920), may be set off against the hostile Protestant views in A. Fawkes's article on the "Papacy" in Hastings's *Encyclopaedia* and E. Denny's *Papalism* (London, 1912). There is no English equivalent for the collection of Latin and other texts massed in C. Mirbt's *Quellen zur Geschichte des Papsttums und des römischen Katholizismus* (4th ed., Tübingen, 1924), illustrating the whole history of the Papacy; but the crucial texts of the first four centuries relating to the historic claims of the Papacy are conveniently translated in Shotwell and Loomis's *The See of Peter* (New York, 1927). Useful introductory bibliographies of the mediæval church will be found in Paetow's *Guide* and the *Cambridge Mediæval History;* but Vossler is concerned with religious feeling and not with ecclesiastical politics.

Those who feel the need of the most elementary information in regard to the organization and ceremonies of the Catholic Church, which the reader of a great Catholic poem should surely possess, can find it in the convenient little textbook of J. F. Sullivan, *The Visible Church* (2nd ed., New York, 1922), or in greater detail in Addis and Arnold's *Catholic Dictionary* (9th ed., London and St. Louis, 1917). The ceremonies are elaborately described in A. Fortescue's *Ceremonies of the Roman Rite Described* (London, 1898); and their history may be studied in such works as L. Duchesne's *Christian Worship, its Origin and Evolution* (transl., 5th ed., London and New York, 1919), which extends to the time of Charlemagne, A. Fortescue's *The Mass: A Study of the Roman Liturgy* (London, 1912), P. Batiffol's *History of the Roman Breviary* (transl., London, 1912), W. O. E. Oesterley's *Jewish Background of the Christian Liturgy* (Oxford, 1925), and E. Bishop's *Liturgica Historica* (Oxford, 1918); Fortescue's articles in the *Catholic Encyclopedia* on "Canon of the Mass," "Liturgical Books," "Liturgy," "Mass, Liturgy of the," "Rites," etc., are excellent summaries; for the popular mediæval conception, see Coulton's *Five Centuries of Religion* (vol. 1, chapters 7–8). The hymns of the church are considered below in the section on Mediæval Latin Literature. Mediæval preaching is dealt with at second hand in E. C. Dargan's *History of Preaching, A.D. 70–1572* (New York, 1905) and at first hand in G. R. Owst's *Preaching in Mediæval England* (Cambridge, 1926), which may serve in a measure as substitutes for A. Lecoy de la Marche's *La chaire française au moyen âge* (2nd ed., Paris, 1886) and similar works; and extracts from representative sermons may be read in English in J. M. Neale's *Mediæval Preachers and Mediæval Preaching* (London, 1856) and G. C. Lee's popular *Orators of the Early and Mediæval Church* (*The World's Orators*, vol. iii, New York, 1900). T. F. Crane's edition of Jacques de Vitry's *Exempla* (London, 1890) and his article in the *Proceedings of the American Philosophical Society*, vol. xxi (Philadelphia, 1884) may be consulted for the manuals of anecdotes and stories for the use of the mediæval preacher.

Henry Adams's *Mont-Saint-Michel and Chartres* (Boston, 1913), E. Mâle's *Religious Art in France in the Thirteenth Century* (transl., London, 1913), and Y. Hirn's *The Sacred Shrine: A Study of the Poetry and Art of the Christian Church* (transl., London, 1912) emphasize in widely divergent ways the relation between mediæval art and the religious thought and feeling of the time, the first as a Puritan troubadour of the Virgin, the second as a specialist in mediæval art and religious literature, and the third as a student of aesthetics. The second volume of E. Moore's *Studies in Dante* (4 vols., Oxford, 1896–1917) contains an important essay on "Dante as a Religious Teacher, especially in Relation to Catholic Doctrine," and the first volume contains a careful investigation of his indebtedness to the Scriptures; other works on Dante's relation to Catholic theology include F. Hettinger's still useful though partisan *Dante's Divine Comedy, its Scope and Value* (abridged transl., 2nd ed., London, 1894) and A. F. Ozanam's sympathetic but antiquated *Dante and Catholic Philosophy* (transl., New York, 1897), originally published in 1839. The more general works on Dante's religious ideals, such as C. A. Dinsmore's *Teachings of Dante* (Boston, 1901), W. T. Harris's *Spiritual Sense of Dante's Divina Commedia* (Boston, 1896), W. Boyd Carpenter's *Spiritual Message of Dante* (London, 1914), and P. H. Wicksteed's *Dante: Six Sermons* (2nd ed., London, 1890), though often suggestive, are seldom of real importance. Many of the commentaries, expositions, and summaries in which the *Divine Comedy* has been threshed over, such as J. S. Carroll's *Exiles of Eternity* (London, 1903), *Prisoners of Hope* (1906), and *In Patria* (1911), which are concerned respectively with the *Inferno*, *Purgatorio*, and *Paradiso*, emphasize Dante's moral and religious teaching.

SAINTS, MYSTICS, AND HERETICS

Among the great canonized (or, in the case of Albertus Magnus, beatified) figures of the church mentioned in the *Divine Comedy*, there are biographies or studies of St. Augustine by J. McCabe (New York, 1903) and L. Bertrand (transl., New York, 1914); of St. Jerome by E. L. Cutts (London, 1878) and C. Martin (London, 1888); of Gregory the Great by F. H. Dudden (2 vols., London, 1905) and R. Hudleston (London, 1924), the former a valuable work; of St. Anselm by R. W. Church (London, 1870) and M. Rule (2 vols., London, 1883); of St. Bernard of Clairvaux by R. S. Storrs (New York, 1892) and J. C. Morrison (revised ed., London, 1868); of Albertus Magnus by J. Sigwart (abridged transl., London, 1876); of St. Bonaventura by L. Costelloe (London, 1911) and R. R. Thaddeus (London, 1908); and of St. Thomas Aquinas by R. W. B. Vaughan (2 vols., London, 1871–72) and P. Conway (New York, 1911); see below for St. Dominic and St. Francis. All the legends that had gathered about the lives of the saints were collected by Dante's elder contemporary, Jacobus de Voragine, in his *Golden Legend*, Caxton's version of which is reprinted in the Temple Classics (7 vols., London, 1900); and with this should be compared H. Delehaye's *Legends of the Saints* (transl., London, 1907), G. H. Gerould's *Saints' Legends* (Boston, 1916), H. Thurston's article on "Saints and Martyrs, Christian," E. von Dobschütz's on "Charms and Amulets, Christian," and J. A. MacCulloch's on "Relics" in Hastings's *Encyclopaedia of Religion and Ethics*, and for convenient reference, F. G. Holweck's *Biographical Dictionary of the Saints* (St. Louis and London, 1924).

The most sympathetic and suggestive study of Catholic mysticism, despite its labored and ponderous style, is F. von Hügel's *Mystical Element in Religion* (2nd ed., 2 vols., London, 1923); H. Joly's *Psychology of the Saints* (transl., London, 1898), which in the original bears the imprimatur of the Archbishop of Paris, is a much slighter but more lucid contribution to the subject; with these may be compared, as of opposing worlds, the analysis of the church fathers and mediæval theologians in C. G. Jung's *Psychological Types* (transl., London and New York, 1923) and the chapters on "Saintliness" and "Mysticism" in W. James's *Varieties of Religious Experience* (London and New York, 1902). There is a considerable but not always reliable literature on the history of Christian mysticism, including W. R. Inge's *Christian Mysticism* (London, 1899), an interesting historical sketch emphasizing the Platonic tradition, but least adequate for the period between Augustine and Eckhart, E. G. Gardner's *Dante and the Mystics* (London, 1913), which deals with the influence of mystical writers on the *Divine Comedy*, E. C. Butler's *Western Mysticism* (London, 1922), which is concerned chiefly with St. Augustine, Gregory the Great, and Bernard of Clairvaux, R. M. Jones's *Studies in Mystical Religion* (London, 1909), essays on Christian mystics from St. Paul to George Fox, and E. Lehmann's *Mysticism in Heathendom and Christendom* (transl., London, 1910), a rapid and somewhat unsympathetic sketch of Oriental, Greek, and Christian mysticism; there is a useful bibliography in Evelyn Underhill's *Mysticism* (London, 1911) and in the notes to J. Bernhart's *Die philosophische Mystik des Mittelalters* (Munich, 1922). There is no thorough monograph in English on the work of Dionysius the Areopagite, which was so influential throughout the Middle Ages, but J. Stiglmayr's article on "Dionysius the Pseudo-Areopagite" in the *Catholic Encyclopedia*, in conjunction with J. H. Lupton's article in Smith and Wace's *Dictionary of Christian Biography* (4 vols., London, 1877–87), is a good introduction to the subject, and further light may be obtained from B. F. Westcott's *Essays in the History of Religious Thought in the West* (London,

1891) and the books by Inge and Jones just mentioned; for his influence on Dante see Gardner's *Dante's Ten Heavens* (2nd ed., London, 1904) and *Dante and the Mystics*, and the article on "Dionisio" in Toynbee's larger *Dante Dictionary;* for the translations of Rolt and Parker, the former containing an appendix on "The Influence of Dionysius in Religious History" by W. J. Sparrow-Simpson, see the section on Translations under Mediæval Thought below.

On mediæval heresy and the Inquisition, H. C. Lea's *History of the Inquisition of the Middle Ages* (3 vols., New York, 1887) is still authoritative, but should be read in conjunction with the divergent views expressed in E. Vacandard's *The Inquisition* (transl., London, 1908), A. S. Turberville's *Mediæval Heresy and the Inquisition* (London, 1921), A. L. Maycock's *The Inquisition from its Establishment to the Great Schism* (London, 1927), and the articles on "Heresy" and "Inquisition" in the *Catholic Encyclopedia.* For the theological or doctrinal details of mediæval heresy, the reader may consult, in addition to Turberville's summary, the histories of Christian doctrine such as Harnack's or Seeberg's, Bussell's *Religious Thought and Heresy in the Middle Ages*, J. H. Blunt's *Dictionary of Sects* (7th ed., London, 1903), and the articles on individual heresies in the encyclopaedias of religion.

THE MENDICANT ORDERS; THE FRANCISCAN MOVEMENT

A sketch of the rise of the Mendicant Orders will be found in J. Herkless's *Francis and Dominic* (London, 1901) and in Lea's *History of the Inquisition of the Middle Ages* (chapters on "The Mendicant Orders" and "The Spiritual Franciscans"); and the second volume of Coulton's *Five Centuries of Religion* and his *From St. Francis to Dante* (see above) are important contributions to their history, especially on its less amiable side; but P. Mandonnet's article on "Preachers, Order of" (Dominicans), M. Bihl's on "Friars Minor" (Franciscans), M. Heimbucher's on "Hermits of St. Augustine" (Augustinians), and B. Zimmermann's on "Carmelite Order" in the *Catholic Encyclopedia*, with their bibliographies, are still probably the best accounts of these four orders in English. The influence of the Mendicant Orders on the intellectual life of the Middle Ages is summed up in sections 150–153 of De Wulf's *History of Mediæval Philosophy* (1926 edition; see below). Further information concerning the Dominicans may be sought in A. T. Drane's *Spirit of the Dominican Order* (London, 1896), E. Barker's *Dominican Order and Convocation* (Oxford, 1913), G. R. Galbraith's *Constitution of the Dominican Order, 1216–1360* (Manchester, 1925), the thirteenth century *Lives of the Brethren* (transl., London, 1896), and the biographies of St. Dominic by A. T. Drane (London, 1891), J. Guiraud (transl., London, 1901), and B. Jarrett (London, 1924).

E. Gebhart's *Mystics and Heretics in Italy at the End of the Middle Ages* (transl., London, 1922) is an admirable account of the spiritual ferment produced by the Franciscan movement in the age preceding Dante; and Ellen S. Davison's *Forerunners of St. Francis* (Boston, 1927) indicates some of its origins. P. Sabatier's *Life of St. Francis* (transl., New York,

1894) still remains the most interesting and valuable biography of the saint (compare E. C. Butler's strictures in the *Encyclopædia Britannica*, 11th ed., vol. x, page 939, and P. Robinson's in *The Real St. Francis*, 1904). Other lives, especially those by Father Cuthbert (London, 1912) and J. Jörgensen (transl., London, 1912), may be read as correctives; both of these contain discussions of the sources. The famous *Little Flowers of St. Francis*, which reflects what has been called "the temperament of the early Franciscan movement," and two early biographies, the *Mirror of Perfection* and St. Bonaventura's *Life of St. Francis*, have been gathered together in one volume of Everyman's Library (London, 1910); T. W. Arnold's version of the *Little Flowers* (6th ed., London, 1903), A. G. F. Howell's of the *Lives of St. Francis by Thomas of Celano* (1908), and E. Gurney-Salter's of the *Legend of St. Francis by the Three Companions* (1902) have been published in the Temple Classics. P. Robinson has translated the *Writings of St. Francis* (London, 1906), and has written a useful *Short Introduction to Franciscan Literature* (New York, 1907); there is also a brief *Guide to Franciscan Studies* by A. G. Little (London, 1920). A bibliography of the vast literature, English and foreign, called forth by the recent celebration of the seventh centenary of St. Francis's death has been published by C. Pitollet in the *Revue d'histoire franciscaine* (Paris, July-December, 1926); one of these volumes, *St. Francis of Assisi, 1226–1926: Essays in Commemoration* (London, 1926), contains an essay by E. G. Gardner on "St. Francis and Dante." The influence of St. Francis on mediæval art is discussed in Anna Jameson's popular *Legends of the Monastic Orders* (1850; ed. by E. M. Hurll, Boston, 1895), J. Kerr-Lawson's essay on "The Influence of the Franciscan Legend on Italian Art" appended to Mrs. Robert Goff's *Assisi of St. Francis* (London, 1908), E. Gurney-Salter's *Franciscan Legends in Italian Art* (London, 1905), B. Berenson's *A Sienese Painter of the Franciscan Legend* (London, 1909), and other works, but nowhere in English with as much insight as in H. Thode's *Franz von Assisi und die Anfänge der Kunst der Renaissance in Italien* (2nd ed., Berlin, 1904). See also the section on Italian Literature below.

THE HEREAFTER

All the histories of religion discuss the idea of a future life, but the articles on "Eschatology" and "State of the Dead" in Hastings's *Encyclopaedia of Religion and Ethics* are useful introductions to the whole field. On the Egyptian, Babylonian, and Persian conceptions of the hereafter, E. A. Wallis Budge's *Egyptian Ideas of the Future Life* (London, 1899) and *Egyptian Heaven and Hell* (3 vols., London, 1906), A. Wiedemann's *Ancient Egyptian Doctrine of the Immortality of the Soul* (transl., London, 1895), M. Jastrow's *Hebrew and Babylonian Traditions* (New York, 1914) and his other works already cited, Dhalla's *Zoroastrian Theology*, and S. H. Mills's *Avesta Eschatology compared with the Books of Daniel and Revelation* (Chicago and London, 1908) may be consulted; but Mills's exaggerated views of Zoroastrian influence have been corrected by Moulton's *Early Zoroastrianism* and other works. The Greek conception is dealt with in Rohde's *Psyche*, the main authority, and

L. R. Farnell's *Greek Hero Cults and Ideas of Immortality* (Oxford, 1921); and the Roman in C. H. Moore's *Pagan Ideas of Immortality during the Early Roman Empire* (Cambridge, Mass., 1918), F. Cumont's *After Life in Roman Paganism* (transl., New Haven, 1922), and the chapter on "Hades" in T. R. Glover's *Virgil* (2nd ed., London, 1912). For Hebrew eschatology, the chief authorities are R. H. Charles's *Critical History of the Doctrine of a Future Life in Israel, in Judaism, and in Christianity* (2nd ed., London, 1913) and W. O. E. Oesterley's *Doctrine of the Last Things, Jewish and Christian* (London, 1908) and *Immortality and the Unseen World: A Study of the Old Testament* (London, 1921). Two of these works, as their titles indicate, deal also with the Christian conception, and to these should be added S. D. F. Salmond's *Christian Doctrine of Immortality* (5th ed., Edinburgh, 1903), F. von Hügel's rather muddled sketch, *Eternal Life* (Edinburgh, 1912), Harnack's *History of Dogma*, H. L. Jackson's *Eschatology of Jesus* (London, 1913), E. von Dobschütz's *Eschatology of the Gospels* (transl., London, 1910), H. A. A. Kennedy's *St. Paul's Conceptions of the Last Things* (London, 1904), and E. C. Dewick's *Primitive Christian Eschatology* (Cambridge, 1912). The eschatology of the scholastic period is summed up in Otten's *Manual of the History of Dogma* (vol. ii, chapter 24); and the articles in the *Catholic Encyclopedia* on "Hell," "Purgatory," "Heaven," "Eschatology," "Judgment, Divine," "Resurrection," "Millennium," "Angels," "Devil," "Demonology," etc., also contain useful information. The doctrine of Thomas Aquinas may be found in the final section of the *Summa Theologica* (part iii, questions 68–119); and the popular mediæval conception of the hereafter is described in Coulton's *Five Centuries of Religion* (vol. i, chapters 4–5, and appendix 2). For Mohammedan eschatology, the reader may consult D. B. Macdonald's *Development of Muslim Theology, Jurisprudence, and Constitutional Theory* (London and New York, 1903) and E. Sell's concise exposition in *The Faith of Islam* (London, 1880). There is an extensive bibliography of eschatological literature up to 1862, by Ezra Abbott, appended to W. R. Alger's *Critical History of the Doctrine of a Future Life* (10th ed., Boston, 1880). Monographs on Dante's relations to these various conceptions are cited below in the section on Apocalpytic Literature.

III. Mediæval Thought

The first volume of J. E. Erdmann's *History of Philosophy* (transl., 3rd ed., London, 1898) is still probably the best summary of ancient and mediæval philosophy available in English; the briefer and radically different treatment in W. Windelband's *History of Philosophy* (transl., New York, 1893) is also good. R. Eucken's *The Problem of Human Life as Viewed by the Great Thinkers* (transl., London and New York, 1909) discusses the great Greek and Christian philosophers with special reference to their attitude to the "spiritual life." Of the many brief manuals, W. Turner's Catholic *History of Philosophy* (Boston, 1903) is the only one that gives adequate, or perhaps more than adequate, space to the scholastic philosophers; but the briefer treatment in A. Weber's *History of Philosophy* (transl., New York, 1897), by reason of its French lucidity, may be more helpful to the beginner. As for works devoted exclusively to mediæval philosophy, Maurice de Wulf's *History of Mediæval Philosophy* (transl. from the 5th French ed., 2 vols., London, 1926; earlier editions inferior) and his more popular lectures on *Philosophy and Civilization in the Middle Ages* (London and Princeton, 1922) present the subject with real learning but with strong neoscholastic partisanship; and it may seem to many, as to Guido de Ruggiero (*La filosofia contemporanea*, 2nd ed., Bari, 1920, vol. ii, page 204), that "a vast and profound knowledge of mediæval thought is in De Wulf's *History* falsified and annulled by an obstinate determination to treat history according to a criterion that is completely anti-historical." Taylor's *Mediæval Mind* is useful in placing the mediæval philosophers as elements in an historic culture rather than in unravelling their thought: "it is enough," its author says (2nd ed., vol. ii, page 449), "to witness the spiritual attitude of these men without tracking them through the 'selva oscura' to their lairs of meditation."

Of all these works De Wulf's *History* contains by far the best bibliographies, but there is nothing in English so rich in bibliographical information as the tenth edition of F. Ueberweg's *Grundriss der Geschichte der Philosophie der patristischen und scholastischen Zeit*, edited by M. Baumgartner (Berlin, 1915); there is an English version of an earlier edition of his *History of Philosophy* (transl., 4th ed., 2 vols., London, 1885), but its bibliographical material is very much scantier and more or less antiquated. Nor is there in English so thorough a study of the scholastic method as M. Grabmann's *Die Geschichte der scholastischen Methode* (vols. i–ii, Freiburg i. B., 1909–11), which has not yet reached the period of Aquinas; nor any work quite like Guido de Ruggiero's *La filosofia del cristianesimo* (3 vols., Bari, 1920), a history of mediæval philosophy written from the standpoint of modern Italian idealism. The second volume of G. Brett's *History of Psychology* (3 vols., London,

1912–21) is devoted to the mediæval and early modern period. It may be worth adding that the articles on the mediæval philosophers in the *Catholic Encyclopedia* (for example, Augustine, Bonaventura, Duns Scotus, Hugh of St. Victor, Thomas Aquinas, etc.) are for the most part vastly superior to those in any other English work of reference; some of the articles in the *Encyclopaedia Britannica* (for example, Albertus Magnus, Hugh of St. Victor, etc.) are pathetically inadequate.

CLASSICAL SOURCES

For the Graeco-Roman background of mediæval thought, the reader may prefer a brief survey like W. Windelband's *History of Ancient Philosophy* (transl., New York, 1899) or W. T. Stace's lucid *Critical History of Greek Philosophy* (London, 1920), before proceeding to more comprehensive works like A. W. Benn's *Greek Philosophers* (2 vols., London, 1882) and especially T. Gomperz's brilliant though somewhat diffuse *Greek Thinkers* (transl., 4 vols., London, 1906–12), which closes with Aristotle and his immediate successors. E. Zeller's history of Greek philosophy remains unrivalled, however, as a storehouse of information; it has been translated in sections as the *History of Greek Philosophy before the Time of Socrates* (2 vols., London, 1881), *Socrates and the Socratic Schools* (1868), *Plato and the Older Academy* (1876), *Aristotle and the Earlier Peripatetics* (2 vols., 1897), *Stoics, Epicureans, and Sceptics* (1870), and *History of Eclecticism* (1883); but for the fullest bibliographies the reader must consult the twelfth edition of F. Ueberweg's *Grundriss der Geschichte der Philosophie: Die Philosophie des Altertums*, edited by K. Praechter (Berlin, 1926).

As for Aristotle, who is mentioned or referred to by Dante more than a hundred times, A. E. Taylor's *Aristotle* (2nd ed., London, 1919), or the article on Aristotle in E. Boutroux's *Historical Studies in Philosophy* (transl., London, 1912), is a good elementary introduction, and E. Wallace's *Outlines of the Philosophy of Aristotle* (3rd ed., Cambridge, 1883) a brief but very convenient résumé of his thought; for fuller treatment, W. D. Ross's *Aristotle* (London, 1923) and especially the introduction to his edition of Aristotle's *Metaphysics* (2 vols., Oxford, 1924) may be added to the indispensable Zeller, the relevant chapters in Gomperz, and the works cited below under Ethical Theory, Political Theory, and Mediæval Science. Of the translations of his works, mention may be made of W. D. Ross's version of the *Metaphysics* (Oxford, 1908), J. E. C. Welldon's of the *Ethics* (London, 1892), B. Jowett's of the *Politics* (2 vols., Oxford, 1885), and R. D. Hicks's of the *De Anima* (Cambridge, 1907), the first of these forming part of a complete translation of Aristotle's works now being brought out under the editorship of J. A. Smith and W. D. Ross.

The following may be consulted for other phases of ancient philosophy: for the early period, J. Burnet's *Early Greek Philosophers* (3rd ed., London, 1920), which contains translations of many of the early fragments, and his *Greek Philosophy, Part I., Thales to Plato* (London, 1914); for Plato, a good elementary introduction like A. E. Taylor's *Plato* (London, 1908; reprinted 1922) or his larger treatise, *Plato, the Man and his Work* (London, 1926), a sympathetic but temperamental interpretation like W. Pater's *Plato and Platonism* (London, 1893) or P. E. More's *Platonism* (Princeton, N. J., and London, 1917), a standard work monumental yet limited in its outlook like G. Grote's *Plato and the Other Companions of Socrates* (3rd ed., 3 vols., London, 1875), or special studies like J. A. Stewart's *Plato's Doctrine of Ideas* (Oxford, 1909) and his *Myths of Plato* (London, 1905), W. Lutoslawski's *Origin and Growth of Plato's Logic* (2nd ed., London and New York, 1905), and R. L. Nettleship's *Lectures on the Republic of Plato* (2nd ed., London, 1901); for the later period, R. D. Hicks's *Stoic and Epicurean* (London, 1910), E. Bevan's lectures on *Stoics and Sceptics* (Oxford, 1913), T. Whittaker's *Neo-Platonists* (2nd ed., Cambridge, 1918), W. R. Inge's *Philosophy of Plotinus* (2nd ed., 2 vols., London, 1923) and his article on "Neo-Platonism" in Hastings's *Encyclopaedia of Religion and Ethics*, an admirably clear introduction to the whole subject; for the Roman philosophers, E. V. Arnold's *Roman Stoicism* (Cambridge, 1911), the best survey of the subject, Zeller's *History of Eclecticism*, or studies of individual writers, such as J. S. Reid's essay on Cicero as a philosopher prefixed to his edition of Cicero's *Academica* (London, 1885), T. W. Levin's *Lectures Introductory to the Philosophical Writings of Cicero* (Cambridge, 1871), J. Masson's *Lucretius, Epicurean and Poet* (2 vols., London, 1907–09), R. M. Gummere's *Seneca the Philosopher* (Boston, 1922), F. W. Bussell's *Marcus Aurelius and the Later Stoics* (Edinburgh, 1910), T. Whittaker's brief *Macrobius, or Philosophy, Science, and Letters in the Year 400* (Cambridge, 1923), and H. F. Stewart's *Boethius, An Essay* (Edinburgh, 1891).

On Plato's *Timaeus*, which exercised a vast influence on the Middle Ages and is the only Platonic dialogue mentioned by Dante, see the introduction to R. D. Archer-Hind's important edition and translation of the *Timaeus* (London, 1888), A. E. Taylor's *Commentary on Plato's Timaeus* (Oxford, 1928), and perhaps also B. Jowett's introduction to it in his translation of the *Dialogues of Plato* (3rd ed., 5 vols., Oxford, 1892) and the thirty-sixth chapter of Grote's *Plato*. Proclus's commentary on the *Timaeus* (transl., 2 vols., London, 1820) and his *Theology of Plato, Theological Elements*, and *On the Substance of Evil* (transl., 2 vols., London, 1816), which were the main sources of Dionysius the Areopagite and of the mediæval pseudo-Aristotelian *Liber de Causis*, may be read in the translation of Thomas Taylor, as may also three treatises of Porphyry (*Select Works of Porphyry*, transl., London, 1823); but the best translation of their master Plotinus is that of Stephen MacKenna (vols. i–iv, London, 1917–26). For the mediæval Latin translations of Aristotle and other Greek philosophers, which transformed the whole course of mediæval thought, see C. H. Haskins's *Studies in the History of Mediæval Science* (Cambridge, Mass., 1924), the eleventh chapter of his *Renaissance of the Twelfth Century*, and the excellent summary in the 144th section of De Wulf's *History of Mediæval Philosophy;* and for the influence of Greek and Roman philosophers on Dante, see the first volume of Moore's *Studies in Dante* (chapters on Aristotle, Plato, Cicero, and Seneca) and P. Toynbee's larger *Dante Dictionary* (articles on "Aristotile," "Platone," "Stoici," "Pittagore," "Epicuro," "Cicero," "Seneca," etc.), which may serve as general introductions to a motley horde of special monographs.

MONOGRAPHS

Mediæval philosophy is still more or less of an unplumbed sea for English-speaking students; and several of the great lovers of wisdom ("spiriti sapienti") whom Dante, in the tenth canto of the *Paradiso*, has placed in the Heaven of the Sun, still await adequate treatment or translation in English. The thought of the greatest of the scholastics has been the object of renewed interest, and may be studied in E. Gilson's *Philosophy of St. Thomas Aquinas* (transl., Cambridge, 1924), P. H. Wicksteed's *Dante and Aquinas* (London, 1913) and *Relations between Dogma and Philosophy Illustrated from the Works of S. Thomas Aquinas* (London, 1920), and M. de Wulf's *Mediæval Philosophy Illustrated from the System of Thomas Aquinas* (transl., London and Cambridge, Mass., 1922); D. J. Kennedy's article on "Thomas Aquinas" in the *Catholic Encyclopedia* is a good summary. But there is no better introduction to his thought, for those who are competent to receive it, than his own *Summa contra Gentiles*, which may be read in the translation of the English Dominican Fathers (4 vols., vols. i–ii, London, 1924) or in the abridged version of J. Rickaby, *Of God and his Creatures* (London, 1906): Rickaby's *Studies on God and his Creatures* (London, 1924) is a commentary on this treatise in dialogue form; C. C. J. Webb in his *Studies in the History of Natural Theology* (Oxford, 1915) devotes a chapter to it; and many of its thoughts may be traced in Donne, Milton, Sir Thomas Browne, Pope, and a host of lesser English writers. His chief work, the *Summa Theologica*, now completely accessible in English in the translation of the English Dominican Fathers (21 vols. and index, London, 1911–24), is fundamental and indispensable, but is perhaps too vast a structure for the novice to scale.

The philosophy of St. Bonaventura has been dealt with in the histories of Erdmann and De Wulf, Taylor's *Mediæval Mind*, and P. Robinson's article on "Bonaventure" in the *Catholic Encyclopedia*, but there is no study in English as thorough as E. Gilson's *La Philosophie de Saint Bonaventure* (Paris, 1924). Since Dante does not mention Abelard, for reasons which Gardner attempts to explain in *Dante and the Mystics* (pages 112–13), perhaps we need not regret that there is no adequate work in English on his philosophy; J. McCabe's biography, *Peter Abelard* (London and New York, 1901), and G. Compayré's *Abelard and the Origin of Universities* (transl., New York and London, 1893) are of little help from this point of view. But two other philosophers not mentioned by Dante have received more adequate treatment, in C. R. S. Harris's comprehensive *Duns Scotus* (2 vols., Oxford, 1927) and H. Bett's brief *Johannes Scotus Erigena* (Cambridge, 1925); the former incorporates the conclusions of German scholarship in regard to some of the fundamental problems of scholastic philosophy and contains an extensive bibliography. The biographies of the great figures of the church listed in the section on Saints, Mystics, and Heretics under Mediæval Religion, and the histories of philosophy, mysticism, and Christian doctrine already cited, should be consulted for the thought of other mediæval philosophers; but Albertus Magnus, Hugh and Richard of St. Victor, Peter Lombard, Alain de Lille (Alanus de Insulis), and a host of others, even Englishmen like Alexander of Hales and William Ockham,[1] still await the scholar prepared to give them adequate philosophical treatment in English.

Dante's indebtedness to Thomas Aquinas is discussed in Wicksteed's *Dante and Aquinas* and in many other works; to Albertus Magnus, in P. Toynbee's *Dante Studies and Researches* (London, 1902); to St. Bernard, Richard and Hugh of St. Victor, St. Bonaventura, etc., in Gardner's *Dante and the Mystics;* to Boethius and St. Augustine, in Moore's *Studies in Dante;* and to these and others, in Toynbee's larger *Dante Dictionary* under the names of the individual philosophers. Hettinger's *Dante's Divine Comedy, its Scope and Value* is useful in connection with Dante's relations to the mediæval philosophers; and the essay on Dante in G. Santayana's *Three Philosophical Poets* (Cambridge, Mass., 1910) is a brief and brilliant attempt to define the poet's place in the history of thought.

TRANSLATIONS

Many of the great patristic philosophers, including Tertullian, Cyprian, Origen, Clement of Alexandria, St. Augustine, and Gregory the Great, may be found in English in the two collections already referred to, the *Ante-Nicene Fathers* and the *Nicene and Post-Nicene Fathers;* and such mediæval classics as the following have also been rendered into English: Boethius's *Consolation of Philosophy* by innumerable translators from King Alfred and Chaucer to H. R. James (London, 1906) and H. F. Stewart (revision of a seventeenth century version, Loeb Classical Library, 1918); the works of Dionysius the Areopagite by J. Parker (2 vols., London, 1897–99) and *On the Divine Names* and *Mystical Theology* by E. Rolt (London, 1920); Anselm's *Proslogium, Monologium,* and *Cur Deus Homo* by S. N. Deane (Chicago, 1903); the works of Bernard of Clairvaux by S. J. Eales (4 vols., London, 1889–96), and his treatise *On Consideration* by G. Lewis (Oxford, 1908); Abelard's autobiographical *Historia Calamitatum*

[1] Perhaps in no other period has Britain been so rich in philosophers as during the Middle Ages; a considerable number of important thinkers of British birth are mentioned in every history of mediæval philosophy. What has English scholarship contributed to the interpretation of their *thought*—disregarding biographical, editorial, and similar labors, and studies in the history of natural science, as work of another nature? There are a few philosophical monographs, such as those on Duns Scotus and Scotus Erigena already mentioned; but what has been done for Alexander of Hales, William Ockham, Robert Grosseteste, Richard Rolle, Richard Middleton, Adelard of Bath, Robert Kilwardby, John Peckham, William of Ware, and even for John of Salisbury (see below), Roger Bacon (see below), and Richard of St. Victor? Perhaps philosophy, or philosophy such as theirs, has no meaning or value; that is doubtless the reason why we edit their writings or study the facts of their lives.

and his correspondence with Heloïse by C. Scott-Moncrieff (London and New York, 1925), and a portion of his *Ethics, or Know Thyself*, by E. K. Rand, in B. Rand's *Classical Moralists* (Boston, 1909); a large part of John of Salisbury's *Policraticus* by J. Dickinson (New York, 1927); Walter Map's *De Nugis Curialium*, if it may be allowed to edge itself into such company, by Tupper and Ogle (London and New York, 1924); Alain de Lille's *Complaint of Nature* by D. M. Moffat (New York, 1908); Thomas Aquinas's *Summa Theologica* and *Summa contra Gentiles* by the English Dominican Fathers (see above); and the works of Meister Eckhart by C. de B. Evans (London, 1924).

None of the works of St. Bonaventura, except one or two minor tracts and his life of St. Francis, appears to have been translated in recent times; a few brief excerpts are also translated in the appendix of Ozanam's *Dante and Catholic Philosophy;* but extensive selections have been rendered into French (*Théologie séraphique*, 2 vols., Paris, 1853) and a German translation is under way (*Werke des hl. Bonaventura*, vol. i, Munich, 1923). An old English version of part of Richard of St. Victor's *Benjamin Minor* is reprinted in E. G. Gardner's *Cell of Self-Knowledge* (London, 1910). Some of the mystical writings of Dante's Catalan contemporary, Ramón Lull, or Raymond Lully, have been translated by E. A. Peers (*Book of the Lover and the Beloved*, London, 1923; *Art of Contemplation*, 1925; *Tree of Love*, 1926). But the great mass of mediæval philosophy and theology must still be read in the original, as in J. P. Migne's uncritical but extremely valuable *Patrologiae Cursus Completus*, of which Matthew Arnold said, " People talk of this or that work which they would choose if they were to pass their life with only one; for my part I would choose the Abbé Migne's collection." His *Patrologia Latina* (221 vols., Paris, 1844–64) includes all the important writers of the Latin Church to the beginning of the thirteenth century, while his *Patrologia Graeca* (166 vols., Paris, 1857–66) includes the writers of the Greek Church to the fifteenth century.

ARABIC SOURCES

For the Arabian philosophers who influenced mediæval thought, T. J. de Boer's brief *History of Philosophy in Islam* (transl., London, 1903) and De L. O'Leary's rather sketchy *Arabic Thought and its Place in History* (London, 1922) will be found useful; but there is no such systematic synthesis in English as may be found in M. Horten's *Die Philosophie des Islam* (Munich, 1924), and Horten (page 357) casts serious doubts on De Boer's competence. The influence of Averroës, who is placed by Dante among the great pagan philosophers in Limbo, is dealt with in the histories of Erdmann and De Wulf, Turberville's *Mediæval Heresy and the Inquisition*, and other works; but there is in English no full account of mediæval Averroism such as may be found in P. Mandonnet's *Siger de Brabant et l'averroïsme latin au XIIIe siècle* (2nd ed., Louvain, 1911); this contains not only the most authoritative account of the great Averroist Siger de Brabant, whose "eternal light" is enshrined by Dante in Paradise (see P. Toynbee's larger *Dante Dictionary*, article on "Sigieri"), but also an excellent summary of the influence of Aristotle on mediæval thought; E. Renan's pioneer work on *Averroès et l'averroïsme* (3rd ed., Paris, 1869) may be superseded in other languages, but not in ours. Nor is there any full treatment of Avicenna, who shares Averroës's glory in Dante's Limbo: he is also discussed by Erdmann and De Wulf; his famous poem on the Soul may be read in E. G. Browne's *Literary History of Persia from Firdawsi to Sa'di* (London, 1906), and there is an English version, such as it is, of his *Compendium of the Soul* by E. A. Van Dyck (Verona, Italy, 1906!); but there is no English equivalent for B. Carra de Vaux's *Avicenne* (Paris, 1900), though there is a good article on "Avicenna" and another on "Averroës and Averroism" by Carra de Vaux in Hastings's *Encyclopaedia of Religion and Ethics.* The mystic Al Ghazali, who was known to the Middle Ages as Algazel, has fared somewhat better: S. M. Zwemer's *A Moslem Seeker after God* (New York, 1920), D. B. Macdonald's life of him in the *Journal of the American Oriental Society*, vol. xx (1899) and the same author's *Religious Attitude and Life in Islam* (Chicago, 1909), and M. Asín Palacios's *Islam and the Divine Comedy* (transl., London, 1926) summarize his ideas, and two of his books, his *Confessions* and the *Alchemy of Happiness*, are available in the Wisdom of the East series (transl., London, 1909–10), and the *Niche for Lights* in W. H. T. Gairdner's version (London, 1924). The Moslem conception of mystical contemplation is analyzed in R. A. Nicholson's *Mystics of Islam* (London, 1914) and in the essay on "The Perfect Man" in his *Studies in Islamic Mysticism* (Cambridge, 1921). The mediæval Latin translations of Arabic works are dealt with in Haskins's *Studies in the History of Mediæval Science;* and the articles on "Averrois," "Avicenna," "Algazel," "Alfergano," etc., in Toynbee's larger *Dante Dictionary* sum up Dante's indebtedness to these writers. For the mediæval Jewish philosophers, especially Avicebron and Maimonides, whose influence on scholasticism was so considerable that an enthusiast has said, with absurd but not unintelligible exaggeration, "No Maimonides, no Aquinas," I. Husik's *History of Mediæval Jewish Philosophy* (New York, 1918) and C. and D. W. Singer's valuable study of "The Jewish Factor in Mediæval Thought" in *The Legacy of Israel* may be consulted; for the mysteries of the Cabbala, A. Franck's *The Kabbalah, or the Religious Philosophy of the Hebrews* (transl., New York, 1926) or J. Abelson's *Jewish Mysticism* (London, 1913); and for the supposed influence of the Cabbala on Dante and Milton, Moore's *Studies in Dante* (vol. iii, pages 263–83) and D. Saurat's *Milton, Man and Thinker* (transl., New York, 1925, pages 280–322).

ETHICAL THEORY

Many of the works already mentioned, including the histories of philosophy and of Christian doctrine, such as Seeberg's and Harnack's, discuss mediæval ethics at some length, but there are also special histories of the subject, notably C. E. Luthardt's *Christian Ethics before the Reformation* (transl., Edinburgh, 1889) and T. C. Hall's *History of Ethics within Organized Christianity* (New York, 1910), and monographs on special fields, such as H. H. Scullard's *Early Christian Ethics* (London, 1907) and A. B. D. Alexander's *Ethics of St. Paul* (Glasgow,

1910); Alexander's articles on the "Seven Deadly Sins" and "Seven Virtues" in Hastings's *Encyclopaedia of Religion and Ethics* are also useful; and the Jesuit T. Slater, in his *Short History of Moral Theology* (New York, 1909), has attempted to sum up the history of Catholic ethics in fifty pages. The chief ethical loci of Thomas Aquinas, from the second part of the *Summa Theologica*, are translated in J. Rickaby's *Aquinas Ethicus* (2 vols., London, 1892); and there are brief summaries of his ethical theory in Sidgwick's *Outlines* (see below), and in the works of Luthardt and Hall just mentioned. Dante's ethical system is discussed in H. W. V. Reade's *Moral System of Dante's Inferno* (Oxford, 1909), K. Witte's essay on "The Ethical System of the Inferno and the Purgatorio" in his *Essays on Dante* (transl., London, 1898), E. Moore's essay on "The Classification of Sins in the Inferno and Purgatorio" in his *Studies in Dante*, and A. H. Gilbert's *Dante's Conception of Justice* (Durham, N. C., 1925); the last is based on Thomas Aquinas's commentary on the fifth book of Aristotle's *Ethics*.

For the mediæval theory of chivalric love the reader may consult L. F. Mott's rather meagre *System of Courtly Love* (Boston, 1896), W. A. Neilson's *Origins and Sources of the Court of Love* (Boston, 1899), the twenty-fourth chapter of Taylor's *Mediæval Mind*, and especially the first chapter of T. F. Crane's *Italian Social Customs of the Sixteenth Century* (New Haven, Conn., and London, 1920), the footnotes to which point the way to the whole literature of the subject; copious extracts from André le Chapelain's *De Amore* are translated in Crane and in J. F. Rowbotham's otherwise negligible *Troubadours and the Courts of Love* (London, 1895); for the contrast between the ideal and the prosaic reality, see G. G. Coulton's comments in the *Encyclopaedia Britannica* (11th ed., vol. xv, page 859). The moralists of the Middle Ages were prolific in giving advice to women, and this vast literature is digested in A. A. Hentsch's *De la littérature du moyen âge s'adressant spécialement aux femmes* (Cahors, 1903). For the theory of spiritual or divine love, of which, as Burton's *Anatomy of Melancholy* tells us, "St. Dionysius with many Fathers and Neotericks have written just volumes, *De amore Dei*, as they term it, many parænetical discourses," see Gardner's *Dante and the Mystics*, Taylor's *Classical Heritage* (for St. Augustine) and *Mediæval Mind* (for Bernard and Aquinas), J. F. Sollier's article on "Love, Theological Virtue of" in the *Catholic Encyclopedia*, and the histories of philosophy and Christian doctrine; but P. Rousselot's *Pour l'histoire du problème de l'amour au moyen âge* (Münster, 1908) is more systematic than anything in English.

There is no comprehensive survey in English of the whole field of European ethics, like F. Jodl's *Geschichte der Ethik* (3rd ed., 2 vols., Stuttgart, 1920–23) or O. Dittrich's *Geschichte der Ethik* (vols. i–iii, Leipzig, 1926); the older English works are antiquated or inadequate; but there are brief sketches, such as H. Sidgwick's *Outlines of the History of Ethics* (5th ed., London, 1906) and R. A. P. Rogers's *Short History of Ethics, Greek and Modern* (London, 1911), though the latter omits mediæval theory entirely. There are numerous books on Hebrew ethics, including H. G. Mitchell's *Ethics of the Old Testament* (Chicago, 1912) and H. M. Hughes's *Ethics of the Jewish Apocryphal Literature* (London, 1909); and the ethical conceptions of other Oriental religions are discussed briefly by various scholars in *The Evolution of Ethics as Revealed in the Great Religions*, edited by E. H. Sneath (New Haven, Conn., 1927).

H. D. Oakeley's translations of *Greek Ethical Thought from Homer to the Stoics* (London, 1925) furnish a useful introduction to Greek ethical theory; and brief summaries may be found in the books of Sidgwick and Rogers, in the chapter on ancient ethics in Janet and Séailles's *History of the Problems of Philosophy* (transl., 2 vols., London, 1902), and in William Wallace's "Excursus on Greek Ethics" prefixed to his translation of Hegel's *Philosophy of Mind* (Oxford, 1894). There are important chapters on Plato's ethics in J. Martineau's *Types of Ethical Theory* (Oxford, 1885), Zeller's *Plato and the Older Academy*, Gomperz's *Greek Thinkers*, and Caird's *Evolution of Theology in the Greek Philosophers;* and all the essential ethical texts are analyzed in R. C. Lodge's *Plato's Theory of Ethics* (London and New York, 1928). Aristotle's *Ethics*, which is quoted by Dante more than fifty times, has found innumerable commentators: a good introduction to it is J. H. Muirhead's *Chapters from Aristotle's Ethics* (London, 1900), which includes translations of the most important passages and discussions of them; more extended treatment will be found in the works of Zeller and Gomperz, in T. Marshall's *Aristotle's Theory of Conduct* (London, 1906), in G. Grote's *Aristotle* (3rd ed., London, 1883; the chapter on the *Ethics* not in 1st ed.), in the introductions to the editions of the *Ethics* by A. Grant (4th ed., 2 vols., London, 1885) and J. Burnet (London, 1900), and especially, but only for those whom Vossler would call "wissensdurstig," in J. A. Stewart's learned *Notes on the Nicomachean Ethics* (2 vols., Oxford, 1892). Later Greek and Roman ethical theory is dealt with in Hicks's *Stoic and Epicurean*, Arnold's *Roman Stoicism*, Zeller's *History of Eclecticism*, the twentieth lecture of Inge's *Philosophy of Plotinus*, Glover's *Conflict of Religions in the Roman Empire*, Dill's *Roman Society from Nero to Marcus Aurelius*, and similar works; the larger editions of the moral treatises of Cicero, Seneca, Epictetus, and Marcus Aurelius should also be consulted. L. Alston's *Stoic and Christian in the Second Century* (London, 1906) compares the ethical theory of Marcus Aurelius with that of his Christian predecessors and contemporaries. But perhaps more may be learnt from Pater's *Marius the Epicurean* (1885) than from any of these. On the other hand, there is nothing in Lecky's *History of European Morals from Augustus to Charlemagne* (1869) that has not been more adequately treated by others.

POLITICAL THEORY, ETC.

W. A. Dunning's *History of Political Theories, Ancient and Mediæval* (New York, 1902) is a serviceable survey of the ancient and mediæval field; but for those wholly unfamiliar with the subject, even so slight a sketch as C. R. and M. Morris's *History of Political Ideas* (London 1924) or F. Pollock's well-known *Introduction to the History of the Science of Politics* (revised ed., London, 1911) may be helpful; R. G. Gettell's *History of Political Thought* (New York, 1924) is a somewhat larger academic textbook. R. W. and A. J. Carlyle's elaborate *History of Mediæval Political Theory in the West* (vols. i–iv, London, 1903–22) is the main authority for the Middle Ages; O. Gierke's *Political Theories of the Middle Age* (transl. with bibliography by F. W. Maitland, Cambridge, 1900) is a briefer but illuminating sketch; a history of mediæval political ideas by Dino Bigongiari is in preparation; and to these may be added *Social and Political Ideas of Some Great Mediæval Philosophers*, edited by F. J. C. Hearnshaw (London, 1923), J. N. Figgis's *Political Aspects of St. Augustine's City of God* (London, 1921), A. L. Smith's *Church and State in the Middle Ages* (Oxford, 1913), and E. Emerton's *The Defensor Pacis of Marsiglio of Padua* (Harvard Theological Studies, 1920). Thomas Aquinas's political theory is discussed in most of these works, as well as in Poole's *Illustrations of the History of Mediæval Thought* and E. F. Murphy's dissertation on *St. Thomas' Political Doctrine and Democracy* (Washington, 1921); and his disciple, Egidio Colonna (Aegidius Romanus), in S. P. Molenaer's edition of *Li livres du gouvernement des rois* (New York, 1899), a thirteenth century French version of Egidio's *De Regimine Principum*. John of Salisbury's *Policraticus* has been edited by C. C. J. Webb (2 vols., Oxford, 1909), and his theories discussed in the introduction to J. Dickinson's translation (see above), in Poole's *Illustrations*, and Hearnshaw's *Social and Political Ideas*. There is an essay on "The Political Theory of Dante" by W. H. V. Reade prefixed to a reprint of the Oxford text of Dante's *De Monarchia* (Oxford, 1916); see also J. J. Rolbiecki's *Political Philosophy of Dante Alighieri* (Washington, 1921). For Greek and Roman political theory, W. W. Willoughby's *Political Theories of the Ancient World* (London, 1903), J. L. Myres's *Political Ideas of the Greeks* (London, 1927), A. C. Bradley's essay on "Aristotle's Theory of the State" in *Hellenica*, edited by E. Abbott (London, 1880), and E. Barker's earlier sketch of the *Political Thought of Plato and Aristotle* (London, 1906) or its later revision, *Greek Political Theory: Plato and his Predecessors* (London, 1918), may be consulted; the introductory essays in F. W. Newman's monumental edition of Aristotle's *Politics* (4 vols., Oxford, 1887–1902) and in B. Jowett's translation of the same work contain much valuable material.

On Roman law, P. Vinogradoff's *Roman Law in Mediæval Europe* (London, 1909) is a brief but excellent introduction; a fuller treatment of its history and principles may be found in J. Declareuil's *Rome the Law-Giver* (transl., London and New York, 1926) and J. Muirhead's *Historical Introduction to the Private Law of Rome* (3rd ed., London, 1916); but there is no more brilliant summary than the forty-fourth chapter of Gibbon's *Decline and Fall*, which for many years was used as a textbook in the schools of continental Europe; J. B. Moyle's edition of the *Institutes* of Justinian (5th ed., 2 vols., Oxford, 1912–13) contains an English translation; and to these the Dante student may possibly add J. Williams's inconclusive study of *Dante as a Jurist* (Oxford, 1906).

There is no field in which English is weaker than in the vast realm of CANON LAW, but there is a good survey, with bibliography, in the article on "Law, Canon" in the *Catholic Encyclopedia* and that on "Canon Law" in the *Encyclopaedia Britannica*, 11th ed., both by A. Boudinhon. O. J. Reichel's brief *Canon Law of Church Institutions* (London, 1922) is the only history in English worth mentioning at all, and digests of the law may be found in E. Taunton's *Law of the Church* (London and St. Louis, 1906), O. J. Reichel's *Complete Manual of Canon Law* (2 vols., London, 1896), and S. Woywod's *The New Canon Law* (New York, 1918), the last a summary of the revised code promulgated in 1917. But all these seem slight props to lean on in comparison with the works of Sägmüller, Maassen, Schulte, and Tardif, and the massive collections and glosses of the great canonists; the most extensive bibliography is that in the fourth volume of B. Ojetti's *Synopsis Rerum Moralium et Juris Pontificii* (3rd ed., 4 vols., Rome, 1909–14). The *Decretum* of Gratian, who is placed among the "spiriti sapienti" in the tenth canto of *Paradiso*, does not appear to be accessible in any modern tongue, and must be read in the editions of the *Corpus Juris Canonici*, such as E. Friedberg's (2 vols., Leipzig, 1879–81). The second volume of Carlyle's *History of Mediæval Political Theory* is devoted to the political theories of the Roman lawyers and the canonists from the tenth to the thirteenth century.

Mediæval thought on ECONOMIC AND SOCIAL QUESTIONS is summed up in the first chapter of R. H. Tawney's *Religion and the Rise of Capitalism* (London and New York, 1926). For further discussion the reader may be referred to G. O'Brien's *Essay on Mediæval Economic Teaching* (London, 1920), W. J. Ashley's *Introduction to English Economic History and Theory: The Middle Ages* (London and New York, 1888; 4th ed., 1913) and his article on "Aquinas" in Palgrave's *Dictionary of Political Economy*, the Dominican B. Jarrett's discursive *Social Theories of the Middle Ages* (London and Boston, 1926) and *Mediæval Socialism* (London, c. 1912), Coulton's *Five Centuries of Religion* (vol. ii, chapters 2–5; vol. i, appendix 23), and the articles on "Usury" and "Slavery" in Hastings's *Encyclopaedia of Religion and Ethics;* but none of these is quite equivalent to E. Troeltsch's *Die Soziallehren der christlichen Kirchen und Gruppen* (2nd ed., Tübingen, 1919). There is a brief summary of ancient and mediæval economic theories in L. H. Haney's *History of Economic Thought* (revised ed., New York, 1920), and extracts from Thomas Aquinas and Nicole Oresme are given in English in A. E. Monroe's *Early Economic Teaching* (Cambridge, Mass., 1924); for other references, see the section on "Economic Thought" in H. Hall's *Select Bibliography of English Mediæval Economic History* (London, 1914). C. F. Kent's *Social Teachings of the Prophets and Jesus* (New York, 1917) may be consulted for the biblical background.

MEDIÆVAL SCIENCE

The most comprehensive treatment of mediæval magic, and to a lesser degree of mediæval science, may be found in L. Thorndike's *History of Magic and Experimental Science in the First Thirteen Centuries of our Era* (2 vols., New York, 1923), a work of great but ill-digested learning, important despite its lack of intellectual grasp. The extensive bibliography which it contains, and the bibliographical note at the end of the tenth chapter of Haskins's *Renaissance of the Twelfth Century*, should be consulted for histories of the individual sciences; and further information may be obtained from G. Sarton's *Introduction to the History of Science* (vol. i, Washington, 1927), a valuable collection of historical and bibliographical notes extending thus far only to the eleventh century. For general orientation the brief sketch of ancient and mediæval science, from the days of the Babylonians, in Sedgwick and Tyler's *Short History of Science* (New York, 1918), C. Singer's *From Magic to Science* (London, 1928), and possibly T. C. Allbutt's lecture on *Science and Mediæval Thought* (London, 1901), may suffice. Brief accounts of ancient science may be found in C. Singer's *Greek Biology and Greek Medicine* (Oxford, 1922) and J. L. Heiberg's *Mathematical and Physical Science in Classical Antiquity* (transl., Oxford, 1922).

The inevitable German has written the only general study of the mediæval attitude toward "nature" available in English, A. Biese's rather sketchy *Development of the Feeling for Nature in the Middle Ages and Modern Times* (transl., London, 1905). W. Ganzenmüller's more competent work, *Das Naturgefühl im Mittelalter* (Leipzig, 1914), is briefly summarized in Wright's *Geographical Lore* (see below); F. T. Palgrave's *Landscape in Poetry from Homer to Tennyson* (London, 1897) is weakest in the mediæval field. The attitude of the ancients is dealt with in A. Geikie's *Love of Nature among the Romans* (London, 1912) and E. Martinengo Cesaresco's *Outdoor Life in Greek and Roman Poets* (London, 1911), and there are some illuminating pages in L. Friedlaender's *Roman Life and Manners under the Early Empire* (transl., 4 vols., London, 1909–13) and G. Boissier's *Country of Horace and Virgil* (transl., London, 1895). There is no adequate account of mediæval gardens in English; the text of F. Crisp's beautifully illustrated *Mediæval Gardens* (2 vols., London, 1925) is amateurish and discursive, like most books on gardening, but useful for its translations from Pietro de'Crescenzi's *Opus Ruralium Commodorum* (*c.* 1305) and the like.

Important aspects of mediæval science are dealt with in C. L. Beazley's *Dawn of Modern Geography* (3 vols., London, 1897–1906), J. L. E. Dreyer's *History of the Planetary Systems from Thales to Kepler* (Cambridge, 1906), J. K. Wright's *Geographical Lore of the Time of the Crusaders* (New York, 1925), L. O. Wedel's *Mediæval Attitude toward Astrology* (New Haven, Conn., 1920), and M. M. P. Muir's *Story of Alchemy and the Beginnings of Chemistry* (London, 1902); and interesting sidelights are furnished in E. Brehaut's *An Encyclopedist of the Dark Ages* (New York, 1912), which contains an analysis, with extracts, of Isidore of Seville's *Etymologiae*, R. Steele's *Mediæval Lore* (London, 1893), which translates portions of Bartholomew de Glanville's encyclopaedia *De Proprietatibus Rerum*, J. H. Bridges's *Life and Work of Roger Bacon* (London, 1914), *Essays on Roger Bacon*, edited by A. G. Little (Oxford,

1914), and W. L. Curry's *Chaucer and the Mediæval Sciences* (New York, 1926); but there is nothing in English to match P. Duhem's exhaustive and penetrating work, *Le système du monde: Histoire des théories cosmologiques de Platon à Copernic* (5 vols., Paris, 1913–17; left unfinished), which is fundamental for the understanding of Dante's world. Haskins's *Studies in the History of Mediæval Science*, Thorndike's *History*, and Singer's article in *The Legacy of Israel* should be consulted for the diffusion of Greek, Arabian, and Jewish science in the Middle Ages; but for Arabian science itself we must seek some such work as Carra de Vaux's *Les Penseurs de l'Islam* (4 vols., Paris, 1921–23), the second volume of which is devoted to the mathematical and natural sciences. The standard work on mediæval military science is C. W. C. Oman's *History of the Art of War in the Middle Ages* (2nd ed., 2 vols., London, 1924).

There is an important chapter on Albertus Magnus and a slighter one on Thomas Aquinas in Thorndike's *History*, and the scientific theories of Aquinas are defended rather than expounded in G. M. Cornoldi's *Physical System of St. Thomas* (transl., London, 1893); the modern Catholic interpretation of the relations between science and the mediæval church are persuasively presented in J. J. Walsh's *The Popes and Science* (New York, 1908) and the article on "Science and the Church" in the *Catholic Encyclopedia*. Dante's relations to the sciences and to nature are treated in R. T. Holbrook's *Dante and the Animal Kingdom* (New York, 1902), M. A. Orr Evershed's *Dante and the Early Astronomers* (London, 1913), E. Moore's essays on Dante's astronomy and geography in his *Studies in Dante*, and O. Kuhns's slight study of the *Treatment of Nature in Dante's Divina Commedia* (London, 1897). But the reader, weary of learning, may at this point prefer to turn to the swift reconnaissance of the first two chapters of A. N. Whitehead's *Science and the Modern World* (New York, 1926), or to D'A. W. Thompson's delightful essay on Aristotle as a student of natural history in *The Legacy of Greece* (Oxford, 1921), or even, despite its errors, to what Gomperz calls G. H. Lewes's "dazzling show piece," *Aristotle, A Chapter from the History of Science* (London, 1864).

IV. Mediæval Literature

There is no adequate history in English of mediæval literature as a whole; but four volumes in George Saintsbury's "Periods of European Literature"—W. P. Ker's *The Dark Ages* (Edinburgh and London, 1904), Saintsbury's *The Flourishing of Romance and the Rise of Allegory* (1897), F. J. Snell's *The Fourteenth Century* (1899), which includes Dante, and G. Gregory Smith's *The Transition Period* (1900)—furnish the best general, though all too general, conspectus. Some of the Dante handbooks listed below, especially Grandgent's, are useful as elementary introductions to the whole field; but most syntheses, such as may be found in Barrett Wendell's *The Tradition of European Literature from Homer to Dante* (New York, 1921) and similar works, and even the highly suggestive chapter on "The Character and Sources of Mediæval Poetry" in the first volume of W. J. Courthope's *History of English Poetry* (London and New York, 1895), suffer from inadequate knowledge of the subject. The narrative literature of the Middle Ages is admirably treated in W. P. Ker's essays on *Epic and Romance* (London, 1897), while H. V. Routh's *God, Man and Epic Poetry* (2 vols., Cambridge, 1927) is a study of the epic from Homer to Dante in relation to the progressive changes of religious belief and the conceptions of the creation and the hereafter, unconvincing in its arbitrary claims for the epic that would hold equally well for every other form of poetry. E. K. Chambers's *The Mediæval Stage* (2 vols., Oxford, 1903; ample bibliography) is the standard work in English on the mediæval drama; there are briefer sketches of the subject in Gregory Smith's *Transition Period* and Allardyce Nicholl's *Development of the Theatre* (London and New York, 1927; convenient bibliographical note).

Useful bibliographies of mediæval literature may be found in M. Edwardes's *Summary of the Literature of Modern Europe from the Origins to 1400* (London, 1907), Gayley and Kurtz's *Methods and Materials of Literary Criticism: Lyric, Epic, and Allied Forms of Poetry* (Boston, 1920: mediæval Latin, pages 191–203, 688–702; Provençal and Old French, pages 205–14, 703–11; early Italian, pages 225–32, 712–19), and Paetow's *Guide to the Study of Mediæval History* (mediæval Latin, pages 445–52; influence of the classics, pages 410–16; etc.).

CLASSICAL LITERATURE

So far as the classics are concerned, there is still no more attractive introduction to Greek literature than Gilbert Murray's *History of Ancient Greek Literature* (London and New York, 1897), or to Latin than J. W. Mackail's brief history of *Latin Literature* (London and New York, 1895), or to the poetry of Virgil than W. Y. Sellar's *Virgil* (3rd ed., Oxford, 1897). Further criticism of Dante's "altissimo poeta" may be sought in T. R.

Glover's *Virgil* (2nd ed., London, 1912), H. W. Prescott's *Development of Virgil's Art* (Chicago, 1927), the latter a paraphrase and condensation of an important German work, R. Heinze's *Virgils epische Technik* (Leipzig, 1902), and in the admirable essays of F. W. H. Myers (in *Essays, Classical*, 1883), J. W. Mackail (in *Lectures on Poetry*, 1911), H. W. Garrod (in Gordon's *English Literature and the Classics*, 1912), H. Nettleship (1875; reprinted in *Lectures and Essays*, 1885), and G. E. Woodberry (in *Great Writers*, 1907; reprinted in *Literary Essays*, 1920); for background, G. Boissier's *Country of Horace and Virgil*, a charming book, especially in the original; for the poet's life, T. Frank's *Virgil, A Biography* (New York, 1922); and for his literary influence, D. Comparetti's *Vergil in the Middle Ages* (transl., London, 1895), H. Beatty's *Dante and Virgil* (London, 1905), J. W. Mackail's *Virgil and his Meaning to the World of Today* (Boston, 1922), and E. Nitchie's *Virgil and the English Poets* (New York, 1919).

The following may be consulted in connection with the other Latin poets whom Dante valued most: for Horace, W. Y. Sellar's *Horace and the Elegiac Poets* (2nd ed., London, 1899), J. F. d'Alton's *Horace and his Age* (London, 1917), A. Y. Campbell's *Horace, A New Interpretation* (London, 1924), and G. Showerman's *Horace and his Influence* (Boston, 1922); for Ovid, Sellar's *Horace and the Elegiac Poets*, E. K. Rand's *Ovid and his Influence* (Boston, 1925), and S. G. Owen's essay on "Ovid and Romance" in Gordon's *English Literature and the Classics;* for Lucan, such general works as J. W. Duff's *Literary History of Rome in the Silver Age* (London, 1927), H. E. Butler's *Post-Augustan Poetry from Seneca to Juvenal* (Oxford, 1909), and W. C. Summers's *Silver Age of Latin Poetry* (London, 1920), and especially C. E. Heitland's introduction to C. E. Haskins's edition of Lucan's *Pharsalia* (London, 1887); and for Statius, who figures so prominently in the *Purgatorio*, D. A. Salter's introduction to his translation of Statius's *Sylvae* (Oxford, 1908) and A. W. Verrall's essays on "To Follow the Fisherman" and "Dante on the Baptism of Statius" in his *Collected Literary Essays* (Cambridge, 1913), as well as the general works cited under Lucan. Later Latin literature has been treated most sympathetically, however, in such French works as D. Nisard's *Études sur les poètes latins de la décadence* (5th ed., 2 vols., Paris, 1882), C. Martha's *Les moralistes sous l'empire romain* (6th ed., Paris, 1894), and Boissier's *La fin du paganisme;* and perhaps the high water mark of Virgilian criticism is to be found in Sainte-Beuve's *Étude sur Virgile* (1857).

For literary histories on a large scale, more modern than Mure and Donaldson, we must seek the aid of continental scholars also; there is no English equivalent for A. and M. Croiset's *Histoire de la littérature grecque* (2nd ed., 5 vols., Paris, 1896–99), W. von Christ's *Geschichte der griechischen Literatur* (6th ed., 3 vols., Munich, 1912–24), or M. Schanz's *Geschichte der römischen Literatur* (3rd ed., 7 vols., Munich, 1907–20); there is an English version of an early edition of W. S. Teuffel's *History of Roman Literature* (transl., 2 vols., London, 1890), but this is an imperfect equivalent for the latest German edition (6th-7th ed., 3 vols., Leipzig, 1913–20); all of these, with the brilliant exception of Croiset, are essentially works of reference, and all contain valuable bibliographical information. The *Companion to Greek Studies*, edited by L. Whibley (3rd ed., Cambridge, 1916), and the *Companion to Latin Studies*, edited by J. E. Sandys (3rd ed., Cambridge, 1921), although only in part literary, will be found helpful. Dante's indebtedness to classical writers from Homer to Boethius has been exhaustively studied in the first series of E. Moore's *Studies in Dante;* see also Toynbee's larger *Dante Dictionary* under the names of individual authors, and the works of Comparetti and Beatty already mentioned. As a first step in connection with the study of any "influence" on Dante, the reader may safely turn to Toynbee's dictionary.

MEDIÆVAL LATIN AND GREEK LITERATURE

There is no general survey of mediæval Latin literature in English, such as M. Manitius's valuable *Geschichte der lateinischen Literatur im Mittelalter* (3 vols., vols. i–ii, Munich, 1911–23) and A. Ebert's *Allgemeine Geschichte der Literatur des Mittelalters im Abendlande* (3 vols., Leipzig, 1874–80; French transl., 3 vols., Paris, 1883–89), although even these do not extend beyond the eleventh century. Segments of the field are covered in F. J. E. Raby's *History of Christian-Latin Poetry from the Beginnings to the Close of the Middle Ages* (Oxford, 1927), which is almost an anthology as well as a history, and Helen Waddell's *The Wandering Scholars* (London, 1927), a vivacious but somewhat overwritten account of the goliardic poets and their spiritual ancestry; both have good bibliographies. Portions of the field are also covered in Teuffel's *History of Roman Literature*, which extends to the eighth century, P. de Labriolle's *History and Literature of Christianity from Tertullian to Boethius* (transl., London and New York, 1925), W. P. Ker's chapter on "Latin Authors" in *The Dark Ages*, the first chapter of Gaspary's *History of Early Italian Literature* (see below), and Taylor's *Classical Heritage of the Middle Ages* and *Mediæval Mind;* and the first volume of J. E. Sandys's *History of Classical Scholarship* (2nd ed., Cambridge, 1906) is an encyclopaedia of information in regard to mediæval scholars and other writers.

The greatest of the mediæval hymns may be read in Latin and in English in M. Britt's *Hymns of the Missal and Breviary* (revised ed., New York, 1924), and Raby's *History of Christian-Latin Poetry* gives the text of many of them; Adam of St. Victor's *Liturgical Poetry* has been completely translated, and published with L. Gautier's text, by D. S. Wrangham (3 vols., London, 1881); the articles on the Latin "Hymns" in Hastings's *Encyclopaedia of Religion and Ethics* and the *Catholic Encyclopedia* are respectively by G. M. Dreves and C. Blume, who are co-editors of the *Analecta Hymnica Medii Aevi* (55 vols., Leipzig, 1886–1922), the most extensive of all the collections of mediæval hymns. The goliardic poets have been charmingly translated in J. A. Symonds's *Wine, Woman, and Song* (London, 1884), and English versions of philosophical treatises and other mediæval Latin works have been referred to in the section on Translations under Mediæval Thought and elsewhere. Some flavour of the originals may be obtained from such elementary anthologies as S. Gaselee's *Anthology of Mediæval Latin* (London, 1925), K. P. Harrington's *Mediæval Latin* (New York, 1925), and C. H. Beeson's *Primer of Mediæval Latin* (Chicago, 1925): "no one," says Émile Mâle, "knows the Middle Ages if he knows it only through its vernacular literature," or, it may be added, if he knows its Latin literature only through translations.

The influence of the Greek and especially of the Latin classics in the Middle Ages is discussed in Sandys's *History of Classical Scholarship* (see especially vol. i, chapter 32), Taylor's *Classical Heritage of the Middle Ages* (especially chapter iv), Haskins's *Renaissance of the Twelfth Century* and *Studies in the History of Mediæval Science*, L. J. Paetow's *The Arts Course at Mediæval Universities* (Urbana, Ill., 1910), and Comparetti's *Vergil in the Middle Ages*, which traces the history of Virgil's reputation among the unlearned more satisfactorily than among the learned up to the time of his appearance in the *Divine Comedy*, and sheds light on numerous other phases of mediæval culture. The bibliographies in Manitius, Raby, Waddell, Paetow, Haskins, and Sandys may be supplemented by that in U. Ronca's *Cultura medievale e poesia latina nei secoli XI e XII* (2 vols., Rome, 1892).

As for mediæval Greek literature, there is no English equivalent for K. Krumbacher's *Geschichte der byzantinischen Literatur* (2nd ed., Munich, 1897). The Greek fathers of the church and the Byzantine historians have been the objects of considerable study, but for other matters the reader must consult Sandys's *History of Classical Scholarship* and the later chapters of Müller and Donaldson's *History of Greek Literature* (3 vols., London, 1858), or must seek the aid of the encyclopaedias, among which K. Dietrich's article on "Byzantine Literature" in the *Catholic Encyclopedia* and K. Krumbacher's on "Greek Literature: Byzantine" in the *Encyclopaedia Britannica*, 11th ed., may be specially commended. The first volume of Saintsbury's *History of Criticism* (see below) contains a brief chapter on "Byzantine Criticism."

PROVENÇAL AND FRENCH LITERATURE

There is in English no first-rate history on a large scale of either Provençal or mediæval French literature. J. H. Smith's book of travel, *The Troubadours at Home* (2 vols., New York, 1899), contains the most interesting account of early Provençal poetry; L. F. Mott's lecture on *The Provençal Lyric* (New York, 1901) and J. Chaytor's slight sketch of *The Troubadours* (Cambridge, 1912) are useful but elementary; and F. Hueffer's *The Troubadours* (London, 1878), though somewhat antiquated, is readable and still worth reading. Ezra Pound's essays on *The Spirit of Romance* (London, 1910) indicate with a certain perverse wilfulness the charm of Provençal and early Italian poetry, and here and elsewhere he has rendered specimens of both into a sort of English paraphrase. Other translations of Provençal poetry may be found in the books of Smith and Mott, and in Barbara Smythe's anthology of *Trobador Poets* (London, 1911). Ida Farnell has translated the ancient *Lives of the Troubadours* (London, 1896); and the romance of *Flamenca* has been charmingly paraphrased and condensed by W. A. Bradley

(New York, 1922). The theories of love found in Provençal, Old French, and early Italian poetry are summarized in Crane's *Italian Social Customs*, Mott's *System of Courtly Love*, and other works (see the section on Ethical Theory above). The music of Provençal and Old French songs is studied in P. Aubry's *Trouvères and Troubadours* (transl., New York, 1914), and a collection of songs in modern notation may be found in J. Beck's *Chansonniers des troubadours et des trouvères* (2 vols., Paris, 1927). For the Provençal influence on Dante the reader may consult Toynbee's larger *Dante Dictionary* under the names of individual troubadours, and the works cited by Gayley and Kurtz (page 229). The originals may be savoured in H. J. Chaytor's *Troubadours of Dante* (Oxford, 1902), which contains selections from the Provençal poets mentioned by Dante, or preferably in J. Anglade's *Anthologie des troubadours* (Paris, 1927), which includes the Provençal text and a French translation of a representative selection of troubadour poetry. Those who seek a more extensive bibliography may be referred to D. C. Haskell's *Provençal Literature and Language: A List of References in the New York Public Library* (New York, 1925) as well as to the general bibliographies of mediæval literature already mentioned.

As for the literature of the "langue d'oïl," Gaston Paris's very brief sketch of *Mediæval French Literature* (transl., Temple Primers, 1903), which is a mere chronological skeleton of his excellent manual, *La littérature française au moyen âge* (5th ed., Paris, 1914), and L. Foulet's even briefer chapter on "Literature" in *Mediæval France: A Companion to French Studies*, edited by A. Tilley (Cambridge, 1922), appear to be the only independent surveys of the field; and the reader who is not a "specialist" and is repelled by the pedantry of the usual academic monograph will be inclined to seek further information in such books as Saintsbury's *Flourishing of Romance* and Ker's *Epic and Romance* or in the elementary histories of French literature, such as Nitze and Dargan's (2nd ed., New York, 1928), C. H. C. Wright's (New York and London, 1912), and Saintsbury's (7th ed., Oxford, 1917). Mention should be made, however, of the important series of works by English-speaking students on the "matter of Britain" (for English scholarship has very naturally concentrated on Arthurian romance) from H. L. D. Ward's *Catalogue of Romances in the Department of MSS. in the British Museum* (3 vols., London, 1883–1910) and A. Nutt's *Studies on the History of the Holy Grail* (London, 1888) to J. D. Bruce's *Evolution of Arthurian Romance* (2 vols., Göttingen, 1923); E. K. Chambers's *Arthur of Britain* (London, 1927) is a brief sketch; the reader may be referred to the bibliographies in the last two. A number of notable works by Gaston Paris, Bédier, Langlois, Jeanroy, and other French scholars, some of them among the glories of French scholarship, also cry out for mention; how much easier is the scholar's task when he is not obliged to confine himself to English! Toynbee's study of "Dante and the Lancelot Romance" in his *Dante Studies and Researches* and J. L. Weston's *Legend of Sir Lancelot du Lac* (London, 1901) may be consulted for the sources of Dante's knowledge of the story of Lancelot and Guinevere. Such works as A. Luchaire's *Social France at the Time of Philip Augustus* (transl., London, 1912), Joan Evans's *Life in Mediæval France* (Oxford, 1925), and F. Funck-Brentano's *The Middle Ages* (transl., London, 1922), like Tilley's *Mediæval France*, are also more or less concerned with literature in connection with its social background. Wright's and Nitze and Dargan's histories contain useful bibliographies; there is a well-selected but all too brief *Bibliography of Mediæval French Literature for College Libraries* by L. Foulet (New Haven, Conn., 1915), which, significantly, does not mention a single work of literary history in English; the bibliographical material in Gaston Paris's manual is much ampler, but hardly more flattering to our scholarship.

A few translations of Old French literature may be selected for mention here. The *Song of Roland* has been translated most recently by C. K. Scott-Moncrieff (London, 1919) and L. Bacon (New Haven, Conn., 1914); the *Huon of Bordeaux* was translated by Lord Berners in the early sixteenth century (ed. by S. Lee, 4 vols., Early English Text Society, 1882–87), the *Romance of the Rose*, which Dante probably knew, in part by Chaucer and more recently by F. S. Ellis (3 vols., Temple Classics, 1908), *Aucassin and Nicollette and other Mediæval Romances and Legends* by E. Mason (Everyman's Library, 1910), the *Châtelaine of Vergi* by A. Kemp-Welch (London, 1903), four Arthurian romances of Chrestien de Troyes, *Érec*, *Cligés*, *Ivain*, and *Lancelot*, by W. W. Comfort (Everyman's Library, *c.* 1913), and the prose Perceval romance, *Perlesvaus*, by S. Evans under the title of *High History of the Holy Grail* (London, 1898; reprinted in Temple Classics and Everyman's Library); nor must the popular retellings of mediæval romance be forgotten, notably J. Bédier's of *Tristan and Iseult* (transl. by H. Belloc, London and New York, 1927), and possibly R. Steele's of *Renaud of Montauban* after Caxton (London, 1897), *Huon of Bordeaux* after Berners (1895), and *The Story of Alexander* (1894). Those who wish to sample the racy flavour of Old French can find no better introduction to the whole field than the excellent little anthology of G. Paris and E. Langlois, *Chrestomathie du moyen âge* (8th ed., Paris, 1912), which contains selections, in modern French versions as well as in the originals, of virtually every type of literature.

ITALIAN LITERATURE

The *History of Italian Literature* by Francesco de Sanctis, which is soon to appear in English (New York: Harcourt, Brace & Co.), is one of the supreme works of literary history: "there is none, according to my taste," said Brunetière, "that is better, or more philosophic, or more agreeable to read." But, as this quotation suggests, the work is critical and philosophic rather than merely informative; it is in fact a history of the spiritual life of the Italian people interspersed with superb criticisms of their great writers; and on the side of information, the manual of Italian literature by F. Flamini, which is available in English (transl., New York, 1907), and that of H. Hauvette (Paris, 1906), which may soon be available, are more trustworthy than R. Garnett's (London and New York, 1898), despite the literary grace of the last. The most competent treatment of the earlier literature, however, is to be found in A. Gaspary's *History of*

Early Italian Literature to the Death of Dante (transl., London, 1901), the first section of an important work which even in the German original does not extend beyond the sixteenth century. The first chapter of J. A. Symonds's *Renaissance in Italy: Italian Literature* (2 vols., London, 1881), a work in which many of the ideas of De Sanctis are incorporated without acknowledgment, sums up the literature before Dante in some fifty pages, which is twice as many as Garnett devotes to it; and there are chapters on the subject in some of the Dante handbooks listed below, in Sedgwick's *Italy in the Thirteenth Century*, and in other works. The religious poets of the thirteenth century are dealt with in Gebhart's *Mystics and Heretics* and in F. Ozanam's somewhat antiquated but still charming *Franciscan Poets in Italy of the Thirteenth Century* (transl., London, 1913). D. G. Rossetti has translated the chief lyric predecessors and contemporaries of Dante in *Dante and his Circle* (new ed., London, 1900; also included under its original title of *Early Italian Poets*, with his version of the *Vita Nuova*, in the Temple Classics). Ezra Pound has translated the poems of Guido Cavalcanti (Boston, 1912), with the originals and translations on opposite pages; the chief "laude" of Jacopone da Todi are given in Italian and English in Evelyn Underhill's *Jacopone da Todi: A Spiritual Biography* (London, 1919); and a selection of early Italian poems is also given in the original and in translation in Lorna de' Lucchi's *Anthology of Italian Poems* (London, 1922). A. J. Butler's *Forerunners of Dante* (Oxford, 1910) is an anthology of early Italian poetry in the original, with English notes, and not a monograph on Dante's eschatology, as Taylor (*Mediæval Mind*, 2nd ed., vol. ii, page 569, note) and after him Paetow (*Guide*, page 482) oddly imagine! W. M. Rossetti's paper on *Early Italian Courtesy Books* (Early English Text Society, 1868) contains translations of Bonvesin da Riva's *Fifty Courtesies of the Table* and of extracts from Francesco da Barberino's *Documenti d'Amore* and other early works. A list of Italian bibliographies and literary histories will be found in Gayley and Kurtz's *Methods and Materials of Literary Criticism* (pages 810–13); and rather full references for early Italian literature are given in Gaspary's *History*, G. Bertoni's *Il Duecento* (Milan, *c.* 1911), and D'Ancona and Bacci's *Manuale della letteratura italiana* (new ed., 6 vols., Florence, 1908–10; see vol. i and the bibliographical supplement in vol. vi).

APOCALYPTIC LITERATURE

The works on the various conceptions of the future life, cited in the section on The Hereafter under Mediæval Religion, furnish the essential preparation for the study of Apocalyptic Literature; and most of the books on Jewish and Christian eschatology given there, notably those by Charles and Oesterley, deal specifically with this subject. Many of the Jewish apocalyptic writings may be read in English in R. H. Charles's elaborately edited version of the *Apocrypha and Pseudepigrapha of the Old Testament* in two very bulky volumes (Oxford, 1913); several early Christian apocalypses (including the *Apocalypse of Paul*, which James asserts and Vossler denies to have been in Dante's mind in *Inferno*, ii, 28, and elsewhere) are translated in M. R. James's *Apocryphal New Testament;* and perhaps the most convenient introduction to the field is Charles's article on "Apocalyptic Literature" in the *Encyclopaedia Britannica*, 11th edition. F. C. Porter's *Messages of the Apocalyptic Writers* (New York, 1911) contains paraphrases and discussions of several Jewish apocalypses; and other works dealing with these Hellenistic Jewish and early Christian writings include W. Bousset's *The Antichrist Legends* (transl., London, 1896), Fairweather's *Background of the Gospels*, W. O. E. Oesterley's *Books of the Apocrypha* (London, 1914), Schürer's *History of the Jewish People in the Time of Jesus Christ*, I. T. Beckwith's *Apocalypse of John* (New York, 1919), and J. Estlin Carpenter's *Johannine Writings: The Apocalypse and the Fourth Gospel* (London, 1927).

For the influence of this apocalyptic literature on Dante and for an account of the numerous mediæval visions of heaven and hell which preceded the *Divine Comedy*, the reader may consult M. Dods's *Forerunners of Dante* (Edinburgh, 1903), a rather sketchy survey of the whole field, T. Wright's *St. Patrick's Purgatory* (London, 1844), E. Becker's *Mediæval Visions of Heaven and Hell* (Baltimore, 1899), J. A. MacCulloch's *Early Christian Visions of the Other-World* (Edinburgh, 1912), and C. S. Boswell's *An Irish Precursor of Dante* (London, 1908); but an adequate work on this subject still remains to be written. Professor Lawton, the translator of the present work, has published an essay on "The Underworld in Homer, Virgil, and Dante" in the *Atlantic Monthly* (July, 1884); and this theme plays an important part in Routh's recent work on *God, Man, and Epic Poetry*. Stewart's *Myths of Plato* points out certain resemblances between Plato's and Dante's eschatology. Mohammedan eschatology and apocalyptic literature, and their supposed influence on Dante, are dealt with in M. Asín Palacios's *Islam and the Divine Comedy* (transl., London, 1926), but its conclusions with respect to Dante have not been accepted by Vossler, Torraca, and other scholars. For Dante's conception of heaven, E. G. Gardner's *Dante's Ten Heavens* (2nd ed., London, 1904), an interesting study of the *Paradiso*, the ninth chapter of Wicksteed's *Dante and Aquinas*, the eighth chapter of Gilson's *Philosophy of St. Thomas Aquinas*, and the articles on "Paradiso" and "Gerarchia" in Toynbee's larger *Dante Dictionary* will be found helpful. A mediæval Hebrew vision of hell and heaven, written apparently in imitation of the *Inferno* and *Paradiso* by a contemporary and probable friend of Dante, Immanuel Romi's *Tophet and Eden*, has been translated by H. Gollancz (London, 1921); see Moore's *Studies in Dante* (vol. iii, pages 277–83). For the influence of apocalyptic literature on mediæval art, see Mâle's *Religious Art in France in the Thirteenth Century* (book iv, chapter 6).

MEDIÆVAL THEORIES OF LITERATURE

The first volume of G. Saintsbury's *History of Criticism* (3 vols., Edinburgh, 1900–04) contains a tantalizing chapter on "Mediæval Criticism before Dante" and an extended analysis of Dante's *De Vulgari Eloquentia;* and there are some cursory studies of Dante's theory of poetry such as C. H. Herford's in the *Quarterly Review*, vol. ccxiii (London, 1910), T. H. Warren's in his *Essays of Poets and Poetry* (London, 1909), and C. H.

Grandgent's in the final lecture of his *Power of Dante* (Boston, 1918). A few suggestive pages in B. Croce's *Aesthetic* (transl., 2nd ed., London, 1922; 1st ed. incomplete), two discursive chapters in B. Bosanquet's *History of Aesthetic* (London, 1892), and the first chapter of J. E. Spingarn's *History of Literary Criticism in the Renaissance* (New York, 1899; 5th ed., 1925) also touch our field; but there is nothing in English like the general survey of mediæval theories of art and literature in the first two volumes of M. Menéndez y Pelayo's *Historia de la ideas estéticas en España* (2nd ed., 9 vols., Madrid, 1890–96), and no study of the aesthetic theories of Thomas Aquinas such as may be found in M. de Wulf's *Études historiques sur l'esthétique de S. Thomas* (Louvain, 1896) and other works of the kind. Small segments of the field have very recently been covered by M. W. Bundy's study of *The Theory of Imagination in Classical and Mediæval Thought* (University of Illinois Press, 1927) and C. S. Baldwin's notes on *Mediæval Rhetoric and Poetic* (New York, 1928), devoted mainly to mediæval survivals of ancient rhetorical theory and practice.

There is a convenient summary of the history of ALLEGORICAL INTERPRETATION in J. Geffcken's article on "Allegory, Allegorical Interpretation" in Hastings's *Encyclopaedia of Religion and Ethics*. A fuller treatment, for the classical and early Christian periods, may be found in A. B. Hersman's *Studies in Greek Allegorical Interpretation* (Chicago, 1906), Hatch's *Influence of Greek Ideas and Usages upon the Christian Church* (lecture iii), Bigg's *Christian Platonists of Alexandria* (lecture iv), Zeller's *Stoics, Epicureans, and Sceptics* (chapter xiii), and the important Excursus on Allegory in Stewart's *Myths of Plato;* and for the mediæval period in general, in Comparetti's *Vergil in the Middle Ages* (chapter viii), F. W. Farrar's *History of Interpretation* (London, 1886, lectures iii–v), Taylor's *Classical Heritage of the Middle Ages* (chapter v), Grandgent's *Dante* (New York, 1916, chapter xi), and Mâle's *Religious Art in France in the Thirteenth Century;* and in connection with these the caveat in the second chapter of Ker's *Dark Ages* should be borne in mind. Dante's own discussion of the subject may be found in the *Convivio* (treatise ii, chapter 1), or more briefly in the Letter to Can Grande; and Thomas Aquinas's, in the *Summa Theologica* (part i, question i, article 10). The most radical analysis of the nature of allegory and of its place in Dante's poem, having much in common with that in the present work, is contained in the introduction to B. Croce's *Poetry of Dante* (transl., London and New York, 1922). A whole bibliography might be devoted to the innumerable interpretations of the allegory of the *Divine Comedy*, for commentaries, expositions, and monographs are filled with them; but, as Croce says elsewhere ("Sulla natura dell' allegoria," in *La Critica*, vol. xxi, page 56, Naples, 1923), "I for my part leave such investigations and disputes to those who have time to waste." Those who disagree with this point of view, however, or who desire to see how the thing is done, may consult F. Flamini's *Introduction to the Study of the Divine Comedy* (transl., Boston, 1910), which summarizes the elaborate interpretation in his work on *Il significato e il fine della Divina Commedia* (2nd ed., 2 vols., Leghorn, 1916), or J. B. Fletcher's *Dante* (Home University Library, 1916).

A brief account of the mediæval theory of the drama, which explains Dante's conception of his own work as a comedy, may be found in Spingarn's *Literary Criticism in the Renaissance* (pages 64–67), and Dante's immediate source has been pointed out in Toynbee's *Dante Studies and Researchers* (pages 102–4); there is also a suggestive discussion of this subject in J. W. Mackail's *Lectures on Poetry* (London, 1911, pages 154–78). Aristotle's *Poetics* was unknown to Dante, and its influence was negligible in the Middle Ages, as may be seen from the brief chapter on the subject in Lane Cooper's *Poetics of Aristotle, its Meaning and Influence* (Boston, 1923); but the tradition of Roman criticism, and some knowledge of Horace's *Ars Poetica*, were never wholly lost, and for an understanding of that tradition the reader may consult the essay on "Literary Criticism at Rome" in W. R. Hardie's *Lectures on Classical Subjects* (London, 1903) and that on "Literary Criticism in Latin Antiquity" in H. Nettleship's *Lectures and Essays*, second series (Oxford, 1895). On the struggle between grammar and dialectics (that is, classical literature and scholastic philosophy) in mediæval universities, see H. Rashdall's *Universities of Europe in the Middle Ages* (3 vols., Oxford, 1895) and L. J. Paetow's translation of the thirteenth century poem of Henri d'Andeli, *The Battle of the Seven Arts* (Berkeley, Cal., 1914), which contains a good introduction and bibliography. The chief mediæval Latin treatises on the art of poetry are collected in E. Faral's *Les arts poétiques du XIIe et du XIIIe siècle* (Paris, 1924); and O. Bacci's *La Critica letteraria dall'antichità classica al Rinascimento* (Milan, *c.* 1910, pages 255–64) contains extensive bibliographical references for the further study of the criticism and literary theory of Dante's time.

V. Dante

Numerous monographs on special phases of Dante study have already been mentioned, and should be sought where they properly belong, that is, in the appropriate section under Mediæval Religion, Thought, and Literature. Some of the books cited, such as E. Moore's *Studies in Dante* (4 vols., Oxford, 1896–1917), P. Toynbee's *Dante Studies and Researches* (London, 1902) and his *Dante Studies* (Oxford, 1921), and K. Witte's *Essays on Dante* (transl., London, 1898), contain other more or less important contributions besides those referred to elsewhere. The allegorical interpreters have naturally been consigned to the section on Mediæval Theories of Literature; and many other questions of the minor commentators and investigators (*γωνιοβόμβυκες μονοσύλλαβοι*) will receive no answer here except Milton's words: "Let any gentle apprehension that can distinguish learned pains from unlearned drudgery imagine what pleasure or profoundness can be in this."

HANDBOOKS AND BIOGRAPHIES

There is no lack of elementary handbooks to Dante's life and works, each with its special virtues and defects. Some of these, like C. H. Grandgent's *Dante* (New York, 1916), K. Federn's *Dante and his Times* (transl., London and New York, 1902), and L. Ragg's *Dante and his Italy* (London, 1907) are chiefly concerned with the poet's epoch rather than with his poetry, while others, like E. G. Gardner's *Dante* (new ed., London, 1923), P. Toynbee's *Dante Alighieri: His Life and Work* (4th ed., London, 1910), and C. A. Dinsmore's useful collection of *Aids to the Study of Dante* (Boston, 1903), are concerned more strictly with the poet and his work. J. A. Symonds's older *Introduction to the Study of Dante* (3rd ed., London, 1893; 1st ed., 1872), though naturally inferior to these serviceable manuals as a compendium of accurate information, is superior to all of them in critical taste. Nothing in English, however, approaches such vast monographs as F. X. Kraus's *Dante, sein Leben und sein Werk* (Berlin, 1897) and N. Zingarelli's *Dante* (Milan, *c.* 1903) as storehouses of information. The *Early Lives of Dante*, by Boccaccio and Lionardo Bruni, have been translated by P. H. Wicksteed (London, 1907) and J. H. Smith (New York, 1901), and should be read in conjunction with E. Moore's *Dante and his Early Biographers* (London, 1890); practically the whole of Smith's version of Boccaccio is reprinted in Dinsmore's *Aids*, and the latter has written the latest *Life of Dante* (Boston, 1919).

DICTIONARIES, CONCORDANCES, BIBLIOGRAPHIES, ETC.

Paget Toynbee's larger *Dictionary of Proper Names and Notable Matters in the Works of Dante* (Oxford, 1898), and his condensed and revised *Concise Dictionary* (Oxford, 1914), are extremely useful and reliable works, containing information in regard to every person, place, book, etc., mentioned in Dante's works; but Toynbee is not wholly at home except in the realm of "facts." There is a concordance to the *Divina Commedia* by E. A. Fay (London, 1894), to the *Canzoniere* and Italian prose works by Sheldon and White (Oxford, 1905), and to the Latin works by Rand and Wilkins (Oxford, 1912). Many of the Italian editions of the *Commedia*, for example C. Steiner's (Turin, *c.* 1921), contain a "rimario," or concordance of rhymes. T. W. Koch's *Catalogue of the Dante Collection presented by W. Fiske to Cornell University* (2 vols., Ithaca, N. Y., 1898–1900; also supplement of *Additions, 1898–1920*, by M. Fowler, Ithaca, 1921), with his *List of Danteiana in American Libraries* (Dante Society, Cambridge, Mass., 1901), and W. C. Lane's *The Dante Collections in the Harvard College and Boston Public Libraries* (Cambridge, Mass., 1890) are valuable bibliographies. P. Toynbee's *Britain's Tribute to Dante in Literature and Art* (London, 1921) contains a complete list of British Dante literature up to 1920; and T. W. Koch's *Dante in America* (Boston, 1896) has a similar list of American Dante literature from 1807 to 1896. Grandgent's edition of the *Divina Commedia* (Boston, 1913) and several of the Dante handbooks mentioned in the preceding section, such as Gardner's and Toynbee's, include useful bibliographies. Vossler specially recommends, as bibliographical guides, B. Wiese's "Hilfsmittel zum Dantestudium" in the *Germanisch-Romanische Monatsschrift* (1911, vol. iii, page 108 sq.), A. Bassermann's "Dante-Literatur der Neuzeit" in the *Deutsche Vierteljahrsschrift* (Halle, 1924, page 852 sq.), and F. Schneider's "Neuere Dante-Literatur" in the *Historische Zeitschrift* (1924–25). For the portraits of Dante and the iconography of his works, R. T. Holbrook's *Portraits of Dante from Giotto to Raffael* (London, 1911) and L. Volkmann's *Iconografia Dantesca* (transl., London, 1899) may be consulted.

TRANSLATIONS

The editions of Dante are legion, but their titles should be sought in the above bibliographies and handbooks, and not here. A few hints concerning translations may be given for convenience of reference. One of the earliest translations of the *Divine Comedy* into English verse, H. F. Cary's (London, 1814; reprinted with notes by E. G. Gardner in Everyman's Library), though rather free, still retains much of its vigour; H. W. Longfellow's (3 vols., Boston, 1867–71; reprinted in one volume) is a cool substitute for Dante's passion, but has its own literal virtues, and has been used throughout the present work. Both of these, as well as H. Johnson's (New Haven, Conn., 1915), are in blank verse; and those who miss Dante's lovely rhymes may sample the rhymed versions of F. K. H. Haselfoot (London, 1887; 2nd ed., 1899) and E. H. Plumptre (*Commedia and Canzoniere*, 2 vols., London, 1886–87), both in Dante's own "terza rima." The best version in prose is probably C. E. Norton's (3 vols., Boston, 1891–92; reprinted in one volume); but J. A. Carlyle's of the *Inferno* (London, 1849; reprinted in Temple Classics edition) is more or less of a classic. Prose versions which also contain the Italian text of the

Commedia and useful notes are A. J. Butler's (*The Hell of Dante*, London, 1892; *Purgatory*, 1880; *Paradise*, 1894), W. W. Vernon's, which cites, translates, and comments on the text, passage by passage (*Readings on the Inferno of Dante*, 2 vols., 2nd ed., London, 1904; *Readings on the Purgatorio*, 2 vols., 3rd ed., 1907; *Readings on the Paradiso*, 2 vols., 2nd ed., 1909), and the Temple Classics edition with translation by Carlyle, Okey, and Wicksteed (3 vols., London, 1899–1900), the last perhaps the most convenient of all for the average reader. The *Vita Nuova* has been translated by Rossetti (see above), C. E. Norton (Boston, 1867), and T. Okey (Temple Classics, 1906; with Italian text); the *Canzoniere* by Wicksteed (Temple Classics, 1906; with Italian text), Plumptre (see above), and Lorna de' Lucchi (London, 1927); the *Convivio* by W. W. Jackson (Oxford, 1909), P. H. Wicksteed (Temple Classics, 1903), and K. Hillard (London, 1889); the complete *Latin Works* by Wicksteed and Howell (Temple Classics, 1904); the *De Monarchia* by A. Henry (Boston, 1904) and F. J. Church (London, 1879); the *De Vulgari Eloquentia* by A. G. F. Howell (London, 1890; reprinted in revised form in the Temple Classics version of Dante's *Latin Works*); the *Letters* by P. Toynbee (Oxford, 1920; with Latin text) and C. S. Latham (Boston, 1891); the *Eclogues* by Wicksteed and Gardner (*Dante and Giovanni del Virgilio*, Westminster, 1902; with Latin text) and Plumptre (see above); and the *Quaestio de Aqua et Terra* by C. L. Shadwell (Oxford, 1909; with Latin text). The standard text of Dante's complete works is the "Oxford Dante," *Le opere di Dante Alighieri*, edited by E. Moore (4th ed., revised by P. Toynbee, Oxford, 1924).

LITERARY CRITICISM

Four essays may illustrate the critical approach to Dante's poetry in English during the nineteenth century: Macaulay's (1824), Carlyle's (in *Heroes and Hero-Worship*, 1841), J. R. Lowell's (1872; reprinted in the fourth volume of his *Literary Essays*), and R. W. Church's, perhaps the most comprehensive of all (1850; reprinted in *Dante, An Essay*, 1878, and *Dante and Other Essays*, 1888); and to these may be added the critical portions of Symonds's *Introduction to the Study of Dante* (1872), the brief but more mature study in his *Italian Literature* (1881), and Maria F. Rossetti's sympathetic résumé of the *Divine Comedy* in her *Shadow of Dante* (London, 1871). Allusion has already been made to Santayana's essay on Dante as a philosophical poet (1910); and the casual wisdom of J. J. Chapman's brief *Dante* (Boston, 1927) is more illuminating than a bushel of handbooks and essays by most professional Dante scholars. Three distinct types of modern Italian criticism may be represented by G. Mazzini's essay "On the Minor Works of Dante" (in his translated *Essays* in the Camelot Series), originally published in 1844, G. Carducci's brief study of *Dante's Work* (transl., London, n. d., but printed in Italy in 1923), and Benedetto Croce's *Poetry of Dante;* but the chapters on Dante in Francesco de Sanctis's *History of Italian Literature*, and some of his untranslated essays, still remain the high water mark of Dante criticism, and have influenced all the critics from Symonds to Croce and

Vossler. A popular but stimulating restatement of this point of view may be found in I. Goldberg's *Dante: An Aesthetic View* (Little Blue Books, 1923), and a criticism of Croce's interpretation is included in the last lecture of L. Abercrombie's *The Idea of Great Poetry* (London, 1925). W. P. Ker's "Notes on the Similes of Dante" in his *Essays on Mediæval Literature* (London, 1900) may be compared with the treatment of the same subject by Croce and others; and the famous comparison of Dante and Milton in Macaulay's essay on Milton should be read in connection with W. J. Courthope's "Consideration of Macaulay's Comparison" in the *Proceedings of the British Academy* for 1908 and C. H. Herford's essay on "Dante and Milton" in his *Post-War Mind of Germany, and other European Studies* (Oxford, 1927). The assaults on Dante's fame have been more or less continuous, and the diatribes of Voltaire and others (see Moore's *Studies in Dante*, vol. ii, pages 2–5) find a not very effectual echo in A. Mordell's *Dante and Other Waning Classics* (Philadelphia, 1915). There is a short sketch of the history of Dante criticism in the appendix of Croce's *Poetry of Dante;* and the earlier English criticism may be traced in P. Toynbee's *Dante in English Literature from Chaucer to Cary* (2 vols., London, 1909). But criticism before the nineteenth century need not detain us here, for as De Sanctis says (*Saggi Critici*, ed. by M. Scherillo, Naples, 1914, vol. i, page 3), "it could not and it did not understand Dante; the *Divine Comedy* was too much above and too much outside all its rules."

Perhaps this Bibliographical Note, which is hardly more than a gesture of friendship and admiration for the author of this book, may best close with the tribute of a distinguished Italian philosopher: "The work of Vossler remains the most powerful instrument which we possess for helping us to understand the art of Dante" (Giovanni Gentile, *Frammenti di estetica e letteratura*, Lanciano, n. d., page 250).

February, 1928.

INDEX

INDEX